Music and Decadence
in European Modernism:
The Case of
Central and Eastern Europe

Decadence is a crucial yet often misunderstood aspect of European modernism. This book demonstrates how decadence as an idea, style or topic informs Central and Eastern European music of the late nineteenth and early twentieth centuries. Combining close analysis with hermeneutic interpretation and cultural critique, Stephen Downes examines works by composers including Wagner, Richard Strauss, Scriabin, Rachmaninov, Mahler and Bartók, considering structural and expressive forms of decay, deformation, mannerism, nihilism, sickness and convalescence. Through the use of critical and cultural theory these musical works are contextualized, and the relationship of music and musical discourse to wider cultural issues is scrutinized. The study will enhance the understanding of musical forms and aesthetics for the reader. Exploring crucial aspects of modernism and the place of music in the development and diversity of decadence, Downes refines and redefines our understanding of musical modernism.

STEPHEN DOWNES is Reader in Musicology at the University of Surrey. He is the author of *Szymanowski as Post-Wagnerian* (1994), *Szymanowski, Eroticism and the Voices of Mythology* (2003) and *The Muse as Eros: Music, Eroticism and Male Creativity in the Romantic and Modern Imagination* (2006). In 1999 he was awarded the Karol Szymanowski Memorial Medal.

Music and Decadence in European Modernism: The Case of Central and Eastern Europe

STEPHEN DOWNES

CAMBRIDGE
UNIVERSITY PRESS

CAMBRIDGE UNIVERSITY PRESS

Cambridge, New York, Melbourne, Madrid, Cape Town, Singapore,
São Paulo, Delhi, Dubai, Tokyo

Cambridge University Press
The Edinburgh Building, Cambridge CB2 8RU, UK

Published in the United States of America by Cambridge University Press, New York

www.cambridge.org
Information on this title: www.cambridge.org/9780521767576

First published 2010

Printed in the United Kingdom at the University Press, Cambridge

A catalogue record for this publication is available from the British Library

Library of Congress Cataloguing in Publication data
Downes, Stephen C., 1962–
Music and decadence in European modernism: the case of Central and Eastern
Europe / Stephen Downes.
    p.   cm.
Includes bibliographical references and index.
ISBN 978-0-521-76757-6
1. Music – Europe, Central – 19th century – History and criticism.   2. Music – Europe, Eastern –
19th century – History and criticism.   3. Music – Europe, Central – 20th century – History and
criticism.   4. Music – Europe, Eastern – 20th century – History and criticism.
I. Title.
ML240.4.D69   2010
780.9′034–dc22

2009050501

ISBN 978-0-521-76757-6 Hardback

In Memoriam
Clive Randolph Downes
1933–2007

Contents

Examples

Acknowledgements

Substantial parts of this book have developed out of materials presented at conferences and invited seminars over several years. I am indebted to the organizers and audiences of these events; without their work and responses writing the book would have been a far harder task. Chapter 2 incorporates material from 'Karłowicz and Russian Pessimism', delivered at the inaugural meeting of the BASEES Russian and East European Music Study Group (University of Bristol, June 2006); 'Divergent Russian Decadents: Rachmaninov and Scriabin', at the Fifth Biennial International Conference on Music since 1900 (University of York, July 2007); and 'Bartók's Elegiac Modernism', at 'Bartók's Orbit' (Institute for Musicology, Hungarian Academy of Sciences, Budapest, March 2006), attendance at which was supported by a British Academy Overseas Conference Grant.

Chapter 3 includes revised versions of 'Wagner, Strauss and the Operatic Double Ending', delivered at the Interdisciplinary Nineteenth-Century Studies Conference (University of Durham, July 2006); 'Forgetful Music and Music for Amnesiacs: Wagner, Strauss and Nietzsche's Dionysian Doubleness', at 'Musical Culture and Memory', the Eighth International Symposium of the Department of Musicology (University of Arts, Belgrade, April 2006); and 'Double Endings in Wagner and Strauss', at an invited research seminar (Keele University, December 2005). Chapter 4 subsumes material from 'Modern Musical Waves: Technical and Expressive Aspects of Post-Wagnerian Form', delivered at the Forty-Second Royal Musical Association Annual Conference (University of Nottingham, July 2006); 'Modern Musical Waves: Technical and Expressive Aspects of Fin-de-Siècle Form', at an invited seminar (Department of Musicology, University of Ljubljana, October 2006); 'Wave Deformations: An Aspect of Post-Wagnerian Form and Expression', at an invited seminar (Institute of Musical Research, London, October 2006); 'Development and Degeneration in Berg's Piano Sonata', at 'Music and Evolutionary Thought' (Institute of Advanced Study and the School of Music, Durham University, and the Centre for Music and Science, University of Cambridge, June 2007); 'Musical Form and Decadence', at the Sixth European Music Analysis Conference (Höchschule für Musik,

Freiburg, October 2007); and 'Decadence and Musical Form', at an invited seminar (University of Birmingham, February 2008).

Parts of Chapter 5 derive from 'Avant-Garde and Decadence: Extremes Touch?', given as part of the colloquium 'Pursuing the Musical Avant-Garde' (University of Surrey, November 2007); 'Mannerism, Decadence and the Chopinesque in the Russian Fin de Siècle', at the Fifteenth Biennial International Conference on Nineteenth-Century Music (University College, Dublin, June 2008); and 'Hearing Decadence in Schoenberg', at an invited research seminar (University College, Dublin, February 2009). Finally, Chapter 6 includes developments of 'Nietzsche contra Schumann', given at 'Schumann Perspectives: A View across the Disciplines' (Texas Tech University, Lubbock, September 2006), for which Texas Tech kindly provided a travel grant; and 'On Polish Musical Decadence', at 'Decadence in Central and Eastern Europe' (The Harriman Institute and the Department of Slavic Languages, Columbia University, New York, March 2007), the travel costs of which were covered by the University of Surrey Research Support Fund.

Completion of the book took place during research leave funded by the Arts and Humanities Research Council and was possible only through the generous support of the University of Surrey, and in particular my colleagues in the Department of Music and Sound Recording.

Many thanks to Victoria Cooper and all her staff at Cambridge University Press for expert editorial guidance in turning my manuscript into its final published form. I am grateful to Neil Luck for producing the music examples with consummate skill and efficiency. Excerpts from the following works are reproduced by permission:

Béla Bartók, *Elegy*, Op.8b No.1: © Copyright 1910 by Rozsnyai Karoly, Budapest; © Copyright assigned 1950 to Edito Musica Budapest.

Sergei Rachmaninov, 'Veter perelyotnïy', Op.34 No 4: © Copyright 1913 by Hawkes & Son (London) Ltd. Reproduced by permission of Boosey & Hawkes Music Publishers Ltd.

Sergei Rachmaninov, *The Bells*, op.35: © Copyright 1920 by Hawkes & Son (London) Ltd. Revised Version © Copyright 1936 by Hawkes & Son (London) Ltd. Reproduced by permission of Boosey & Hawkes Music Publishers Ltd.

Arnold Schoenberg, 'Erwartung', Op.2 No.1, Piano Piece Op.11 No.1, 'Ich darf nicht dankend', Op.14 No.1, *The Book of the Hanging Gardens*, Op.15, *Herzgewächse*, Op.20, *Pierrot lunaire*, Op.21; Franz Schreker, *Der ferne Klang*; Richard Strauss, *Stimmungsbilder* Op.9; Karol Szymanowski, *Three Fragments*, Op.5, *The Love Songs of Hafiz*, Op.24 No.2, *King Roger*,

Op.46b: Reproduced by kind permission of Universal Edition, AG, Wien. All rights reserved.

Richard Strauss, *Elektra*: © Copyright 1908, 1909 by Adolph Furstner. US copyright renewed. Copyright assigned 1943 Hawkes & Son (London) Ltd. (a Boosey and Hawkes company) for the world excluding Germany, Italy, Portugal and the former territories of the USSR (excluding Estonia, Latvia and Lithuania). Reproduced by permission of Boosey & Hawkes Music Publishers Ltd.

Richard Strauss, *Der Rosenkavalier*: © Copyright 1910, 1911 by Adolph Furstner. US copyright renewed. Copyright assigned 1943 Hawkes & Son (London) Ltd. (a Boosey and Hawkes company) for the world excluding Germany, Italy, Portugal and the former territories of the USSR (excluding Estonia, Latvia and Lithuania). Reproduced by permission of Boosey & Hawkes Music Publishers Ltd.

Richard Strauss, *Salome*: © Copyright 1905 by Adolph Furstner. US copyright renewed. Copyright assigned 1943 Hawkes & Son (London) Ltd. (a Boosey and Hawkes company) for the world excluding Germany, Italy, Portugal and the former territories of the USSR (excluding Estonia, Latvia and Lithuania). Reproduced by permission of Boosey & Hawkes Music Publishers Ltd.

Finally, to my family – Rachel, our sons Adam and Thomas, and our daughter Alice, born just weeks before the manuscript was finished – deepest, heartfelt thanks and love. I dedicate the book to the memory of my father, who sadly died in the summer of 2007.

1 | Decadence, music and the map of European modernism

… nothing is more modern than this total sickness, this lateness and overexcitement of the nervous mechanism …

Friedrich Nietzsche, *The Case of Wagner* (Leipzig, 1888)

Introduction

This book presents an analysis and interpretation of the role played by musical composition, aesthetics and criticism in Central and Eastern European decadence from the mid-nineteenth century to the immediate aftermath of the First World War.[1] Decadence is usually associated with themes of despair, deviance, decay, degeneration and death. Its artistic styles are characteristically described as excessive, epicurean, artificial, darkly comic or esoteric, and its structural strategies commonly understood as based upon processes of fragmentation, dissolution, deformation and ornamentation. The principal aim was a pessimistic critique of the bourgeois affirmation of subjective, psychological, physical and social progress and unity through the denigration of wholeness and wholesomeness and the celebration of the toxic and taboo. The energetics of the early riser were rejected in a turn to a protracted twilight of the idle. The work ethic and hopes of self-improvement were replaced by the provocative pose of the hedonist, the delights of *ennui* and lassitude, and the perverse pleasures of self-debasement. Decadence plays a complex, multifaceted role in the polemics and agendas of modernism. It is also notably ambiguous. Its spokesmen delighted in smokescreens. Its projects and purposes were altered according to regional and national context. These circumstances generated diverse cultural, aesthetic or political motives for either posing or creating as a decadent and for evoking or resisting the term as a descriptor of artistic style or content. The task ahead, therefore, is

---

[1] Reflecting the often cataclysmic events in politics and society during the 1920s and 1930s, the discourses of decadence which developed during interbellum Central and Eastern Europe are in many important ways radically different from those which form the focus of this book. Music's role in this discourse demands a separate study.

challenging, but as Henry Winthrop argues, the slippery pluralism of
decadence is 'both legitimate and desirable'; it liberates analysis from the
restrictions of conservative censure and moralistic indictment.[2]

Art historians, cultural theorists and literary scholars have sustained full
and fervent debates concerning the functions and characteristics of decadence in European modernism. By contrast, there is no book-length study
devoted to defining and interpreting the styles, themes and forms of
musical decadence. Furthermore, the role of decadence in Central and
Eastern Europe remains rather less well explored than the French or
British varieties, which often, of course, functioned as models or stimuli
for artists working in Austria, the Czech lands, Germany, Hungary, Poland
and Russia.[3] The shift of decadent ideas back and forth across political and
ideological boundaries generated striking new artistic developments. In the
final years of the Habsburg, Prussian, and Tsarist Russian Empires, decadence acquired new and potent resonances which interacted, influenced
and resisted each other in complex ways. For example, decadence assumed
an important role in the repertory of 'ethnosymbolisms', to use Anthony
D. Smith's influential term,[4] where the formation of national identities,
histories and cultures evokes forces of decline and regeneration through
moulding, institutionalizing and modernizing the image of the 'ethnic'
under the impact of bourgeois discourses of language, race and physiognomy. This was typically manifest in a debate between decadence and a
neoclassical revival of national mythologies and pagan primitivisms, one
which raised the stakes invested in the regressive–progressive polarity.
In this, and other ways, decadence played a critical role in artistic

---

[2] Henry Winthrop, 'Variety of Meaning in the Concept of Decadence', *Philosophy and Phenomenological Research* 31 (1971), 510–26.

[3] In the twenty-three chapters of his 'Baedeker' of decadence George C. Schoolfield devotes just four to these regions – one to Austria, one to Germany and two to 'Poland/Prussia' (to cover the movements of Stanisław Przybyszewski); Russia, in particular, is notably absent. See *A Baedeker of Decadence: Charting a Literary Fashion 1884–1927* (New Haven: Yale University Press, 2003). Erwin Koppen's *Dekadenter Wagnerismus: Studien zur europäischen Literatur des Fin de Siecle* (Berlin: de Gruyter, 1973) moves from Germany westwards – to France, England – and to the south – Italy – but not the east (though he also considers Przybyszewski as a 'German' decadent).

[4] See Anthony D. Smith, *Myths and Memories of the Nation* (Oxford University Press, 1999) and 'When is a Nation?', *Geopolitics* 7 (2002) 5–32. Athena S. Leoussi discusses, among a range of examples illustrating Smith's theory, the depictions of nostalgia, decline and rebirth in Alphonse Mucha's *The Slav Epic* (1900–28), a Pan-Slavic, anti-Habsburg vision of ethnicity from origin through to apotheosis, and the allegorical, personified figures of the Polish nation in canvases by Jacek Malczewski: 'The Ethno-Cultural Roots of National Art', in Montserrat Guibernau and John Hutchinson (eds.), *History and National Destiny: Ethnosymbolism and its Critics* (Oxford: Blackwell, 2004), 143–59.

constructions of self-identity and national iconography and became central to the expression of modern social and political predicaments.

Jacques Barzun has put it simply: 'all that is meant by Decadence is "falling off"'. But this does not imply a weakening of artistic creative vigour. Barzun continues:

It implies in those who live in such a time no loss of energy or talent or moral sense. On the contrary it is a very active term, full of deep concerns, but peculiarly restless, for it sees no clear lines of advance. The loss it faces is that of Possibility. The forms of art as of life seem exhausted, the stages of development have been run through. Institutions function painfully. Repetition and frustration are the intolerable result. Boredom and fatigue are great historical forces.[5]

Charles Baudelaire expressed similar sentiments when, in response to the critical use of the phrase 'a literature of decadence!' as a derogatory cry of warning, he declared:

In the changing splendours of this dying sun, some poetic minds will find new joys; they will discover dazzling colonnades, cascades of molten metal, a paradise of fire, a melancholy splendour, nostalgic raptures, all the magic of dreams, all the memories of opium. And the sunset will then appear to them as the marvellous allegory of a soul, imbued with life, going down beyond the horizon, with a magnificent wealth of thoughts and dreams.[6]

The sense of 'falling off' which Barzun identifies, with its subjective anxieties and sensational thrills, might be called cultural 'vertigo'.[7] Dizzying, disorientating and destabilizing, it has insecurities which are produced by the threat of precipitous or prolonged (or even endless) descent into a fetid underworld. Maurice Barrès, in his *Amori et dolori sacrum: La Mort de Venise* (1902), put it, with a symptomatic allusion to Wagner, thus: 'Vertigo – the intoxication of high places and extreme emotions! At the height of the waves to which *Tristan* bears us let us recognise that pestilence which rises from the lagoons at night.'[8] The inevitable complement to the rise of the new is the discomforting displacement from the 'natural' ground of being. The modern ascends to high artifice. The loftier it becomes, the

[5] Jacques Barzun, *From Dawn to Decadence: 500 years of Western Cultural Life, 1500 to the Present* (New York: HarperCollins, 2000), xx.

[6] Charles Baudelaire, 'Further Notes on Edgar Poe' [1853], in *Selected Writings on Art and Literature*, trans. P. E. Charvet (Harmondsworth: Penguin, 1972), 189.

[7] On this metaphor see Philipp Blom, *The Vertigo Years: Change and Culture in the West, 1900–1914* (London: Weidenfeld and Nicolson, 2008).

[8] Maurice Barrès, *Amori et dolori sacrum: La Mort de Venise* [1902], trans. from Raymond Furness, *Wagner and Literature* (Manchester University Press, 1982), 49.

greater the sense of imminent decline and fall. From the highpoint the approaching sunset is sooner in view. Modernism's apparently upward progress leads towards a precarious, isolating predicament as its foundations are tested to breaking point. In spite of the achievements of modern bourgeois society, collapse into the abyss seems increasingly at hand. The sense of decadence is encapsulated by Mann's Thomas Buddenbrook, who at the height of his professional and personal development confessed that 'I feel older than I am ... When the house is finished, death comes. It doesn't need to be death. But the decline, the falling-off, the beginning of the end ... the signs and symbols of happiness and success only show themselves when the process of decline has set in.'[9] Edifices of comfort and prestige crumble. The bourgeois romantic project disintegrates in the fall of the house of Utopia. Hopes of regenerative, renewing powers in a cyclic relationship of naïve immediacy and sentimental self-reflection, in a reactivation of innocent play in the face of potentially debilitating self-awareness, are also dashed in the irreconcilable alienation of humanity from all that seemed 'natural'.[10] Nonetheless, the wounded spirit of romanticism might be perversely perpetuated, raised against realism and naturalism, and the outer world repulsed in the solipsistic, narcissistic turn inwards, with solace sought in shadowy simulacra. The elevated view is spurned; the curtains are drawn in to hide dark and private interiors.

Of course the sense of alienation from nature and pessimism about mankind's cultural progress are not exclusive to late nineteenth-century thought. Neither is the sense of decadence, which in part is an extreme manifestation of these feelings. But the artistic intensifications and transformations of these concerns as they became crucial in the case of Central and Eastern Europe at a time of political and social upheaval represent some of the period's most fascinating and often magnificent achievements. The restrictive use of the term 'decadence' to mainly French, or French-inspired, literature of the 1890s is myopic. A broader and more comprehensive view of decadence is one which sees the work of Joris-Karl Huysmans and his contemporaries as an extreme, influential or perhaps paradigmatic example of a topic which is of wide and profound importance in the second half of the nineteenth century and up to the First World War. Nietzsche emerges as a seminal figure. Decadence preoccupied him in the

---

[9] Thomas Mann, *Buddenbrooks* [1902], trans. H. T. Lowe-Porter (London: Vintage Books, 1999), 352.

[10] For discussion of these issues see Richard Sheppard, 'The Problematics of European Modernism', in Steve Giles (ed.), *Theorizing Modernism: Essays in Critical Theory* (London: Routledge, 1993), 1–51.

years before his final mental collapse. With Wagner, the French *décadence*, Christianity, and Greek and Roman antiquity as central stimuli he saw decadence as the major modern cultural malaise, but one which is not simply to be equated with, or defined by, decline. He threw out the traditional identifications of decadence with the collapse and excesses of the Roman Empire, as represented by Edward Gibbon's *The Decline and Fall of the Roman Empire* (1788) and Thomas Couture's canvas *Les Romains de la décadence* (1847) – a construction of decadence often extended into images of Byzantium. He shifted decadence from abject marginality to ambivalent prominence in modernity. Decadence thus rises above the merely topical or fashionable.[11] Nietzsche's diagnosis was hugely influential. Music's role within these wider discourses of decadence, as compositional artefact, metaphor or inspiration, was often crucial.

Music and decadence

In recent decades much of the repertory which this book considers has attracted substantial analytical and theoretical interest. Writing in 1989, Christopher Lewis noted that analysis of a 'distinct musical style' which he calls 'post-romantic music' (Lewis identifies this as 'essentially post-*Tristan* music') has burgeoned with the development of new methods, particularly in harmonic analysis.[12] This analytical project gained further impetus in the neo-Riemannian enthusiasms of theorists from the mid-1990s.[13] This development was contemporaneous with the heyday of the so-called 'new' musicology. *Pace* some important essays on Wagner's *Parsifal* and Strauss's *Salome* in particular, however, the hermeneutic and critical projects which emerged from this musicological climate tended to skirt the issue of decadence, or consider it too briefly or superficially. Although 'decadence' has been identified as 'a term that moved easily across disciplinary boundaries, settling in different contexts with distinct connotations and

---

[11] See Michael Silk, 'Nietzsche, Decadence, and the Greeks', *New Literary History* 35 (2005), 587–606.

[12] Christopher Lewis, 'Into the Foothills: New Directions in Nineteenth-Century Analysis', *Music Theory Spectrum* 11 (1989), 15–23.

[13] See in particular the work of Richard Cohn: 'Introduction to Neo-Riemannian Theory: A Survey and an Historical Perspective', *Journal of Music Theory* 42 (1998), 167–80; 'Maximally Smooth Cycles, Hexatonic Systems, and the Analysis of Late Nineteenth-Century Triadic Progressions', *Music Analysis* 15 (1996), 9–40; and lately, with a more strongly hermeneutic element, 'Uncanny Resemblances: Tonal Significance in the Freudian Age', *Journal of the American Musicological Society* 57 (2004), 285–323.

effects',[14] it has been little employed in any sustained way in interdiscipli-nary studies which are broadly centred on musicological methods and concerns. This is especially surprising, given music's prominent position in many of the seminal discussions of decadence from leading writers of the modernist period. Perhaps the neglect is to some degree related to ques-tions of taste. Lewis quotes Charles Rosen's dictum that 'good taste is a barrier to our understanding and appreciation of the nineteenth century'.[15] The issue becomes acute in some of the musical styles which flourished at the end of the nineteenth century, which may seem to flirt dangerously with hyper-emotionalism, excessive ornament or over-complexity. Something of this last quality is reflected in the jargon of theory, for example where rich functional 'multiplicity' in nineteenth-century harmony is described as leading to the 'functional extravagance' of Wagner's so-called 'Tristan chord'.[16] If this is extravagance, then what happens to functionality and coherence in those pieces which take Wagner's *Tristan* and seek to pursue its chromaticism to further 'extremes'? The control, moral restraint, civility, and ideas of beauty and seemliness that were associated with what the self-appointed arbiters of cultural worthiness deemed to be 'good taste'[17] were prime targets for decadents. Indicators of 'bad' or 'poor' taste – the man-nered, kitsch, flamboyant, voluptuous, debased, debauched and indulgent – were flaunted and celebrated. Their audience's offence, where taken, was always intended. 'The intoxicating thing about bad taste', Baudelaire famously declared, 'is the aristocratic pleasure in giving offence'.[18] Baudelaire provocatively proposed an 'unhealthy appetite' for the lasciv-ious or obscene which 'threatens the assumption that "virtue is knowl-edge"'.[19] This can challenge the strongest of palates.

There are other barriers to overcome. The problems which arise on attempting to relate music to prominent aspects of modernism in other

---

[14] Liz Constable, Dennis Denisoff and Matthew Potolsky, 'Introduction', in Constable, Denisoff and Potolsky (eds.), *Perennial Decay: On the Aesthetics and Politics of Decadence* (Philadelphia: University of Pennsylvania Press, 1999), 21.

[15] Lewis, 'Into the Foothills', 23; Charles Rosen, 'New Sound of Liszt', *New York Review of Books* 29 (12 April 1984).

[16] Charles J. Smith, 'The Functional Extravagance of Chromatic Chords', *Music Theory Spectrum* 8 (1986), 94–139.

[17] See, for example, Daniel Cottom, 'Taste and the Civilized Imagination', *The Journal of Aesthetics and Art Criticism* 39 (1981), 367–80; Marcia Cavell, 'Taste and the Moral Sense', *The Journal of Aesthetics and Art Criticism* 34 (1975), 29–33.

[18] Charles Baudelaire, 'Rockets', from 'Journals and Notebooks', in My Heart Laid Bare *and Other Prose Writings*, trans. Norman Cameron, ed. Peter Quennell (London: Soho Books, 1986), 167.

[19] E. S. Burt, '"An Immoderate Taste for Truth": Censoring History in Baudelaire's "Les Bijoux"', *Diacritics* 27 (1997), 31.

artistic media (for example, symbolism, impressionism, *art nouveau*, *Jugendstil*, expressionism) have been widely attested. Carl Dahlhaus, for example, wrote of the 'ineffable tie' between works by Mahler, Schoenberg, Zemlinsky and Schreker and the art of *Jugendstil* and the Viennese Secession, but argued that 'we cannot pinpoint it technically without doing interpretative injustice to these pieces'. Dahlhaus acknowledges that 'connotations' of decadence 'have left their mark' on the subject matter of several important works (for example, Debussy's *Pelléas and Mélisande* or Strauss's *Salome*) but dismisses these 'marks' as representing mere 'details in the overall picture of the age'.[20] In this view decadence is limited to topical aspects of certain operas and is the reflection of a very limited aspect of the modern *Zeitgeist*. Decadence's potential to play a major role in musical modernism is highly restricted. Indeed, for Dahlhaus, it is actually potentially misleading to attempt to identify 'decadent' aspects of musical style and structure. Other work by Dahlhaus, however, identifies character- istics of late nineteenth-century and early twentieth-century musical struc- tures and aesthetics which are strongly resonant of decadent styles and themes. In *Between Romanticism and Modernism* the topics he covers include the Nietzsche–Wagner polemic on the relationship of language and music, constructions of nationalism in music, techniques of 'develop- ing variation', 'endless melody', 'expanded' or 'wandering tonality' and the 'individualization of harmony.'[21] All these subjects can be related to concepts central to decadence. They invoke the perceived modern decline and disunity of expressive media, the polarities of organic growth and decay, unity and fragment, esotericism and exotericism, the delights of ambiguity and harmonic 'vagrancy', the preoccupation with origins, genealogy, memory, inheritance, the heroic resistance to decline, and the search for a regenerative, primitive pastoral. Yet in this book Dahlhaus uses the term 'decadent' to describe only musical 'kitsch' – the anachronistic and empty pretensions of some of romanticism's late 'flowerings' (note here the metaphor of evolutionary or biological over-ripeness).[22] The association of decadence and kitsch needs unpacking. But Dahlhaus's polemical use of the term 'decadent' is too restrictive and negative. It sustains its employment in music criticism to denote tasteless sentimen- tality, sensuality or stylistic indiscrimination, or simply as a word for outing

[20] Carl Dahlhaus, *Nineteenth-Century Music*, trans J. Bradford Robinson (Berkeley: University of California Press, 1989), 334.

[21] Carl Dahlhaus, *Between Romanticism and Modernism*, trans. Mary Whittall (Berkeley: University of California Press, 1980).

[22] Dahlhaus, *Between Romanticism and Modernism*, 11–14.

the *outré*. It thus dismisses or ignores potential employments of the term to vitally useful and freshly illuminating musicological ends.

There are, however, examples in recent musicology where decadence's significant role in modernism is recognized. A fruitful discussion of music and decadence has emerged in recent interpretations of Tchaikovsky's *The Queen of Spades* (1890) by Simon Morrison and Boris Gasparov. For Morrison the opera 'addresses the decline of Imperial Russia, the sense – prevalent in the symbolist movement – that the nation was undergoing a transition'. He notes how the work exemplifies the *fin-de-siècle* move to the modern, expressed in musical allusions to eighteenth- and nineteenth-century pasts. Morrison concludes that Tchaikovsky was 'the only composer at the time to give voice to the growing sense of unease in Russian society', a feature which assured his posthumous status among the symbolists as prophet of their world view.[23] For Gasparov the opera is a 'quintessentially Petersburgian tale' containing 'symbolist and expressionist traits'. But Gasparov's description of St Petersburg as the 'symbolist city', as the site of an existence overburdened with allusions and memories,[24] where the 'inner world of a person is dissolved into mutually incompatible images, postures, actions, each provoked by ubiquitous precedents …', also intimates a world of decadence. This decadent element is further suggested when he describes Hermann, the main character, as a 'sum of … incoherent parts', a person who 'turned out to be a "man without qualities", a disoriented neurotic self incapable of comprehending how and for what purpose he ended up in the place in which he finds himself'. For Gasparov, Tchaikovsky's transformation of Hermann 'reflects the perceived malaise of the *fin de siècle*'. In the opera's 'dizzying' stylistic shifts of 'chronotypes' Hermann becomes 'lost in time': through a 'maze of temporal mirrors' he appears as 'eighteenth-century seducer, an early nineteenth-century Byronic figure, a Tristanesque character for whom love means death … a Dostoevskian killer with an obsessive idea, or a Chekhovian man of the age

---

[23] Simon Morrison, *Russian Opera and the Symbolist Movement* (Berkeley: University of California Press, 2002), 'Introduction', 14; 'Chaikovsky and Decadence', 45–114. Decadence is also an important aspect of Alexandra Wilson's *The Puccini Problem: Opera, Nationalism and Modernity* (Cambridge University Press, 2007), particularly in her discussion of *Madama Butterfly* and the 'superficial', 97–124; see also Byron Adams, 'Elgar's Later Oratorios: Roman Catholicism, Decadence and the Wagnerian Dialectic of Shame and Grace', in Daniel M. Grimley and Julian Rushton (eds.), *The Cambridge Companion to Elgar* (Cambridge University Press, 2004), 81–105.

[24] Morrison notes how 'signs of decadence, the social malaise that presaged the tumults of the modern era', appear in those works by Gogol and Pushkin which 'portray St. Petersburg as being suspended between natural and supernatural worlds, but also between the recent and distant past': *Russian Opera*, 46.

of twilight afflicted by a deep spiritual malaise'. If, as Gasparov concludes, the opera is 'an overture to the symbolist drama of an imperial city on the road to its collapse' then it is equally the prelude to decadence. The result is 'self-annihilating symbiosis that betrays the decadent world of incoherent obsessions and perpetual disturbances'.[25] Once this pessimistic, 'proto-decadent' tone is recognized in Tchaikovsky's music, its attractiveness as a model for Karłowicz and Rachmaninov (discussed in Chapter 2) becomes more clearly understood.

Morrison's and Gasparov's insights relate music to cultural and historical discourses. In neither is there any sustained musical analysis. In his magisterial history of Western music, Richard Taruskin offers a short discussion of musical decadence which includes observations of harmonic and formal aspects in music by Richard Strauss and Arnold Schoenberg. As an example of 'mild and pretty' musical decadence he analyses Strauss's early piano piece 'Rêverie', Op.9 No.4, from *Stimmungsbilder* (1882–4). The piece's topic, a musical image of a 'mood' produced by a dream, is one typical of high romanticism. Taruskin locates a decadent tone in the musical preoccupation with an 'oscillation' between the tonic chord and a chord of 'chromatic neighbours' which according to harmonic theory is unclassifiable (Example 1.1). This play with the unnameable is, according to Taruskin, 'endlessly repeated until it sounds "normal"'. But this is not quite right. Taruskin's focus on the unusual chromatic detail is apposite: the chord is returned to rather obsessively (fetishistically perhaps), and by the final section it is certainly normalized. But the piece is not 'endless'. It is constructed as a series of sentence forms, with a strongly closural final phrase in which the opening gesture returns one last time to act as a frame for the *Stimmungsbild*. Thus, in its formal clarity, convention and simplicity the piece seems remote from what one might expect of a musical example of decadence. Taruskin provides no discussion of what decadent musical form might involve, but does offer a striking image to illustrate the kind of 'perverse' pleasures that decadent forms might provide. He asks us to imagine a 'child at play with an "erector set"':

For a while, if intelligent and interested, or at least well-behaved, the child will follow the instruction book and connect the pieces "structurally", producing the expected buildings and bridges. Later, however, in order to maintain interest, the child might start connecting the pieces with one another in ways the instruction book does not prescribe, creating wierd shapes that have no practical application,

---

[25] Boris Gasparov, *Five Operas and a Symphony: Word and Music in Russian Culture* (New Haven: Yale University Press, 2005), 133–4, 142–4, 158, 160.

Example 1.1 Richard Strauss, 'Rêverie', *Stimmungsbilder*, Op.9 No.4, bars 1–4

Example 1.2 Arnold Schoenberg, 'Erwartung' (Dehmel), Op.2 No.1, bars 1–2

but give pleasure (to the maker, at least). Really curious children might even stick the pieces in places their mothers might not care to hear about.[26]

Childish wilfulness, boredom and perverse pleasures in deformation – all might describe the psychological state and motivations of Salome. Indeed, Strauss's famous operatic treatment of this character seems an obvious place to look for decadent forms. (Chapter 4 will explore how, in response to one of Oscar Wilde's most overtly decadent poetic lines, Strauss sets up the 'normal' dynamics and shape of the bar form only to dissolve, distort and deform them by decadent play on the harmonic characteristics of chromatic neighbour chords.) Taruskin's second example of 'mild and pretty' decadence is Schoenberg's setting of Richard Dehmel's 'Erwartung', Op.2 No.1 (1899). The similarities between the opening of this song (Example 1.2), introducing the 'sea-green pond beside the red villa' in which is seen the

---

[26] Richard Taruskin, *The Oxford History of Western Music*, vol.IV: *Early Twentieth Century* (Oxford University Press, 2005), 31–3, 36.

reflection of the moon (a favoured symbolist and decadent image), and that of Strauss's 'Rêverie' are unmissable. It too is based on chromatic neighbour-note motion around the tonic triad. Taruskin points out the obvious debt to the chromaticisms of Wagner's *Tristan and Isolde* but also notes that, by contrast with Wagner, in this song the desired effect is the overt presentation of sex without a philosophical or metaphysical 'mask'. Idealist burdens are jettisoned for 'polymorphously perverse' delight in erotic pleasures.[27] The Strauss and Schoenberg also share a common initial emphasis on the flat sixth, raising it to the prime motivation for the decadent, 'individualized' harmonic detail.[28] In both openings this initial motif – a common romantic musical symbol of yearning – is followed by contrasting material suggesting delight, in the Strauss by the melodic peak on the major submediant (G♯), in the Schoenberg by the filigree arabesque which emphasises the major ninth, a decorative figure which led Taruskin (as it has others) to compare the song with the curvaceous ornaments typical of *Jugendstil* canvases.[29] Yearning moves into voluptuous shape shifting. The conjunction suggests algolagnia, that pleasure in pain which is the sado-masochistic mark of much decadence.

Taruskin's readings are somewhat brief because of the small space he allows for decadence in his historical survey (admittedly, the competition for space is fierce, despite the gargantuan size of the multi-volume project). One of the most sustained attempts to offer an analysis of decadent musical style within a critical examination of cultural and historical contexts is Lawrence Kramer's comparison of Goethe settings by Schubert and (the Slovenian-born) Hugo Wolf.[30] Kramer argues that when romantic subjectivity – based on inwardness and pain – 'wears out' there is an increasing tendency for 'the inner resonances of both desire and suffering to merge with intimations of solipsism, morbidity, and self-destructiveness', to move into what Nietzsche called the 'desire for the

[27] Taruskin, *The Oxford History*, 34–5.

[28] See Dahlhaus, 'The "Individualization" of Harmony', *Between Romanticism and Modernism*, 71–5.

[29] See Walter Frisch, 'Music and *Jugendstil*', *Critical Inquiry* 17 (1990), 138–61; and Reinhold Brinkmann, 'On the Problem of Establishing "Jugendstil" as a Category in the History of Music – with a Negative Plea', in *Art Nouveau and Jugendstil and the Music of the Early Twentieth Century*, *Adelaide Studies in Musicology* 13 (1984), 31–5; Frisch returns to the topic in *German Modernism: Music and the Arts* (Berkeley: University of California Press, 2005), 106–12. For a wider attempt to relate music and *Jugendstil* see Robert Schollum, 'Kodaly, Marx, Szymanowski: Drei Komponisten im Jugendstilbereich', in *Wort und Ton im europäischen Raum: Gedenkschrift für Robert Schollum* (Vienna: Böhlau, 1989), 147–65.

[30] Lawrence Kramer, 'Decadence and Desire: The *Wilhelm Meister* Songs of Wolf and Schubert', in Joseph Kerman (ed.), *Music at the Turn of Century* (Berkeley: University of California Press, 1990), 115–28.

nothing',[31] or into perverse paralysis in the manner of Baudelaire. He concludes that 'when this devaluation of the ego is coupled with a certain masochistic pleasure, a heightened sensuousness, and a love for artifice, we can begin to speak of decadence'. For Kramer, Wolf's compositional 'critique' of Schubert in setting the same texts from Goethe's *Wilhelm Meister* points out the musical techniques which can express this decadent subjectivity. For example, the piano introduction to Wolf's 'Wer sich der Einsamkeit ergibt' (1888) recalls piano material from Schubert's setting, which Schubert 'dwells on briefly, then abandons' after the vocal cadence at the end of the first stanza (bb. 11–14; see Example 1.3).[32]

Wer sich der Einsamkeit ergibt,
Ach! der ist bald allein;
Ein jeder lebt, ein jeder liebt
Und lässt ihn seiner Pein.

He who surrenders himself to solitude,
Ah! He is soon alone;
Everyone lives, everyone loves
And leaves him to his pain.

Wolf's song opens and expands from this musical evocation of a painful ending which was abandoned, left undeveloped in Schubert's romantic model. The descending motif is now presented within a sentence form – or Wagnerian *Satz* – whose harmony is 'shadowed', as Kramer notes, by the tendency to fall to the subdominant minor and is coloured by the tragic dark Neapolitan (Example 1.4). All the material of Wolf's song is derived from obsessive transformations of this phrase (most greatly expanded on the long dominant which sustains the image of the lover 'stealing up' on his mistress). A thematic statement – of intertextual allusion to painful abandonment – is thus fetishistically repeated and unpicked. All the while the tonic is undermined or shadowed by the threat of a fall to the sub-dominant. This is coupled with a strategy in which the initially structural B♭ (the third scale degree of G minor) becomes reinterpreted as the main carrier of the chromatic burden of the introduction, inflecting (in different ways) the dominant chords at the end of bars 1, 2 and 5. This pitch's chromatic alternatives – B♮ and B♭♭ – take over this expressive role in bars 3 and 4, the latter most pungently marking the expressive moment of greatest

[31] Friedrich Nietzsche, *The Will to Power*, trans. Walter Kaufmann and R. J. Hollingdale, ed. Walter Kaufmann (New York: Vintage, 1968), 66.
[32] Kramer, 'Decadence and Desire', 118.

Example 1.3 Franz Schubert, 'Wer sich der Einsamkeit ergibt' (Goethe), bars 1–14

intensity in this material, when the aspirations of melodic ascent turn back to repeated, fatalistic descent. In summary, the relationship of Wolf's setting to Schubert's suggests a kind of 'hyperbolic' rewriting of romantic effect, where the source of decadent style and expression lies in extending the 'romantic agony'.[33]

Kramer notes that the 'replacement of a romantic by a decadent model of the self' exhibited by this song was a 'process that begins in music with

---

[33] The classic text is Mario Praz, *The Romantic Agony*, trans. Angus Davidson (Oxford University Press, 1970). On the sources of decadence in romantic fancy and agony see Jean Pierrot, *The Decadent Imagination 1880–1900*, trans. Derek Coltman (Chicago University Press, 1981). On decadence as a 'paradoxical' or 'hyperbolic' rewriting of romantic themes see Michael Riffaterre, 'Decadent Paradoxes', in Constable, Denisoff and Potolsky (eds.), *Perennial Decay*, 65–79.

Example 1.4 Hugo Wolf, 'Wer sich der Einsamkeit ergibt' (Goethe), bars 1–12

Wagner'.[34] Wolf's debt to Wagner hardly needs reasserting.[35] Inevitably, a study of musical decadence in Central and Eastern Europe is also a study (in large part) of the artistic emulation of, or resistance to, Wagner.[36] The

[34] Kramer, 'Decadence and Desire', 118.

[35] See Amanda Glauert, *Hugo Wolf and the Wagnerian Inheritance* (Cambridge University Press, 1999) and Chapter 6 below.

[36] On Wagner and Eastern Europe see, for example, Rosamund Bartlett, *Wagner in Russia* (Cambridge University Press, 1995); Boris Gasparov, '*Khovanshchina*: A Musical Drama, Russian-Style (Wagner and Musorgsky)', in *Five Operas and a Symphony*, 95–131; Richard

incredibly powerful impact of the Venusberg music from *Tannhäuser*, the eroticism-death symbolism of *Tristan and Isolde*, the image of the debased and degraded Siegfried as he succumbs to the decadent Gibichungs in *Twilight of the Gods*, the sickness–redemption oppositions in *Parsifal* and (to a lesser degree) of Wagner's theoretical writings (for example, those from the 1850s describing artistic production and 'national' types of opera according to cultural decay or sexual deviance, impotence and healthy virility) have all been widely studied.[37] Wagner's legacy in decadent art and thinking has also been richly documented and closely analysed.[38] For example, Baudelaire's description of Wagner's Venus music in terms of 'will, desire, concentration, nervous intensity, explosion' in his essay 'Richard Wagner and *Tannhäuser* in Paris' (1861)[39] is widely recognized as a crucial text, not only in the move of Wagner reception into decadent thematics, but also for the fundamental definition of decadence. The figure

Taruskin, 'Scriabin and the Superhuman', in *Defining Russia Musically* (Princeton University Press, 1997), 308–59; and my *Szymanowski as Post-Wagnerian* (New York: Garland, 1994).

[37] A productive survey of the recent musicological literature would start with the work of Kramer: *Opera and Modern Culture: Wagner and Strauss* (Berkeley: University of California Press, 2004), and 'Musical Form and *Fin-de-Siècle* Sexuality', in *Music as Cultural Practice, 1800–1900* (Berkeley: University of California Press, 1990), 135–75; and that of Marc A. Weiner; 'Opera and the Discourse of Decadence: From Wagner to AIDS', in Constable, Denisoff and Polotsky (eds.), *Perennial Decay*, 119–41, and *Richard Wagner and the Anti-Semitic Imagination* (Lincoln: University of Nebraska Press, 1995), ch.5, 'Icons of Degeneration', 307–47.

[38] See Erwin Koppen's section on Wagner and decadence in his 'Wagnerism as a Concept and Phenomenon', in Ulrich Müller and Peter Wapnewski (eds.), *Wagner Handbook*, trans. and ed. John Deathridge (Cambridge, Mass.: Harvard University Press, 1992), 348–50, and Koppen's substantial study of German, French, English and Italian *fin-de-siècle* literature in *Dekadenter Wagnerismus*. See also the essays in David C. Large and William Weber (eds.), *Wagnerism in European Culture and Politics* (Ithaca: Cornell University Press, 1984); Raymond Furness, *Wagner and Literature*, ch.2, 'Wagner and Decadence', 31–68; Thomas Grey, 'Wagner the Degenerate: *Fin de Siècle* Cultural "Pathology" and the Anxiety of Modernism', *Nineteenth Century Studies* 16 (2002), 73–92. For Wagner's impact on aspects of 'Western' decadence see also Emma Sutton, *Aubrey Beardsley and British Wagnerism in the 1890s* (Oxford University Press, 2002); Steven Huebner, *French Opera at the Fin de Siècle: Wagnerism, Nationalism and Style* (Oxford University Press, 1999); Nachum Schoffman, 'D'Annunzio and Mann: Antithetical Wagnerians', *Journal of Musicology* 11 (1993), 499–524; Gail Finney, 'Self-Reflexive Siblings: Incest as Narcissism in Tieck, Wagner, and Thomas Mann', *The German Quarterly* 56 (1983), 243–56. On the attraction for *fin-de-siècle* homosexual audiences of the 'dissident' sexualities which Wagner's operas seemed to explore see Mitchell Morris, 'Tristan's Wounds: On Homosexual Wagnerians at the *Fin de Siècle*', in Sophie Fuller and Lloyd Whitesell (eds.), *Queer Episodes in Music and Modern Identity* (Urbana and Chicago: University of Illinois Press, 2002), 271–91.

[39] Charles Baudelaire, 'Richard Wagner and *Tannhäuser* in Paris', in *Selected Writings on Art and Literature*, 355. For recent work on this text see Margaret Miner, *Resonant Gaps between Baudelaire and Wagner* (Athens: University of Georgia Press, 1995) and Susan Bernstein, *Virtuosity of the Nineteenth Century: Performing Music and Language in Heine, Liszt and Baudelaire* (Stanford University Press, 1998).

of Venus was widely significant and problematic. Seductive, arousing, inspiring, terrifying and extreme, Venus achieved a pre-eminence and pervasive 'libidinal sway' which led to her being raised as the pinnacle of sexual beauty.[40] Yet, as the ideal nude, Venus seemed unrepresentable. She was the ultimate challenge to the mastery of the artist, and the inevitable source of anxieties about the power of masculine creativity. Wagner's 1861 rewriting of Venus's music in the 'modern' *Tristan* style for the Paris production is in part a reflection of her exalted status and the composer's desire to match her heightened qualities. She demanded more and more from the composer.[41] Wagner rewrites Wagner, reworking his romantic music into decadent effects. More widely, in the mid- and late nineteenth century the seductive profile of the Muse as Venus problematized notions of male artistic identity, leading to the adoption of perverse, typically decadent positions such as masochism.[42] Prostration before the dominatrix in the male's contractual alliance with the cold, radical otherness of the cruel woman was most famously explored in Leopold von Sacher-Masoch's *Venus in Furs* (1870). In illusion and fantasy man stages his servitude, in a projection of his narcissistic ideal. Trauma and sickness become the mark of the true modern (and Wagnerian) man. But in masochistic role-play masculinity could be redefined and thus reassert its hegemonic power. This was not a new position for woman, nor a dissolution of the male subject. Rather, a re-branded form of masculine self-control and definition was affirmed: 'it claims its own undoing as the precondition of its very existence'. A new norm was raised in the name of deviance and marginalization – the wounded, the fragmented, the tormented, the enslaved.[43] Stooped and staggering stands the decadent.

As John Daverio states, for the leading literary lights of decadence – Mann, Gabriele D'Annunzio, Joséphin Péladan and others – *Tristan and*

[40] Caroline Arscott and Katie Scott, 'Introducing Venus', in Caroline Arscott and Katie Scott (eds.), *Manifestations of Venus: Art and Sexuality* (Manchester University Press, 2000), 5.

[41] She was similarly demanding on the painters of the age. The Paris salon of 1863 was replete with efforts at Venus's representation, a project 'symptomatic of a need to assert the primacy of masculine creativity and control, both of which were perceived – consciously or not – as under threat'. Jennifer Shaw, 'The Figure of Venus: Rhetoric of the Ideal and the Salon of 1863', in Arscott and Scott (eds.), *Manifestations of Venus*, 90–2.

[42] Caroline Arscott, 'Venus as Dominatrix: Nineteenth-Century Artists and their Creations', in Arscott and Scott (eds.), *Manifestations of Venus*, 109.

[43] Suzanne R. Stewart, *Sublime Surrender: Male Masochism at the Fin-de-Siècle* (Ithaca: Cornell University Press, 1998), 1–15. On notions of 'masculinity' in decadent writings see George L. Mosse, 'Masculinity and the Decadence', in Roy Porter and Mikuláš Teich (eds.), *Sexual Knowledge, Sexual Science: The History of Attitudes to Sexuality* (Cambridge University Press, 1994), 251–66.

Isolde 'was a prime symbol of morbid desire, spiritual corruption, and feverish hedonism'. Daverio argues that this attraction was primarily based on the seductive allure of Wagner's exquisite and complex musical 'surfaces'. However, the opera's formal 'austerity', noted by Nietzsche, its simplicity and clarity of design, 'contrasts sharply with the sensual and luxurious surface of the finished score, which so captured the later decadent imagination'. Daverio concludes that 'the "decadent" exterior of *Tristan* is held in check by a solidly architectural (one is tempted to say classical) foundation'. In support, he deploys Friedrich Hölderlin's dialectic between appearance (*Schein*) and essence (*Grundton*), an opposition especially tense in *Tristan* because of the often overwhelming seductive beauty of its surface.[44] Decadent delight in surface detail is unquestionable. The strain this places on formal clarity and function is frequently intense. But decadence need not remain 'shallow', and its practitioners were not inappreciative of structural 'depth'. The relationship of decadence to formal organization is a neglected field of enquiry. And in music this is especially vital: formal processes of intensification and dissolution (so central to the structure and expressive character of Tristan's 'delirium' scene[45]), deformation, miniaturism and the preoccupation with 'ending' all possess powerfully decadent potential. 'Classical' musical forms are thereby transformed into new and fascinating designs. To return to Taruskin's 'playful' imagery, the forms so produced may be 'weird', apparently 'impractical' or solely designed for the arousal of 'pleasure', but this does not make their aesthetic or technical significance negligible or disreputable.

The decadent character of *Parsifal* is frequently related to Wagner's famous letter to Mathilde Wesendonck of 30 May 1859 where he described Amfortas as 'my Tristan of the third act with an inconceivable intensification [*Steigerung*]'. Wagner continued, 'more terribly than ever the sinful wounds flare up in him – *His* [i.e. Christ's] wound! His very devotions become a torment! Where is the end to it, where is redemption? The sufferings of humankind endlessly drawn out!'[46] In this description of Amfortas several themes which became central in decadence are evoked: the repeated yearning for the end to apparently endless torment, the coexistence of the highest religious devotion with the most piercing physical pain, the source of all this in erotic transgression. The musical details

---

[44] John Daverio, '*Tristan und Isolde*: Essence and Appearance', in Thomas S. Grey (ed.), *The Cambridge Companion to Wagner* (Cambridge University Press, 2008), 115–18.

[45] See Thomas S. Grey, *Wagner's Musical Prose* (Cambridge University Press, 1995), 342–7.

[46] Wagner, letter to Wesendonck, 30 May 1859, trans. in Richard Wagner, *Selected Letters*, trans. and ed. Stewart Spencer and Barry Millington (London: Dent, 1987), 457.

Example 1.5 Richard Wagner, *Parsifal*, Prelude to Act 1, bars 1–6

operating within the opera's redemptive narrative have been traced by William Kinderman. In a description relating the forces of evolution, the moment, doubleness, cleansing and concentration of complexity, Kinderman also points out stylistic features which can be seen as reflecting decadence. He begins by identifying in the opening phrase of the Prelude to Act 1 (Example 1.5) a 'striking inflection' as the A♭–G semitone descent 'sounds, momentarily, like the flat sixth of C minor', a motif presenting, in 'germinal form', the tonal pairing of A♭ and C which parallels the relationship between the Grail's purity and anguished torment. A transformation of this motif into a 'poignant' rising appoggiatura subsequently supports the enunciation of the word 'Wunde' and informs the crucial moment in Act 2 of Kundry's kissing of Parsifal, when the source of the wound and the 'pollution of the sanctuary' in her previous seduction of Amfortas is revealed. Kinderman describes how in Act 3 this sinful semitonal wound is 'purged' from the communion theme, how it is 'cleansed' as the semitone is replaced by a rising whole-tone. In this he suggests a powerful similarity between *Parsifal* and *Tristan and Isolde*: in both music dramas Wagner presents an opening theme which contains in remarkable concentration 'elements of musical tension and complexity which are identified throughout with the drama, and resolved only at its conclusion'. According to Kinderman, then, the work is not decadently inorganic, but teleologically organic; the resolution of the A♭–C tonal pairing and the cadences of the closing bars offer a 'completing and perfecting' of the 'musical form as an audible symbol for the utopia of redemption'.[47]

For Nietzsche, however, the opera's redemptive yearnings and conclusion represented a fundamental aspect of the decadent 'sickness' of the work. Nietzsche provocatively declared *Parsifal* to be Wagner's 'greatest masterpiece'. He explained that this was because he heard it 'as *the stroke of genius* in seduction', as the supreme example of Wagner's 'persuasion of

---

[47] William Kinderman, 'Wagner's *Parsifal*: Musical Form and the Drama of Redemption', *Journal of Musicology* 4 (1985), 431–46. On *Parsifal* and themes of decadence see also Linda Hutcheon and Michael Hutcheon, *Opera: Desire, Disease, Death* (Lincoln: University of Nebraska Press, 1996), 61–93.

sensuousness which in turn makes the spirit weary and worn-out'. In *Parsifal*, Nietzsche continues,

the cunning in his alliance of beauty and sickness goes so far that, as it were, it casts a shadow over Wagner's earlier art – which now seems too bright, too healthy ... Never was there a greater master in dim, hieratic aromas – never was there a man equally expert in all small infinitudes, all that trembles and is effusive, all the femininisms from the *idioticon* of happiness! – Drink, O my friends, the philters of this art! Nowhere will you find a more agreeable way of enervating your spirit, of forgetting your manhood ...[48]

Here and elsewhere *The Case of Wagner* summarizes many central decadent themes. Famously, Nietzsche declares the crucial role of decadence in modernity and its central significance in his own development: 'I am, no less than Wagner, a child of this time; that is, a decadent.' He repeatedly warns that 'one pays heavily for being one of Wagner's disciples', principally in the 'corruption' of one's taste and nerves. Wagner, the 'greatest name' in the spread of European decadence from Paris to St Petersburg, produces art of sickness, neurosis, recovery, resistance, miniaturism, atomization, artifice, sensuousness and the 'histrionics' which are 'an expression of physiological degeneration'. In all this, 'Wagner sums up modernity'.[49] As we shall see, Nietzsche's notion of 'convalescence' from Wagnerian sickness and the necessity of a full experience of decadence are powerfully resonant in the styles, topics and critical reception of many ambivalently 'post-Wagnerian' works of the late nineteenth and early twentieth centuries. In Nietzsche's own more overtly 'poetical' work this overturning, or overcoming, of *Parsifal* is manifest in Part IV of *Thus Spake Zarathustra* (1883–5), which is a travesty of the opera's redemptive, religious quest and emphasis on sin and pity. Nietzsche's scene of temptation and seduction inverts the model of Parsifal's encounter with Kundry and the Flower Maidens in Act 2 and leads, by contrast with Wagner, to the repudiation of pity. The 'higher men' who seek to divert and seduce Zarathustra are figures parallel to the Flower Maidens (Nietzsche even calls them 'flowers'), and their cry of anguish mimics that of Kundry's hysteria. The final banquet and arcane rites are clearly a parody of Wagner's Grail scene. Wagner, as Zarathustra's adversary, is the 'wicked sorcerer', the 'evil spirit of deception' and the 'melancholy devil'. In a portrait, as Roger Hollinrake

---

[48] Nietzsche, *The Case of Wagner*, in The Birth of Tragedy *and* The Case of Wagner, trans. with commentary by Walter Kaufmann (New York: Vintage, 1967), 183–4.
[49] Nietzsche, *The Case of Wagner*, 155–6, 165, 169.

states, 'drawn from the acuteness of disappointed veneration',[50] Wagner is identified with the magical, mutilated Klingsor.

Klingsor's magic garden in Act 2 of *Parsifal* is a site rich with expressions and figures suggesting the decadent. It is also one where the relationship emerges between decadence and avant-garde. The Flower Maidens are often dismissed as little more than fragrant, flagrant floozies. Thomas Grey's description of them as 'an alluring vision without real substance, a seductive conjurer's trick in which artifice merely apes the ideal of nature' raises their transparently decadent characteristics. They are, Grey continues, 'products of necromantic artifice', and their music, 'with its little aromatic arabesques and sensuously mild chromatic inflections of a smooth harmonic exterior, is the musical equivalent of the exotic Parisian scents and fabrics by which Wagner was seduced'.[51] In their music's filigree patternings chromatic motions reach immediate local, circular completion, suggesting the pleasure of ephemeral delights. But these figures play an important role in crucial transformational aspects of this scene, the turning point of the drama. First Kundry, upon being mistaken by Parsifal for another Flower Maiden (the stage directions describe the appearance 'through an opening of flowers' of a 'young and very beautiful woman – Kundry in altered form – lying on a flowery couch, wearing a light veil-like robe of Arabian style'), transforms their ornamental style as she dismisses them as 'withered' creatures. After Kundry has named Parsifal, the 'pure fool', the Flower Maidens' motivic wriggle is again transformed, now into gradually more disturbingly dissonant contexts. What had previously seemed easy (as in cheaply available sex) is now uneasily disquietening. The passage is shown in Example 1.6. Parsifal, fearful of the knowing Kundry, asks if she is a bloom from the flower garden. Triplet arabesques derived from the Flower Maiden music now combine to form descending chromatic lines. These lines echo the inner-part chromatic descents in the motif of Parsifal as 'pure fool', but they are now the harbingers of his desire to know. The harmonic progression which controls Parsifal's lines is based on a descending A♭–D♭ fifth in the bass, the latter pitch decorated by its upper neighbour D (which is itself prolonged by its upper neighbour E♭). Kundry answers Parsifal's query by telling him of her remote origins, but her chromatic motif is heard over a bass line which is a varied restatement of that which underpinned Parsifal's

---

[50] Roger Hollinrake, *Nietzsche, Wagner and the Philosophy of Pessimism* (London: George Allen and Unwin, 1982), 153. Hollinrake explores the parallels between Part IV of *Zarathustra* and *Parsifal* in great detail, pp. 123–71.

[51] Grey, *Wagner's Musical Prose*, 174–7.

Example 1.6 Wagner, *Parsifal*, Act 2, Parsifal: 'Nie sah ich nie träumte mir …'

question. Now the fall from G♯ (enharmonic A♭) is fully chromaticized and halts on D, which becomes the dominant of the key of Kundry's following 'lullaby' ('Ich sah das Kind an seiner Mutter Brust'). After this lullaby the chromatic instability created from the transformation of Flower Maiden motifs into Kundry's reply is intensified to generate the musical idiom employed after the famous kiss, at Parsifal's recognition of the source of Amfortas's pain, the moment of his acquisition of knowledge, where erotic yearning explodes into ferocious and forceful flux. This effect is then powerfully concentrated in Kundry's motif of extreme, dissonant collapse, which becomes more broadly symbolic of psychological

Example 1.6 (cont.)

and physical anguish. Thus the style has been transformed from decadent amorality to avant-garde agonies. Wagner's virtuoso art of transition allows him to move between apparently opposite aesthetic and stylistic categories.

The gnomic, sententious character of *Parsifal* has often been noted. Nietzsche remarked that in the Prelude to Act 1 'every nuance of feeling' is 'expressed with epigrammatic concision'. In Wagner's prose Dieter Borchmeyer has noted the 'manifest tendency towards hieratic utterance' and 'emotionally intensified words'. Reduction and atomization lead to allusive condensation but also, occasionally, to evaporation, to a sense of 'nothing here and nothing there', as Wagner wrote in 1880.[52] *Parsifal* sounded to Adorno as the dying 'echo' of music rather than as music itself; its motives are 'ascetic, emaciated, desensualized'.[53] Otto Weininger's *On Last Things* (1904), posthumously published after his notorious suicide, reflected on the powerful experience of hearing *Parsifal* in 1902. Weininger was particularly moved by the 'magnificent' second act, especially the Parsifal–Kundry exchanges. More specifically, he declared that 'what appealed to me so strongly about it was just the way the passion is muted, the colours are not heavy and yet are vivid ... everything seems muffled ...'.[54] He heard these qualities of understatement, tracery and elusiveness captured in the motif of the Flower Maidens, which he described as the 'emerging of a Will-o'-the-wisp from nothingness, and its submerging', and even in Kundry's cries, in which he heard 'the faint residue of the sense of doom'.[55] But these comments contrast with the characterization of Wagnerian motifs elsewhere in these collected notes where Weininger writes of their 'maximum of musical density ... They are never diluted, but always say everything. Wagner's motifs are characterized by the extreme succinctness, concentration and irresistibility of his melodies, by their great remoteness from any lack of oxygen, and by the opposite of any thinning of the atmosphere and absence of mass.'[56] There is some contradiction here: are Wagner's motifs densely packed or lightly ephemeral? In Weininger's ears they may tend to opposite extremes of 'weight', but what is constant is their miniature concentration of effect. Here Weininger beholds the feature which had led Nietzsche to castigate Wagner as the 'greatest *miniaturist* in music who crowds into the smallest space an infinity of sense and sweetness'.[57]

Weininger famously raised Wagner's Kundry as a prime example of the 'hysterical' woman. In the vocal exclamations of this character he heard revealed the essence of his understanding of the essential character of woman.[58] Hysteria – with its all-too-clear misogyny – was a topic of wide

---

[52] See Dieter Borchmeyer, *Richard Wagner: Theory and Theatre* (Oxford: Clarendon Press, 1991), 379, 383. Nietzsche's comment was made in a letter to Peter Gast, 21 January 1887.

[53] Theodor W. Adorno, 'On the Score of *Parsifal*', trans. with commentary by Anthony Barone, *Music & Letters* 76 (1995), 384.

[54] Otto Weininger, *A Translation of Weininger's 'Über die letzten Dinge' (1904/1907)/'On Last Things'*, trans. Steven Burns (Lewiston, NY: The Edwin Mellen Press, 2001), 76.

[55] Weininger, *On Last Things*, 75.   [56] Weininger, *On Last Things*, 74.

[57] Nietzsche, *The Case of Wagner*, 171 (Nietzsche's emphasis).

[58] Otto Weininger, *Geschlecht und Charakter* (Vienna, 1902); see Julie Brown, 'Otto Weininger and Musical Discourse in Turn-of-the-Century Vienna', in Juliè Brown (ed.), *Western Music and Race* (Cambridge University Press, 2007), 84–101.

interest. Its significance was considered to extend beyond the psychological. Hystericism was broadly understood by Nietzsche to lie at the root of
the 'decay' of artistic expression into hyperbole.[59] But for Mann this
hysteria in Wagner was an essential and powerful aspect of the transition
from romanticism to modernism: 'There is about all Wagner's heroines a
touch of grand hysteria, something somnambulistic, enraptured and
visionary, which lends a curious and disquieting modernity to their romantic posturings.' Kundry is the extreme, most modern manifestation of this
trend; she is 'nothing less than an exercise in mythical pathology; in her
agonizingly schizoid condition, an instrument of the Devil and penitent
hungering after redemption, she is portrayed with an unsparing clinical
accuracy, an audacious naturalism in the exploration and representation of
a hideously diseased emotional existence'.[60] Thus Mann hears Kundry as a
figure in which the move from romanticism through naturalism to expressionism is achieved. But we have seen how this expressionistic audacity is
reached through the transformation of decadent musical material. Mann
seems to have missed a crucial aesthetic and stylistic component of
Wagner's transformative music. However, while in his great 1933 essay
on Wagner Mann never uses the term 'decadence', several passages raise it
in all but name. Mann writes that the

> general spiritual tenor of Wagner's music is marked by a certain pessimistic
> heaviness and measured yearning, a sense of fragmentation in its rhythms, of forces
> struggling out of dark confusion to find deliverance in beauty; it is the music of an
> oppressed soul, not a music that speaks dancingly to our muscles, but the toiling,
> heaving and struggling of northern drudgery.

The characteristics of bleak pessimism, disintegration into fragments,
physical lassitude and even 'northern-ness', as we shall see, amount to a
checklist of decadent features. This list expands to include permissiveness
and algolagnia when Mann identifies the 'intensification' of Tristan's
suffering which Wagner felt he had expressed in Amfortas as 'the involun-
tary and ultimately self-indulgent law by which all his work lives and
grows'. Mann's extended discussion of Wagner's image of his own ill-
health turns the composer into a decadent hypochondriac: 'his was a
constitution that felt itself to be constantly on the edge of exhaustion …
Constipated, melancholy, insomniac, afflicated in every kind of way', so
that already by the age of thirty-nine Wagner felt his nerves were 'in an

[59] Nietzsche, *The Case of Wagner*, 169.
[60] Thomas Mann, 'The Sorrows and Grandeur of Richard Wagner' [1933], in *Pro and Contra
      Wagner*, trans. Allan Blunden (London: Faber, 1985), 99.

advanced state of decay … my dying has already begun'. Mann describes this ailing Wagner as 'breathing the air' of his bourgeois age in an atmosphere of 'moralistic pessimism' and a 'mood of decline', and as demonstrating a bourgeois taste for a fastidious, opulent elegance which 'shows a tendency to degeneracy'. And finally he identifies the pairing of Baudelaire's two 'gods', Poe and Wagner, as a 'propinquity' which 'suddenly places Wagner's art in a new light', that of romanticism in its 'high and late periods, intoxicated with death and beauty – a world of pessimism, of intimate acquaintance with exotic drugs and an over-refinement of the sense that indulges rapturously in all manner of synaesthetic speculation … Such is the world into which Richard Wagner must be projected.'[61] This is the world of decadence.

Alexander Scriabin compared *Parsifal* with *Tristan* through a typical eroticization of the creative process – with the aging Wagner characterized as approaching impotance: 'the weaker he is in the sexual area, the weaker his art. Maximum creativity; maximum eroticism. Look at Wagner. *Tristan* is his maximum, and *Parsifal*, already it has dropped. It's the work of a worn out old man.'[62] Mann, pairing *Parsifal* with Ibsen's *When We Dead Awaken* (1899), saw a work 'filled with a majestic sclerotic weariness, having that sense of the now-routine about all their artistic devices, and all the marks of lateness: recapitulation, retrospective, self-quotation and dissolution'.[63] Interpretations of *Parsifal* have often evoked decadence through its status as the quintessential 'late work', grounded, as Adorno noted, on the work's 'excess and extravagance, its peculiarity and mannerism'. For Adorno, however, the work's style reflects declining artistic vigour to remarkable effect: 'from out of the waning of his original inventive powers, Wagner's force produces the virtue of a late style [*Altersstil*]', a style that 'withdraws from appearance' and is based upon 'the phenomenal decomposition of the musical language'. Adorno identifies the Flower Maidens as the 'first *Jugendstil* ornaments'.[64] And here, in summary, is the image of a 'young' style emerging out of the old: the late flowers of post-romantic artifice produce the blooms of a new season. As Anthony Barone has demonstrated, concepts of late style are produced by the confluence of two intellectual tributaries: teleological or periodic historiography, especially as codified by Winckelmann and Hegel, and natural history, the construction of

[61] Mann, 'The Sorrows and Grandeur of Richard Wagner', 112–14, 135, 146.
[62] Faubion Bowers, *Scriabin: A Biography*, vol.II (New York: Dover, 1996), 226.
[63] Mann, 'The Sorrows and Grandeur of Richard Wagner', 95.
[64] Adorno, 'On the Score of *Parsifal*', 384–6.

Example 1.7 Wagner, *Tristan and Isolde*, Prelude to Act 1, bars 1–3

organic narratives of human development and their application to the lives of artists. Winckelmann's model necessarily includes a period of inevitable decline, the 'unstable late phase of decay, the least explicable, the most ineffable'. This was a stage that Winckelmann failed to name, in a significant manifestation of his fear of the end.[65] Towards the end of the nineteenth century and into the new one concepts of lateness and evolution, of mannerism and the decline of style, informed the way in which Wagner's works shaped 'developmental' narratives of music history. In Lorenz Kraussold's lectures (*Die Musik in ihrer kulturhistorischen Entwickelung und Bedeutung*) delivered at Bayreuth in 1876, German music's 'evolution' was inevitably viewed as triumphantly assuming its position as the Universal art when 'all lines of evolution meet in Wagner, with Liszt at his side'.[66] But by the early twentieth century, in the first part of his *The Decline of the West* Spengler identified Wagner as culmination but also as marking the moment of imminent decadence, manifest in his taste for the 'gigantic' as the 'dissimulation' of the 'absence' of 'inward greatness', and also for miniature, colouristic effect. Inspired by Baudelaire, Spengler makes a comparison with Manet to argue that 'the end and the culmination of art was the conjuring up of a world in space out of strokes and patches of colour'. Wagner achieved this in the concentrated symbolic tone 'painting' exemplified by the first three bars of *Tristan* (Example 1.7):

A whole world of soul could crowd into these three bars. Colours of starry midnight, of sweeping clouds, of autumn, of the day dawning in fear and sorrow, sudden glimpses of sunlit distances, world-fear, impending doom, despair and its fierce effort, hopeless hope – all these impressions which no composer before him had

---

[65] Anthony Barone, 'Richard Wagner's *Parsifal* and the Theory of Late Style', *Cambridge Opera Journal* 7 (1995), 39–41.

[66] Quoted in Warren Dwight Allen, *Philosophies of Music History* [1939] (New York: Dover 1962), 119, 208, 285.

thought it possible to catch, he could paint with entire distinctness in the few tones of a motive … Everything emerges in bodiless infinity, no longer even does a linear melody wrestle itself clear of the vague tone-masses that in strange surgings challenge an imaginary space. The motive comes up out of dark terrible depths. It is flooded for an instant by a flash of hard bright sun. Then, suddenly, it is so close upon us that we shrink. It laughs, it coaxes, it threatens, and anon it vanishes into the domain of the strings, only to return again out of endless distances, faintly modified in the voice of a single oboe, to pour out a fresh cornucopia of spiritual colours.

Spengler's description is indulgently poetic, but we can see several aspects that evoke the 'decadent', in particular the density of symbolic resonance in miniature forms and the appearance and vanishing of figures. Spengler's concluding opinion of the art of Wagner and Manet is further replete with key themes of decadence: 'As a step, it is necessarily the last step'; it is 'an artificial art', and 'has no further organic future, it is the mark of the end'. Thus, music practised 'after Wagner' is marked by 'impotence and falsehood'. For Spengler, what 'died' in *Tristan* was 'Faustian' art, the dynamic work produced by the 'Faustian man' who 'sees in a history a tense unfolding towards an aim'. The illusion or 'lie' that this dynamism is not 'exhausted' is for Spengler the very 'foundation of Bayreuth'.[67] Spengler's myth of 'decline' in the post-Wagnerian West is, of course, myopic and prejudiced. But it is an important manifestation of powerful anxieties in European culture of the early twentieth century, deploys a range of terms central to the conception of decadence, and raises the question of what is possible 'after Wagner', a question which vexed so many artists in this period.[68] Mann, pursuing his

[67] Oswald Spengler, *The Decline of the West* [*Der Untergang des Abendlandes*, 1918, 1922], trans. Charles Francis Atkinson (London: George Allen and Unwin, 1932), 291–3, 364.

[68] Michael P. Steinberg has couched the relevant question to include a terrible but irresistible pun: 'music trauma, or, is there life after Wagner?' Steinberg argues that the recovery or restoration of subjectivity after the Wagnerian trauma is a subversive one because through it the centre is claimed 'from the vantage point of the periphery', an act achieved by establishing a heroic femininity which is sung by the pure voice of nature: 'if post-Wagnerian opera is post-traumatic opera, it must be understood according to the regeneration of voice'; this 'equals the regeneration of non-Germanness'. This is manifest in 'minor modernisms' which reclaim the centre from the periphery – an idea which Steinberg appropriates from Deleuze and Guattari's notion that in Kafka, for example, a minority constructs a literature within a major language. In music the 'minor' subverts the major, and is figured, for example, as the feminine, the melancholic. This can be employed as a way of interpreting projects such as Bartók and Balázs's *Duke Bluebeard's Castle* (where the masochism in the relationship between the operatic protagonists reflects masochistic self-enslavement in the political relationship of Hungary to Austria in the Habsburg Empire) and Janáček and Capek's *The Makropoulos Case* (whose main character's 300-year torment has the same span as the subjection of Bohemia within the Habsburg Empire). See Michael P. Steinberg, *Listening to Reason: Culture, Subjectivity, and Nineteenth-Century Music* (Princeton University Press, 2004).

pairing of Wagner's *Parsifal* with the 'late' work of Ibsen, is pessimistic: 'As for what was termed *fin de siècle*, what was it but the paltry satyr play of a minor age to the century's true and awesome finale, encountered in the last works of these two sorcerers?'[69] The art of the end of the century is condemned as *too* late, its magic as worn-out trickery, its message a tautological postscript. However, Adorno, in unusually positive mood, noted that Spengler 'over-looks one thing – the forces released by decay. "Wie scheint doch alles werdende so krank" ['How sick seems all becoming'] – Georg Trakl's line transcends Spengler's landscape. In a world of brutal and oppressed life, decadence becomes the refuge of a potentially better life ...'[70] Similar sympathies are expressed in more fullsome manner by Robin Holloway:

By the turn of the modern century this [Austro-German] tradition was decadent, although astonishingly fecund in its decay. A rating circa 1880 would still have been 'supreme': Wagner, Brahms, Bruckner, three giants at the height of their powers. Yet decay ran alongside: what is latent in the gods grows explicit in the succeeding demi-gods, the generation of the 1860s – Mahler, Strauss, Wolf – and the 70s – Reger, Schoenberg. These composers, heirs to a wealth of resources used with complete technical mastery, tend towards excess in all things – length, performing forces, volume (and later, exaggerated brevity, barely audible dynamics from a tiny group of players inside or without an enormous orchestra). Nervous intensity is the expressive goal; head and heart alike are liable to explode with approaching over-cerebration and overkill ... Our sense now is, 'What a wonderful way to go!' – feasting, debauchery, fireworks, squandering the savings of centuries in a riot of conspicuous consumption; sunsets and love-deaths by the dozen, nightmares and blasphemies, heads on dishes and corpses under the bench ...[71]

Artists who identified with decadent aesthetics and styles fought constantly against the charge of epigonism, and the shadow cast over this battlefield by the work of Wagner was of course especially long and dark. Musical decadence in Central and Eastern Europe is a shifting cultural phenomenon, at times post-, anti-, semi- or pointedly non-Wagnerian, and sometimes an ambiguous combination of these within the one work. In the German modernist tradition, Nietzsche, Mann and Spengler have long been recognized as the major analysts of decadence. And in the work of each of them, music is especially prominent. Analysis of the relationship of this German decadence to that found in the music of Austrian, Polish,

[69] Mann, 'The Sorrows and Grandeur of Richard Wagner', 95.
[70] Adorno, 'Spengler after the Decline', in *Prisms*, trans. Samuel and Shierry Weber (Cambridge, Mass.: MIT Press, 1983), 71.
[71] Robin Holloway, 'Customised Goods' [1997], in *On Music: Essays and Diversions 1963–2003* (Brinkworth: Claridge Press, 2003), 329.

Russian, Hungarian and Czech composers is crucial to understanding the repertory of late romanticism and early modernism. In recent musicology Taruskin, Kramer, Morrison, Gasparov, Kinderman, Barone and even the profoundly sceptical Dahlhaus have opened up important areas in this slippery terrain. Following the work of these and other authors who will appear in due course, the challenge now lies in constructing a broader range of readings in which defining facets of decadence can be persuasively identified in musical forms and expressions. The contribution of decadent musical features to wider discourses in nineteenth-century and early twentieth-century Central and Eastern European modernity can then be more fully appreciated. But the development of an understanding of how decadence is artistically manifest and the extent of its significance and relationship to other related and conflicting trends in modernism has vexed many scholars in literary history and cultural theory. Some indeed have concluded that the term 'decadence' is useless, even dangerous. If defining decadence is tough, then defending it is sometimes equally testing.

Defining and defending decadence

Recently, historians have treated the term 'decadence' with extreme caution and a high degree of suspicion. Historical narratives incorporating notions of decadence or decline, which Winckelmann and Spengler famously exemplify, have long fallen into disrepute. There has been disciplinary resistance to grand narratives of cyclical historical change based on cultural rise and fall and the deployment of organic metaphors such as 'decay' and 'regeneration'. The histories which draw on these strategies and metaphors are viewed as stimulated by the writer's subjective feelings of lateness and decline, with the resulting historical narrative formed to justify this sense of decadence. (For example, A. L. Rowse saw Spengler as drawing tendentious inspiration from German *Schadenfreude* – German defeat engendering the sense of ending.) For many historians, 'decadence' is too literary, nostalgic, pejorative, ideologically loaded (as are its antonyms – 'progress', 'regeneration'), pathological, and associated with troubling concepts of nature (barbarism) and culture (civilization).[72] 'Decadence' is a term 'damaged, or vulnerable,

---

[72] See Neville Morley, 'Decadence as a Theory of History', *New Literary History* 35 (2005), 573–85, which, among other issues, discusses the dismissal of Spengler in Rowse's classic *The Use of History* (London: Hodder & Stoughton, 1946).

from the start', declared Richard Gilman in his coruscating essay of the late 1970s. 'Its existence', he argues, is 'purely negative. It is a word chosen to fill a space.' For Gilman, who considers progress and decadence to be two sides of an 'illusion', the important question is whether such metaphors can be employed to create an artistically useful 'other-worldly' space, that is, whether the notion of 'decadence' can function productively as a 'lie' that 'must lead to truth'. There are familiar usages which, for Gilman, fail this test: for example, cultural history based on the metaphor of the life cycle of the human body or ages of man (as in Spengler's *Decline of the West*) or as a fictional construct designed to support an ideal (as in the image of the end of the Roman Empire brought about by decline through decadence or old age). Gilman is ultimately dismissive: 'decadence' is a 'portmanteau stuffed with emptiness', and 'will go on recommending itself to the shallow, the thoughtless and imitative, the academically frozen: monkey minds'.[73] *Contra* Gilman, this study will demonstrate, by means of contextualization, critical interrogation and stylistic analysis, that the term can be employed without the resulting work becoming that of a simian simpleton. In fact, Gilman's book itself suggests a way of moving forward with what seems such a 'backward' term (his comic-derogatory evolutionary imagery is telling). Gilman writes:

what history appears to show, instead of a law of decadence, are the simultaneity of decline and advance ... and the potential convertibility of one form of human enterprise into another. The evidently powerful produces the secretly so; the appearance of weakness is discovered as actual strength, and the reverse; culture wanes in order to renew itself; empires 'die' so that their parts may live; the immoral is the proof of the moral.

Gilman is also suggestive of a productive critical angle when he states that the term 'decadence' has been deployed to cover what is really 'fluctuation', since standards do not fall: they 'shift'. The analysis of decadence in cultural history as a crucial state of flux, manifesting complex dialectical relationships with development and progress, is the basis of David Weir's study, in which he asserts that decadence 'provides a conceptual focus that helps to unify the cultural transition from romanticism to modernism'. Weir argues that the 'various nineteenth-century movements that proliferated in the period between romanticism and modernism (naturalism, symbolism, Parnassianism, Pre-Raphaelitism, aestheticism, *décadisme*, and others)

[73] Richard Gilman, *Decadence: The Strange Life of an Epithet* (New York: Farrar, Straus and Giroux, 1979), 150–2, 157–62, 180.

can be best understood if they are all seen as grounded in some concept of decadence or decadentism'. Within this transition decadence plays a 'dynamic', 'generative' role; it is 'developmental'.[74]

If decadence can be defined within transition, then the characteristic decadent position has normally been viewed as occupying the last or the next-to-last phase, a moment before final decline or demise in which looking back to earlier, stronger states is the preoccupying state of mind. Nietzsche, unavoidably a towering presence in studies of decadence because of the term's central role in his influential diagnosis of modern culture, writes in *Twilight of the Idols* (1889) that 'we moderns' are living in an age of 'decline' and weakness by comparison with the last 'great' or 'strong' age, which he identifies as the Renaissance. But under the pervasive 'unconscious influence of *décadence*', Nietzsche declares, we cannot go back, and 'retrogression' is impossible: 'one has to go forward, which is to say step by step further into *décadence* (– this is my definition of modern "progress" …). One can retard this development and, through retardation, dam and gather up degeneration itself and make it more vehement and sudden: more one cannot do.'[75] This apparent paradox of an impetus to move forward generated through the experience of decadence is not one found solely in Nietzsche. Gilman characterizes Joris-Karl Huysmans's *À Rebours* (1884), the heretical bible of French literary decadence, as a book representing a beginning, something new which, by contrast with its topics and characters, is not old and tired but fresh and vital. Thus Huysmans emerges as a prophet of the modern. Oscar Wilde, the most famous victim of the use of 'decadent' as a term for moral and legal condemnation, similarly wrote works whose decadent style can be understood to point forwards.[76] Indeed, as Renato Poggioli noted, decadent discontent with the present as the result of the negative consequences of apparent progress in the modern world is closely comparable with the distinctively antihistorical, prospective view of the avant-garde; the end of the series meets the beginning of the new. Thus extremes touch.[77] Decadence and the avant-garde are two sides of modernism's discontent with bourgeois positivism. Both seek to *épater le*

[74] David Weir, *Decadence and the Making of Modernism* (Amherst: University of Massachusetts Press, 1995), xvi–xvii.

[75] Nietzsche, *Twilight of the Idols* [1889], trans. R. J. Hollingdale (Harmondsworth: Penguin, 1990), 101–2, 108. On the 'sudden' and Nietzsche see Karl Heinz Bohrer, *Suddenness: On the Moment of Aesthetic Appearance*, trans. Ruth Crowley (New York: Columbia University Press, 1994), 113–72.

[76] Gilman, *Decadence*, 67.

[77] Renato Poggioli, *The Theory of the Avant-Garde*, trans. Gerald Fitzgerald (Cambridge, Mass.: Harvard University Press, 1968), 75–6.

bourgeois. The distinction lies in decadence's preoccupation with the transitory by contrast with the avant-garde's determined delight in disjunction.

There are other ways in which decadence is strikingly transitional. It can be understood as straddling an aesthetic transition between the apparently polar extremes of naturalism and symbolism, as inhabiting ambiguous positions between analysis and synthesis, object and subject, a position typified by obsessions with the detailed portrayal of perverse deformations or esoteric transfigurations (often, narcissistically, in the self-portrait). Furthermore, degeneration – a central process in decadent formal descriptions and symbolic imaginations – can be understood as a process that can operate either from the surface inwards or from the depths to outer appearance.[78] These transitory forces move towards the grotesque, sacrilegious, or perversely erotic, in the adoption of intermediate or hybrid states (e.g. androgyne), in human figures blending into natural or artificial forms – for example, women as waves, plants, or dying swans – and in modern (often misanthropic or misogynist) visions of Ovidian metamorphoses.[79]

This entwinement with states of transition highlights decadence's defining position within the modern concept of time. Matei Calinescu makes a distinction between the 'classical' idea of decadence (as found in Plato's *Republic*) and its 'modern' version, based on the latter's dependence on a 'linear and irreversible' view of time in the Judaeo-Christian tradition, which works towards the judgement of the 'last day'. Modern decadence is the 'anguishing prelude to the end of the world' in which every single instant or moment is decisive and deliberated. In the experience of modern temporality the heightened sense and mistrust of apparently inexorable 'progress' leads to anxiety concerning loss, a feeling of alienation, and thus to a withdrawal into a state in which 'decadence becomes self-consciously modern'.[80] The experience of transitionality which underpins this temporality informed the nineteenth-century development of a periodic conception of history, with 'zones of indeterminacy' identified between classical or normative periods of 'organic wholeness'. These

---

[78] The creations of Mann's Gustave von Aschenbach exhibited 'aristocratic self-command that is eaten out from within and for as long as it can conceals its biological decline from the eyes of the world' or 'the sere and ugly outside, hiding the embers of smouldering fire', where 'the pallid languors of the flesh ... contrasted with the fiery ardours of the spirit within': *Death in Venice* [1911], in Thomas Mann, *Death in Venice; Tristan; Tonio Kröger*, trans. H. T. Lowe-Porter (Harmondsworth: Penguin, 1955), 15–16.

[79] See, for example, the essays in Peter Barta (ed.), *Metamorphoses in Russian Modernism* (Budapest: Central European University Press, 2000).

[80] Matei Calinescu, *Five Faces of Modernity: Modernism, Avant-Garde, Decadence, Kitsch, PostModernism* (Durham: Duke University Press, 1987), 153–7.

periods were retrospectively identified and interpreted within a governing concept of history which was dynamic and teleological. Although interest grew in the periods of transition, in the chaotic or transformative historical gaps between ages of coherence, 'in the aesthetic realm … such periods are generally thought to produce forgettable art that has degenerated into bad taste and succumbed to the vulgar charms of a hybrid, flamboyant, or decadent style'.[81] In a climate of *le mal du siècle*, which was felt with the Restoration after the great revolutionary period (a shift famously analysed by Stendhal and Nietzsche), the defining experience was one of a dissatisfactory state of limbo, with romanticism's Utopia painfully and protractively vanishing into the increasingly remote past or unattainable future, a condition reflected in the polar visions of the 'nostalgic' and the 'messianic'. Modernity became defined as a 'transitional period', characterized by the double process of decay and renewal, and also therefore as a period of doubt with regard to the outcome, as these dialectical forces waxed and waned in strength. This was an ambiguity encapsulated in Alfred de Musset's startling 1836 image of the spirit of the age as an 'angel of twilight … half mummy, half fetus'.[82] Goran Blix argues that this uncertain doubleness was 'tamed' by Baudelaire's invention and celebration of the term 'modernity' in the *Salon of 1845* and *The Painter of Modern Life* (1863), for in this famous definition of the modern as 'the transitory, the fugitive, the contingent' Baudelaire bestowed upon it the 'reassuring constancy of a stable term' in a time of anxiety over apparently constant flux and fluidity. Transition is raised as norm, and the modern as an endless period of transition, of an 'ambivalent, hopeful, dreadful, final, open-ended character', one of both 'imminent closure and endless expansion'.[83] There are of course suggestive resonances here with Wagner's 'endless melody' and 'art of transition', but in the modern predicament it is unclear whether through these transitions we will see worlds end, begin or both (as in the double ending of Brünnhilde's final monologue at the climax of *Twilight of the Gods*). Transitional modernity undermines the authority of synthetic-redemptive endings: it is a culture of 'apocalyptic overtures'[84] which reach their most developed state in decadent art of the *fin de siècle*,

---

[81] Goran Blix, 'Charting the "Transitional Period": The Emergence of Modern Time in the Nineteenth Century', *History and Theory* 45 (2006), 55.

[82] Musset, *La Confession d'un enfant du siècle* [1836], trans. from Blix, 'Charting the "Transitional Period"', 63.

[83] Blix, 'Charting the "Transitional Period"', 71.

[84] See Richard Dellamora, *Apocalyptic Overtures: Sexual Politics and the Sense of an Ending* (New Brunswick: Rutgers University Press, 1994).

where the aim is endlessly to postpone, and hence intensify the inevitability of ending, and to challenge the hope placed in an ultimate, higher state of unification. Decadence might therefore be understood as the 'other' to teleology and metaphysics, those fictional, constructed 'natural' and Ideal 'norms' which are themselves revealed to be 'no more than an illusory projection, a false turn away from the materiality of an allegorical world without redemption'.[85]

Decadence and modernism are thus ambiguously entwined. Decadence is not merely a parodic hiatus before the inception of modernism.[86] It is a vital part of what defines the modern, what makes modernism so paradoxical and at times apparently self-contradictory. There is, therefore, an urgent need to move out of the restrictive legacy of Max Nordau's hugely influential and widely translated *Entartung* (*Degeneration*) (1892), which defined decadence as second-rate and retrograde, as an exoticized or 'localized' and dangerous 'other' (e.g. Byzantium).[87] In recent years there has been important work in literary criticism revealing how decadent textual strategies 'interfere with the boundaries and borders (national, sexual, definitional, historical, to name but a few)' and how the tropes and characters of decadence, and their uses, cultivation and illusions in various 'inversions, displacements, and qualifications', seek to 'problematize orthodox critical measures of decay and degeneracy and to destabilize the binary oppositions in cultural discourse' (nature/artifice; male/female; regression/progress, etc.). Baudelaire, Huysmans, Nietzsche and Wilde are prime examples of writers appropriating or developing strategies which challenged and reinvigorated the tired and clichéd 'organic, historical, and aesthetic metaphors' which attach to decadence.[88]

But an apparent paradox appears, for as a stylistic category decadence can be seen to be based on the desire to inhibit transition. Indeed, this is one feature through which decadence and symbolism, so closely entwined, might be differentiated. For Clive Scott, symbolist poetry characteristically explores moments of relativity in 'seamless transition'; decadence, by contrast, characteristically seeks to capture the fleeting moment as valorized in the influential 'Conclusion' to Walter Pater's *Renaissance* (1873). Pater's words are very familiar: 'Not the fruit of experience, but experience itself, is

---

[85] Charles Bernheimer, 'Unknowing Decadence', in Constable, Denisoff and Potolsky (eds.), *Perennial Decay*, 50–63.

[86] See the introduction to Constable, Denisoff and Potolsky (eds.), *Perennial Decay*.

[87] Max Nordau, *Degeneration*, trans. of 2nd (1895) edn with an introduction by George L. Mosse (Lincoln: University of Nebraska Press, 1993).

[88] Introduction to Constable, Denisoff and Potolsky (eds.), *Perennial Decay*, 9–16.

the end … To burn always with this hard, gem-like flame, to maintain this ecstasy, is success in life.' Crucially, the experience Pater describes is ephemeral – 'While all melts under our feet, we may well grasp at any exquisite passion … For art comes to you proposing frankly to give nothing but the highest quality to your moments as they pass, and simply for those moments' sake.'[89] The intense but isolated moment is cherished in 'its awful brevity': it is doomed, shrinking, immanently lost. While symbolists characteristically delight in what Scott calls an 'elastic' time, decadents delight in the exploration of paralysis and stagnancy.[90] But the epigraph (from Heraclitus) at the head of Pater's 'Conclusion' – 'All things are in motion and nothing at rest' – is telling. As Pater writes:

To such a tremulous wisp constantly re-forming itself on the stream, to a single sharp impression, with a sense in it, a relic more or less fleeting, of such moments gone by, what is real in our life fines itself down. It is with this movement, with the passage and dissolution of impressions, images, sensations, that analysis leaves off – that continual vanishing away, that strange, perpetual, weaving and unweaving of ourselves.[91]

The moment is always passing; and each and every one of them may or may not be the last. Decadent movement is a vibration which weakens; under the threat of paralysis it seeks to sustain this moment in quivering stasis, for it may be the delectable last shudder of pleasurable experience. In the face of decay, the compulsion is to preserve. Indeed, Pater's view of history, *contra* Hegelianism and Darwinism, is one which emphasizes the need for preservation: 'the intensification of experience comes out of the need for an isolated self to take on the fatality of its own re-composition and to do so at every moment'.[92] Transition is feared because the present experience may be the moment that immediately precedes final extinction. But the inevitability and imminence of this demise are precisely why the transitory sensuous pleasures are heightened and beautified. Such ideas inform, for

[89] Walter Pater, *The Renaissance: Studies in Art and Poetry* [1873], ed. Adam Phillips (Oxford University Press, 1986), 151–3.
[90] Scott identifies other contrasts: symbolism transfigures, transforms, transcends; decadence disfigures, deforms, descends. Symbolist art is depersonalized, in the Baudelairean 'vaporization of the self' as in the hashish dream; the decadent 'remains imprisoned in personality, either as a defensive strategy, or as part of an ethos of self-cultivation (dandyism) or as inability to escape ironic self-consciousness'. See Clive Scott, 'The Poetry of Symbolism and Decadence', in Patrick McGuinness (ed.), *Symbolism, Decadence and the Fin de Siècle: French and European Perspectives* (University of Exeter Press, 2000), 57–71.
[91] Pater, *The Renaissance*, 151–2.
[92] Brad Bucknell, *Literary Modernism and Musical Aesthetics: Pater, Pound, Joyce, and Stein* (Cambridge University Press, 2001), 41, 43.

example, Béla Bálasz's 'Death Aesthetics' (1907), where the emphasis is placed on the immanent demise of every moment, one which is perceived or valued as beautiful precisely as we already mourn its inevitable loss: the beautiful is the promise of memory, of a mourning that has already begun, its becoming into appearance is bound to its withdrawal, to its absence.[93]

The sources and styles of modern decadence

Having outlined the main contexts and concerns of decadence, we are faced with the question: how are these preoccupations manifest in artistic style? In a classic study Jean Pierrot traced the sources of the decadent aesthetic in the romantic 'fancy' and romantic 'agony' of the work of Baudelaire, Poe, De Quincey, Flaubert, Théophile Gautier and Schopenhauer. Based on pessimism, a loss of traditional or orthodox faith (variously reflected in the heretical and hysterical, in aesthetic Catholicism, mysticism, occultism) and an abhorrence of nature as an unfeeling mechanism, decadence sought escape from both the redemptive and the 'natural' through moving into the artificial, deviant, perverted or abnormal. The decadent wished to stand solitary, to appear aloof from society's demands, from the political and social movements whose progress was illusory at best, damaging at worst, and move into an inner sensation, the rare, the new, the strange, the nervous, the hallucinatory, the sexual unconscious, the fantastic, *les paradis artificiels* or the elemental *rêverie* (invoking images of water, gemstones, vegetable matter, often in decay or metamorphosis).[94] When decadence as a 'style' was influentially described in Gautier's preface to the 1868 edition of Baudelaire's notorious *Les Fleurs du mal* (first published in 1857), although it was identified as the product of an aged culture its aim was the generation of new styles and forms which express psychological areas until now artistically elusive:

The style inadequately called of decadence is nothing but art arrived at the point of extreme maturity yielded by the slanting suns of aged civilizations: an ingenious, complicated style, full of shades and of research, constantly pushing back the boundaries of speech, borrowing from all technical vocabularies, taking colour from all palettes and notes from all keyboards, struggling to render what is most inexpressible in thought, what is vague and most elusive in the outlines of form,

---

[93] For further commentary see Thomas Harrison, *1910: The Emancipation of Dissonance* (Berkeley: University of California Press, 1996).
[94] Pierrot, *The Decadent Imagination*.

listening to translate the subtle confidences of neurosis, the dying confessions of passion grown depraved, and the strange hallucinations of the obsession which is turning to madness.[95]

Thus, in Gautier's understanding the decadent style pushes art into territories unknown, feared or prohibited. Part of the motivation for this heroic stylistic adventure, as Robert Pynsent notes, was the desire to shock the arbiters of taste (*épater le bourgeois*). In such a style traditional modes of organic connection and narrative, and the expected unity of tone, are all likely to be eschewed. Instead, apparently incompatible coexistences are pursued; for example, the playful and the profound, pessimism and pleasure, enthusiasm and *ennui*.[96] Such juxtapositions generate new frissons, for within such determinedly 'inorganic' works there also lies the threat (deliberately raised) of disintegration or degeneration.

'Degenerate' is of course an especially controversial word. Daniel Pick has analysed the language of degeneration from Plato's *The Republic* (where 'decay' is the 'lot of everything that has come into being') through Rousseau's *The Discourse on the Origin of Inequality* (1755) to Hegel's *Lectures on the Philosophy of World History* (1822–30), which identified the categories of development, over-refinement and degeneration functioning in an overall progressive narrative of national histories. For the second half of the nineteenth century it was the discussion of degeneracy in Benédict Augustin Morel's *Traité des dégénérescences physiques, intellectuelles et morales de l'espèce humaine* (1857) which became widely influential, spawning some notorious tracts (for example, Cesare Lombroso's *Genius and Insanity* of 1863 and Richard von Krafft-Ebing's *Psychopathia sexualis* of 1886). As Pick notes, after Morel 'degeneration' assumed a central role in cultural discourse as the focal term for the 'conceptions of atavism, regression, relapse, transgression and decline within a European context so often identified as the quintessential age of evolution, progress, optimism, reform or improvement'. Pick emphasizes the 'historical specificity of the model of degeneration which, in the shadows of evolutionary naturalism, inflected so much writing of the period'. This model is developed, for example, in the context of disillusioned utopian revolutionaries in the 1850s or the pain of French defeat in the Franco-Prussian War. (Émile Zola, for example, is 'the great novelist of heredity and degeneration' who 'not only disseminates but also interrogates ideas about

---

[95] Trans. from Calinescu, *Five Faces of Modernity*, 164.

[96] Robert B. Pynsent (ed.), *Decadence and Innovation: Austro-Hungarian Life and Art at the Turn of the Century* (London: Weidenfeld and Nicolson, 1989), 142.

degenerescence and medical authority' and exhibits an 'obsession with naming perversions or disorders – manias, philias, phobias', those 'which constitute terrains of degeneration'.) Thus, Pick concludes, degeneration is not reducible to a single theory, definition or ideology; it is dependent upon contexts (those national, disciplinary, racial and urban pathologies, etc.) and moves by slippages and transgressions. The problem is highlighted in the shifting stylistic identity of the 'face of the degenerate'.[97] Images of degeneracy were often incorporated into decadent descriptions of the faces in portraiture. In the facial image framed as an artistic object a moment in a life or a genealogy is captured on canvas, collected as an exhibit and then presented for observation. The transitional condition of degeneration is preserved or halted in imaginary painted forms. In the famous opening of *À Rebours* the founders of the Des Esseintes family appear in their portraits as 'sturdy', with 'bulging chests', but this is followed by images of 'degeneration' in later portraits, 'with the men becoming progressively less manly', as, through 'intermarrying', they lose 'what little vigour they had left'. Thus the one remaining descendant, the Duc Jean des Esseintes, is a 'frail young man of thirty who was anaemic and highly strung, with hollow cheeks, cold eyes of steely blue, a nose which was turned up but straight, and thin, papery hands'.[98] But these pictures of degeneracy are a narcissistic mirror image; as Wilde wrote, 'It is the spectator, not life, that art really mirrors.'[99] Realization of this reflected identity is what shocks the bourgeois observer.

In another aphorism Wilde states: 'The nineteenth century dislike of Realism is the rage of Caliban seeing his own face in a glass. The nineteenth century dislike of Romanticism is the rage of Caliban not seeing his own face in a glass.'[100] Caliban, described in *The Tempest*'s dramatis personae as a 'savage and deformed slave', is primitive, undeveloped, yet also an ugly,

---

[97] Daniel Pick, *Faces of Degeneration: A European Disorder c.1848–1918* (Cambridge University Press, 1989), 2–11. On Krafft-Ebing see Renate Hauser, 'Krafft-Ebing's Psychological Understanding of Sexual Behaviour', in Porter and Teich (eds.), *Sexual Knowledge, Sexual Science*, 210–27. The Austrian Krafft-Ebing offered anecdotes of how female masochism is defined by regional and class origin: 'It is said that lower class women in all Slav peoples are unhappy when they do not get beaten up by their husbands': from the 1890 edn of *Psychopathia sexualis*, quoted in Hauser, 'Krafft-Ebing's Psychological Understanding', 213. Important studies of degeneration include Sander L. Gilman and J. Edward Chamberlin (eds.), *Degeneration: The Dark Side of Progress* (New York: Columbia University Press, 1985); Sander L. Gilman, *Disease and Representation* (Ithaca: Cornell University Press, 1988) and *Difference and Pathology* (Ithaca: Cornell University Press, 1985) especially ch.9, 'Sexology, Psychoanalysis and Degeneration'.

[98] Joris-Karl Huysmans, *À Rebours [1884]*, trans. Robert Baldicj as *Against Nature* (Harmondsworth: Penguin, 1959), 17.

[99] Oscar Wilde, 'Preface' to *The Picture of Dorian Gray* [1891] (Harmondsworth: Penguin, 1994), 6.

[100] Wilde, 'Preface' to *The Picture of Dorian Gray*, 5.

semi-human product of a degenerative process, the son of a witch whose name may be derived from 'cannibal'. It is hard to fathom whether Caliban's rage might have been assuaged or intensified by decadence's transitional stylistic paradoxes, in which hyperbolic romanticism and 'realist' grotesqueries often provocatively coexist. The link between the 'ugly' and the characteristic features of decadence is clear, however, from Nietzsche's discussion in *Twilight of the Idols* of notions of beauty and ugliness in aesthetic judgement. Nietzsche states that the ugly

recalls decay, danger, impotence ... The effect of the ugly can be measured with a dynamometer ... The ugly is understood as a sign and symptom of degeneration ... Every token of exhaustion, of heaviness, of age, of weariness, every kind of unfreedom, whether convulsive or paralytic, above all the smell, colour and shape of dissolution, of decomposition, though it be attenuated to the point of being no more than a symbol – all this calls forth the same reaction, the value judgement 'ugly'.

What this ugliness arouses in the observer is 'the profoundest hate there is' because it springs from a recognition, the foresight that this is the 'decline of his type'.[101] As in Wilde's aphorism, the ugly, as manifestation of processes of decay and deformation, reflects the anxieties of the shocked bourgeois spectator. The critic's rage is as intense as Caliban's hatred of the portrait mirrored in the ugly image. Clearly, rather than an outraged, bourgeois turning away, a sustained critical reflection is required. Paul Bourget wrote in 1876: 'We accept ... this terrible word decadence ... It is decadence, but vigorous; with less accomplishment in its works, decadence is superior to organic periods because of the intensity of its geniuses. Its uneven, violent creations reveal more daring artists, and audacity is a virtue which despite ourselves elicits our sympathy.'[102] Horrific, cruel, intense, inorganic – decadence would seem inevitably to lead to the observer's abhorrence. But disgust can coexist with admiration as the bravery of the decadent is recognized by the enlightened critic. Tastelessness is the test of courageously decadent truth.

It was Bourget's 1881 essay on Baudelaire, reprinted in *Essais de psychologie contemporaine* (1883), which provided the most famous definition of decadent style (one which, as is well known, Nietzsche virtually reproduced in *The Case of Wagner*): 'A style of decadence is one in which the unity of the book breaks down to make place for the independence of the page, in

---

[101] Nietzsche, *Twilight of the Idols*, 90.
[102] From Bourget, *Le Siècle littéraire* (1876); trans. from Calinescu, *Five Faces of Modernity*, 169.

which the page breaks down to make place for the independence of the sentence, and in which the sentence breaks down to make place for the independence of the word.'[103] For Bourget, the decadent sensibility and aesthetic, one based on physical and nervous exhaustion, produced an 'advanced' state of disharmony, where the emphasis lies on expanding, capturing and analysing the moment. An anonymous text published in *Le Décadent* (15 December 1888) stated: 'These emotions once felt, the decadent analyzes them. He cultivates them in the recollection of his reverie, he brings them into focus, molds his thought to them in order to capture their most delicate convolutions …'[104] Bourget was a key influence on Nietzsche's work. As Charles Bernheimer notes, Nietzsche 'reacted with unique vigour to [decadence's] stimulating force as an intellectual *agent provocateur*' and reflected the characteristics of decadent style which Bourget identified. Thus *The Case of Wagner*, with its overt borrowings from Bourget, 'is itself a fragmented artifact' – episodic, idiosyncratic, histrionic.[105]

Nietzsche's earlier, celebratory essay 'Richard Wagner in Bayreuth' (1876) raised important issues concerning stylistic development. In a text couched in evolutionary terms, Wagner is here raised as an exceptional artist, first because of the speed of his artistic progress, and second because of the dramatic and organic nature of the resulting artwork. As prophet of the new and vigorously healthy art, Wagner 'unites what was separate, feeble and inactive; if a medicinal expression is permitted, he possesses an *astringent* power'.[106] For Nietzsche, Wagner's art is, to pursue his medicinal metaphor, styptic (it stops bleeding) and contracting (strengthening through tightening). Wagner's art can then function as antidote to the 'degeneration', 'degradation' and 'corruption' symptomatic of modern art. In particular, Nietzsche turns to the debilitated state of language: 'everywhere language is sick, and the oppression of this tremendous sickness weighs on the whole of human development'. It is exhausted, incapable of revealing the 'needs' and 'distress' of man, and artists are no longer the masters of linguistic expression:

---

[103] Trans. from Calinescu, *Five Faces of Modernity*, 170.

[104] Quoted in Pierrot, *The Decadent Imagination*, 123.

[105] Charles Bernheimer, *Decadent Subjects: The Idea of Decadence in Art, Literature, Philosophy, and Culture of the Fin de Siècle in Europe* (Baltimore: Johns Hopkins University Press, 2002), 8, 19. For further critique of Nietzsche see Calinescu, *Five Faces of Modernity*, 178–95 and Andrea Gogröf-Voorhees, *Defining Modernism: Baudelaire and Nietzsche on Romanticism, Modernity, Decadence, and Wagner* (New York: Peter Lang, 2004).

[106] Nietzsche, 'Richard Wagner in Bayreuth', in *Untimely Meditations*, trans. R. J. Hollingdale (Cambridge University Press, 1983), 208.

Just as when every art goes into decline a point is reached at which its morbidly luxuriant forms and techniques gain a tyrannical domination over the souls of youthful artists and make them their slaves, so with the decline of language we are the slaves of words; under this constraint no one is any longer capable of revealing himself, of speaking naively ...[107]

Wagner's art holds the regenerating and redemptive answer, first through the reunification of man with fellow man and with a 'purified' nature, and second through the redemption of word by tone in musical style and technique. Wagner's musical qualities contrast with the visual experience of the modern world and the clothing which disguises the decadent body of modern man:

unspeakable poverty and exhaustion, despite the unspeakable gaudiness which can give pleasure only to the most superficial glance ... the agitated play of colours, does the whole not appear as the glitter and sparkle of countless little stones and fragments borrowed from earlier cultures? Is everything here not inappropriate pomp, imitated activity, presumptuous superficiality? A suit of gaudy patches for the naked and freezing? A dance of seeming joy exacted from sufferers? An air of haughty pride worn by one wounded to the depths? And amid it all, concealed and dissembled only by the rapidity of the movement and confusion – hoary impotence, nagging discontent, industrious boredom, dishonourable wretchedness! The phenomenonon of modern man has become wholly appearance; he is not visible in what he represents but rather concealed by it ...[108]

Nietzsche contrasts this decadent image with the depth and true formal qualities whose corresponding shape is a 'gymnastic' body, one which dives vigorously into turbulent waves of passion: 'Gradually we notice that the inner general movement has become more powerful, more compelling; the convulsive restlessness has passed over into a broad, fearfully strong movement towards an as yet unknown goal; and suddenly the whole breadth of the stream ends by plunging down into the depths with a demonic joy in the abyss and in its seething waves.'[109]

Nietzsche's view of this kind of oceanic movement shifted as his later writings turned to a critique of the 'decadent' Wagner. In *Nietzsche contra Wagner* he writes of the effect of 'endless melody': 'One walks into the sea, gradually loses one's secure footing, and finally surrenders oneself to the elements without reservation: one must *swim*.' In the kind of movement

[107] Nietzsche, 'Richard Wagner in Bayreuth', 215.
[108] Nietzsche, 'Richard Wagner in Bayreuth', 215–16.
[109] Nietzsche, 'Richard Wagner in Bayreuth', 243.

evoked by these waves Nietzsche argued that Wagner 'overthrew the physiological presupposition of previous music. Swimming, floating – no longer walking and dancing.'[110] Thus the 'musical' body is no longer gymnastic, self-supporting and powerful: it is reliant on the support and movement of a water bed. Nietzsche's description, in the preface to *The Case of Wagner*, of his convalescence from Wagnerian decadence ('I comprehended this, I resisted it') reflects a wider statement in *The Will to Power*: 'Waste, decay, elimination need not be condemned, they are necessary consequences of life, of the growth of life. The phenomenon of decadence is as necessary as any increase and advance of life: one is in no position to abolish it.'[111] Such statements place Nietzsche's work as part of a *rhetorique obsédante* and thus link it to work by Baudelaire, Nordau, Huysmans, Freud and D'Annunzio. Barbara Spackman has analysed how 'the rhetoric of sickness and health, decay and degeneration, pathology and normalcy … passed first through the sick body of the degenerate: sick bodies produced sick thought': decadent writers 'valorize physiological ills and alteration as the origin of psychic alterity'. In particular, 'convalescence' was raised as the scene of artistic and philosophic creation. In the experience of convalescence – a transitional state between sickness and health – the diseased past is at first so threatening that it has to be forgotten, but this 'first moment in Baudelaire's, Nietzsche's and D'Annunzio's portrayals of convalescence is followed by a second moment of total, and arbitrary recall'. In his preface to the second edition of *The Joyful Wisdom* Nietzsche writes of the 'intoxication of convalescence', experienced as a rebirth into a 'more childlike' state, but he also seeks to perpetuate the passage of convalesence, holding the state of health as a continuous hope rather than reaching complete fulfilment.[112] This transitional state heightens the sense of double

---

[110] Nietzsche, *Nietzsche contra Wagner*, in *The Portable Nietzsche*, trans. Walter Kaufmann (New York: Viking, 1959), 666.

[111] Nietzsche, *The Case of Wagner*, 155–6; *The Will to Power*, 25.

[112] Barbara Spackman, *Decadent Genealogies: The Rhetoric of Sickness from Baudelaire to D'Annunzio* (Ithaca: Cornell University Press, 1989), vii–viii, 37, 94. For further cultural reference see Susan Sontag's modern classic, 'Illness as Metaphor' (1978), in *Illness as Metaphor and Aids and its Metaphors* (Harmondsworth: Penguin, 1991). Sontag writes of a 'dual citizenship, in the kingdom of the well and in the kingdom of the sick'. She argues that the kingdom of the ill has been 'landscaped' by 'lurid metaphors' from which we must seek liberation. Sontag argues that many of Nietzsche's comments on decadence and sickness are an extension of the traditional metaphors attached to tuberculosis, whose names are resonant with etymological meaning: 'consumption', that which consumes and corrupts, or 'tuberculosis' that of morbid growth. Tuberculosis is characterized as a 'disease of extreme contrasts: white pallor and red flush, hyperactivity alternating with languidness'. Its 'euphoria, increased appetite, exacerbated sexual desire' are illustrated by the patients in Mann's *The Magic*

character. In the opening section of *Ecce homo*, 'Why I am so Wise', Nietzsche proclaimed his 'twofold origin': 'at once *décadent* and beginning'. He explains:

convalescence means with me a long, all too long succession of years – it also unfortunately means relapse, deterioration, periods of a kind of décadence. After all this do I need to say that in questions of *décadence* I am experienced? … To look from a morbid perspective towards healthier concepts and values, and again conversely to look down from the abundance and certainty of rich life into the secret labour of the instinct of decadence – that is what I have practised most …

He also declares himself 'the antithesis of the decadent', as one who is 'fundamentally healthy' and 'knows how to forget'. 'This twofold succession of experiences, this accessibility to me of apparently separate worlds, is repeated in my nature in every respect – I am a *Doppelgänger*.'[113] This doubleness is a radically different relationship from that found in a dialectic, for dialectical systems are themselves a 'symptom' of decadence for Nietzsche. This is because in dialectics the antithesis is the negation of the thesis's prior affirmation, rather than a radically stimulating polarity, and the system is based upon the striving and hopes for a redemptive, higher synthesis which is illusory and ultimately debilitating to life.[114] The stylistic implications of this lie in the valorization of paradox, polarity, unresolved doubleness, the undoing of apotheosis, the celebration of the eternal return of suffering.

These decadent stylistic features – miniaturism, fragmentation, hysterical hyperbole, sensuality, ornament and degenerate ugliness – assumed differing shades of character and function as they sprang up and spread in the artistic communities, and solitaries, of Central and Eastern Europe. A survey of the main protagonists and centres in this development provides the final contextual groundwork.

Mountain (a 'late, self-conscious commentary on the myth of TB'), and contrasts with Aschenbach's 'degradation' on succumbing to cholera in *Death in Venice*.'When Hans Castorp is discovered to have tuberculosis, it is a promotion'; more mysterious than syphilis, tuberculosis's symptoms are 'deceptive'. It appears as an aphrodisiac, but is a disease of 'disintegration, febrilization, dematerialization', a disease of liquids, mythically reduced to a coughing of blood from diseased lungs. The romantic conception of the disease was as a transformation of the powers of passionate, sexual love, but one ending in frustration, as in Turgenev's *On the Eve* (1860) and its frustrated Bulgarian exile in Venice. 'Chopin was tubercular at a time when good health was not chic' (so wrote Saint-Saëns in 1913).

[113] Nietzsche, *Ecce homo*, trans. R. J. Hollingdale (Harmondsworth: Penguin, 1979), 38–41.
[114] *The Genealogy of Morals*. See John Burt Foster Jr, *Heirs to Dionysus: A Nietzschean Current in Literary Modernism* (Princeton University Press, 1981), 42–51.

Themes of decadence in Central and Eastern Europe

At this point Orientalism may seem to be the elephant in the room. Titular use of the terms 'Central' and 'Eastern' (which of course imply their opposites, 'periphery' – or 'margin' – and 'Western') brings with it ideological baggage in particularly heavy sacks. These are terms raising identities which bolstered, from both sides of a shifting, imaginary divide, the construction of familiar West–East oppositions (some of which have undermined understanding so painfully in the history of European modernism[115]). Conjoining these terms with the equally encumbered word 'decadence' only compounds the burden. The gaze of the Orientalist decadent, a widely studied topic,[116] was most characteristically drawn to locations such as Byzantium, Babylon or the court of King Herod, mythologized and aestheticized places lying seductively and dangerously just beyond the boundaries of the European continent. On the Orientalist's imaginary map of Europe the relationship of decadence, the 'East' and notions of 'centre' and 'periphery' are parts of influential yet ambiguous mythologies. In the European continent the 'region' was often viewed from the imaginary centre as a potentially revitalizing antidote to the decadence of that centre. Thus the image of Italy in Winckelmann ('Wiedergeburt und Neues Leben') and in Burckhardt (*Kultur der Renaissance in Italien*) and especially of Sicily, where Stendhal (and later Szymanowski) found (or imagined) that peoples were still moved by fires of passion and hatred, the authentic remnant of what was dead or buried in Paris, Berlin or London. By contrast with the dead centre, the margin became the site of origin, the location of the Goethean *Ur-Pflantze*, the source of new life.[117] Thus also Nietzsche's call to Mediterraneanize, to move to warmth and light in order to recover from the damp, decadent, twilight world of the north. Tilting the axis towards the West–East polarity, Nietzsche's image of the 'Dionysian'

---

[115] See Geoffrey Chew, 'Introduction: The Geography of Modernism: Reflections on the Theme "New Music for a New Europe"', in Chew (ed.), *New Music in the "New Europe" 1918–1938: Ideology, Theory, and Practice, Colloquia musicologica Brunensia 38, 2003* (Prague: Koniasch Latin Press and Institute of Musicology, Masaryk University Brno, 2007), 7–14.

[116] For representative, stimulating essays from among the voluminous literature see: Emily Apter, 'Acting Out Orientalism: Sapphic Theatricality in Turn-of-the-Century Paris', in Elin Diamond (ed.), *Performance and Cultural Politics* (London: Routledge, 1996), 15–34; and Stavros Stavrou Karayanni, 'Dancing Decadence: Semiotics of Dance and the Phantasm of Salomé', in *Dancing Fear and Desire* (Waterloo, Ont.: Wilfrid Laurier University Press, 2004), 99–119.

[117] See Roberto M. Dainotto, *Place in Literature: Regions, Cultures, Communities* (Ithaca: Cornell University Press, 2000).

Poland (which he constructed as his 'real' homeland) was an antidote to decadent German culture, and on this recuperative axis also lie Russia's artistic images of the marginal Caucasian region as pastoral stimulant, or the Tatra mountains around Zakopane as a region emblematic of 'Polish' artistic renaissance and recovery, especially through the perceived, mythic link to ancient Greek pastoralism. In his prose poem 'Anywhere out of the World' Baudelaire evokes a continent-wide geography of decadence and convalescence. 'Life is a hospital, in which every patient is possessed by a desire to change his bed … It always seems to me that I'd be better off somewhere else, and this question of changing my place of abode is one that I continually discuss with my soul.' The convalescent's desire is to move to extreme locations of life and death – to Lisbon, for example, a land of 'warmth' and 'light', or, by contrast, to 'the limits of the Baltic', where there are 'countries that are analogies of Death'. If we draw a line between these two points – contrasting sites of recovery and demise, the heat of life and the cold of the dead – we cross, at roughly the mid-point, an area where 'Central' moves towards 'Eastern' Europe. Baudelaire's diagonal is thus poised between the north–south polarity, so crucial for Nietzsche's decadent–healthy doubleness, and the Enlightenment's West–East dichotomy in which 'Eastern' Europe was 'discovered' by Western travellers, or 'invented' by the imaginations of those who moved no further than the comfortable drawing rooms of their bourgeois domesticity, as an exhilarating yet dangerous and possibly diseased location.[118]

Paradoxical characteristics attach to the polar points of this cultural cartography. Nietzsche's vibrant south is also the location of Mann's deathly Venice. The predicament of Mann's Tonio Kröger (who declares: 'I stand between two worlds') is symptomatic. He is part southern, part northern in origin. Through his parentage these origins are identified with the feminine (maternal) and masculine (paternal) respectively. He complains of the exhaustions brought about by the clash of hot and cold in his artistic imagination: he is 'half worn out by the fevers and frosts of creation' (he is also a transitional figure between the 'finesse and melancholy and the whole sickly artistocracy of letters' and life as a bourgeois *manqué*).[119]

---

[118] Baudelaire, *My Heart Laid Bare*, 150–1. On constructing the European 'East' see Larry Wolff, *Inventing Eastern Europe: The Map of Civilization on the Mind of the Enlightenment* (Stanford University Press, 1994). French decadence has been well examined, the classic texts in English being A. E. Carter, *The Idea of Decadence in French Literature, 1830–1900* (Toronto University Press, 1958) and Koenraad W. Swart, *The Sense of Decadence in Nineteenth Century France* (The Hague: Nijhoff, 1964).

[119] Mann, *Tonio Kröger* [1903], in *Death in Venice; Tristan; Tonio Kröger*, 159, 189–90.

Paradox is also manifest in the oppositions between the view of the 'East' as site of both the revitalizing and the deleterious. It was a home of the noble savage (the figure of nature not yet 'degenerated' by the hand of man, as Rousseau put it) or of those whose glorious hour was yet to come (Herder, for example, on the Slavs), by contrast with the decaying, declining, decadent West.[120] But it was also the source of possible contagion, of fearfully perverse and primitive drives which in the West were strictly policed or sanitized. The latter is exemplified by Bram Stoker's decision to move the location of his *Dracula* (1897) further east, from his original idea of the Austrian Styria to the Transylvanian Carpathians, an imaginary location more suitable for his erotic and supernatural tale since travel writing of the time described it as lying beyond the reach of the world of science, a place to expose and exorcise fears over sexuality and disease.[121] As a 'decadent fantasy' of the 'thrills and terrors of blurred sexual, psychological, and scientific boundaries', Stoker's Transylvania was drawn to lie 'on the border of three states' – the living, the dead and the undead.[122]

Such were the European sites and characteristics of decadence when the 'West' looked Eastwards. For artists working in or identifying their origins in these 'Eastern' lands, notions of 'Centre' and 'East' remained crucial in arguments over self-definition. Whether they looked in the mirror, or turned to consider their position with regard to a beloved or (more likely) mistrusted neighbour (Austria and Hungary; Austria and Germany; Germany and Poland; Poland and Russia; the provocative pairings multiply), returned the Occidental Orientalist's gaze, or developed their own discourses of Orientalism, the oppositional forces of decline and revitalization operated across fraught cultural mappings. In this discourse alterity and identity are symbolic, social and cultural constructions based on invented boundaries. Identity desires, their meanings and anxieties, are situated and contingent, negotiated through notions of place and history.[123] Geographical self-perception, constructions of cultural hierarchy and national identity and

---

[120] The Balkans, for example, were a site of touristic liberation from Western decadence: see Andrew Hammond, 'The Escape from Decadence: British Travel Literature on the Balkans 1900–45', in Michael St John (ed.), *Romancing Decay: Ideas of Decadence in European Culture* (Aldershot: Ashgate, 1999), 141–53.

[121] See Christopher Frayling, *Nightmare: The Birth of Horror* (London: BBC, 1996), 66–113.

[122] Elaine Showalter, *Sexual Anarchy: Gender and Culture at the Fin de Siècle* (London: Bloomsbury, 1991), 179.

[123] See Markus Reisenleitner, 'Tradition, Cultural Boundaries and the Constructions of Spaces of Identity', *Spaces of Identity: Tradition, Cultural Boundaries and Identity Formation in Central Europe and Beyond* 1/1 (2001) https://pi.library.yorku.ca/ojs/index.php/soi/article/view/8052/7229 (accessed 16 December 2008).

the concomitant rivalries and aspirations all played crucial roles in the differing manifestations of decadence. In 'Central' and 'Eastern' locations of European modernism decadent poses, styles and identities developed as reflections of this complex geography; they responded to and reshaped the writing of histories and construction of ideologies, and expressed anxieties for the future. For example, Kirsten Lodge has shown how preoccupation with the 'Roman paradigm', that 'mythopoetic construct' of imperial decline and fall which Nietzsche and then Gilman have debunked, was manifest in differing forms according to political and cultural context. Czech decadents, she argues, tended to highlight weary collapse because of their status as subjects of the Habsburg Empire, exhausted by the wait for political and linguistic equality. By contrast, Russian symbolists emphasized imperial collapse through barbarian bellicosity, with decadence flourishing later, between 1905 and 1911, 'precisely when the Russians began to see themselves as a once powerful empire shaken by both external and internal undermining forces'.[124] In Vienna, Budapest, Prague and Cracow the artistic urge to be cosmopolitan and modern often conflicted with heritage-based national identities and self-perceptions. Thus contrasts emerge between the imagery and technique in Klimt's Secession *Jugendstil* and symbolism and decadence in Polish and Czech art, where a frequent concern was the transformation of certain national mythologies in the new aesthetic climate of decadence. In Hungarian painting, by further contrast, decadence played a lesser role, and thus the *femme fatale* – typical obsession of the decadent or symbolist – is a less frequent artistic figure.[125] The cultural status of language also strongly inflected the functions and character of decadence. Pynsent argues that if linguistic deformation is a defining stylistic feature of decadence then it is easier to explore this style in Germanic works, for in the case of Czech and Hungarian it is complicated by the histories of the language, its 'purification' and 'petrification' as it plays a symbolic role in national revival and identity creation.[126]

The idea of a pervasive sense of decay in the Habsburg Empire after the political changes of 1867 culminating in a decadent mood at the *fin de siècle* is very familiar. It is crucial, however, to recognize that this was counterpointed by the sense of having caught up and now overtaken the artistic

[124] Kirsten Lodge, '"The peak of civilization on the brink of collapse": The "Roman paradigm" in Czech and Russian Decadence', unpublished PhD thesis, Columbia University, 2004.

[125] Ilona Sarmany-Parsons, 'The Image of Women in Painting: Clichés and Reality in Austria-Hungary, 1895–1905', in Steven Beller (ed.), *Rethinking Vienna 1900* (New York: Berghahn Books, 2001), 220–63.

[126] Pynsent (ed.), *Decadence and Innovation*, 168–9.

achievements of the 'West'. In this climate, in which Pynsent identifies egocentricism as central,[127] the exterior signs of decline contrast with interior worlds of innovation. Hermann Bahr was the crucial Austrian disseminator and analyst of decadence. He observed, practised, mastered, parodied and ultimately rejected it. After moving to Munich in the late 1880s he visited Paris, and in his essay 'Die Décadence', in his *Studien zur Kritik der Moderne* (1894), he described the French overcoming of Naturalism in favour of the artificial, the bizarre, the inner and the mystical. Maurice Maeterlinck was the great example, and Bahr struggled with the ambiguous relationship of decadence and symbolism. Bahr's definitions of decadence emphasized extremes of 'inwardness' and disguise, the nerves and costumes – the psyche and the masquerade.[128] He noted the crucial significance of Wagner in this decadent project. His novel *Die gute Schule* (1890) reflects the Parisian decadent world, with sections on 'The Dandy', 'Ennui', 'Expectation' and 'The Sign of the Whip'.[129] Ultimately, Bahr envisaged naturalism and decadence – the two extremes of modern art – moving towards a future productive synthesis and rejected the decadence of Vienna for the 'healthy' provincial alternative.

In Robert Musil's Kakania, that Viennese state of smooth bureaucratic systems and unobtrusive yet pervasive administration, the subject is dissolved away; he is hollowed out and drained. What remains is the interior 'passive fantasy of spaces yet unfilled' which does not allow the Kakanian subject to take seriously the petty obligations and fulfilments of bourgeois life. In this fantastic inner space the genius – whom the bureacrats of Kakania regard as 'insolent' – finds a 'negative freedom'. Thus, despite its outwardly humdrum conventionality 'Kakania was, after all, a country for geniuses; which is probably what brought it to its ruin.'[130] From around 1900 the Viennese artistic project of identity reconstruction was manifest in what Jacques Le Rider calls 'radicalized individualism'. This focused on the symbolic figures of the genius, the mystic and Narcissus. These figures are, however, always under threat: 'bound to fleeting moments', they are destined to 'inevitable collapse'. As 'compensation' for the rise of exoteric Germanic power and the decline of the Habsburg monarchy, artists turned 'inwards',

---

[127] Pynsent (ed.), *Decadence and Innovation*, 113, 143.

[128] See Donald G. Daviau, 'Hermann Bahr and Decadence', *Modern Austrian Literature* 10 (1977), 53–109.

[129] See the sections trans. in Ray Furness (ed.) and Mike Mitchell (trans.), *The Dedalus Book of German Decadence: Voices of the Abyss* (Sawtry: Dedalus, 1994), 60–81.

[130] Robert Musil, *The Man without Qualities*, trans. Sophie Wilkins and Burton Pike (London: Picador, 1997), 29–31.

into decadence's moment and arena of truth. The 'Habsburg myth' of a 'beautiful and harmonious lost order', 'sapped' by 'destructive forces', became widespread, and yet, as Le Rider is principally concerned to emphasize, it was a culture of vitality, fecundity, one which 'kept a strong awareness of loss, of a decadence which must be fought, for a world in a state of collapse and a still undefined future'.[131] Musil points out the paradox: there was, he writes, a 'veneer of morbidity and decadence: but both these negative definitions were only contingent expressions for the will to be different, to do things differently from the way people had done in the past'. The aim looked forward; it was vital and innovative.[132] The Czech decadent Arnošt Procházka wrote in Prague in 1910: 'an important chapter remains to be written on the relationship between progress and decay, about their close interconnections, their inseparability. Once careful research has been carried out into the points of contact between evolution and decadence, it will be found … that they are synonyms.'[133]

The perceived decline of powers of the ruling Viennese bourgeois was counterpointed by Hungary's accession to a position of greater self-determination and strength. (Externally, they are thus transitional states moving in opposite directions.) But which direction along the axes of geography marked the way forward? In Budapest the title of the important journal *Nyugat* (*The West*) declared the standpoint of many leading artists. This affirmation of belonging or looking to the West is embodied in Hungary's most important symbolist poet, Endre Ady, who was described as 'a son of Paris'. Hungarian 'translations' of French symbolists were typically rather free adaptations created for Hungarian ends. Hence, Pynsent argues, 'the paradoxes of this literary reception. Though lassitude, morbidity and artificiality characterized the adepts of Decadence, these deserters from a feudal world were keen to re-evaluate all values in a reinvigorated country, and so they also introduced vitalism and affirmed

---

[131] Jacques Le Rider, *Modernity and Crises of Identity: Culture and Society in Fin-de-Siècle Vienna*, trans. Rosemary Morris (Cambridge: Polity Press, 1993), 12–17, 23. See also Gerald N. Izenberg, *Modernism and Masculinity: Mann, Wedekind, Kandinsky through World War I* (Chicago University Press, 2000).

[132] Musil, 'Der deutsche Mensch als Symptom' (1923), trans. from Scott Spector, 'Marginalizations: Politics and Culture beyond *Fin-de-Siècle Vienna*' in Beller (ed.), *Rethinking Vienna 1900*, 145. Spector's essay, as its title reveals, is part of the critical re-evaluation of the legacy of Carl E. Schorske's seminal *Fin-de-Siècle Vienna: Politics and Culture* (New York: Knopf, 1979), whose central thesis, that with the failure of political liberalism artists withdrew into an aesthetic modernism, has been challenged by many scholars. See also Spector's *Prague Territories: National Conflict and Cultural Innovation in Kafka's Fin-de-Siècle* (Berkeley: University of California Press, 2000).

[133] Trans. from Pynsent (ed.), *Decadence and Innovation*, 112–13.

their complicity with modern renewal'.[134] The 'imaginary geographies' of
the Czech modernism in the 1890s set internationalist integrationism
against parochial, claustrophobic and chauvinistic nationalism. A close
relationship developed between the iconoclastic journal *Rozhledy*
(*Outlooks*) and the Viennese *Die Zeit* (in which several *Rozhledy* articles
were published). A contrast developed, meanwhile, between the *Moderní
Revue* and the work of Stanisław Przybyszewski in Berlin. These notably
conflicting projects established two poles in Prague modernism, one
socially engaged, the other amorally decadent. František Václav Krejčí
saw Bohemia as a weak centre, as peripheral to European modernist
developments. A rethinking of the image of Vienna, from hated centre of
the Empire to centre of radicalism, was focused in particular on an
enthusiasm for Bahr's notion of *Nervenkunst* and his ethical, regenerative
programme. The counterpole is represented by Procházka's turn to
Berlin and the erotomaniac Przybyszewski, the notorious 'high priest' of
Berlin decadence in the late 1890s.[135] *Moderní Revue* published many of
Przybyszewski's works. There was disdain for the political interests of the
Moderna, and a countering espousal of scandalously licentious, demonic,
anti-bourgeois decadence. As with Bahr's *Nervenkunst*, there was a focus
on nervous response to the modern age, but with a radically different
emphasis. Przybyszewski's idea was that the condition of 'neurasthenia',
'despite its physically debilitating effects, is a positive stage of evolution
for the individual in which the brain becomes more sensitive and therefore
more creative'.[136] It was hugely influential. But Przybyszewski's extravagant decadence was unusual for artists and writers working in Germany,
where an ambivalent attitude to decadence was a more common strategy.[137] This is reflected in the work of Theodor Fontane in the early 1890s,
whose use of the French term *décadence* – as opposed to the German
Dekadenz – denotes a certain distance and irony (Nietzsche, too, of course,
strategically deployed the French term). In Fontane, characteristically for
German letters, the term is never employed neutrally: it is imbued with an

---

[134] Pynsent (ed.), *Decadence and Innovation*, 70.

[135] On Przybyszewski in Berlin see Anna Czarnocka, 'Nietzsche, Przybyszewski and the Berlin
Bohême from the Circle of the *Kneipe "Zum schwarzen Ferkel"*', in Piotr Paszkiewicz (ed.),
Totenmesse: Modernism in the Culture of Northern and Central Europe (Warsaw: Institute of Art
and Polish Academy of Sciences, 1996), 41–50; and, in the same volume, Edward Boniecki,
'Stanisław Przybyszewski's Berlin Essays on Artists and Art', 51–64.

[136] Katherine David-Fox, 'Prague–Vienna, Prague–Berlin: The Hidden Geography of Czech
Modernism', *Slavic Review* 59 (2000), 735–60.

[137] See Robert Vilain, 'Temporary Aesthetes: Decadence and Symbolism in Germany and Austria',
in McGuinness (ed.), *Symbolism, Decadence and the Fin de Siècle*, 209–24.

ambivalent character, and there is an implied polemical edge. Later in the decade an important essay by Adolf Bartels, 'Dekadenz' (1897), associated decadence particularly with disease and decay, but most crucially viewed it as a necessary stage and as a herald of the new. This overcoming of decadence into renewal became a common theme in 1890s debates. Carl Hasse, in his 'Naturalismus und Décadence' (1895), for example, saw decadence as the radical anti-realist strand of modernism but concluded that 'the line of the decadents must perish so that a new race may rise from it'.[138] (The perils of pursuing such 'racial' uprisings are obvious.) After Nietzsche, Mann was the great German analyst of decadence. In *Reflections of a Nonpolitical Man* (1918) he remarked: 'Intellectually, I belong to that generation of writers, spread over the whole of Europe, which, emerging from decadence, destined to be chroniclers and analysts of decadence, simultaneously bore the emancipatory wish to turn away from it (or, let us pessimistically say, bore an inactive awareness of this renunciation), and at least experimented with the conquest of decadence and nihilism.'[139] His Aschenbach was the 'poet-spokesman of all those who labour at the edge of exhaustion; of the overburdened, of those who are already worn out but still hold themselves upright; of all our modern moralizers of accomplishment, with stunted growth and scanty resources, who yet contrive by skilful husbanding and prodigious spasms of will to produce, at least for a while, the effect of greatness'.[140] Mann observed the decadent bohemianism which characterized certain social circles in turn-of-the-century Munich and drew upon an intimate knowledge of a wide range of decadent literature.[141] *Buddenbrooks*, *Tristan*, *Tonio Kröger* and *Death in Venice* are all steeped in decadent themes – the cult of beauty, disease, decline and especially, of course, Wagner. A mixture of *ennui* and nervous over-excitement raises Mann's Siegmund in *Blood of the Wälsungs* (1906) as a paradigmatic decadent figure:

The accoutrements of life were so rich and varied, so elaborated, that almost no place at all was left for life itself. Each and every single accessory was so costly and

---

[138] See Florian Krobb, '"Die Kunst der Väter tödtet das Leben der Enkel": Decadence and Crisis in *Fin-de-Siècle* German and Austrian Discourse', *New Literary History* 35 (2005) 547–62.

[139] Thomas Mann, *Reflections of a Nonpolitical Man*, trans. Walter D. Morris (New York: Ungar, 1983).

[140] Mann, *Death in Venice*, 12.

[141] Mann's work resonates with important decadent literary examples. The figure of Spinell, the central male character in the sanatorium in *Tristan*, is based on Arthur Holitscher, the Budapest-born author of *The Poisoned Well* (1900). The incest and narcissism of *Blood of the Wälsungs* (1906) carry echoes of D'Annunzio's *Il piacere* (1889) and Élémir Bourges's *Le Crépuscule des dieux* (1884).

beautiful that it had an existence above and beyond the purpose it was meant to serve – confusing the observer and absorbing attention. Siegmund had been born into superfluity, he was perfectly adjusted to it. And yet it was a fact that this superfluity never ceased to thrill and occupy him, to give him constant pleasure.[142]

Siegmund's reaction to seeing Act 2 of *The Valkyrie*, with his beloved sister eating chocolates by his side, is that of the archetypal decadent Wagnerian:

He saw the pale, spent woman hanging on the breast of the fugitive to whom she had given herself, he saw her love and her destiny, and felt that life, in order to be creative, must be like that. He saw his own life, and knew its contradictions, its clear understanding and spoilt voluptuousness, its splendid security and idle spite, its weakness and witticisms, its languid contempt; his life, so full of words, so void of acts, so full of cleverness, so empty of emotion and he felt again the burning, the searing anguish which yet was sweet – whither, and to what end? Creation? Experience? Passion?[143]

And finally, Mann's description of the siblings' re-enactment of Wagner's incestuous love scene on the rug in their own home encapsulates the experience of taboo eroticism which lies at the heart of decadent desire:

They loved each other with all the sweetness of the senses, each for the other's spoilt and costly well-being and delicious fragrance. They breathed it in, this fragrance, with languid and voluptuous abandon, like self-centred invalids, consoling themselves for the loss of hope. They forgot themselves in caresses, which took the upper hand and turned into an urgent thrashing and then just sobbing.[144]

When Przybyszewski returned to his native Poland at the end of the 1890s he took his decadent theories to a new and receptive artistic community. Despite the Partition, in which Poland was fractured and submitted to imperial rule from Berlin, Vienna and St Petersburg, towards the end of the nineteenth century a unifying impulse emerged in Polish arts. As Czesław Miłosz notes:

underneath the buoyant expansion of capitalism, destructive forces were at work, and the more sensitive minds felt this. The enigma we have to cope with is the genesis of a new approach to reality and art, emerging simultaneously in various European countries despite their respective differences in economic and social development. Whether we speak of a mutual 'contamination' or of a 'natural

---

[142] Mann, *Blood of the Wälsungs*, in Furness (ed.) and Mitchell (trans.), *The Dedalus Book of German Decadence*, 265.
[143] Mann, *Blood of the Wälsungs*, 276.   [144] Mann, *Blood of the Wälsungs*, 282.

growth' out of local conditions or simply refer to an unidentifiable *Zeitgeist*, the fact is that similar tendencies in France, Germany, Poland and Russia sprang up more or less at the same time.[145]

Miłosz's metaphors, of cultural contamination or natural growth, reveal how he views cross-border influences as potentially decadent or generative. This was an anxiety reflected in *fin-de-siècle* Polish criticism. Stanisław Szczepanowski's 'The Disinfection of European Currents' (1898), for example, advocated an isolationist stance, particularly calling for resistance to the 'French illnesses' of impressionism and decadence (a stance attacked by Artur Górski's *Młoda Polska*, or 'Young Poland', articles). Ludomir Benedyktowicz's *Genealogy of the Secession in Painting and Sculpture: Its Flowers and Fruits on our Soil* (1905) railed (note the book's organicist title) against the 'decadent' turn away from Polish traditions to the art of the East (especially Japan – note the political importance of the date of publication for Russo-Japanese relations!) and argued for a healthy alternative in art whose form and content reflected the nation's body and soul.[146]

Miłosz considers 'decadence' to be too vague a term to be useful as a descriptor of Polish art of this time, for it was just one within a *mélange* of current labels. But the term is especially useful in pinpointing the double nature of Polish modernism. References to Young Poland modernism, which appeared in the writings of Górski from 1898, came to cover widely differing aesthetics, of which decadence is one important, but often underestimated, strand. Young Poland artists were characteristically obsessed with contradictory visions of transfiguration and degeneration, erotic ecstasy, 'messianic' eschatology and the bleakest oblivion.[147] They returned to themes and ideas drawn from romanticism, a move motivated by a resistance to and distaste for bourgeois confidence in positivistic 'progress' and a critical disdain for the scientific world view. Manifest at first in anarchic iconoclasm and pessimistic negation (frequently using images of desertification, wastelands and

---

[145] Czesław Miłosz, *The History of Polish Literature* (Berkeley: University of California Press, 1983), 320.

[146] Stanisław Szczepanowski, 'Dezynfeksja prądów europejskich', *Słowo Polskie* 40 (1898); Ludomir Benedyktowicz, *Rodowód Secesyi w malarstwie i rzezbie: Jej kwiaty i owoce na naszej grzędzie* (Cracow, 1905). See Jan Cavanaugh, *Out Looking In: Early Modern Polish Art, 1890–1918* (Berkeley: University of California Press, 2000), 28–9, 104. If one recalls the traditional Polish Francophilia it is telling to contrast French decadent Catholicism with the Polish link of the Catholic Church and national identity.

[147] See Wojciech Gutowski, *Mit-Eros-Sacrum: Sytuacje Młodopolskie* (Bydgoszcz: Homini, 1999).

decrepit vegetation), but also in a Byronic revolt or rebellion, it soon
led to a call for resurrection and revitalization, particularly as social and
patriotic issues became more heated after the 1905 revolution, which
affected the territories occupied by Russia. There was also a liberation
from the artistic duty towards national themes and styles – a move
towards an art for art's sake, absolute and cosmopolitan outlook which
represented a new development in partitioned Poland, one which led to
conservative critical attacks as 'sick' or 'decadent' art.[148]

Between 1897 and 1900 translations of Poe, Baudelaire, Verlaine and
Swinburne appeared in the Warsaw and Cracow *Życie* periodicals (the
latter held close ties with Prague's *Moderní Revue* through Procházka's
relationship with Przybyszewski). Schopenhauer and Nietzsche were
avidly read. On his return to Cracow from Berlin in 1898 Przybyszewski
became a central, magnetic figure. On 1 January 1899 the Cracow *życie*
published his famous 'Confiteor', in effect a manifesto of the Polish
Moderna. Przybyszewski was convinced that, as part of a chain in the
evolutionary process, man's destiny is determined by blind, instinctive
forces, the carnal and animalistic 'naked soul' which is manifest in
'abnormal' states of hysteria, hallucination and possession, those
which are manifest when the illusion of consciousness is destroyed.
Nevertheless, he drew up a redemptive 'Absolute' characterization of
'Art'.[149] Stanisław Wyspiański envisaged a resurrection of Polish culture
symbolized by the return of old gods. The contrasting pessimistic side
of Young Poland thinking is clear from Górski, who wrote: 'Over all
souls a terrible darkness is spreading in which even doubt is extinguished; nothing is more certain but horror and pain; all the walls
between the real and the incomprehensible are broken. There is nothing
but a dust of souls tossed about by fate and crashing against each other
over the abysses.'[150] The characteristic response to the decadence of
modern society was hedonism or withdrawal, for many in a recourse to
the usual stimulants and addictions of the bohemian life (alcohol, sex,
drugs). Cracow, enjoying the relative freedoms of the Austro-Hungarian

---

[148] Maria Podraza-Kwiatowska, 'Polish Literature in the Epoch of Symbolism: *Młoda Polska*', in
Cynthia Newman Helms, A. D. Miller and Julia Henshaw (eds.), *Symbolism in Poland: Collected
Essays* (Detroit Institute of Arts, 1984), 12. As Miłosz notes, the influence of Russian thought
in Polish modernism is often difficult to identify; in the Russian territories such interests
would characteristically be privately held but not publically espoused: *The History of Polish
Literature*, 326–7. See also Lija Skalska-Miecik, 'Echoes of Russian Art in the Work of Polish
Modernists', in Helms, Miller and Henshaw (eds.), *Symbolism in Poland*, 45–53.

[149] For more on Przybyszewski see Schoolfield, *A Baedeker of Decadence*, 117–31, 182–97.

[150] Trans from Miłosz, *The History of Polish Literature*, 327.

occupation and its history of 'aristocratic' dissidence, in particular saw artists adopting a decadent lifestyle after the Parisian manner, publicly centred on the 'Paon' (Peacock) café and the 'Zielony Balonik' (Little Green Balloon) cabaret at Jan Michalik's Den, which may themselves have been modelled on the 'Schall und Rauch' in Berlin or the 'Elf Scharfrichter' in Munich.[151] The diversity of the art which emerged from this milieu – satirical humoristic works contrasting, for example, with the morbidly melancholic – should not mask the underlying artistic themes, of which the opposition of decadence and revitalization was the prime example. Since its inception the Cracow *Życie* had reflected the political and national atmosphere of that city. Modernists accused the conservatives of a debilitating and limited definition of patriotism – a stagnancy which could be revitalized by cosmopolatin-ism. Revitalization was the aim. Ludwik Szczepański, its first editor, declared in his 1897 column 'In Regard to Life': 'Resignation begone! It so happens that we love life … to the point of madness, to the point of mortal sin.'[152] Early in the new century there was a strong feeling of 'literary convalescence' – after the example of Nietzsche – where Schopenhauerian pessimism was replaced by a return to life, achieved through pantheistic therapies of 'nature', or 'discovering' a recuperative pastoral location, especially the Tatra mountains around Zakopane.[153]

According to John E. Bowlt, a 'distinct, cohesive school of decadents' is very hard to identify in Russia: many of the characteristic themes, topics and techniques of decadence were certainly explored, but there was ambivalence and complexity in their function and deployment.[154] As in the reaction of some Polish critics, in Russia decadence was often critically characterized as a foreign infection – sustaining the traditional ambivalence towards the West since the reforms of Peter the Great. Vladimir Stasov's 1899 diatribe on decadence was overtly proposed as an attempted defence of national honour. He was appalled by Sergei Diaghilev's 'World of Art' exhibitions.[155] Despite his declared 'deca-dence' Valery Bryusov 'occasionally adopted the typical Russian tone of

---

[151] Cavanaugh, *Out Looking In*, 42–4. Munich was often characterized as the Bavarian 'decadent' by contrast with the image of Prussian military strength.

[152] Trans. from Cavanaugh, *Out Looking In*, 28–9.

[153] Podraza-Kwiatowska, 'Polish Literature in the Epoch of Symbolism', 12.

[154] See John E. Bowlt, 'Through the Glass Darkly: Images of Decadence in Early Twentieth-Century Russian Art', *Journal of Contemporary History* 17 (1982), 93–110.

[155] See Rosamund Bartlett, 'Stravinsky's Russian Origins', in Jonathan Cross (ed.), *The Cambridge Companion to Stravinsky* (Cambridge University Press, 2003), 9–10.

moral superiority toward a new trend from the decaying West'. But during 1893–6, as new ideas from France gradually, and fragmentarily, became disseminated in Russian lyrical poetry, Bryusov attempted a definition of symbolism and decadence and an assessment of their Russian significance. He considered 'decadence' to be a term relating to world view and lifestyle, with 'symbolism' relating to artistic technique or method. Decadence was valued as an advance, characterized as vibrant individual experience, so that in 1893 Bryusov declared that 'the future belongs to decadence': for him, it defined the content of the modern spirit. Balmont was important here as the primary Russian example of this forward-looking mode, as the epitome of the decadent 'new man', a characterization based on Balmont's close identification with Poe (he published two volumes of Poe 'translations' in 1895).[156] Morrison groups Balmont and Bryusov along with Hippius and Dmitri Merezhkovsky as the 'decadent generation' of symbolists, but does not offer a definition of decadent, beyond Bryusov's Mallarmé-inspired desire for a poetry of suggestion and enigmatic allusion. The second, 'mystic generation' (Bely, Blok, Ivanov) sought a transfiguring, utopian emancipating revelation related to German Idealism – a project to which Scriabin was closely alligned.[157] But renewal through the Dionysian was also a common theme in the first generation, especially in Merezhkovsky, who saw the new age in terms of a Nietzschean recurrence of the Peter epoch, with the Tsar cast as Anti-Christ. He envisaged an apocalyptic 'third testament', which would bring about the end of history.[158] For many Russian writers and artists 'decadent fears' and 'utopian hopes' were 'filtered through an apocalyptic lens', so that Olga Matich can identify 'decadent utopianism' as a defining feature, a pursuit of 'an economy of desire that would overcome … degeneration', where death might be conquered by 'resisting nature's procreative imperative', for in birth lies the seeds of inevitable death. Nothing less than an erotic revolution was required to transcend the individual, overcome the crisis of sexuality and dismantle divisions of gender. In a (sometimes explicitly Dionysian) 'religious' turn to metaphysics the notion of 'progress' was disavowed in favour of an 'apocalyptic rupture'

---

[156] Joan Delaney Grossman, *Valery Bryusov and the Riddle of Russian Decadence* (Berkeley: University of California Press, 1985).

[157] Morrison, *Russian Opera*, 2.

[158] See Bernice Glatzer Rosenthal, 'Stages of Nietzscheanism: Merezhkovsky's Intellectual Evolution', in Rosenthal (ed.), *Nietzsche in Russia* (Princeton University Press, 1986), 69–93.

which would stop the cycles of growth and degeneration, of a utopianism which would bring history to an end.[159]

Thus, at its highpoint in the 1890s and the first decade of the twentieth
century, decadence provoked and permeated a range of Austrian,
German, Polish, Czech, Hungarian and Russian artistic projects. The
survey above is, of course, a highly condensed summary of the key
themes and a cast of the main characters involved in their development.
Its strong literary focus is a reflection not only of the vitality of 'decadent' letters but also of the comparative neglect of musical decadence in
recent studies. But it also reveals the central, often driving position of
music in the decadent imagination, whatever the medium in which this
is artistically manifest. The readings which follow are collected under
thematic pairings, some of which bring together closely related terms,
while others juxtapose apparent opposites. Together, these themes create
a broad picture of decadence during this period, from its inception in
romantic pessimism in the mid- to late nineteenth century through to
its complex relationships with the early twentieth-century avant-garde
and primitivism. A thematic organization, rather than a chronological
or geographical one, allows for coherent analysis by avoiding the
dangers of repeatedly moving back and forth among key topics, and
enables close comparison to be made of related decadent preoccupations
as they are manifest in music composed and heard in different national
contexts.

Chapter 2 focuses on pessimism and nihilism. It begins by analysing
the discussion of these 'symptoms of decadence' in influential texts by
Nietzsche and then explores examples of their manifestation in music by
Wagner, Tchaikovsky and Richard Strauss. This leads to a consideration
of the work of the Polish composer Mieczysław Karłowicz, whose worldview approached a nihilist position as Nietzschean affirmation and the
hedonisms of the dandy were both rejected. This is related to the pessimistic strand of Young Poland modernism. In a series of symphonic
poems written in the first decade of the twentieth century Karłowicz
presents musical images of defeated love, suicidal drives and Dionysus
as enervated dandy in melancholy scenarios derived from the pessimistic
philosophy of Schopenhauer, the tragic literature of Turgenev and musical models drawn from Wagner, Strauss and Tchaikovsky. The themes of
the symphonic poem *Returning Waves* (1904), for example, derive from

---

[159] Olga Matich, *Erotic Utopia: The Decadent Imagination in Russia's Fin de Siècle* (Madison:
University of Wisconsin Press, 2005).

Wagnerian musical symbols of surging intoxication, but images of past longing and rapture yield to voicings of the eternal song of annihilation, to repeated failure or corruption of the processes of Straussian *Steigerung* with the melancholic aspects of Tchaikovsky's *Pathétique* Symphony drawn upon as a pessimistic alternative to Nietszchean Dionysianism. In this scenario the musical future is as bleak as the image of returning waves which toss the hero into the abyss and must themselves crash, self-destructively, into the rocky coast.

Chapter 2 also offers a reconsideration of Rachmaninov by comparing his semiotic and syntactical treatments of the flat sixth and tritone as motif and harmony with those found in the music of Scriabin. A symbolic interpretation is developed by employing Richard Drake's distinction between 'decadent romanticism' and 'decadenticism' and Yakovlev's 1911 contrast between the 'Byronic' Rachmaninov and the 'Nietzschean' Scriabin. A range of examples from Scriabin's 'transitional period' demonstrate the flat sixth's function as the approach towards, or prelude to, a hovering, tritonal prolongation of the dominant function, in which lie the seeds of Nietzschean ecstasy. The closing strategies of the Third, Fourth and Fifth Piano Sonatas reveal Scriabin's move from Byronism to Nietzscheanism. In the Third Sonata's final section the heroic transformation of the 'decadent' slow movement is reached out of the resolution of the augmented sixth chord on the flattened sixth, but in the final bars the tragic 'Byronic' tone of the opening movement returns. The eternal struggle through adversity to apotheosis must start again. In the Fourth Sonata the 'floating' dance moves to apotheosis and thematic transformation, with the flattened sixth less prominent than the alternative major sixth. Through this the Byronic tone has been eliminated and replaced by erotic ecstasy. In the Fifth Sonata a similar but even more ecstatic apotheosis now leads to de-materialization in an explosive return to the opening chaos. The tragic, pessimistic, Byronic descent from the flattened sixth has been displaced.

In Rachmaninov, by contrast, as examples from his piano sonatas, *The Bells* and Balmont songs reveal, emphasis is placed on the flat sixth's precarious structural position as signalling the beginning of the end through its inevitable resolution, down a semitone, to the dominant. Rachmaninov's closing gestures represent an array of structural and expressive responses to this 'endful-ness'. Those which evoke the tone of Byronic fateful resignation reveal how Rachmaninov's 'decadent' apocalypticism emerges from the same romantic semiotics and musical syntax as Scriabin's but diverges towards an artistic vision in which the subject comes to a completely different 'end'. The last section of Chapter 2 considers the elegiac in Bartók's *Elegy*, Op.8b No.1, First String Quartet and *The Miraculous Mandarin*, which illustrate processes of decay and degeneration in modern works of mourning, and the relationship of decadence and the grotesque.

Chapter 3 considers the manipulation of processes of degeneration and regeneration in the 'double endings' of Wagner's *Twilight of the Gods* and Strauss's *Salome* and *Elektra*. The problem of 'ending' is acute in romanticism. This is hardly surprising given the prominence of becoming and 'endless longing', the Hegelian dialectic of thesis, antithesis and synthesis, and belief in dynamic historical progress, in the utopian fantasy of revolutionary transformations. The problem is compounded in an aesthetic in which completion and fulfilment are repeatedly deferred, or in which the meaning of events is apparently defined only by self-fulfilling, teleological impulses, or (as in Goethe's organic view of form) in which polarities and intensification (*Steigerung*) engage in a restless striving towards higher synthetic levels. In these works by Wagner and Strauss, where decadent processes are evoked, these features of romantic form and aesthetics are further problematized. The familiar romantic notion of the double can be employed as a way of analysing the crisis in endings and the anxieties over competing forces of decay and development as musical romanticism moves into decadence and modernism. Brünnhilde's two closing cadences in the final scene of *Twilight of the Gods* express the outcomes of polar forces of decadence and Dionysian revitalization. The first is marked by debilitating regression, the second by a Dionysian, reanimating experience. They are approached by different types of movement – in the first sinking, slowing, shrinking of power, and, by contrast, in the second rising, accelerating, energizing, expansive reinivigoration. Salome's famous monologue is closely modelled on this doubled structure as the two C sharp cadences in the final section also invoke these polar forces. But they are now in complex interactions which emphasize their interdependence and illusory status. In the final part of *Elektra* the central character's double role as degenerate and maenad underpins another double ending whose harmonic and motivic contents are the final stage in the complex manipulation of musical symbols of degeneration and revitalization.

Chapter 4 considers examples of 'wave deformation' as manifestations of decadence in Central European music from the first decade of the twentieth century. In musical waves the height of energetic expression is followed by an end which may be felt as a decline or disintegration as much as a resolution of tension. Ernst Kurth famously described Wagner's and Bruckner's music in terms of the 'internal energetic will of surging under-current' which produces, by contrast with classical periodic structures, 'developmental waves' that become the 'basic formal principal'. But post-Wagnerian musical idioms were to interrogate this legacy through deformations of inherited formal structures and narrative processes. Wave deformations are a vital part of the modernist questioning of heroic formal paradigms and the post-Kantian Romantic sublime, as cultural anxieties were manifested in the resistance or counterforce to degeneration and stagnation, or, by contrast, in the obsession with decay and dissolution in the aesthetics of decadence. The chapter illustrates key aspects of this formal procedure with examples from Strauss's *Salome* (the dissolution of *Steigerung*, or intensification, as a marker of Salome's perverse eroti-cism), the finale of Mahler's Sixth Symphony (where an 'oceanic' second thematic section occurs within a movement whose overriding tone is one of crushing loss and denial), Berg's Piano Sonata, Op.1 (which opens with an ending and is based on a dialectic between post-*Tristan* intensifications to the *Höhepunkt* and what Adorno called 'permanent dissolution' (*Auflösung*)), and the Count's ballad from Act 2 scene vi of Schreker's *Der ferne Klang* (where a melancholic ballad turns to 'artificial' wave movements at the poetic image of the crown being thrown into the waves and the pale woman dragging the king into the sea).

Chapter 5 explores the relationship of decadence to two apparently conflicting cultural phenomena: mannerism and the avant-garde. Decadence and mannerism are often closely associated. They are fre-quently deemed to share debilitating obsessions with old or dying styles, artificially sustaining and extending the 'lifespan' of an aged idiom, suffusing their work with the problematics of over-ripeness and 'late-ness'. Mannerism is examined in relation to Russian miniaturism, in particular the 'Chopinesque' miniatures of Anatoliy Lyadov and Scriabin, and to structural complexity, stylistic anachronism and kitsch in Strauss's *Der Rosenkavalier*. Decadence and avant-garde are then analysed as polar cultural tendencies which meet at their 'extremities', or engage in a powerful dialectic with productive and explosive results. Strauss returns as a figure in whose work these extremes touch. The last section of Chapter 5 proposes that decadent tones play a vital role in many of Schoenberg's 'avant-garde' scores composed during the years leading up to the First World War. These decadent aspects, often underestimated, neglected or silenced in the critical literature, are cru-cial to the innovations and ambiguities of these famous works.

The final chapter explores convalescence from decadent disease and decay. It begins with consideration of Nietzsche as convalescent composer, as one spurred to write music against the decadence he saw exemplified by the 'case' of Schumann. Nietzsche declared that his youthful enthusiasm for the music of Schumann was something that he had to overcome. *Manfred-Meditation* (1872) was, he stated, a creative act of furious vengeance, composed as a counter to Schumann's *Manfred* melodrama (1848), which he deemed to be a fundamental misunderstanding of Byron. But the piece is also much more than a contradiction of Schumann. Nietzsche's attempts at musical composition in the early 1870s can be heard as an adumbration of his critique of decadence in the later writings. Nietzsche's Manfred music is a reaction against the self-reflective unity, the themes of incestuous narcissism and solipsism and the narrative of romantic pessimism moving to other-worldly redemption in Schumann's overture, all of which Nietzsche would later bring together as characteristics of decadence. Finished four months after the publication of *The Birth of Tragedy*, *Manfred-Meditation* not only foreshadows the denunciation of Schumann in *Beyond Good and Evil*, but also marks the transformation of Manfred into an early version of Nietzsche's Dionysus, into a figure of double birth and character which adumbrates the notions of 'Dionysian pessimism' and childish 'forgetfulness' which were to be set up in later writings in opposition to romantic pessimism and decadence, of which Schumann, among others, was accused.

The third and fourth sections of Chapter 6 explore recoveries from Wagnerian 'sickness' in the music of Wolf and Szymanowski. The musical portrayal of Amfortas's suffering in *Parsifal* Act 1 is analysed as a paradigmatic example of the decadent musical expression of agony and the yearning for convalescence through the manipulation of leading-note energies in a harmonic idiom of intensive alteration. Wolf's Mörike songs 'Seufzer' and 'An den Schlaf', and 'Schon streckt' ich aus im Bett die müden Glieder' from the *Italian Songbook* present related examples of recovery from various intense forms of suffering, heavily indebted to the Wagnerian model. Szymanowski's 'convalescence' involved moving out of Schopenhauerian pessimism and decadent narcissism through appropriating Dionysian concepts drawn from Nietzsche, Pater and Merezhkovsky, and re-appropriating Chopin's legacy for the regeneration of Polish culture. Chopin is rescued from his disfigurement in decadent imagery (e.g. in Mann and Albert Giraud) and in the 'pale imitations' of Chopin derided by leading musical authorities of the Polish *fin de siècle* (Władysław Żeleński and Zygmunt Noskowski), and his revitalized legacy is fused with a re-imagining of the 'healthy' culture of the Tatra mountain region. This is most powerfully symbolized in the final pages of *King Roger*. By contrast with Karłowicz's dark tones of decadence, this is modern Polish music resonating, even glittering, with erotic ecstasy and the promise of regeneration as a tradition, legacy or genealogy is reconstructed and coexists with eclectic 'affiliations' achieved through 'Pan-Europeanism', a utopian, optimistic alternative to the pessimistic diagnosis of decadent modern culture.

2 | Pessimism and nihilism

> We are weary. In vain we await our repose; we no longer believe in hope …
>
> Alexander Blok (St Petersburg, 1899)

Introduction

During the nineteenth century various forms of cultural pessimism developed in response to tragic political events, national defeats, disenchantment with the scientific rational world view, the failures of revolutionary heroism, boredom with the bourgeois ethic or the apparent decline in artistic vitality.[1] Mann summed up the double aspect of the century: its 'faith in reason and progress' was 'counterbalanced, indeed outweighed, by its deep pessimism, its musical attachment to night and death, which will probably come to be seen as the dominant characteristics of the age'. The 'grandeur' which Mann saw as the 'essence and hallmark' of the nineteenth-century artwork was a 'gloomy and afflicted' one. (This melancholy 'monumentalism', Mann points out, 'curiously enough, goes hand in hand with a love of the very small and painstaking, the psychologically detailed'.)[2] The utopian hopes of romantic idealism were shadowed by dystopian nightmares. Artistic reflections on the themes of pessimism expressed certain morbid psychological tendencies, the alienation from, or corruption of, 'natural' energies, the fatalistic attractions of nihilism, the breakdown of amorous relationships and, as they moved into the psychoanalytically explored territory of traumatic loss, the melancholy works of mourning. Within such reflections decadence can emerge as a perverse perpetuation and intensification of the pessimistic side of romanticism.

---

[1] Pessimism in its various forms and motivations is explored at length in Swart, *The Sense of Decadence*. In his eighth chapter Swart expands his view beyond French borders to consider pessimism in, among other areas, nineteenth-century Germany and Russia (213–57).

[2] Mann, 'The Sorrows and Grandeur of Richard Wagner', 92. On 'miniaturism' see Chapter 5 below.

Decadence is, however, not necessarily the outcome of such deliberations. Josef Suk's *Asrael* Symphony, Op.27 (1906), for example, a powerfully extended work of profound mourning composed after the deaths, in tragically quick succession, of Dvořák (his teacher and father-in-law) and his wife, Otylka, contains none of the topics, narratives or idioms of decadence. The five-movement symphony concludes with two Adagios (Otylka died as Suk began writing the first of these). The second, a Maestoso, ends with consolatory tones in C major. Even though it was written in Suk's darkest personal hour the symphony ultimately is not pessimistic. This working through grief and suffering to renewal reaches greater heights in the symphonic poem *Ripening*, Op.34 (1912–17), expressed in a trajectory through recollections to transcendence over life's struggles and tragedy. Suk's inspiration came from Antonín Sova, whose collections of poems, *A Broken Soul* (*Zlomená duše*) (1896) and the following *Embers of Grief* (*Vybouřené smutky*) of the same year, together represent, according to Arne Novák in her obituary for the poet, a 'breviary of Czech decadence'. But Sova's aim was to 'rise above the pessimism of the title', to express 'belief in a new and noble future, of faith in the new century and the men it will bear'.[3] Sova's later, overt turn to social engagement and concern for national renewal appears to be typical of figures in Czech decadence, who characteristically spurned narcissism and solipsism to embrace the world.[4] For the pessimist, the title of Vítězslav Novák's symphonic poem *Eternal Longing*, Op.33 (1903–4), seems more promising, as does its inspiration, a story by Hans Christian Andersen in which the moon tells us of still waters, strange plants and a falling swan. But in the second half of Novák's piece the expressions of unfulfilled desire and despondency are transformed into moods of soaring exultation. The swan revives and its ascendant flight is symbolic of spiritual deliverance.[5]

---

[3] Arne Novák, 'Antonín Sova', *The Slavonic and East European Review* 7 (1929), 418–22.

[4] Robert B. Pynsent argues that among Czech writers it was only Arthur Breisky who remained devoted to the ideals of decadent aesthetics: 'A Czech Dandy: An Introduction to Arthur Breisky', *The Slavonic and East European Review* 51 (1973), 517–23.

[5] Decadence is hardly directly present in the music and musical-critical discourse emerging from the Czech lands during the *fin de siècle* and first decade of the twentieth century (though it is felt in its absence or resistance: Janáček's mature style is in many ways a polar opposite of the styles typical of contemporaneous post-Wagnerian decadence). It becomes a much more prominent concept in polemics after the First World War (and thus lying outside the chronological scope of this book), for example in the critical reception of Dvořák's *Rusalka* (1900) and Otakar Ostrčil's *Legenda z Erina* (begun in 1913, completed in 1919). The latter was based on a drama by the symbolist Julius Zeyer, who by the first performance of the opera (1921) was widely dismissed as an unfashionable decadent. See Brian Locke, 'Decadence, Heroism and Czechness: The Reception of Ostrčil's *Legenda z Erinu*', in Mikuláš Bek, Geoffrey Chew and Petr Macek (eds.), *Socialist Realism and Music* (Prague: KLP, 2004), 71–82.

The contrasting move from romantic pessimism into decadence was most influentially analysed by Nietzsche. In this chapter discussion of Nietzsche's analysis leads into discussion of music by Karłowicz, Rachmaninov, Scriabin and Bartók. These musical interpretations are contextualized by comparative analyses of influential examples of romantic pessimism from the music of Wagner, Tchaikovsky and Strauss. Karłowicz remains little known outside Poland. His work therefore requires more extensive introduction than that of either Rachmaninov (one of the most popular of all composers, if not in some of academia's loftier ivory towers) or Scriabin and Bartók (who have both long secured places in the modern canon).

In a pioneering study of Karłowicz's symphonic poems Leszek Polony comes to an early but important conclusion. He demonstrates how several of Karłowicz's themes derive from Wagnerian musical symbols of whirling intoxication, madness and frenzy. Polony argues, however, that in Karłowicz's symphonic tragedies the yearning for de-individualization, inseparable from enthralment with love's desire and ecstasy, is one inevitably condemned to end in fiasco or destruction. Dionysian intoxication – the polar opposite of depressive stagnation – is a transitory, passing moment in the experience of the lyrical subject of Karłowicz's musical poems. This subject is enveloped in mists of nostalgic reminiscence, mired in a melancholy psychological state: images of love's longings and raptures yield to the eternal song of annihilation.[6] Manifestations of this subjective crisis in Karłowicz's symphonic poems are based on programmatic narratives of tragic love, beauty's ephemeral pleasures, pessimism and death. In these works Karłowicz's primary musical models were Wagner, Tchaikovsky and Strauss. Nietzsche provided a crucial philosophical and literary context. Nietzsche's vision of a 'strong', 'Dionysian pessimism', the affirmative alternative to various important literary and philosophical responses to the existential crisis of nihilism, was a response to the despair and renunciation pervading the work of Schopenhauer and Turgenev[7] and a riposte to the ultimately pessimistic poses of the hedonist and the dandy, as most famously described by Baudelaire. Karłowicz's music can be heard as anti-Nietzschean in its allegiance to Schopenhauer. Drawing inspiration also from Russian versions of romantic pessimism, it approaches the black hole of nihilism. Rachmaninov's post-Tchaikovskian

---

[6] Leszek Polony, *Poetyka muzyczna Mieczysława Karłowicza: Program literacki, ekspresja i symbol w poemacie symfonicznym* (Cracow: PWM, 1986), 20–21.

[7] Karłowicz's attraction to the work of Turgenev is widely acknowledged. See Henryk Anders, *Mieczysław Karłowicz: Życie i dokonania* (Poznań: Abos, 1998), 307ff., and Alistair Wightman, *Karłowicz, Young Poland and the Musical Fin-de-Siècle* (Aldershot: Scolar Press, 1996), 41, 80, 90.

idiom sustains and scrutinizes the Russian pessimistic tradition in a 'Byronic' mode which contrasts with Scriabin's transition through the overcoming of suffering into an ecstatic brand of Nietzschean modernism. Bartók's elegiac music expresses the depth of despair which sparks the rise of the new. Bartók wrote in August 1905: 'You are rebuking me for being a pessimist?!! Me, a follower of Nietzsche?!!'[8] The extent of Nietzsche's influence on Bartók has been disputed, but the height of his enthusiasm for the philosopher of 'strong pessimism' around the years 1905–7 was crucially timed, for he subsequently developed an elegiac tone of great symbolic significance in, for example, the First String Quartet, Op.7, and *Elegy*, Op.8b No.1. This was further pursued and intensified in the Ady songs, Op.16, and in sections of *The Miraculous Mandarin*, Op.21.

Nietzsche's symptoms of decadence: Turgenev, Baudelaire, Schopenhauer

The fullest treatment of nihilism in Nietzsche's writings is found in the notes collected in the first section of *The Will to Power*. Nihilism is a crucial symptom of the malaise of modern civilization. Nietzsche is concerned with responding to the situation 'in which the romantic faith in love and the future is transformed into the desire for nothing, 1830 into 1850'. His 'signposts to nihilism' consist of the pessimism which he sees as the logical result of decadence, with its predominance of either suffering over pleasure or its hedonistic opposite. Along the road to nihilism it is confirmed 'that becoming has no goal', that there is no truth, no morality, no 'why', only 'how'. It is the path of the exhausted, weary modern subject. This section will focus on three of Nietzsche's chief manifestations of decadent pessimism – Russian pessimism (of which Turgenev, although not mentioned by name in Nietzsche's writings, can confidently be considered a representative), aesthetic pessimism or *l'art pour l'art* (epitomized by Baudelaire, who again is not mentioned in *The Will to Power* but is clearly in Nietzsche's mind here) and epistemological pessimism (Schopenhauer) – and examine the manner in which they are contrasted with Nietzsche's self-portrait as the modern embodiment of the strong pessimism of the Dionysian.[9]

Nietzsche appropriated and reinterpreted vital and energetic aspects of the Dionysian developed by German romantics. From the works of Goethe,

[8] Letter to Irmy Jurkovics, in Béla Bartók, *Letters*, ed. János Demény, trans. Péter Balabán and István Farcas (London: Faber, 1971), 50.
[9] Nietzsche, *The Will to Power*, Book I, 'European Nihilism', 9–82.

Herder and Johann Hamann he took the notion of the ecstatic, intoxicated dithyramb, and he turned to poetic expressions of this image in the work of Hölderlin and Novalis. He also drew upon Dionysus as the figure of abundance and joy described in Friedrich Schlegel's romantic mythology, and Heinrich Heine's resurrected god of sensuality and voluptuousness, as saviour of the senses and destroyer of the romantic equation of Dionysus and Christ. Thus in Nietzsche the Dionysian ecstasy of the German romantics 'reached its final culmination'.[10] Dionysus was reborn (once more) as Nietzsche's hero in the modern, decadent world. He returns to show the Will to power of eternal recurrence as the affirmative alternative to oblivion or Nirvana. Nietzsche's overcoming of Schopenhauer, made possible by this power, was part of his deep concern for countering the prevailing views of pessimism. 'Dionysian pessimism' as described in Nietzsche's *The Joyful Wisdom* contrasts with Schopenhauer's 'romantic pessimism', and, indeed, in later formulations the association of Dionysus with pessimism is dropped altogether.[11]

Through his romantic transformation from a frolicking figure in bucolic settings to a dynamic idea of the imagination, Dionysus no longer appears as an inebriated wine god in human form, but becomes an abstract metaphor for a higher state of intoxication.[12] Thus the Dionysian shifted from the phenomenal to the noumenal, from an external world inhabited by figural representations, to a non-figural or metaphysical realm, one where Schopenhauer famously and influentially located the workings of the Will. By contrast with the illusory formal appearances created in cool, contemplative thought, the surging kinetic forces of the Schopenhauerian Will are perpetually striving, desiring, straining. Perhaps paradoxically, these forces are inseparable from the body, and thus the Will is connected to the erotic. But the Will is not an object-related desire; rather it is a blind, impulsive force of nature. Willing is brutish, inchoate, undisciplined, and is the universal urge to combine, to de-individualize. Manifestations of the Will in the phenomenal world, for example the illusory objectification of its universal force as erotic desire, are the source of unmitigating misery. In the earthly life of the individual man, the woman as erotic object of desire is, in

[10] Max L. Baeumer, 'Nietzsche and the Tradition of the Dionysian', trans. Timothy F. Sellner, in James C. O'Flaherty, Timothy F. Sellner and Robert M. Helm (eds.), *Studies in Nietzsche and the Classical Tradition* (Chapel Hill: University of North Carolina Press, 1976), 165–89.

[11] See Ivan Soll, 'Pessimism and the Tragic View of Life: Reconsiderations of Nietzsche's *Birth of Tragedy*', in Robert C. Solomon and Kathleen M. Higgins (eds.), *Reading Nietzsche* (Oxford University Press, 1988), 104–31.

[12] Albert Henrichs, 'Loss of Self, Suffering, Violence: The Modern View of Dionysus from Nietzsche to Girard', *Harvard Studies in Classical Philology* 88 (1984), 218.

Schopenhauer's decidedly misogynist world view, destabilizing and disorderly, a maenadic source of discontent, despair and ultimate destruction. True and lasting contentment is impossible for the individual under the sway of the Will.

Nietzsche's notion of the Dionysian is often associated with the Schopenhauerian Will, but there are significant differences. It is a comparably powerful and apparently uncontrollable drive, but it leads to enchantment, charm and ecstasy. The associations with the erotic point up this distinction. In Part II of *The World as Will and Representation* Schopenhauer describes erotic love as directed to an individual object; it is therefore an individualizing, desiring force. But this is an illusion. It is actually a force driven by the Will, whose only interest lies in the species, and ultimately demands renunciation of the individual figure of love. By contrast, the Nietzschean Dionysian is a creative energy through which the individual is transformed by the experience of being made a work of art; the erotic is an artistic force, the satyrs of *The Birth of Tragedy* are subtly creative artists. Thus Nietzschean art is not an attempted detachment from life, the body and sensuality; it is not based on renunciation. Dionysus is finally figured as Eros, and unlike the Schopenhauerian unintelligible force of the Will, this Eros is a revitalizing artist. Schopenhauer's pessimism is thus refuted by the glorification of the madness of intoxicating erotic love.[13]

These distinctions between the character of the Dionysian and the Will therefore reflect different understandings of the functions of art. For Schopenhauer, escape from the particular erotic love object may be promised through the general, abstract, contemplative relation to art. But the aesthetic attitude is unstable, a momentary distraction from affliction, a magical illusion which inevitably will be dispelled as man's awareness of his dreadful predicament returns. In the condition of pessimism, tragedy in high art is viewed as 'metaphysical consolation through mimesis of human destruction'. It offers this moment of comfort because its content, experienced as a cathartic encounter with images of pain and destructive forces, is a reminder of why we turn to art in 'tragic spectatorship'. For Nietzsche, 'Art' is figured as saving sorceress, expert at leading to an overcoming of the traumas of life, and Dionysian intoxication is hailed as the transforming power of love and stimulus to life through which the heroic subject becomes

---

[13] See Martha C. Nussbaum, 'Nietzsche, Schopenhauer and Dionysus', in Christopher Janaway (ed.), *The Cambridge Companion to Schopenhauer* (Cambridge University Press, 1999), 344–74. See also Nussbaum's 'The Transfiguration of Intoxication: Nietzsche, Schopenhauer, and Dionysus', in Salim Kemal, Ivan Gaskell and Daniel W. Conway (eds.), *Nietzsche, Philosophy and the Arts* (Cambridge University Press, 1998), 36–69.

stronger, more perfect and more valuable. Here lies tragedy's profound relationship with the existential challenges posed by the encounter with the sublime. For Schopenhauer, the sublime aesthetic experience reveals the illusory nature of representation and the phenomenal world's basis on the *principium individuationis*. In *The Birth of Tragedy*, by contrast, Nietzsche argues against the belief that instability leads inexorably to pessimistic anxiety and nihilism, for this is itself an illusory representation. Nietzsche turns the employment of the sublime on its head: rather than leading to passive nihilism in the momentary consolations of aesthetic representation, it is informed by the Will to live, the Will to love and the Will to power.[14]

As Lyotard famously concluded, the aesthetic and experience of the sublime lie at the heart of modernism's characteristic preoccupations with nostalgia and the futile strivings of the Will in the face of the power-lessness of the faculty of representation. Sublime moments are where 'modern art finds its impetus'. They are experiences in which the unrepresentable idea of the coincidence of pleasure and pain may lead to 'neurosis' or 'masochism'. Two possible alternative 'modes' arise in Lyotard's sublime modernity: 'jubilation' at the overcoming of old laws and assumptions, and a concentration on 'the powerlessness of the faculty of presentation, on the nostalgia for presence felt by the human subject, on the obscure and futile will which inhabits him in spite of everything'.[15] By contrast with nostalgia for a Kantian restoration of reason, for formal recuperation and recovery, in Nietzsche's later formulations, where the Dionysian becomes a metonym for the Dionysian–Apollonian dialectic, form is neither therapeutic nor a turning away: it is a product of a tragic and sublime moment invoking both the Will to form and the Will to dissolution. Nietzsche contrasted this with the formlessness arising from the passive nihilism of decadent modernity, the disintegration of part–whole relationships and the fetishism of the fragment, most seductively exemplified by Wagner's magical-musical miniaturism. This disintegration is a sign of exhausted Will, of a pessimism of the weak which is marked by mourning at the loss of transcendent truth, the neuroticism of romanticism, ascetic renunciation and degeneration. By contrast, active nihilism accepts the contingency of knowledge; it is marked by an absence of nostalgia and by the revitalizing moment of Dionysian intoxication, which is indispensable if art is to exist.[16]

[14] Matthew Rampley, *Nietzsche, Aesthetics and Modernity* (Cambridge University Press, 2000), 80–97.
[15] Jean-François Lyotard, 'Réponse à la question: Qu'est-ce que le postmoderne?', *Critique* 419 (1982), trans. Régis Durand as 'Answering the Question: What is Postmodernism?', in *The Postmodern Condition: A Report on Knowledge* (Manchester University Press, 1984), 71–82.
[16] See Rampley, *Nietzsche, Aesthetics and Modernity*, 120, 163, 218–20.

As pessimism and nihilism became increasingly widespread in the decades after the crushing blow dealt to romantic optimism by the revolutionary failures of 1848–9, an important part of Nietzsche's polemic with this world view was based on his discovery of Turgenev through his friend Paul Rée (who had known Turgenev in Paris). Nietzsche met Rée in 1873, and their friendship marked the end of Nietzsche's Wagner idolatry. Turgenev's work epitomized the Russian existential crisis as the idealism of the 1840s turned to the nihilism of the 1860s. The tone is already set in Turgenev's first attempts at verse in the 1830s, based on Byron's *Manfred*, which lead to the later concept of the 'superfluous man', with renunciation viewed as the door to the secret meanings of life. Love is viewed as an enriching experience, but one which happens only once; the rest of life is a postscript, and the momentary balance and unity and happiness which love confers serve only to confirm the tragic or comic impermanence of life.[17] After 1848 Turgenev's work turns determinedly elegiac and nostalgic. Turgenev's avid reading of Schopenhauer is especially manifest in *Enough! An Extract from the Memoirs of a Deceased Man* (1862–4). Recounting the reminiscences of a love affair long over and the impotence of man in the face of intractable forces of nature, it confirms that the beauties of art can provide only momentary consolation. Man's imaginative life is at the mercy of the recalcitrant, impassive, implacable forces of nature which cause horror as the melancholic turns to the threatening presence of death. The inevitably tragic fate of man leads to profound and insurmountable pessimism. Love is not ultimately a positive force; it is seen as an illness, a destabilizing force which can take hold like a fever. By contrast with the intoxications described by Nietzsche, love leads only to death. Thus Turgenev highlights the irreconcilable contrasts between lovers: though happiness seems promised, the affair is always doomed and leads to the lovers' destruction.[18] Love is illusory or nullified in Turgenev's works, which are preoccupied with themes of isolation and the finality of loneliness.[19] Life is viewed as hard and endless toil, whose hidden meanings are discovered not in dreams fulfilled but in repeated and crushing denials.

A contemporaneous but strikingly contrasting response to the culture of pessimism emerged in the work of Baudelaire. In 1883–4 Nietzsche

---

[17] See A. V. Knowles, *Ivan Turgenev* (Boston: Twayne, 1988), 13, 39, 43.

[18] See Richard Freeborn, *Turgenev: The Novelist's Novelist* (Oxford University Press, 1963). In his own life, for the hours of sublime happiness at his beloved Pauline Viardot's operatic successes, Turgenev suffered years of misery and amorous unfulfilment; see the classic account given in Nicholas N. Segievsky, 'The Tragedy of a Great Love: Turgenev and Pauline Viardot', *American Slavic and East European Review* 5 (1946), 55–71.

[19] See Edgar L. Frost, 'Turgenev's "Mumu" and the Absence of Love', *The Slavic and East European Journal* 31 (1987), 171–86.

discovered Paul Bourget's psychological analysis of decadence, the 'Théorie de la décadence' in *Essais de psychologie contemporaine* (1883), which included an important discussion of Baudelaire. (Nietzsche drew heavily on Bourget for his description of decadent style in *The Case of Wagner*.) If pessimism in Germany was exemplified by the work of Schopenhauer, and in Russia by Turgenev, then in France the example was Baudelaire, whose response was a search for new fleeting sensations through which, according to Bourget, Baudelaire 'reveals in pessimism a positive dynamic quality, thanks to his ability to penetrate its inner logic, critically and creatively, and infuse it with novelty'.[20] In particular, the dandy is a key figure in the cultural climate of decadence, and Baudelaire's *The Painter of Modern Life* (1863) contains one of the most influential descriptions of this character. In the face of the demoralizing breakdown and denial of joyful unity, the dandy defies established morality and divine law in a critique of romantic optimism. Baudelaire considered dandyism to be 'the last flicker of heroism in decadent ages'. The dandy is splendid, brilliant, but cold and ultimately melancholic. Under the constant threat of subjective disintegration, he retreats in cool detachment behind a mask of preservation. Thus he is tied to asceticism, amorality and the cultivation of outer appearance at the expense of inner nature. 'It is a kind of cult of the ego which can still survive the pursuit of that form of happiness to be found in others, in woman for example; which can even survive what are called illusions.' Love, the 'natural occupation of men of leisure', is pursued, but crucially it is done so in 'ephemeral reverie', in a 'fantasy', one which 'can scarcely be translated into action'. The dandy's 'beauty' consists of a 'cold exterior', his 'determination to remain unmoved'.[21] Through this tactic the dandy outwardly seeks to avoid the despair of delusion and dejection. His smile is blasé. It is a smirk of aristocratic superiority, and his body is a temple to the religion of art for art's sake. In flagrant artifice, in ironic, ludic withdrawal from society, he declares a heretical mockery of the forces of nature, or drapes a veil over nature's baseness in flaunting the beautiful façade of the poseur.[22] If the dandy wears his hedonist heart displayed on his exquisite sleeve then the sensation must also be kept at arm's length. You may look but you may not touch. The dandy's creation of a world of glittering art objects and the decadent swerve away from sexual experience are both responses to the horrific dangers of the female liquid realm, a

[20] Gogröf-Voorhees, *Defining Modernism*, 157.
[21] Baudelaire, 'The Painter of Modern Life', in *Selected Writings on Art and Literature*, 420–1.
[22] For more, see Gogröf-Voorhees, *Defining Modernism*, 53–60, 79.

withdrawal or attempt to ironize the surging Dionysian forces of the chthonian. His pose is of the Apollonian androgyne.[23] In the dandy's world the Dionysian dance becomes atrophied as its vitality is drained away into empty elegance and steps of pretence. His antithesis is the passionate man of the crowd, who seeks 'dwelling in the throng, in the ebb and flow'.

> He, the lover of life, may also be compared to a mirror as vast as this crowd; to a kaleidoscope endowed with consciousness, which with every one of its movements presents a pattern of life, in all its multiplicity, and the flowing grace of all the elements that go to compose life. It is an ego athirst for the non-ego, and reflecting it at every moment in energies more vivid than life itself, always inconstant and fleeting.[24]

It is empty, an exoteric appeal to narcissistic protection.

Nietzsche was scathing of the dandy's pose. In *Beyond Good and Evil* he wrote: 'paralysis of the will: where today does one not find this cripple sitting? And often in such finery! How seductive his finery looks!' By contrast with Baudelaire, Nietzsche emphasized life, not a withdrawal into a hermetic art or isolation behind the seductive artifice of the masked ball. He posited the Will to power as the alternative to hedonism, which is embraced by the weakly pessimistic to avoid the struggles of the pessimist of strength.[25] The hedonist seeks to delight in the moment, the exquisite, ephemeral pleasure, the presentness which correlates with Baudelaire's famous 'transient', 'fleeting', 'contingent' experience of 'modernity'.[26] Nietzschean forgetting is motivated by a desire to affirm the present, in a defiant recoil from nostalgia – the impossibility of ever achieving a moment of true present or of radical forgetting which is the mark of modernity. This is used as a 'strategy to counteract the paralyzing and deadly accumulation of memory and knowledge'.[27]

Nietzsche knew that failure to establish new libidinal connections and to hanker nostalgically for the return of the dead object of desire leads only to abject melancholia. By contrast with the affirmations of strength in the artwork of the modern moment, this failure is expressed in the morosely elegiac. In such nostalgic works the heroic work of mourning, through which suffering and loss is ultimately overcome, must be deemed to be unsuccessful. 'Heroic' models of artistic creation condemn this elegiac art

---

[23] Camille Paglia, *Sexual Personae: Art and Decadence from Nefertiti to Emily Dickinson* (Harmondsworth: Penguin, 1992), 430.

[24] Baudelaire, 'The Painter of Modern Life', 400.

[25] See Soll, 'Pessimism and the Tragic View of Life', 128.

[26] Baudelaire, 'The Painter of Modern Life', 403.

[27] Gogröf-Voorhees, *Defining Modernism*, 134–7.

as degenerate and effeminate. Thus there is a mourning or elegy for a dying image of a self that seems to fail the Nietzschean heroic test and succumbs to seductive beauty and to indulgent, hyper-emotional subjectivity and thus lacks disciplined, 'masculine' objectivity. As Melissa Zeiger has pointed out, however, the work of elegy is a 'primary site of critical negotiation' with 'cultural norms of sexuality, gendered identity, cultural inheritance, and permissible response to death'. The modern subject's defining fear is of an emasculating failure to establish new libidinal connections and achieve creative originality, of succumbing to the nostalgic weakness of the backward glance towards the lost Euridice and therefore becoming melancholic, 'effeminate', deviant and weak. Thus 'cultural misogyny' lies in the artist's dread of the destruction at the hands of insane maenads, the 'multiple threats to his vocation' which are overcome in his 'triumphant apotheosis' over her dead body.[28] Karłowicz's elegiac music is pervaded by eternally unfulfilled longing and themes of loss, death and nostalgia (and, it should be added, hints of a misogynistic tendency). The next section considers examples which crucially influenced Karłowicz's development of a musical semiotic of pessimism.

Musical pessimism: Wagner, Tchaikovsky and Strauss

The influence of Wagner on Karłowicz was profound. Wagner provided Karłowicz with powerful models for the musical expression of pessimism. This is best demonstrated by focusing on one aspect of *Twilight of the Gods*, the music drama which Nietzsche heard as the romantic-artistic 'preparation of nihilism'.[29] The protracted history of Wagner's writing of the *Ring* cycle is well known, but it had a critical impact on the ambiguous tone of its ending. His initial invention of the *Ring* story in late 1848 came as revolutionary enthusiasms still rang true. Its complements were the essays of 1848–52 which advocated the utopian artwork of the future achievable through Young Hegelian radicalism, a recovery of a Hellenic ideal and a historical, teleological process of liberation in tandem with a Feuerbachian guiding love.[30] But this optimism turned to Schopenhauerian pessimism as

---

[28] Melissa F. Zeiger, *Beyond Consolation: Death, Sexuality, and the Changing Shapes of Elegy* (Ithaca: Cornell University Press, 1997), 1–25. On functions of elegy and mourning and the *Grablied* see also my *Szymanowski, Eroticism and the Voices of Mythology*, Royal Musical Association Monograph 11 (Aldershot: Ashgate, 2003), 19–37.

[29] Nietzsche, *The Will to Power*, 8.

[30] See James Treadwell, 'The "Ring" and the Conditions of Interpretation: Wagner's Writing, 1848 to 1852', *Cambridge Opera Journal* 7 (1995), 207–31.

his reading of *The World as Will and Representation* in 1854 coincided with the decline of the utopian romantic world view after the failures of the 1848–9 revolutions. Schopenhauer's example allowed Wagner to articulate pessimistic themes for which he seemed to have long been striving: the emptiness of the phenomenal world is revealed in its destruction, the heroic revolutionary man of the future (Siegfried) succumbs to a vacuous and deceptive decadent world (the Gibichungs), and nature is corrupted and decaying, exemplified in miniature by the derivation of the motif of the twilight of the gods as an inversion of the theme of Nature, the decaying, downward curve of the wave, the opposite of the upwardly striving will to life.[31]

By the time of the cycle's first complete performance (1876) there was a willing audience of the variants (or deviants) of cultural pessimists – melancholics, nihilists and proto-decadents. The portrayal of the apparent failure of redemptive love relationships, and the tragically destructive link with the degenerate world of the Gibichungs leading to the *dénouement* at the death of the romantic hero Siegfried, were both heard as signposts to an inevitably nihilist conclusion. As first noted by Nietzsche, the modern hero Siegfried is subject to what Kramer terms 'progressive debasement'. Kramer describes the process of Siegfried's degeneration from 'exemplary immoralist' and 'Promethean, liberating law-breaker', as from Brünnhilde's rock he 'blunders into the modern world' and 'utopian optimism dies into the murk of Schopenhauerian pessimism'. The corrupt Gibichung world is reflected in Gunther's 'tortured *ressentiment*' and Gutrune's 'abject wheedling'. In such company Siegfried's mien turns to one of 'tedious vanity'.[32] Under the influence of Hagen's potion Siegfried is transformed from the vital hero of the previous night's passionate duet with Brünnhilde into a dandified hedonist who falls for the vacuous charms of Gutrune (and who through the tricks of the Tarnhelm can fool Brünnhilde into thinking he is the feeble-minded, egotistic Gunther). Wagner associated Gutrune's character with light music – the 'prostituted music' of French *opéra comique*. Her frivolous character aligns her with the coquette who symbolizes this genre in *Opera and Drama*. She is the female equivalent of the dandy, one who desires admiration, but seeks to resist being overcome with love for the admiring object: her pleasures derive from her vanity, a delighting in her self-image.[33] Meanwhile, the 'impressive exterior' of

[31] See Warren Darcy, 'The Pessimism of the *Ring*', *Opera Quarterly* 4 (1986), 24–48.
[32] Kramer, *Opera and Modern Culture*, 9, 36–7, 77.
[33] See Jean-Jacques Nattiez, *Wagner Androgyne*, trans. Stewart Spencer (Princeton University Press, 1993), 84–7.

Gunther's motive is heroism which is all show: it masks a weakness revealed through his debilitating concern for appearance and reputation. Just as Gutrune can be considered Brünnhilde's 'inverted double',[34] so also the decadent recognizes that Gunther is part of Siegfried's 'shadow'.[35]

As the depiction of Siegfried's journey to the Gibichung realm reaches its climax Hagen sees the heroic figure approaching. Siegfried appears as the strong man able to tame the mighty waters which carry his boat. It is an image of heroic, muscular strength which will progressively decay through the scenes which follow. At the beginning of Act 1 scene ii Hagen hails the hero in the notes of the C major triad, but underneath this vocal line the harmony is a fateful half-diminished F sharp chord which is gradually transformed into the dominant of the Gibichung key, B minor (Example 2.1). Over this harmonic transformation there appears a fragmentary motif of sweetly seductive sensuality (E–F♯–G–G♯), a chromatic shape which steals, or degrades, Brünnhilde's passionate falling seventh. (Hagen's hailing of Siegfried might also be heard as a fateful stealing of Brünnhilde's hail to the sun when she was woken by Siegfried on the mountain.) At this moment Gutrune stares at Siegfried in astonishment. This motif had been heard in the previous scene during Hagen's and Gutrune's discussion of how to charm Siegfried and make him forget Brünnhilde. Later it becomes increasingly prominent as, thanks to Hagen's amnesiac-aphrodisiac potion, Siegfried falls for the beguiling Gutrune. Nietzschean heroic forgetfulness – Siegfried's lack of concern for, or knowledge of, the past – turns to the different forgetfulness of the decadent Gibichung world, the surrender to indolence, the lack of resilience to Gutrune's charms. When, at the climactic ending of Act 2 scene iv, Siegfried celebrates his marriage to Gutrune the sensual motif is transformed into celebratory music in C major (Example 2.2). But we know that these are the empty festivities of decadent hedonists.

In Act 3 scene ii, when Hagen delivers another potion to Siegfried to allow the memory of the beloved Brünnhilde to return, this recollection of love is the tragic precursor of Siegfried's demise. (In his student days Karłowicz expressed dissatisfaction with Wagner's recourse to magic potions at these crucial moments, perhaps because he felt that the device gave a supernatural aura to a psychological truth which was all too real in the bleakly pessimistic world view he was already developing.[36]) The massive recapitulation of

[34] Carolyn Abbate, *Unsung Voices: Opera and Musical Narrative in the Nineteenth Century* (Princeton University Press, 1991), 219.

[35] Robert Donington, *Wagner's 'Ring' and its Symbols* (London: Faber, 1979), 222–4.

[36] See Wightman, *Karłowicz*, 16.

Example 2.1 Wagner, *Twilight of the Gods*, Act 1 scene ii, Hagen: 'Heil! Siegfried theurer Held!'

Example 2.2 Wagner, *Twilight of the Gods*, Act 2 scene iv, celebration as Siegfried embraces Gutrune

music from the love scene at the end of *Siegfried* suspends time as Siegfried recalls his love for Brünnhilde with no trace of awareness of his tragic position. The subsequent tonal shift from C major to the C minor of the funeral march intensifies the pathos. The memory of love is one of the shadows which haunt the whole of the final drama of the *Ring* tetralogy. This is confirmed from its opening dark E flat minor version of the chords of Brünnhilde's awakening which in *Siegfried* preceded the white heat of the love duet.[37] As he dies, and the awakening memories begin to plague him,

37 See William Kinderman, 'Dramatic Recapitulation in Wagner's *Götterdämmerung*', *19th-Century Music* 4 (1980), 101–12.

the nostalgic images of the love flood back. There is a parallel here with Turgenev's view of love as an enriching experience which happens only once, to which the rest of life is all too likely to be a depressing postscript. The momentary balance and unity and happiness which love confers only serve to confirm the tragic (or comic) impermanence of life.

Turgenev's opinion of Wagner's work was at best ambivalent,[38] but both Turgenev's and Wagner's depictions of love's failure were vital examples for Karłowicz. The Russian psychological tradition, of which Turgenev is a leading literary example, is strongly reflected in the 'morbid' or 'despondent' quality often heard in passages of Tchaikovsky's music.[39] Tchaikovsky's influence on both Karłowicz and Rachmaninov was crucial. Much recent scholarship has been focused on a critical revaluation of Tchaikovsky's music. Henry Zajaczkowski, for example, hears skilful and purposeful 'inorganic structures', 'breaks' and 'longueurs', all of which contrast with the pervasively connective, developmental mode of the organic ideal. He also identifies processes which deliberately close too much and too soon. Tchaikovsky's characteristic developmental techniques are 'designed as enforced hiatuses … they stultify organic growth and replace it with a cunningly constructed build-up of tension, finding its release in an ultimate climax of sometimes overwhelming force'. Zajaczkowski argues that this musical process is linked to the dramatic or expressive workings of 'fate': Tchaikovsky's 'most compelling and profoundly inspired compositions are those that depict malign predestination', with 'peaks [that] are an unleashing of suppressed dynamicism'. In the *Pathétique* this 'suppressive-propulsive' technique is seen to 'extend its grip over the whole composition', across the first movement's resignation, the perverted limping waltz, the feverish self-delusion of the third movement and the 'underlying malaise' of the finale.[40] Zajaczkowski's analysis facilitates the rehabilitation of stylistic features that had fuelled the derogatory view of Tchaikovsky as melodramatic, sentimental, neurotic, lyrically yielding, melancholic, exhibitionist, formally weak, effeminate, homosexual composer. The negative construction of this reputation was built, of course, on the marked contrast with the heroically 'masculine', Beethovenian mythology of what was required of the 'symphonic'

---

[38] See Bartlett, *Wagner and Russia*, 54–6.

[39] For Alexander Poznansky it is this tradition that is the source of the tone of 'passionate nostalgia' and 'disaffection' in Tchaikovsky's music, not – as popularly assumed – the composer's personal grief or anguish; see *Tchaikovsky's Last Days: A Documentary Study* (Oxford: Clarendon Press, 1996), 223.

[40] Henry Zajaczkowski, *Tchaikovsky's Musical Style* (Ann Arbor: UMI Research Press, 1987), 1–2, 25, 45.

composer. As Taruskin points out, Tchaikovsky's allegiances to the 'Mozartian' symphonic tradition, to the aspiration towards 'classical' mastery in all genres, to expressions of beautiful 'pleasure' and 'delight', all bypass the Beethovenian image of the symphonic sublime and are thus characterized as non-heroic according to Germanic iconography. According to Taruskin, Tchaikovsky further distances himself from German late romanticism by eschewing 'esoteric metaphysical hand-wringing' and manifesting a 'typically Russian aversion' to 'exhausting' Wagnerian nervousness.[41] But Tchaikovsky's symphonic works have also been heard to contain subversions of Wagnerian redemptive narratives. James Hepokoski has described Tchaikovsky's *Pathétique* Symphony as a tragic deformation of what he calls the '*Flying Dutchman* model', after Wagner's overture, where the minor mode seeks resolution into major at the recapitulation of the 'feminine' second subject. According to this model, the exposition of the redeeming second subject is soft, but its gloriously transformed return in apotheosis confirms the telos in a utopian masculine erotic fantasy.[42] Tchaikovsky's symphony can be read to express the pessimistic dismissal or denial of such fantastic redemption. This aspect of the *Pathétique* and the closely related *Manfred* Symphony made a profound impact on Karłowicz, who in many ways represents an attempted synthesis of Wagnerian and Tchaikovskian species of pessimism. It is useful at this point, then, to examine how Tchaikovsky's music generates a fatalistic tone (which, of course, was not the only one, or even the most commonly found one in his music, but is here the most pertinent).

The *Pathétique*'s tragic end is pessimistically foreshadowed by its slow introduction, which is replete with symbols of melancholy – falling seconds, a lamenting bass descent from E to B, a grief-ridden ♭6–5 in the final statement of the motif of the opening phrase (in the viola, G♮ to F♯ over the dominant of E minor) and a harmonic emphasis on what proves to be the traditionally melancholic subdominant minor. It is a 'dual subject', a contrapuntal combination of pathos and lament, and thus a distant relative of the slow introduction to Beethoven's *Les Adieux* Piano Sonata, Op.81a, which similarly configures a 'farewell' motif over a lamenting bass.[43] By contrast with Beethoven's sonata, however, there is no prospect of a joyful return. Tchaikovsky's slow introduction also sounds like an enervated version of the slow introduction to Beethoven's *Pathétique* Piano Sonata,

---

[41] Taruskin, 'Chaikovsky and the Human', in *Defining Russia Musically*, 251–8.

[42] James Hepokoski, 'Masculine–Feminine', *The Musical Times* 135 (1994), 494–9.

[43] See Carl Dahlhaus, *Ludwig van Beethoven: Approaches to his Music*, trans. Mary Whittall (Oxford: Clarendon Press, 1991), 36.

Op.13. According to eighteenth-century aesthetics, the 'pathetic' may shift 'up' to the sublime, or 'down' into the sentimental, as it may be expressed in grand, tragic style or gentler lamentations.[44] Michaelis proposed a pathetic sublime which resembles the lyric, an intense form of the pathetic, a second-order sublime presented in softer forms and tender sensibility. But as Kramer argues, the sensibility of the eighteenth century (Tchaikovsky's beloved eighteenth century) is transformed in the course of the nineteenth century into destructive psychopathology.[45] By contrast with the revolutionary, heroic power, the elevated and energetic tone, the resistance to suffering and the struggle for mastery over the sighs and sobs in Beethoven's 'Schillerian' pathetic,[46] Tchaikovsky's tone in this symphony is one of mournful introspection, sympathetic sighs and lingering expressions of grief.

Emerging out of this image of despair and enfeeblement, the first subject group of the main expository section is characterized by tonally unstable, 'scherzando-fantasy' material.[47] It is a subject which seems to cry out the need of resolution and redemption. The Andante second subject (bb.89ff.), which offers a momentary promise of redemption through amorous fulfilment, contains inversions of or alternatives to the melancholic musical symbols of the slow introduction. Melodic emphasis is on the natural rather than flat sixth (B in D major), and chromatic motions in inner parts of the accompaniment rise, a motion emphasized by the altered dominant at the close of the phrase (bb.96–100). Timothy Jackson hears this as an ideal image, a 'languorous portrait' of the beloved muse evoked through bucolic, pastoral topoi.[48] But the middle section of this secondary thematic area evokes for Taruskin a 'hallucinatory atmosphere', and he hears the whole thematic group as an 'uncanny *lyrisches Intermezzo*'.[49] This theme, then, offers an unreal, fantasy image of love which cannot last. This is rudely confirmed as it is interrupted by a descent into hellish turmoil at the start of the development. Literal or close recapitulation of the first subject group is avoided. Rather, a developed version leads to a structural dominant supporting what Jackson calls a

---

[44] Elaine R. Sisman, 'Pathos and the *Pathétique*: Rhetorical Stance in Beethoven's C-minor Sonata, Op.13', *Beethoven Forum* 3 (1994), 90–1.

[45] Lawrence Kramer, 'Primitive Encounters: Beethoven's "Tempest" Sonata, Musical Meaning, and Enlightenment Anthropology', *Beethoven Forum* 6 (1998), 44, 65.

[46] Sisman, 'Pathos and the *Pathétique*', 94, 102.

[47] Timothy Jackson, *Tchaikovsky: Symphony No.6 'Pathétique'* (Cambridge University Press, 1999), 30.

[48] Jackson, *Tchaikovsky: Symphony No.6*, 41.

[49] Taruskin, *Defining Russia Musically*, 257–8, 304.

new 'Oracle' theme, creating an effect of breakthrough and speaking a deathly tone, with the coincident string descent (bb.284–9) foreshadowing the collapse of the finale. Definitive arrival on the tonic major is delayed until the recapitulation of the second group, where Jackson hears the warm, seductive, idyllic tone of this subject in the exposition now transformed by the chilling embrace of death.[50] The first movement's coda is a chorale over pizzicato falling strings, one which adumbrates the Adagio lamentoso of the finale. This lament follows the sublimely precipitous thrills of the third-movement march. Its effect recalls Michaelis's description of how the subjective dangers posed by the torrent and tumult of the musical sublime can function as a precondition for a response in the 'pathetic' signs of sympathy – the sorrowful voicing of sighs and sobs.

The *Pathétique* is closely related to the *Manfred* Symphony, Op.58 (1885). Byron's *Manfred* was widely attractive for the post-1848 pessimists, as it was for the young Turgenev and Nietzsche. It is easy to see why, if we recall the hero's contemplation of life's tragic end on top of the sublime Jungfrau, the gloomy opening and the theme of doomed and transgressive love. As Manfred famously declares near the opening of the drama:

But great grief should be the instructor of the wise;
Sorrow is knowledge: they who know the most
Must mourn the deepest o'er the fatal truth,
The Tree of Knowledge is not that of Life.[51]

In a programmatic model for a symphonic version of the story which Stasov sent to Balakirev, the hero's beloved Astarte returns in the finale as an ideal oasis amid the orgiastic pandemonium of a bacchanal. Some time later Balakirev suggested the project to Tchaikovsky, lauding the profundity and contemporary resonance of the subject of Manfred, for 'the sickness of modern mankind lies in the fact that man cannot preserve his ideals. They are shattered, nothing is left for the satisfaction of the soul except bitterness.'[52] Tchaikovsky's portrait of the tragic hero includes a stirring string theme initiated by passionate but gloomy falling sevenths (a dark, pessimistic alternative to the erotically charged falling sevenths of the glance motif from *Tristan*?). At the climax of the first thematic

---

[50] Jackson, *Tchaikovsky: Symphony No.6*, 63. Jackson proposes that the *Pathétique* is a negative trope of *Tristan*, a narrative of the destined death of lovers which ends not in redemption but in oblivion, where the transfiguring ascent of *Liebestod* is replaced by irrevocable descent or collapse.

[51] George (Lord) Byron, 'Manfred', in *Complete Poetical Works* (Oxford University Press, 1970), 390.

[52] See Gerald Abraham's preface to the score, Tchaikovsky, *Manfred* Symphony Op.58 (London: Eulenburg, n.d.).

complex (bb.150–4) a chromatic upper voice descent outlines a plunge from heights into abyss, recalling the similarly tragic gesture from bar 284 in the first movement of the *Pathétique*. The second subject, Astarte's theme (bb.171ff.), is characterized by a short, breathy melodic emphasis on B (the hopeful natural sixth of its D major key) but also repeated allusion to E minor (the melancholic minor subdominant of the symphony's home key of B minor). Rising chromatic inner parts also suggest comparison with the second subject of the *Pathétique*. A climactic statement follows with heavenly harps (b.260) but this peters out into silence, after which Manfred's tormented theme returns (b.289) and builds to the deathly introduction of the tam-tam (b.324). Astarte's theme does not return in this movement: there is no rapprochement or dialectical synthesis, just irreconcilable opposition or contrast. There is no sonata resolution, not even a narrative deformation of one. It is a mighty symphonic version of Turgenev's vision of tragically doomed love.

In the finale Astarte's shadow at first appears as diminished-seventh-based fragments (b.303) but then leads to the return of the heavenly harps. After another silence which threatens decadent fragmentation her theme is restated, but now in D flat (b.337) – the shadow key of her original D (recalling perhaps the similarly deathly shadow tonal relationships in *Tristan* and *Twilight of the Gods*). The function of the opening bacchanal in the finale is entirely negative (one can compare it with the finale of Berlioz's *Symphonie fantastique*, which was a model for Tchaikovsky), and the darkening and fragmentation of Astarte's music continue the pessimistic prognosis. The final return of Manfred's existential torment leads to the tam-tam marking his death (b.390), the sonority which signals the similar moment in the finale of the *Pathétique*. By contrast with the demise of the subject in the *Pathétique*, however, Manfred is redeemed in the after-life, a fate signalled by the organ-led chorale of the final pages.[53]

The third of the trinity of major musical models for Karłowicz consists of Strauss's tone poems. Strauss will feature prominently in later sections of this book, so at this point only a brief identification of those stylistic characteristics most pertinent to the music of Karłowicz is offered. In several of the tone poems the problems of maintaining formal coherence and sustaining a semblance of teleology in the face of the perils of decadent collapse are frequently evoked. The music's individual parts suggest the fragmentation of traditional forms, shattered by the intensification and

---

[53] The popularity of the figure of Manfred was a leading factor in the 'Byronism' which attracted many artists of apparently pessimistic bent, not least, as we shall see, Rachmaninov.

juxtaposition of episodal contrast. In Strauss's familiar *Schwung* the sweeping, swelling waves of cumulative energy are invested with the power to counter the inertia of decadent decay and lifelessness. Strauss builds upon the tone of Wagner's eroticism, the sensual alternative to Schopenhauerian asceticism, heard for example in Isolde's loss of individual identity in an ecstatic, surging flood ('in dem wogenden Schwall'), her 'höchste Lust',[54] and in the exuberant, energetic passion of the Siegfried–Brünnhilde love duet, a blissful release suggestive of the Nietzschean Dionysian. (But the post-Wagnerian's 'requirement for the sublime, the profound, the overwhelming' was, of course, ridiculed by Nietzsche as the art of 'histrionics', an 'expression of physiological degeneration' inaugurated by Wagner.[55]) Wagner expressed his characters' *Verklärung* through musical processes of *Steigerung* (intensification). As Goethe influentially described it, this is driven by an increasing urge towards a desired synthesis: although opposite extremes (*Polarität*) 'are attracted to each other, they cannot rest, because the principle of intensification causes all things to strive upward toward higher levels of organization'. Where this striving fails the 'pathetic' might be evoked. In the slow introduction to Beethoven's *Pathétique* Sonata, for example, phrases climb (*steigen*) but fall in the 'pathetic' gesture of the yearning appoggiatura.[56] In the mythologized image of Beethoven's 'heroic', 'revolutionary' narratives the striving upwards is maintained (even as polarities are heightened). In this regard Wagner sought to emulate and surpass Beethoven's achievement. In Strauss, this narrative and structural process is repeatedly problematized: its heroic idealism no longer rang true. In Strauss's *Don Juan* the *Steigerung* waves are negated, unfulfilled; they dissolve or collapse.[57] After this, a different sort of redemption might be sought in 'modern' structural process of 'breakthrough' and an 'attempted resacralization' of the neo-romantic metaphysical after a 'realistic' embracing of the 'merely material'.[58] But where such processes once

54 See Linda and Michael Hutcheon, *Opera: The Art of Dying* (Cambridge, Mass.: Harvard University Press, 2004), 64–5, 69.
55 Nietzsche, *The Case of Wagner*, 167–9.
56 Michael Spitzer, *Metaphor and Musical Thought* (Chicago University Press, 2004), 294, 296–7.
57 For a case study in Strauss's influence on Karłowicz which employs Harold Bloom's theories of the 'anxiety of influence' to read Op.12 as a 'misprison' of *Don Juan*, see Michael Murphy, 'An Aesthetical and Analytical Evaluation of the Music of Mieczysław Karłowicz', unpublished PhD thesis, University College, Cork (1994), Part II, 175–92.
58 James Hepokoski, 'Fiery-Pulsed Libertine or Domestic Hero? Strauss's *Don Juan* Reinvestigated', in Bryan Gilliam (ed.), *Richard Strauss: New Perspectives on the Composer and his Works* (Durham: Duke University Press, 1992), 166. Hepokoski also discusses examples of *Steigerung* in Strauss in his review of Walter Werbeck, *Die Tondichtungen von Richard Strauss* (Tutzing: Hans Schneider,

again 'fail' the ascent to the noumenal is dragged down to earth, the euphoric wave sinks into its watery grave. By contrast, one of the most influential redemptive 'ascents' in Strauss was that in *Death and Transfiguration*, Op.24 (1890). Strauss outlined the programme in a letter of 1894 – 'the dying hours of a man who had striven towards the highest idealistic aims', the bed-ridden 'sick man' 'racked with horrible agonies' who has nostalgic flashbacks to childhood and 'youthful striv-ings and passions'. 'As the pains already begin to return, there appears to him the fruit of his life's path, the conception, the ideal which he has sought to realize, to present artistically, but which he has not been able to complete, since it is not for man to be able to accomplish such things.'[59] In the tone poem's famous ending the Ideal theme receives its transfiguration in C, in an apotheosis after the suffering man's death, an ending achieved through a synthesis of deformations of traditional design with processes of 'teleological genesis'.[60] The preparatory 'wave forms' which precede this redemptive ending contain the 'failures' which must be overcome. The first, only partially realized statement of the musical image of the Ideal occurs after a climactic arrival on a structural dominant pedal of C minor (b.149). Falling chromatic motions in the upper parts (*molto agitato*) are reiterated over a dom-inant 6–4 chord. They repeatedly resurge upwards (from b.157), but the dominant does not resolve: the bass slips down to F (b.161) and the striving chromatic lines halt on a half-diminished Tristan chord. The Ideal theme's first appearance (bb.163–4) subsides and leads to nostalgic images of youth – to an evocation of the beautiful. In such moments Strauss displays the techniques of concentration, intensification, abundance, evo-lution and dissolution that Polony identifies as central to Karłowicz's symphonic technique.[61] But *Death and Transfiguration* offers a model of musical processes, materials and symbolism to which Karłowicz alludes only in order to invert or subvert. This technique of subversion is central to how he generates his own *pathétique* tone, to speak of a twilight world in which pessimistic negation crushes the hopes of Dionysian revivifica-tion, in which the drive to a desired higher union is dissolved, obstructed or denied.

1996), *Journal of the American Musicological Society* 51 (1998), 617–23. I will return to consider this topic more fully in Chapter 3.
[59] Quoted in Norman Del Mar, *Richard Strauss: A Critical Commentary on his Life and Works*, vol.I (London: Faber, 1986), 77–8.
[60] Hepokoski, review of Werbeck, *Die Tondichtungen von Richard Strauss*, 621.
[61] Polony, *Poetyka muzyczna Mieczysława Karłowicza*, 160–78.

Dionysus debilitated: the symphonic poems of Karłowicz

As he completed his studies in Berlin in 1899 and 1900, with the music of
Wagner, Strauss and Tchaikovsky resonating in his imagination, Karłowicz
began to compose the *Rebirth Symphony*, Op.7. The symphony begins with
a requiem, the shattering grief of which moves into an awakening of the
will to life over inertia. This shift is the first step along what the programme
describes as an 'infinitely long grey road' towards heroic rebirth. After the
slow(ish) introduction the first movement's main Allegro creates an effect
of turbulent striving in E minor. In the traditional manner of romantic
sonata form, the lyrical idiom of the second subject, a song of the beloved
'other', offers a marked contrast. However, according to the programme,
this is an 'illusion' of the 'ardently desired future'. After the exposition of
these polarized moods the music builds towards the movement's mightiest, most sublime climax (b.206). The intensification seems to promise an
approaching moment of synthesis. But the process is brought to an awe-
struck halt on a dissonant A♯–C–E–G chord. Over this hiatus sound fateful
fanfares portentous of doom. The programme reads: 'a stroke delivered by
the hand of destiny falls like a thunderbolt, crushing all the dreams'. The
climactic chord is one of tragic initiation. In the collapse of rising expectation it is also a moment of pathos (and, it should also be said, one which
in the composer's relatively inexperienced hands only just escapes bathos).
The chord, which will become a Karłowicz fingerprint, resolves onto a
dominant 6–4 in E (the bass A♯ rising to B) as the tension is released
towards recapitulation. But the move into recapitulation provides no
heroic glories. It is a return to 'futile striving' of the opening. When the
storm subsides, solo melodic lines suggest a tragic focus on the lone
suffering figure before his striving energies regain some momentum.
After this the return of the illusory 'other' with the recapitulation of the
second subject is disappointingly routine: a more mature Karłowicz would
surely have considered radical recomposition of this theme, to reflect the
subjective crisis and pursue the implications of the tragic and pathetic
sublime which conjoined at the movement's climax.

A scene of amorous reverie is evoked by the second movement, but this is
also dismissed as hallucination when the third movement launches into an
image of the Dionysian. Karłowicz's programmatic description at this
point makes several Nietzschean allusions: 'Come, plunge into life! Forget
everything, lose oneself! Love, revelry! On and on, not thinking, not
reflecting! May fleeting impressions flash past one after another; may

seething life go to the head like wine, may reason never make an impression; may one be sucked in and lost in this whirlpool!'[62] Here we might hear the living for the now and the new, the effects of de-individualization as the subject drowns in a maelstrom of intoxicating sensations. This is an intimation of the radical modernism of Nietzschean forgetting and the liberation from the laws of logic and rational succession. For Wightman, 'the attempt to portray immersion in the ephemeral experiences of life drew from [Karłowicz] some of his most progressive and vital music to date'.[63] The musical symbolism of Dionysian existence is achieved through kaleidoscopic harmonic effects in the tempo of a rapid waltz. The movement's opening bars, the moment of arousal from the previous movement's illusory reveries, seek to establish the dominant of B through movement from the minor submediant (G) to the dominant, with the pitch G suspended over the F sharp triad to form the dominant minor ninth. With much subsequent emphasis on the diminished seventh 'subset' of this chord (A♯–C♯–E–G) in whirling rhythmic figures there is more than a hint of the erotic revelries of Wagner's Venusberg. When the tonic B is finally secured it is major (b.87 – the minor ninth has also been altered to major by raising the G to G♯), and this leads rapidly to fleeting allusions to E flat (enharmonically D sharp, the major mediant) in bars 103ff. This enharmony initiates a *Steigerung* to a sustained C major triad underpinned by B♭ (bb.127ff.), an enharmonic version of the first movement's tragic chord, whose close relationship to the progressions of the opening ensures that beneath the kaleidoscopic surface there is a single harmonic impulse. However, this leads to chains of altered dominant chords, a passage of dissolution, liquidation or harmonic breakdown. The subject, and formal security, are redeemed only by the introduction of 'Her' music with the Trio in E flat major.[64] The programme reads: 'But stop here a little longer! Look longer into these eyes and drink without ceasing from these cherry-red lips! It is she, the longed-for, dreamed-of woman. May a broad, passionate love-song resound for her; there is nothing but her in the world!' The section is constructed around an ardent climax in the broader triple metre of a moderato waltz, so that the gaze can be more lingeringly focused on her. Through the contemplation of beauty a moment of calm moves into feelings of rapture, but in true Schopenhauerian fashion, these

---

[62] Trans. from Polony, 'Preface' to Karłowicz, *Rebirth Symphony*, Op.7, *Mieczysław Karłowicz: Complete Edition*, vol.IV (Cracow: PWM, 1993), xxv–xxvi.

[63] Wightman, *Karłowicz*, 32.

[64] Wightman hears this image of dream woman as a 'vulgar, ungainly melody', suggesting a misogynistic impulse; see *Karłowicz*, 32.

consolations prove ephemeral and illusory: 'But no! Enough of that! Move on, move on again! The whirlpool sweeps the soul far away; everything becomes smaller, vanishes, fades away, expires ...' The ecstatic pleasures of the dancing lovers quickly disappear.

After this pessimism, the heroic rebirth of the finale's chorale, after the manner of the end of Tchaikovsky's *Manfred*, is an unconvincing *deus ex machina* salvation. According to the programme, at 'the longed-for moment' the 'trials' are 'overcome' and 'the soul stands triumphant and serene ...'. But the finale's bombast and optimism are unpersuasive as Karłowicz's level of inspiration sinks, frankly, into the bathetic and banal. The expressive and structural function of the chord of tragic initiation as an ultimately deceptive sonorous symbol suggests, however, a pessimistic alternative to the optimism of the redemptive narrative, one which will preoccupy the works which follow. Its recurrences and resolutions in the symphony secure the association of the Dionysian image with expressions of the tragic and pathetic sublime, the ephemeral pleasures and wistful recollections of the erotic and the conviction that the intoxications of Dionysian delights pass with the final cadence of the last waltz.

The title of *Returning Waves*, Op.9 (1904), refers to the recurring figures which define the nostalgic tone of the work. Karłowicz was fascinated by seascapes, which he saw as an inspiring combination of sublime and tragic in the eternally reshaping and returning waves.[65] The composer wrote to Adolf Chybiński on the programme: 'Amid the bitter thoughts of a man who was being preyed upon by his fate and who was drawing to the end of his days, memories suddenly revive of the springtime of his life, irradiated with the sunny smile of happiness. Pictures pass one another. Everything vanishes however and bitterness and sorrow grip the tired soul in their claws.'[66] Polony has suggested that Turgenev's *An Unhappy Girl*, with its tale of unfulfilled love and striking images of ice crystals forming on a window-pane, acted as a model for the programme (the ice crystal motif reappears in Karłowicz's description). In this scenario death plays no consolatory role. The chord of tragic initiation from the *Rebirth Symphony* returns and functions as a deceptive version of the harmony which characterizes the Ideal motif from Strauss's *Death and Transfiguration*. The sublime, which in the Strauss provides a route out of suffering and nostalgia to apotheosis in an after-life of heavenly

---

[65] See Wightman, *Karłowicz*, 39–40.
[66] Letter of 20 April 1904, quoted in Polony's 'Preface' to Kartowicz, *Returning Waves*, Op.9, *Mieczystaw Karłowicz: Complete Edition*, vol.VI (Cracow: PWM, 1988), xv.

fulfilment, is in Karłowicz's profoundly nihilistic world view turned into a totally negative experience. In this way his alliance lies with Turgenev's dismissal of the utopian-romantic hopes of redemption. As we shall see, he is also with Nietzsche in condemning the dandy's masquerade, but he cannot envisage a heroic alternative to either profound pessimism or this decadent figure.

The work evokes and problematizes Straussian formal processes of intensification. These contrast with the freezing of returning musical images as the sublime and tragic coexist with the decadent and lifeless. The structural returns heighten the question of how music might create an illusion of pastness. They also heighten questions of form and coherence, of part–whole relationships in a world of deformation, recollection and denial.[67] In his preface to the score Polony quotes Aleksander Poliński's 'condescending' opinion after the work's first performance (28 November 1904) that 'although the whole consists merely of pieces, some of them are admittedly beautiful'. Polony counters this view by arguing that the form is a many-stranded 'stream of consciousness' underpinned by an organic, developmental process which unifies the structural levels of theme and tonal structure. Polony's argument of harmonic logic in a 'free, multi-thematic form' is based on a large-scale V–VI–VII–VIII, as presented in miniature in the opening theme, a sort of ascending *Urlinie*.[68] But Polony's structural interpretation is based on a mishearing of the role of the E–C–A♭ augmented triad in bar 481 as an altered dominant in A minor. This sonority actually leads via an F–A–C♯ augmented triad (b.510) to resolution (b.557) on an F major triad, which then becomes an augmented sixth chord (F–A–D♯, b.569) leading to the return of the opening theme over dominant 6–4 harmony (b.570). Within this harmonic progression there is a large-scale expression of an E–F–E neighbour relation – a structural expansion of the traditional 5–♭6–5 motif of grief (see Example 2.3).

---

[67] For Murphy, the form is a rondo whose sections possess differing temporal qualities; the A section (bb.1–95) equals the tragic 'present', while the B and C episodes are nostalgic, representing the lost joys of the 'past' through an 'illusory stability'. The formal complexity is reflected in Murphy's hearing of the B episode as a 'guest' sonata design embedded within the 'host' rondo. This sonata is itself deformed, with a first theme in C major, transition in A/A flat, a second theme in G flat, a misplaced coda in bb.223–36 in G flat, followed by a chorale in bb.237–52 leading to a truncated mirror reprise of the two themes in bb.253ff.; see Murphy, 'An Aesthetical and Analytical Evaluation', 15–30. Aspects of this provocative reading are persuasive, but I find the embedded 'sonata' design hard to accept.

[68] Polony, 'Preface' to *Returning Waves*, xv–xvi. For more detail see Polony's analytical graphs in his 'Program literacki i symbolika muzyczna w twórczości symfonicznej Karłowicza', in Jadwiga Ilnicka (ed.), *Muzyka Polska a modernizm* (Cracow: PWM, 1981), 141–55.

Example 2.3 Mieczisław Karłowicz, *Returning Waves*, Op.9, bars 481–570, harmonic progression

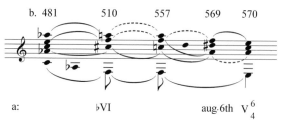

The pessimistic tone of the opening is generated by two ideas presented over the dominant E: a mournful brass chorale is followed by a yearning, miniature wave-form melody on cellos and horns. Like the opening of Tchaikovsky's *Pathétique*, it is a dual subject, but with its topics presented in succession rather than in counterpoint. The fleeting comforts of the nostalgic images which follow are harmonically based on modal mixture: the major alternative to the minor sixth (F sharp) is, enharmonically (G flat), the key of the image of 'Her'; the tonic major (A) is the key of the image of the Dionysian as a waltzing dandy. As in the *Rebirth Symphony*, pessimistic and optimistic narratives coexist, but now the pessimism of nihilism crushes any hope of a positive outcome. In this scenario the subversion of *Steigerung* and the promised sublime moment once more play vital roles in the creation of expection and denial, of hope and delusion. The first of these moments is suggested soon after the deeply melancholic opening. This is started by the ephemeral appearance of Karłowicz's favoured chord of tragic initiation. In a characteristically decadent focus on detail, the symbolic chord (here an F major triad over a bass D♯ which functions as lower neighbour note to the dominant E) stimulates a miniature surge promising the successful process of *Steigerung*. But this leads to sinking chromaticisms once again begun by the tragic semitonal resolution of F to E (bb.37–8). Larger waves generate further intensification and weakening through more chromatic sinking before a return of the opening theme (from b.80) via another resolution of F to the dominant of A minor.

At the tragic chord's next appearance (b.96) the bass note is 'spelt' as E♭, and it leads to Allegro agitato material (b.104) with sinking augmented triads which Wightman hears as a depiction of 'psychological disturbance'.[69] Subsequently, F is more strongly implied as a tonal centre

---

[69] Wightman, *Karłowicz*, 44.

through arrivals on its dominant. At the next highpoint (b.152, Allegro moderato) a dominant 6–4 in F suggests an ecstatic state, the promised consequence of the line in the programme – 'life erupted in laughter full of strength and gaiety' – the first allusion to Dionysian joys and vitality. The call to reinvigoration, previously heard on the trumpet at the tragic chord of its first main appearance (bb.97ff.), is transformed as part of an alluring cadence on the dominant of F (b.156). But the flat submediant is a doomed key in nineteenth-century symphonism. The joys and pleasures it promises are unstable and contain the seeds of their own demise. The F major predictably subsides to A minor and, more subversively, a semitone further to A flat, a 'shadow' flattened tonic which is more deeply darkened into A flat minor and then, with the melodic emphasis on F, an allusion to the Tristan chord (F–A♭–C♭–E♭). From here there is a smooth transition into 'Her' theme as F moves to F sharp/G flat and the A♭–C♭–E♭–F chord is held over a pedal D♭ to form the dominant ninth of G flat (b.169). She, therefore, is a figure who emerges from dark shadows.

The programme describes how 'the youthful figure of a girl who seemed to be meant for him appeared standing in the sunshine'. 'Her' G flat is the enharmonic of F sharp, the bright alternative to the grief-ridden E–F–E association. It is also, being a semitone higher than the doomed F, an attempt to counterbalance the previous wave's decline into the flattened tonic. But the spelling as G flat is significant – this key had, by the end of the nineteenth century, strong associations with the sensuous and the amorous.[70] There is also a dimension of the Ideal or other-worldly attached to its symbolism.[71] When 'Her' G flat moves to C (b.193) there is a more joyously expressive tone. The bass then moves from C to B♭ (b.197) to form the initiating tragic chord, whose local resolution promises more joy at bar 208 in A major, with F supporting augmented sixth chords. This prepares for a grand *Steigerung* to a climactic 6–4 of G flat with soaring strings offering a redemptive vision (b.219), complete with heavenly harps. The chorale which follows (bb.238ff.) begins as an apparent consecration of the amorous relationship, but it poignantly turns to mournful dissonances, subsiding into a soft return of 'Her' theme for eight bars, into a new version of the call to reinvigoration, this time counterpointed with chromatically falling high strings and (again) the heavenly harp. But ultimately there is only denial (b.269) as the Wagnerian Tristan or Fate chord is formed by an

---

[70] See Hugh MacDonald, 'G♭', *19th-Century Music* 11 (1988), 221–37.
[71] Wightman considers the theme of young girl in G flat to resemble the Ideal theme from *Death and Transfiguration*: Karłowicz, 45.

A minor triad over an F♯ bass (enharmonic G♭). Across a large paragraph Karłowicz assembles a range of musical figures of hope, only to leave such promises denied.

The Andantino introduction to the waltz (bb.299–303) plays with the E–F–F♯ motif and augmented triads (E♯–A–C♯ in the melody; D–F♯–A♯ in the altered dominant chord of bar 303). The music suggests a young dandy establishing his pose with light and elaborate flute arabesques which are mannered rather than energetic. The Allegro energico from bar 304 is in the tonic major (A), which sounds as a false, premature resolution. Chromaticisms in the melody are principally generated by the F♯–F–E relation. Descending and ascending chromatic motions are swooping and swaying, but hardly vigorous, and there is a sense of sensuousness kept at bay. The *pianissimo* statement of the main waltz theme in D from bar 343 is supported in the bass by a diatonic version in rhythmic augmentation of the Reinvigoration motif (A–D–F♯–B–F♯–A), which also relates to the cadential figure of bars 311–12. The first phrase of the waltz theme also alludes to this signal (E–A–C♯–F♯–C♯–E). This is a theme curling in on itself: it is self-contained yet derivative. After this the waltz gains renewed vigour – in the programme we read that 'black diamonds of eyes flashed; oblivious of the world, he flung himself after them in a whirl of desires, torments and frenzy' – but this energy emerges from narcissistic self-reflection and ends in a deathly collapse.[72]

The waltz disintegrates onto the Tristan chord over F (b.372). After a return of the trumpet signal to reinvigoration this chord, as before, easily melts into the dominant ninth on D♭ which supports the nostalgic return of 'Her' theme (b.416). But this nostalgia is a precursor to the work's most pungent interpolation (bb.434–7): in fragments or shards of powerful Tristanesque dissonances the flash of diamond eyes turns to a death-laden glance as the musical narrative reaches the crisis at the heightened

---

[72] Comparison with Mahler's Ninth Symphony is useful. In the second movement's *Totentanz*, the Viennese waltz is a symbol of aristocratic grace, of femininized, subversive sensuality, in whose frenzy and intoxication the dancers become bacchantes – misogynist images of women as deadly seductresses. As Francesca Draughon argues, Mahler's treatment of the waltz is not one of nostalgic retreat, but rather he is utilizing it as a 'marker of disillusionment', and the sophisticated façade of the masquerade marks it as fake, ultimately empty; see 'Dance of Decadence: Class, Gender, and Modernity in the Scherzo of Mahler's Ninth Symphony', *Journal of Musicology* 20 (2003), 388–413. We might also recall the limping or distorted waltz in 5/4 of the second movement of Tchaikovsky's *Pathétique*, with its perverted elegance and sense of impending doom, as the waltz's traditional association with romance and glamour turns to one of negative deception in which love leads to disappointment and demise; see Sevin Yaraman, *Revolving Embrace: The Waltz as Sex, Steps, and Sound* (Hillsdale: Pendragon Press, 2002), 86–90.

threat of disintegration. An altered dominant of F (the chromatic upper-voice C♯ creates an 'A major triad' within the dominant thirteenth before resolving to D, the ninth) moves to an altered dominant of A minor. The allusion to the opening of *Tristan* is clear. When the waltz returns (b.438) it is on a 6–4 of F, and the chromatic C–C♯–D in the melody recalls the C♯–D motion in the pungently dissonant *Tristan* allusion. This is the most vigorous version of the dance (Allegro vivo). Both this waltz topic and 'Her' music attempt to 'resolve' or 'heal' *Tristan* allusions – 'Her' through resolution of F–A♭–C♭–E♭ 'Tristan' chords, 'he' (the dancing dandy) through a light-hearted transformation of the chromatic yearning motif. With the Poco più mosso (b.463) the intoxication of the dance is intensified – in a desperate last chance? – but disintegrates into chains of augmented triads. All is now a show of colour, the shimmering plumage of the dandy's ball costume which dissolves into a return to a bass F as the mournful upper neighbour to E (bb.538–70), resolving into the melancholic coda with the return of the opening theme. This dissolution is a negation of the Baudelairean notion of the artist as convalescent, a denial of a shock-like impulse to the will to life.[73] It is also the negative image of the Nietzschean philosophy of 'recovery' from decadent sickness,[74] or the obverse of the figure who leaps up into a *Tanzlied* in Strauss's *Thus Spake Zarathrustra*.

The death of the Dionysian Eros is confirmed in *Stanisław and Anna Oświecimowie*, Op.12 (1908). The inspiration for this symphonic poem was a portrait of the titular brother and sister, figures from the seventeenth century. Legend has it that, upon reuniting after being separated from young age, they fall desperately in love, struggling against the sinfulness of their love. Stanisław journeys to the Vatican to seek papal blessing – but on his return Anna is dead. He soon dies too, and their illicit love is consummated only after death.[75] *Steigerung* processes promising the synthesis of polarities are played out in a transgressive erotic drama which is fated – *à la* Manfred – to be tragically unsuccessful. Karłowicz spoke of the piece's 'polyphonic intensification'. This works alongside an (incestual) intertwining of thematic oppositions. Stanisław's dynamic, energetic character is represented by a theme whose chromatic signature – an augmented sixth chord moving to a dominant 6–4 preceding a ii–V–I cadence with a prominent melodic role for G♯ (the natural sixth) – contains the essential conflict of G♯ and G♮. The latter is the seed of the augmented sixth's

---

[73] Baudelaire, 'The Painter of Modern Life', 398.
[74] Nietzsche, *The Case of Wagner*, 155.   [75] Wightman, *Karłowicz*, 71–2.

alternative enharmonic function as dominant of C, the key of Anna's theme. Anna's music is based on *Steigerung* processes to climactic 6–4 chords in C major, as the tone builds to one of amorous rapture. The tonality and the ecstatic joy make for more than a passing recollection of Act 3 scene iii of *Siegfried*. The work evokes polarities of anguish and rapture, but the latter leads only to a tragic descent into the abyss, as Anna's theme is repeatedly stated in progressively lower registers. The link into the funeral march which follows is one of Karłowicz's finest and most complex symbolic passages. A prolongation of a dominant minor ninth (F♯–A♯–C♯–E–G) is pathetically coloured as the dissonant G♮s (bb.319–23) become decorated with even more pungent A♮s at the local melodic highpoint (bb.324–7). These pitches combine to form a recollection, amid a tone of painful longing, of Anna's C major materials. This allusion occurs over the dominant of the deathly B minor. Doomed love is expressed in the recalcitrant tonal opposition of B and the remnant echoes of C. Just as Siegfried's recollections of his C major ecstasies with Brünnhilde lead into his funeral march in *Twilight of the Gods*, so this nostalgic moment marks the death of the Dionysian eros, the final extinguishing of the flames of intoxication. Polony hears the end as marking the entry of Polish music into modernism, with the final bars presenting an enigmatic, pessimistic allusion to the Ideal theme of Strauss's *Death and Transfiguration*. If so, then Strauss's apotheosis meets its crushing demise.

A macro-narrative can be identified as operating across Karłowicz's symphonic poems. In *A Sad Story*, Op.13 (1908), with Dionysus now apparently dead, we enter into a mourning process, but if this is unsuccessful the inevitable result is a descent into melancholia, with potentially suicidal consequences. The programme, in which Wightman has spotted reminiscences of Turgenev's Schopenhauerian *Enough*, presents the 'psychology of a suicidal man', a 'struggle between the desire for life, which recalls visions of beautiful moments from the past, and the *idée fixe* of suicide' which leads to the victory of the latter and 'nothingness'.[76] (Karłowicz's original 'realist' idea to have a pistol shot at the moment of death was replaced by the Tchaikovskian symbolic tam-tam.) Polony describes the work as a 'musical study of Young Poland's melancholy'. Drawing upon psychiatric descriptions of melancholia from Antoni Kępiński and poetic versions by Tetmajer, Polony identifies the basic categories and existential experience of melancholia as 'heaviness, stagnation, greyness or darkness, a stopping of time, desolation, a dread of infinity

[76] Wightman, *Karłowicz*, 80.

on the one hand and a desire for it on the other'. For Polony, the work moves from nihilism to the first manifestation of expressionism in Polish music.[77] This usefully relates the work to the 'melancholia' of the German expressionists, which Lyotard identified as the result of a hopeless nostalgia for lost narrative. Murphy's interpretation of the work as based upon a struggle between melancholic and hysterical thematic groups suggests a descent into madness through failure of the Freudian work of mourning.[78] There are also strong Nietzschean resonances in the work's musical processes. Polony's hearing, that 'in place of theme-symbols which are distinctly isolated, tonally stabilized and presented in closed periodic structure or evolutionary arc form, open dynamic structures appear', suggests the dissolution or displacement of the Apollonian by the Dionysian. Furthermore, when Polony describes the melodic and harmonic aspects in terms of a 'clash between contradictory tendencies: introversion and extroversion, activity and passivity'[79] the parallels with Nietzsche's dualism of active and reactive nihilism are striking.

The work's opening, which Polony relates to the opening of the *Pathétique* Symphony but with the tone of gloom and stagnation intensified, invokes *lugubre, sordino* chords of what is later revealed to be the mournful minor subdominant of the tonic, F sharp (B minor), and its mediant minor (D minor). Such chromatic mediant chords have a long romantic tradition of evoking melancholic, mythic realms. The first melodic gesture – Polony' s hero motif – begins on a dissonant D over an F♯–C♯ fifth and outlines a shape again reminiscent of the Ideal theme from Strauss's *Death and Transfiguration*. A melancholically falling seventh motif (Polony's plaint motif, an existential cry to God) outlines B–D–F♯–A, a mournful version of the chord of the Ideal and also an amalgam of the opening two chords (B and D triads). (The falling melodic minor seventh's long semiotic history includes the main theme of the hero's tormented yearning in Tchaikovsky's *Manfred* Symphony and familiar motifs of erotic yearning from *Tristan* and *Twilight of the Gods*.) These two features – the D–C♯ relationship and the chord of mourning – are important seeds of

---

[77] Polony, 'Karłowicz – *A Sad Story*: A Musical Study of Young Poland's Melancholy', preface to *A Sad Story (Preludes to Eternity)*, Op.13 (Cracow, PWM: 2000), 16. This was likely spurred by the suicide of the writer Józefat Nowkiński, on whose dramatic poem *Biała gołąbka* (*The White Dove*) Karłowicz wrote an overture and incidental music. On wider resonances of the suicide theme see Anders, *Mieczysław Karłowicz*, 483. Nordau considered suicide as a phenomenon of social decay in his *Die conventionellen Lügen der Kulturmenschheit* (1883); see Pynsent, *Decadence and Innovation*, 135.

[78] Murphy, 'An Aesthetical and Analytical Evaluation', Part II, 104.

[79] Polony, 'Karłowicz – *A Sad Story*', 17–18.

future materials. But the motif which immediately follows in the horns is
one which Polony identifies as a motif of 'tragic fate', a 'foreboding of the
inevitable catastrophe' which 'appears always in culminations or crisis
points like a tragic memento'. It is a signal of the 'final catastrophe'.[80] The
will to develop new forms is always threatened by crushing annihilation or
inevitable dissolution.

In bars 29–30 the chord of mourning is expanded into a melancholic
melodic gesture emphasizing the dissonant relationship of D–C♯ over B
minor. The succeeding Moderato assai, which marks the beginning of
Steigerung processes to an existential scream, builds from a pungent D–F♯
third over bass C♯, a further reinterpretation of the dissonant D–C♯ association. The first scream (fig.9) is based on the superimposition of a B
minor chord over A♯. This is a chromatic alteration of the initial chord of
mourning (B–D–F♯–A). The immensely long, post-Tchaikovskian climactic descent over the C♯ dominant pedal which follows prolongs the D–C♯
relationship. Contrapuntal working-out of the mournful melodic materials, beginning on D over a C♯ pedal, is accompanied by oracular brass
chords and falling chromatic upper voices which gradually decline as the
texture thins and the dynamic diminishes, to end on slow repetitions of
the D–C♯ dyad. This leads to the reprise of the opening *lugubre* chords. The
melancholic opening theme now returns, but transposed to highlight G♯–A
over F♯, and the chords of mourning are similarly transposed, to outline
first F♯–A–C♯–E and then A–C♯–E–G♯. This last mourning chord is then
transformed into a seductively scored dominant thirteenth, at the opening
up towards ecstatic (erotic?) climax (fig.15). For Polony, this is a 'Tristan-
like apotheosis of love leading to an ecstatic culmination in B major', and
Wightman hears a 'blissful transfiguration of the second theme and a
diatonicized version of the previously chromatic descent'.[81] The unstable
giocoso versions of the hero's melancholic theme evoke for Polony a
pastoral-idyllic episode, as kaleidoscopic orchestral colours and promising
dominant chord formations suggest the bucolic. But these amorous images
function as momentary, Schopenhauerian comforting illusions, not as a
means to overcoming through Nietzschean-Dionysian intoxications. The
vision dissolves away in trilled chromatic descents to the mourning chords.
There is another long lead-up to a second existential cry, based on dissonant C♯ under the D major triad – a cataclysmic return of the dissonance
which pervaded the opening section of the piece. Sinking variants of the
mourning gesture then lead to the final *lugubre* chords. In summary, the

[80] Polony, 'Karłowicz – A Sad Story', 19.   [81] Wightman, *Karłowicz*, 83.

pessimistic, nihilistic narrative of *A Sad Story* can be compared with that of *Returning Waves*. The works display similar overall trajectories, from lament, through preliminary strivings and collapses, to redemptive images of the amorously lyrical and hedonistic dance, leading to crisis, catastrophe and an inevitable return to the lamenting opening. Instead of a Nietszchean *amor fati* embedded in eternal recurrence, Karłowicz's eternal longing is one which leads to total, obliterating despair and self-destruction.

Karłowicz's final, incomplete symphonic poem, *Episode from a Masquerade*, has been heard as a retreat from this expressionistic trauma. Dionysus appears to return from the dead in an even more banal, dandified version. The programme promulgated by Chybiński has often been compared with Turgenev's *Three Meetings*, but this has been disputed.[82] The image is of a banal Dionysian assembly recollected by the saddened lover: strengthened, the lovers become 'forgetful of the world', but the brutal orgy breaks the thread of their reborn love. For this Ariadne there is no Dionysus to whisk her off her island of solitude. The thread as narrative line, as saving, connecting route to the inner, noumenal or amorous idyll is cut; the ring as token of love and symbol of eternal recurrence is shattered. Dionysus no longer holds such powers. He is to be found mingling and merging with the 'boisterous' crowds of 'yelling clowns'.

A glittering, preludial Maestoso with the calls of horns and trumpets moves into a first subject of notable energy and vigour. But this lasts a mere sixteen bars before dissolving into *dolce* solo chromatic lines. There are attempts at revivification (the rapid *crescendo* into fig.2) before *quasi meno mosso* chromatic sliding, in which the tendency to inertia suggests sensual languor. This enervation of Dionysian powers is comparable with that heard in *Twilight of the Gods*. The masquerade's brass fanfares, in *maestoso* F major, resemble a magically transformed recurrence of Siegfried's horn calls, and the debasement into sensual fragments and weary sighs mirrors the seduction of Wagner's hero in the Gibichung hall in the company of the scheming Hagen, the decadent Gunther and the alluring Gutrune. On its return in Karłowicz's *Episode*, the recovered heroic energy is thus seen as a 'Siegfried' whose 'boisterous' passion leads him to resemble a 'yelling clown'. Karłowicz's enervated version also foreshadows the transformation of the energetic theme at the

---

[82] One might note here the dandy aspects of the Turgenev *Three Meetings*, in which, as Wightman suggests, the sexual aspect is all at a distance, an 'erotic element which is no less disturbing for its being presented at one remove': *Karłowicz*, 91.

Andante (8 bars after fig.10), which initiates a passage whose chromaticism and rhythmic contours might suggest erotic lassitide and yearning.

By contrast with *Returning Waves*, 'Her' theme is not one of happy beauty. The beloved is presented in B flat minor (the melancholic minor submediant of the opening F). 'Her' music is based on nested motifs of F–E–F, a variant of the 5–♯4–5 motif which informs the opening energetic theme. At the theme's second statement the F–E–F motif occurs in three versions, including the weaving and decorative triplet accompaniments as well as the theme itself and the chromatic harmonic motion which underpins it. The triplication could symbolize morbid and narcissistic self-absorption, the thread which is turned in on itself. The E–F association is also the basis of the *pianissimo* recollections of the Dionysian motifs at fig.25 which dissolve and dissipate so that the return of the opening Allegro maestoso is an abrupt one: it is not a recapitulation which sounds like a resolution or outcome of organic developmental process. The thread of structural connection breaks down, raising the threat of decadent disintegration into sensual particulars. The sudden appearance of the Dionysian impulse sounds as false as do the nuptial celebrations of Gutrune and Siegfried. Fitelberg's completion of the final section of the work, though its merits as an 'accurate' prediction of how Karłowicz might have continued are questioned, does contain one structural decision which, in the light of the fate of the Dionysian figure in Karłowicz's oeuvre, seems especially appropriate. In the recapitulation 'Her' theme does not return in a transfigured version in the romantic fashion: rather, there is a *fortissimo* and Molto largamente form of the Andante version which initiated the passage of lassitude. This is a deformation of the redemptive 'Dutchman model' which leads to a *morendo* ending in G. Thus the seductive, sensuous version of the Dionysian leads once more to unfulfilment – to amorous, spiritual and material denudation and subjective abandonment. Dionysus's apparent resurrection is a futile comeback. It leads only to a slow, remorseful relapse.

Across these symphonic works Karłowicz's musical semiotic of pessimism is developed through the manipulation of the topoi of the Dionysian fop, the chorale of the requiem, the sensual lost 'Her', the yearning, falling seventh and the rise and collapse of *Steigerung* processes. All of these potentially redemptive, life-giving figures or processes are crushed, dismissed or ironized. The composer's tragic early death in an avalanche cruelly denied us the story of how he might have further developed this symphonic world of pessimism.

Divergent Russian decadents: Rachmaninov, Scriabin and the end

Richard Drake has outlined a distinction, after Walter Binni's *La poetica del decadentismo* (1936), between 'decadent romanticism' and 'decadenticism'. The former is an extreme, agonized last form in the development of, for example, Byronism: it is a popular but terminal stage of morbid romanticism.[83] The latter is a radical transformation of romantic preoccupations into something new and different: it moves into the elitist, esoteric and avant-garde (for example, Schopenhauer into Nietzsche, Baudelaire into Mallarmé).[84] In many ways Rachmaninov and Scriabin represent these two species of the decadent. The dualism is suggested by their contrasting reactions to Tchaikovsky. Rachmaninov was heavily influenced by Tchaikovsky's brand of romanticism; by contrast, Scriabin resisted it, turning instead to radical modernisms inspired by Nietzsche's *Anti-Christ* and Wagner's *Tristan*. Drake's distinction also resonates with the apparently pervasive, morbid pessimism and sentimental nostalgia heard in much of Rachmaninov's music, by contrast with Scriabin's ecstatic, explosive advance: misery versus 'Mystery'. This opposition slips easily into the critical orthodoxy which dismisses Rachmaninov as romantic epigone[85] and hails Scriabin as modernist visionary. This section aims to challenge the value judgements that too often underpin this dualism. Both composers were preoccupied with 'ending', and their approaches to that end share many paths. Decadent romanticism (Rachmaninov) and decadentism (Scriabin) have common origins in pessimism and the struggle to overcome. Both types of decadence are vital dimensions of late nineteenth- and early twentieth-century Russian culture.

Many assessments of Rachmaninov's music have identified characteristics considered to be damning features of decadent stylistic decline. Such judgements begin with César Cui's dismissal of the First Symphony as containing 'sickly perverse harmonization' and a 'complete absence of simplicity and naturalness'.[86] They continue in an extraordinary portrait

---

[83] As richly explored in Praz's classic *The Romantic Agony*.

[84] Richard Drake, 'Decadence, Decadentism and Decadent Romanticism in Italy: Toward a Theory of Decadence', *Journal of Contemporary History* 17 (1982), 69–92. Drake's aim is to provide a workable definition of various manifestations labelled decadent, in response to Gilman's exasperation with the term. On decadence and the avant-garde see Chapter 5 below.

[85] Francis Maes describes Rachmaninov as representing the 'waning phase of romanticism': *A History of Russian Music* (Berkeley: University of California Press, 2002), 203–4.

[86] Cui in 1897, trans. in Geoffrey Norris, *Rakhmaninov* (London: Dent, 1976), 101.

of the composer from 1927 by the Scriabin champion Leonid Sabaneyeff, where Rachmaninov is described as exhibiting 'volitional impotence' and a 'semi-conscious mood characteristic of a "hashish stupor"'. Sabaneyeff describes Rachmaninov's music as 'will-less, motionless, almost never reaches the point of culmination', commenting that 'nothing is new'.[87] Later, on the centenary of Rachmaninov's birth, Stephen Walsh wrote of a 'self pity which haunts, beautifies, but also enervates' and noted Rachmaninov's 'inability to take even a temporary objective position outside his own melancholy'.[88] Such comments, invoking a creativity stifled by neuroses, suggest that a psychoanalytical approach might be illuminating. Such a project has been undertaken by Emanuel E. Garcia, who has analysed Rachmaninov's struggle to overcome the trauma of the catastrophic first performance of the First Symphony[89] and also offered a psychoanalytical comparison of Rachmaninov and Scriabin, one which is none too flattering to the traumatized Sergei. Garcia argues that fate conspired against Rachmaninov's development as a composer, and that after he destroyed the First Symphony – 'an act of artistic self-immolation' – none of his works reached the same heights of originality. Rachmaninov never recovered. Scriabin's modern genius is manifest in 'unparalleled economy of expression, a tremendous concentration of a vast emotional range' and a 'repudation of the sentimental'.[90] Garcia's diagnosis is that Rachmaninov's music is the opposite of this achievement: it is lavish yet limited in expressive scope, indulgent and mawkish.

A more sensitive and potentially productive assessment comes from Donald Mitchell, who suggests that the trauma was dealt with by being allowed to act as a sustaining compositional stimulant. Rachmaninov's melancholia was his muse. Mitchell writes that Rachmaninov remains an 'enigma':

While all the world is aware of Dr Dahl's successful therapeutic-hypnotic séances, which resulted in the freeing of Rachmaninov's creative ability and the composition of the Second Piano Concerto, the cause and nature of the initial depression has been kept top secret. The mystery would hardly matter were it not for the fact that all the musical evidence implies that this spiritual breakdown acted (of course

---

[87] Leonid Sabaneyeff, *Modern Russian Composers* [1927], trans. Judah A. Joffe (New York: Da Capo, 1975), 107.

[88] Stephen Walsh, 'Sergei Rachmaninoff 1873–1943', *Tempo* 105 (June 1973), 17.

[89] Emanuel E. Garcia, 'Rachmaninoff's Emotional Collapse and Recovery: The First Symphony and its Aftermath', *The Psychoanalytic Review* 91 (2004), 221–38.

[90] Emanuel E. Garcia, 'Rachmaninoff and Scriabin: Creativity and Suffering in Talent and Genius', *The Psychoanalytical Review* 91 (2004), 423–42.

after it had been overcome) as Rachmaninov's chief creative stimulant. It was Rachmaninov's fear of his depressive mania which drove him to compose – to keep his mania at arm's length so to speak; and at the same time it was in his music that his mania found an outlet and was able to flower. Hence, no doubt, the extremely narrow range of Rachmaninov's moods, the family (well-nigh incestuous) relationship of his themes, and, in his large scale pieces, the many beautiful lyrical ideas which are never developed, it seems almost through sheer fatigue and inertia. Yet this very fatigued aspect of Rachmaninov's music has a striking fascination of its own. One might say with justice that Rachmaninov cashed in on his neurosis and made something vital out of it; no mean achievement, since it's not every composer who knows what to do with his neurosis.[91]

There is perhaps still some remnant of prejudice here, but what it suggests is that Rachmaninov developed a notable creative courage. (Mitchell's comment that Rachmaninov sought to 'cash in' on his trauma is unfortunate as it sustains the denigration of Rachmaninov's music as commercial, as commodity art, to use Adorno's phrase. It seems unlikely that Mitchell meant to raise such implications.) The image of Rachmaninov as a courageous explorer of the realms of musical pessimism facilitates the reconsideration of Rachmaninov's achievement and its relationship to that of Scriabin. Alongside this it is necessary to refine understanding of how the function and character of their diverging types of musical decadence are manifest in details of musical syntax.

In November 1915 Rachmaninov programmed a concert of Scriabin's piano music in a memorial homage to his recently deceased compatriot. Many critics felt that Rachmaninov did not understand Scriabin's style. The concert, which included the Fifth Sonata, was famously derided by Grigori Prokofiev: 'When Scriabin's music floated in the clouds, Rachmaninov brought it down to earth.'[92] This opposition – the eschatological, air-borne Scriabin versus Rachmaninov's heavy human tread – sustains a symbolic polarity between the two composers in contemporaneous Russian criticism. Rachmaninov is unable to escape the suffering of the human condition; Scriabin soars away into the superhuman. It is an opposition crystallized in V. V. Yakovlev's 1911 contrast between Rachmaninov as 'Byronic' and Scriabin as 'Nietzschean'.[93] Byronism, exemplified by the

---

[91] Donald Mitchell, review of Victor Seroff, *Rachmaninoff* (London: Cassell, 1951), *Tempo* 24 (1952), 35–6.

[92] *Russkaia Muzykal'niaa Gazeta* 49 (6 December 1915), trans. in Robert Palmieri, *Sergei Vasil'evich Rachmaninoff: A Guide to Research* (New York: Garland, 1985), 232.

[93] V. V. Yakovlev, 'S. V. Rachmaninoff' (1911), trans. in Stuart Campbell (trans. and ed.), *Russians on Russian Music, 1880–1917* (Cambridge University Press, 2003), 181–5.

tragic figure of Manfred,[94] played a crucial role in the Russian pessimistic tradition, as romantic idealism turned to nihilism in the 1860s.[95] The post-Schopenhauerian romantic pessimism of Turgenev, whose 'superfluous man' repeatedly finds that love is doomed to fail and whose life is one of recurring melancholic unfulfilment, is a fine example. Yakovlev argues that, because of the 'short history' of Russian secular art music, at the time of Byronism's flowering in the other arts the technique or 'aesthetic' required to express this idea was not then available to Russian composers. In the early twentieth century Byronism has been revived, he continues, because the desire to voice these strivings in music remains unfulfilled and the means to do so have now been developed. In this regard Rachmaninov's Byronism cannot be condemned as anachronistic or weakly nostalgic. It is supremely timely.

The contextualization of lyrical expressions of grief in an arena of heroic human conflict is crucial for expressions of Byronism. Thus, for Yakovlev, Tchaikovsky's symphonies do not represent Byronism, because 'there is too little resisitance or conflict in Tchaikovsky, and too much mundane lyricism'. Rachmaninov (on whom he acknowledges the powerful influence of Tchaikovsky – and, more contentiously, Wagner) is the true musical Byronist, for the 'subject-matter' of his music is 'gloomy protest, indistinct prolonged struggle between the heart and life'. But Rachmaninov's great achievement is that he has 'not turned into the limited, Byronic tendency': this feature is 'characteristic', but Rachmaninov 'goes deeper, and, being moreover alien to aesthetic sectarianism, is more many-sided. From his own sorrow, which is serious and concealed, albeit stylish … he moves to an enchanting sound landscape, from extreme subjectivism to composure, and from the dynamic to the static.' Thus what are most important in Rachmaninov's music for Yakovlev are the transitions from the sorrows and conflicts of Byronism into a new world beyond the strivings of the romantic subject. In Drake's terms, Rachmaninov seeks a route out of decadent romanticism – a task he repeatedly undertakes. Such 'transitionality' is also fundamental to Scriabin's artistic project, which is also notable for its obsessive repetition of a single narrative plot. But there is a contrast in the nature of the transition. In Rachmaninov, Yakovlev notes, 'some

---

[94] There is a lost student work from 1890–91 by Rachmaninov based on *Manfred*.

[95] See Nina Diakonova and Vacuro Vadim, 'Byron and Russia: Byron and Nineteenth-Century Russian Literature', in Paul Graham Trueblood (ed.), *Byron's Political and Cultural Influence in Nineteenth-Century Europe: A Symposium* (Atlantic Highlands, NJ: Humanities Press, 1981), 143–59. For a case study in Russian Byronism see Lewis Bagby, *Alexander Bestuzhev-Marlinsky and Russian Byronism* (Philadelphia: Pennsylvania State University Press, 1995).

kind of austere, ancient vision incomprehensible to the mind burdens his individuality, and, not being a Nietzschean (like Skryabin) but a Byronist, i.e. profoundly human, he, like his spiritual ancestors, is nevertheless going off to some place, where there are no people, where there is silence'.[96] It is a gloomy prospect. For many Russian writers and artists, however, decadence was aligned to an apocalyptic vision: decadent utopianism, rather than pessimism, became the defining feature. Through an erotic revolution the misery of individuation and the conflicting divisions of sex and gender could be overcome and tragic history brought to an end in an 'apocalyptic rupture'.[97] These decadents sought the ecstatic intoxication experienced in Nietzsche's Dionysian state, through which the illusion of individuality was broken, suffering was surmounted, and the Universal Mystery revealed. Thus, for Yakovlev, Scriabin's music moves from heroic struggle and melancholy through ecstatic transfiguration into the Nietzschean superhuman. Rachmaninov's music, by contrast, is encumbered with a grave sense of loss at the inevitable demise of subjective existence. Yakovlev's terms are suggestive, but his polarity is too simplistic. Several works demonstrate how Byronism informs Scriabin's transitional idiom, and how Rachmaninov offers a differently realized ambiguity between Byronic-romantic pessimism and transfiguration.

A unifying narrative across Scriabin's ten piano sonatas has often been identified.[98] The differences manifest in the closing strategies of the 'transitional' sonatas – the Third, Op.23 (1897–8), Fourth, Op.30 (1901–3), and Fifth, Op.53 (1907) – are, however, highly significant as they can be heard to express stages in the struggle to overcome romantic Byronism and promise the move into modern Nietzscheanism. The narrative strategies of Rachmaninov's two piano sonatas (in D minor, Op.28, 1907, and in B flat minor, Op.31, 1913) also evoke a Byronic tone and reveal how Rachmaninov's pessimism emerges from similar romantic semiotics and musical syntax as Scriabin's transition to ecstatic affirmation, but diverges towards an artistic vision in which a 'heroic' subject comes to completely different 'ends' – in the D minor one of fateful resignation, in the B flat minor

[96] Nietzsche believed that Byron's revolutionary heroism was misunderstood by the pessimists, citing it as an example of the decadence which he considered to be the defining mark of decline in the modern age. Nietzsche's complex relationship to Byron is based upon his gradual redefining of the role of suffering and struggle as affirmation of the tragic Dionysian life. In the discussion of convalescence in the final chapter we will see how Nietzsche re-evaluated Byron.

[97] See Matich, *Erotic Utopia*.

[98] See, for example, James M. Baker, 'Scriabin's Music: Structure as Prism for Mystical Philosophy', in James M. Baker, David W. Beach and Jonathan W. Bernard (eds.), *Music Theory in Concept and Practice* (University of Rochester Press, 1997), 53–97.

sonata a more ambivalent tone suggesting the continuing possibilities of overcoming. Before analysing these works it is useful to address once more, in this context of species of pessimism, the question of how decadent features might be pinpointed in harmonic manipulations.

Decadence has been widely defined as a hypertrophic rewriting of romanticism. A favourite structural and expressive device in romantic musical style is the flat sixth, as motif and/or harmony. Susan McClary has noted that the flat submediant harmony possesses a 'fundamental contradiction – acoustical stability versus functional instability' (the need for the sixth to resolve to the fifth). Furthermore,

> if the minor mode context represents some negative emotional state … then the sudden emergence of a stable major-quality area on the [flat or minor] sixth degree represents an unexpected infusion of some positive state. But because of the contrapuntal implication that the function is in need of resolution, this prolongation brings with it from its inception the seeds of its own demise.

Hence it ultimately evokes a 'sense of disillusion and pessimism'. If the flat submediant occurs in a major-key piece then its source lies in modal mixture, or chromatic alteration, and, to use McClary's startling description, this 'deviance' from the diatonic 'intensifies its functional instability – its unnatural generation demands resolution all the more'.[99] So in this hearing the flat sixth is not only precarious; it is also abnormal. In this regard it seems perfect musical material for extending the romantic style into pessimistic-decadent expression. Thus it is hardly surprising that when Wagner wished to encapsulate the endless longing of the ill-fated Tristan and Isolde in the opening of his prelude he employed both the melodic ♭6–5 descent (F–E) and the harmonic function of the submediant fall to the dominant. Wagner's flat-sixth-dominated opening became something of a musical addiction for the decadent generation, a drug of delirium in chromatic tones.

The struggle to overcome the doomed, ephemeral, instability of the flat sixth can be manifest in a number of ways. Two common strategies emerged. One is to emphasize the contrasting natural or raised sixth; the second employs moves to the alternative, more 'uplifting' diatonic mediator, the harmony on the third scale degree. The exploitation of alternative third relationships opens up the possibility of tonal symmetries functioning as potential counter-structures to diatonicism. Much recent theoretical work has focused on symmetrical major third relationships. In this system

---

[99] Susan McClary, 'Pitches, Expression, Ideology: An Exercise in Mediation', *Enclitic* 7 (1983), 78.

the submediant, flat sixth function is operative only if there is an initial descent from the tonic, or if the cycle is broken by semitonal descent to the dominant. In the complete 'ascending' cycle, which overrides the tendency for the flat sixth to fall to the dominant, the effect is more strongly one of successive mediants.[100] In the augmented triad cycle the flat sixth's diatonic function as harmonic mediator is redefined; it is no longer the mid-point in the descent from tonic to subdominant, and neither is it, alternatively, the inevitable precursor to a structural dominant. When the chromatic system breaks free from the demands of diatonicism the 'perfect' symmetry might be a promising vehicle of musical utopianism, for the flat submediant (to retain its diatonic monicker) is also liberated from the semiotic associations of the ♭6–5 motif, which, as Carl Schachter put it, 'has had an age-old association with ideas of death, grief, and lamentation', a meaning whose basis lies in 'the descending half-step … with its goal directed and downward motion, its semitonal intensity, and the "sighing" quality it can so easily assume'.[101] When precariously poised *between* these two systems – between the romantic grievous fall to the closing dominant and the modern possibility of symmetrical, cyclic perfection of equal division – the flat sixth becomes an ideal syntactical basis for musical decadence of either pessimistic or utopian variety, or, more pertinently to the examples which follow, that which is transitional between the two states.

James Baker considers 'the most important harmonic function in Scriabin's tonal music, aside from those of tonic and dominant', to be the supertonic, with the harmony on the flat sixth often functioning as its dominant.[102] Indeed, many works from Scriabin's 'transitional period' exploit the flat sixth as the approach towards a hovering, tritonal prolongation of the dominant function through the flat supertonic. In this dominant stasis lie the seeds of what Taruskin calls the 'extinguishing of the desiring subject',[103] the dissolution of romantic yearning in Nietzschean ecstasy. Taruskin highlights the significance of Scriabin's elimination of the diatonic end, the abolishment of the obligation for the

---

[100] In the most recently published discussion of the topic, Matthew Bribitzer-Stull points out that the 'move from I to ♭VI … relies not only upon the use of mixture, but also upon the falling root motion to evoke the dream-world state so often associated with this progression'. See 'The A♭–C–E Complex: The Origin and Function of Chromatic Major Third Collections in Nineteenth-Century Music', *Music Theory Spectrum* 28 (2006), 168.

[101] Carl Schachter, 'Motive and Text in Four Schubert Songs', in David Beach (ed.), *Aspects of Schenkerian Theory* (New Haven: Yale University Press, 1983), 70.

[102] James M. Baker, *The Music of Scriabin* (New Haven: Yale University Press, 1986), 1–2.

[103] Taruskin, *Defining Russia Musically*, 329.

tritonal prolongation of V to resolve to I. But it is the flat submediant which marks the first move towards that end, and if the ♭II–V tritonal prolongation is to stand alone in symmetrical stasis – marking the final moment of transition away from diatonicism – then the flat sixth's romantic functional and semiotic status as pessimistic sign of the beginning of the end must also be eliminated.[104] In much of Scriabin's music we can hear the struggle to overcome or eschew this function as an expression of the desired transition from Byronic romanticism to Nietzschean modernism.

In 1901 an anonymous Russian reviewer described Scriabin's Third Sonata as a 'history of moods from Byron to Nietzsche', with the finale marking the move out of 'despair, protest and longing' into the 'birth of the "man-god"'.[105] In 1906 Boris de Schloezer similarly identified a Byronic quality in the sonata, quoting the famous lines from *Manfred* – 'the tree of knowledge is not the tree of life' – and noting that the sonata's unfulfilled conversion to Nietzscheanism is expressed in 'the tragedy of a personality unable to bear his own deification into the Man-God'.[106] Schloezer noted that the Third Sonata was written when Scriabin began to discover Nietzsche. Most crucially, the sonata 'discloses to us the psychological and spiritual structure of all the sonatas … which is basically a drama, an action, culminating after various peripeties in the affirmation of free will'.[107] Scriabin subtitled the work 'États d'Âme' – 'moods' or 'soul-states' – and the 1901 review has close resonances with the programme notes supplied for the composer's performance in Brussels on 8 November 1906, written by his second wife, Tatyana:

First Movement: The free, untamed Soul plunges passionately into an abyss of suffering and strife.

Second Movement: The Soul, weary of suffering, finds illusory and transient respite. It forgets itself in song, in flowers. But this vitiated and uneasy Soul invariably penetrates the false veil of fragrant harmonies and radiant rhythms.

Third Movement: The Soul floats on a tender and melancholy sea of feeling. Love, sorrow, secret desires, inexpressible thoughts are wraithlike charms.

---

[104] In this context the exquisite *Feuillet d'album* Op.45 No.1 (1905), with its repeated emphasis on the resolution of the flat sixth to the dominant, can be heard as a nostalgic fragment (recalling erotic effects in Liszt) – a leaf taken from a fading album of romantic musical memories.

[105] Trans. from Ann Lane, 'Balmont and Skriabin: The Artist as Superman', in Rosenthal (ed.), *Nietzsche in Russia*, 213.

[106] Quoted in Bowers, *Scriabin*, vol.I, 256. For Schloezer a link to Byron is also found in Scriabin's courting and conquering of the dangers of diabolism.

[107] Boris de Schloezer, *Scriabin: Artist and Mystic* [1923], trans. Nicolas Slonimsky (Oxford University Press, 1987), 318.

Fourth Movement: The elements unleash themselves. The Soul struggles within their vortex of fury. Suddenly, the voice of the Man-God rises up from within the Soul's depths. The song of victory resounds triumphantly. But it is weak, still … When all is within its grasp it sinks back, broken, falling into a new abyss of nothingness.[108]

The sonata's mood-states can be summarized as a pessimistic cycle: suffering, delusion, melancholy and the heightened return of suffering. The finale's Byronic tone is established by its opening motif – an upward leap followed by chromatic descent from the tonic to the dominant, an expression of struggle and lament which incorporates at its end the grief symbol of ♭6–5. At the arrival of the movement's final structural dominant this motif returns in an inner voice. On its second statement it is transposed to begin on D, the flat sixth of the F sharp major home key, initiating a ♭VI–II–V progression. An apotheosis based on the transfigured theme from the slow movement is reached via increasing harmonic and melodic emphasis on the major sixth alternative, D♯. Dissolution of this affirmative transformation is marked by the return of the flat sixth scale degree, and in the final bars the tragic 'Byronic' tone of the sonata's opening movement returns. The heroic struggle through adversity to transfiguration must, therefore, start over again.

A similar gesture of thematic recall and transformation informs the end of the Fourth Sonata, where the 'floating' dance of the Prestissimo moves to a new majestic version of the sonata's previously languid and tentative opening theme.[109] Here transformational processes also operate on the flat sixth. By contrast with the opening of the sonata, it is no longer the point of dissonant disturbance, and by contrast with the tragic-Byronic tone in the ending of the Third Sonata the effect here is ecstatic. This is achieved not by eschewing the flat sixth but rather by transforming its expressive character – most overtly in the final cadence of the sonata, where an augmented sixth on D resolves directly to the tonic triad. Thus while D♮ still resolves to C♯ the cadence avoids the dominant and also therefore the tragic or pessimistic semitonal harmonic descent from ♭VI to V. In the Fifth Sonata – which is

---

[108] Trans. in Bowers, *Scriabin*, vol.I, 254–5.

[109] Its languid opening theme emphasizes D♯ as part of a four-bar embellishment of the F sharp major tonic chord. This is followed by a ♭VI–II–V progression which ends with a melodic return of D♯. The D♯ is a markedly dissonant presence, emphasized by the triple suspension of the tonic chord. This antecedent phrase is then answered by a consequent which closes on the major mediant (enharmonic B flat), that key which, in the symmetrical augmented triad cycle of thirds, is the optimistic upward move from F sharp, heard here in a rather ethereal resolution, by contrast with the dissonant function of the submediant.

often identified as a recomposition of the Fourth[110] – a comparable but even more ecstatic apotheosis based on the transfigured version of a languid opening theme now leads to a kaleidoscopic return of the sonata's introductory image of chaos. Through this gesture the 'Byronic' descent from the flattened sixth has been banished. But this move leads to disintegration. In the formal articulations preceding this dissolution – the opening of the recapitulation, and the start of the Presto coda – an ambivalent coexistence of flat and natural sixth is operative. This generates an expressive ambiguity which is structurally and ideologically significant. Formal process, function, cohesion and consequence are in part dependent on perpetuating this conflict, the eternally recurring struggle which is the basis of man's move to the superhuman. Through this struggle, which we can identify as originating in Byronic heroism, the pessimistic obsessions of romantic decadence are overcome and lead to explosive disintegration, original chaos, formlessness and stasis.[111] It is an effect of 'apocalyptic rupture', that iconoclastic, utopian end to history which explodes the formal cycles of growth and degeneration.

In Rachmaninov's piano sonatas the flat sixth relationship and the conflicts of Byronism are exploited to different structural and expressive ends. In fact, the sonatas constitute part of something of an obsession with the motif and its expressive and structural potential. For Sabaneyeff, the all-too-famous Prelude in C sharp minor, Op.3 No.2 (1892), 'clearly rings the fundamental leitmotif' of Rachmaninov's music, 'the facing of the terrifying and unconquerable power, fate or destiny'.[112] The piece is dominated by the tragic ♭6–5 motif (A–G♯), so this can confidently be identified as Sabaneyeff's 'leitmotif'. Adorno's dismissal of the prelude as 'commodity music', or kitsch, is based on his hearing of it as 'just one long final cadence', as a 'debasement' of the romantic gesture of ending.[113] This disdainful description is of a piece which Rachmaninov himself came to loathe, but it identifies the pessimistic preoccupation with ending,[114]

[110] For a detailed comparison in this regard see Baker, *The Music of Scriabin*, 194–202.
[111] In *Prometheus*, as Baker notes, there is a parallel climactic move from apotheosis to dematerialization, with the former section (forming the first part of a double ending) based upon a remnant or vestige of the resolution of ♭VI, the second displacing evolution with an 'accelerated involution'. See Baker, 'Scriabin's Music', 88, 95; and *The Music of Scriabin*, 364–5 (especially the graph of the underlying bass progression, his example 140).
[112] Sabaneyeff, *Modern Russian Composers*, 107.
[113] Theodor Adorno, 'Commodity Music Analysed' [1934–40], in *Quasi una fantasia*, trans. Rodney Livingstone (London: Verso, 1992), 38–40.
[114] This emphasis on ending is also apparent in the formal proportions of the Preludes in E flat and G flat, Op.23 Nos.6 and 10 (1903), both of which have codas that, judged by convention, may seem disproportionate and indulgent.

motivically focused on the resolution of the flat sixth. It is a prelude to nothing. The end is already there at its beginning. One of the most extensive exploitations of the ♭6–5 motif is the orchestral opening of the Prologue to the one-act opera *Francesca da Rimini*, Op.25 (first performed January 1906). The opera is burdened by a terribly lame libretto by Modest Tchaikovsky, after Dante's *Inferno*, but there is some fine music. The motivic and chromatic character of this opening music is clearly modelled on similar sections in Tchaikovsky's *Fantasy-Overture* on the same topic (1876). But in Rachmaninov's chromaticism there is an intensification of ambiguity which generates an increased sense of the endless sorrow and suffering experienced by the damned lovers. The opera opens with manifold Largo repetitions of an F–E motif. In the larger tonal framework this is ♭6–5 in A minor, but in the chromatic counterpoint of the opening paragraph the key most overtly suggested is D minor, the romantic's gloomy minor subdominant. The F–E motions sound like repeatedly frustrated attempts to complete 3–2–1 melodic closure in D minor. In this respect they can be heard as the dark melancholic opposite to the endless 3–2 'ewig' motif in the farewell of Mahler's *The Song of the Earth*. In Rachmaninov there is no bright horizon; this is a welcome to hell. When the dominant of A is reached (confirming that the music started out of the home key) the F–E motif returns as the expression of a wailing minor ninth over the dominant chord. Thus the motif sums up the wretchedness of the lover's fate.

Rachmaninov's First Piano Sonata, composed in the year after the performance of *Francesca da Rimini*, exposes a similarly sorrowful tale. Its finale culminates in the mighty statement of a chorale theme which in the first movement occupied the precarious 'redemptive' narrative space of the second subject on the flat submediant, B flat. At the end, however, it resolves to stormy tonic D minor assertions. Redemption is denied. This is the final outcome of a tonal structure summarized in Example 2.4. The exposition of the first movement offers a typical romantic contrast between an energetic, turbulent, heroic first subject in the tonic minor and a contemplative, quasi-spiritual second subject on the unstable flat submediant. But after this traditional polarity the sonata becomes more subversive. The exposition ends on the dominant of C, the minor seventh, which is a large-scale reflection of the influence of Aeolian modality on the sonata's material. The recapitulation, which is 'tragically reversed',[115]

[115] See Timothy Jackson, 'The Finale of Bruckner's Seventh Symphony and Tragic Reversed Sonata Form', in Timothy Jackson and Paul Hawkshaw (eds.), *Bruckner Studies* (Cambridge University Press, 1997), 140–208.

Example 2.4 Sergei Rachmaninov, Piano Sonata No.1, Op.28: harmonic structure

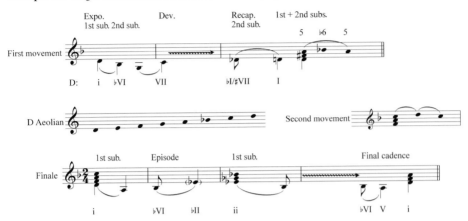

begins with the second subject in D flat – ambiguously functioning as either the flattened tonic or as the sharp seventh, the chromatic alternative to the modal seventh, C♮. After this the return of the first subject reasserts the tonic, with the closing pages in the tonic major tinged by echoes of the flat sixth. The D Aeolian aspect of the first movement is a context for emphasizing, in perhaps 'Russian' or nostalgic colours, the tragic effect of the flat sixth (which is absent, of course, in the Dorian mode). The second movement reinterprets this pitch material to highlight the natural sixth in F major (which we might identify as another potentially redemptive space, particularly as the piece was originally planned as a Faust sonata, so this, one might assume, was partly conceived as a portrait of Gretchen[116]). The finale returns to Aeolian-inflected D minor. As in the first movement, a contrasting, redemptive episode emerges on the flat submediant, but now this B♭ has a consistent tendency to function as V of ♭ii, which in one especially poignant passage allows a cyclic return of the first subject of the first movement in the doubly dark minor Neapolitan. The closing cadence confirms the unstable position of the flat sixth harmony and the 'failure' of its associated themes of redemption.

The tonal structure of the outer movements of Rachmaninov's Second Sonata is summarized in Example 2.5.[117] The opening tonic is

---

[116] Norris, *Rakhmaninov*, 91.

[117] Rachmaninov wrote two versions of the Second Sonata, the 1913 original and a shorter revision, with significant changes in structure and effect, in 1931. There is also a famous version by Vladimir Horowitz which is something of a hybrid of the two published editions, one which apparently gained the composer's approval.

Example 2.5 Rachmaninov, Piano Sonata No.2, Op.31: harmonic structure

prolonged by motion through the flat sixth. An important expressive
gesture (bb.10–11) promises a move to the subdominant (by moving to
a B♭–D–F–A♭ chord) but is deflected to an enharmonically notated
minor submediant chord (F♯–A–C♯–E♯). The transition to the second
subject is based on a move from ♭VI to V with the dominant elaborated
by G♭–F, a motivic echo of the harmonic move. Thus the first section
of the exposition exploits three differing functions of the flat sixth:
prolongational, deceptive and then transitional. The second subject, in
the relative major (D flat), leads into intensification towards the climax
of the exposition in the closing material. At this highpoint there is a
virtuosic, precipitous passage based on the ♭6–5 (B♭♭–A♭) resolution in
the new key. In the recapitulation the deceptive move to the enharmonic flat sixth is postponed until the move into the coda. The second
subject is recapitulated in the flat submediant key (G flat), which in the
long term allows the move to the final structural dominant to be based
on the grief-ridden fall from ♭VI to V. The climactic cadential chords
are strikingly rewritten to hint at the potentially redemptive major
mediant, D, and a reinterpretation of the neighbour-note bass move
as ♭VI–V of III. The slow movement is ambiguously poised between E
minor (♯IV of B flat) and G major (♯VI), a redemptive tonal space which
is emphasized by its later turn to E major, but set awry by its tritonal
relation to B flat. The tritone, rather than serving as part of some utopian
stasis, is employed as a doomed 'other' world, placed a semitone 'under'

the dominant (in this relation, it is symmetrically 'opposite' the flat sixth). The finale begins with celebratory bells in B flat and G flat; the mediant D returns in the transitional material, which leads to the lyrically impassioned second subject in E flat (inevitably tinged with melancholic C♭s). Developmental material leads to a recapitulation of the first subject in the 'wrong' key of D; the effect is to provide a redemptive alternative to the sorrows and struggles of the flat sixth and also to postpone the arrival of the tonic for the climactic recapitulation of the second subject. It is also part of the long-range shift from prolongations of the tonic minor (which invoked the flat submediant) to that of the tonic major. The Presto coda, like the codas of Scriabin's Fourth and Fifth Sonatas, re-ignites the ambiguity between flat and natural sixth, but only as precursor to a final, virtuosic affirmation of the major sixth.

By contrast with the Byronic gloom of the First Sonata, the Second Sonata's tonal structure ultimately expresses a more positive outcome in the struggle between decadent pessimism and redemptive transfiguration.[118] In short, these sonatas offer tonal narratives which, with regard to their treatment of the flat sixth tonal region, are the equal of Scriabin's in complexity and innovation. Scriabin's 'superhuman' music may offer a more radical, sensual, modernist surface, but Rachmaninov hurls harmonic types of romantic origin into a modern arena of fierce 'human' conflict between pessimistic decadence and revitalization. Thus his music is, in these instances, perhaps more fundamentally tensed, teasing and tortuous.

The poet Konstantin Balmont declared that decadents are 'on the border of two periods, one ended, the other not yet born'.[119] It is a characterization which sits rather neatly with Rachmaninov's ambiguously poised pessimism. Balmont has often been linked with Scriabin because of apparently shared interests in aspects of symbolism and Nietzscheanism, but Rachmaninov set Balmont's poems on several occasions. A setting of 'A Passing Breeze' ('Veter perelyotnïy') was published

---

[118] The 1931 version is arguably more decadent in effect: it excises the final, tragic return of the deceptive motivic move to the flat sixth in the first movement and offers a subdued version of the coda to the exposition and recapitulation (the climactically powerful chords and virtuosic descent of the original is removed); there is a nostalgic return of the second subject of the first movement in the slow movement; the 'hopeful' D major recapitulation of the first subject in the finale is cut. These changes result in a simpler, more passive and more uniformly pessimistic effect.

[119] Trans. from Lane, 'Balmont and Skriabin', 202.

as Op.34 No.4 (1912). In this poem the sense of a lingering transitional moment between an ending and new beginning is encapsulated in the image of a passing breeze which tells first of the pessimism of nightfall and then, on changing direction, the optimism of the daybreak emerging from the east.

A passing breeze
Caressed my cheeks
Whispering sadly
'Night is more powerful than day.'
The sun was fading,
Storm-clouds were gathering;
The gloomy fir-trees
Trembled in dismay.
And over the dark ocean,
Where waves roll by,
The passing breeze
Surged ever on.
Night ruleth the earth,
Yet far away across the ocean,
The glow of dawn
Lit up the sky.
Flowers blossomed
Once more in the heavens,
The East was bathed
In a new-born light.
The breeze changed direction
And blew into my face,
Whispering with a smile:
'Day is more powerful than night.'[120]

Rachmaninov's setting opens in A minor with expressive emphasis on its minor submediant, F. The tonal centre then shifts to C sharp (the dark key of the infamous Op.3 No.2), thus turning A into a new flat submediant, with prominence given to the new melodic function of A as flat sixth. The song's most exquisite harmonic transformation occurs at the poetic transition from night to day, when C sharp/D flat moves to C, emphasizing the new flat sixth function of A♭ (see Example 2.6). This flat

---

[120] Trans. from sleeve notes to Elisabeth Söderström and Vladimir Ashkenazy, *Rachmaninov Songs* (Decca 436 920–2, 1975, reissued 1993).

Example 2.6 Rachmaninov, 'A Passing Breeze' (Balmont), Op.34 No.4, bars 27–31

sixth of C is repeatedly echoed in the closing section. The overall tonal structure of the song therefore outlines vi–♭ii–V–I in C, a large-scale cadential progression whose final tonic area is melancholically tinted with the flat subdominant, the chromatic alternative to the A minor of the opening section. Night is the relative minor to day. The inflexions of A♭ in the final C major section are memories of the reign of darkness, or the melancholic's conviction that, inevitably, the day will pass once more into night. Rachmaninov handles tonal structure to especially touching expressive effect.

He achieves a similar mastery on a much larger scale in his setting of Balmont's paraphrases of Poe's *The Bells*, Op.35 (1913), for soloists, chorus and orchestra. The tonal centres of the work's four movements present the succession A flat major–D major–F minor–C sharp minor–D flat major. The D major of the second movement's amorous hopes functions as either the tritonal prolongation of the dominant relationship of A♭ to the final D♭ (this tritone is emphasized in the link between the movements, as the tintinnabulation of sleigh bells changes to the delight of wedding bells) or as a doomed Neapolitan to the finale's C sharp minor. In the finale, in response to Poe's poetic description of

Example 2.7 Rachmaninov, *The Bells* (Balmont–Poe), Op.35, finale, figs.121–2 (texture simplified)

the bells tolled by the king of ghouls – their 'melancholy menace', 'moaning and groaning' and 'muffled monotone' – a deathly C sharp minor is prominently coloured by the minor sixth, as the opening theme, on the elegiac cor anglais, is placed over oscillations between C♯ and A. There are two main climaxes: the first (fig.108) on F♯–A–C♯–E–G♯, the ninth chord on the minor subdominant, the second (4 bars after fig.116) at a move to the Neapolitan D via a modally inflected flat submediant. Both these climaxes possess tensions which are resolved in the exquisite beauty of the orchestral postlude (from fig.121) in the tonic major (enharmonic D flat major) The first part of this coda (whose redemptive effect is heightened by the sounds of the harp and organ) also achieves the final resolution of the flat sixth, A♮ (Example 2.7). It does this by sustaining A through the subdominant minor ninth (the chord of the first climax) and ♭II⁷ (a transformation of the chord of the second climax) to reach, via a half-diminished supertonic chord, the dominant, where the A finally falls to A♭. The subdominant and supertonic alterations are, furthermore, a beautiful alternative to the resolution of the flat sixth via an augmented sixth pre-dominant chord. The second part of the coda, over a tonic D♭ pedal, contains one final flat sixth inflexion. But this is dispelled by the penultimate chord – G♭–B♭–D♭–F–A♭ – the major ninth on the subdominant, emphasizing that A♭ has finally displaced A♮ in a hopeful and sumptuous alternative to the subdominant minor ninth of the first climax.

Bartók's elegiac modernism

Bartók's music resonates with cultural anxieties which pervaded Hungarian artistic thinking in the early twentieth century. This disquiet was characterized by polarizations of organicism and fragmentation, of order and chaos, by a preoccupation with the search for identity within an apparently disintegrating society, and by the demands for renewal or redemption in the face of anxiety, loss and despair. It was exemplified by György Lukács's ethical demands of artistic form, with its contents of suffering and redemption, and by Bartók's modern realism, with its 'duality of polarized contrast and unifying force'.[121] Recent Bartók studies have often emphasized his artistic project of regeneration, interpreted in the contexts of Hungarian political and cultural modernism and contemporaneous discourses of race and class.[122] Too frequently underestimated, however, is the concomitant significance of elegy as expressive of the potentially debilitating pessimism which marks the crisis of the modern subject. This is central to several of Bartók's works of the first two decades of the century, those which mark his transition between romanticism and modernism.

In Bartók's music elegy is a crucial driving force towards radical expressive forms. Elegiac expressions push the musical 'language' to dare to speak of the most profound truth. In this respect Bartók's music reflects the specific concerns of his influential contemporaries. Lukács argued that at great moments, which are 'generally moments of death', there emerges a glimpse of the appearance of the essence of meaning.[123] At the depth of despair there appears 'the most profound meaning of form: to lead to a great moment of silence', to lead to the

---

[121] Judit Frigyesi, *Béla Bartók and Turn-of-the-Century Budapest* (Berkeley: University of California Press, 1998), 165, 194. On the need for critical resistance to hearing Bartók's music according to a 'totalizing organicist paradigm' see John Neubauer, 'Bartók and the Politics of Folk Music: Musico-Literary Studies in an Age of Cultural Studies', in Walter Bernhart, Steven Paul Scher and Werner Wolf (eds.), *Word and Music Studies: Defining the Field* (Amsterdam: Rodopi, 1999), 59–77. Lukács wrote that 'in life, not only those motives play a role which have been accepted for the sake of the final unity, and not every note that has been struck must necessarily be silenced in the end'. See 'The Foundering of Form against Life' (first published in *Nyugat* 2, 1910), in *Soul and Form*, trans. Anna Bostock (London: Merlin Press, 1974), 40.

[122] See for example David Cooper, 'Béla Bartók and the Question of Race Purity in Music', in Harry White and Michael Murphy (eds.), *Musical Constructions of Nationalism: Essays on the History and Ideology of Musical Culture 1800–1945* (Cork University Press, 2001), 16–32; Julie Brown, 'Bartók, the Gypsies and Hybridity in Music', in Georgina Born and David Hesmondhalgh (eds.), *Western Music and its Others: Difference, Representation, and Appropriation in Music* (Berkeley: University of California Press, 2000), 119–42; and most recently David E. Schneider, *Bartók, Hungary, and the Renewal of Tradition: Case Studies in the Intersection of Modernity and Nationality* (Berkeley: University of California Press, 2006).

[123] György Lukács, *The Theory of the Novel*, trans. Anna Bostock (London: Merlin Press, 1978), 149.

'abyss'.[124] In his essay 'Death Aesthetics' (1907) Béla Bálasz laid crucial emphasis on the imminent demise of every moment, so death is always a part of life, which is a vital struggle against the final ending. For Bálasz, exquisite beauty is discovered precisely at the moment when we mourn its inevitable loss: the beautiful is the promise of memory, of a mourning that has already begun, and its becoming into appearance is bound to its withdrawal, to its absence. Elegy shadows the idyllic moment: Lukács sets up a complementary relationship between the elegiac and the idyllic, for they are 'profoundly akin to one another and complete one another'.[125] Also crucial in these pessimistic aesthetics is a concept of sensual love as symbolizing the necessity of being always halfway within an eternal motion, in a perpetual transition, in an unresolved tension between polarized forces, in what the poet Endre Ady called the 'kiss halfway kissed'. Incompleteness is vital, as fulfilment of desire would mean death. Eros, like decadence, is always in the middle, but always desires the end.[126] It is perpetually shadowed by loss.

Elegy is an expression of mourning. In an apparent paradox, mourning demands both remembering and letting go. It generates fidelity and affirmation through relinquishment. Its character, as process or affect, is related to Spinoza's *Sehnsucht*, longing nourished by memory, to *Trauer*, with its etymological suggestions of drooping or lowering, and to Descartes's regret, the sadness at the memory of the joy (*jouissance*) of lost pleasure. Hence it is also typically excessive.[127] Mourning may lead us beyond the knowable, into the perils of the sublime, or even into the realms of the Nietzschean 'frightful'. Of the historical types of elegy – from the ancient classical-pastoral, through the confessional-medieval and beyond – it is the romantic and modern forms of elegy which express

---

[124] Lukács, 'The Moment and Form' (1908), in *Soul and Form*, 111, 114.

[125] Lukács, 'Longing and Form', (1911), in *Soul and Form*, 102–4.

[126] See my *The Muse as Eros: Music, Erotic Fantasy and Male Creativity in the Romantic and Modern Imagination* (Aldershot: Ashgate, 2006), 147–67. We might note here the *fin-de-siècle* infatuation with (and Bartók's personal erotic preference for) the adolescent as a figure on the cusp of 'knowing', held in a precarious betweenness, in a relationship which keeps the door ajar to the enchanted, a figure in discourses of passage, initiation, transition, of emergent sexuality and loss of innocence, of nostalgia and fear. See John Neubauer, *The Fin-de-Siècle Culture of Adolescence* (New Haven: Yale University Press, 1992).

[127] David Farrell Krell, *The Purest of Bastards: Works of Mourning, Art, and Affirmation in the Thought of Jacques Derrida* (Philadelphia: Pennsylvania State University Press, 2000), 1–5.

the breaks and lacunae, the disjunctions, elisions and testings of conventions in an approach towards the taboo. The elegiac tradition registers the revolutions of post-Cartesian epistemology: ultimately the feeling of loss is more profoundly to do with how and what we can know than with loss of an individual. There also emerges a complex relation between the personal response to loss and the control and manners of modern cultural institutions, precepts and practices.[128] Elegy raises the threat of descent into madness and melancholia.[129] As romantic pessimism approaches the abyss of nihilism so it reaches the point of the ultimate meaningless of mourning when God is dead. The apparent impossibility of mourning in modernity is familiar from Adorno. It raises some fundamental questions: how to reinvigorate petrified conventions of past forms of mourning in a godless, post-metaphysical world; how to discover a hope without being sentimental or anachronistic; how to recover the childish experience prior to disenchantment, the absent magical effect, which must reside with the deathly and the aged; how to capture the fading aura of the vanishing figure in a long gaze of farewell (as Adorno heard in Mahler);[130] how to avoid the false refuge of a fading theology, the illusions of totality and meaning grasped through resolution and the struggle to achieve closure.[131] The only possible response to the impossible burden thereby placed on endings is the 'sacred fragment', for 'the fragment is the intrusion of death into the work'.[132] This emerges from Nietzsche's diagnosis of the death of tragedy through a polemic against dramatic examples of closural, mastering narrative telos, which he associated with the false psychology of redemption and Socratic optimism. New forms emerge as secular critiques of the categories of transcendental and the metaphysical, as critical views of how loss and suffering are expressed. These may involve the evocation of a wholeness

[128] W. David Shaw, *Elegy and Paradox: Testing the Conventions* (Baltimore: Johns Hopkins University Press, 1994).

[129] Lawrence Kramer, *Music as Cultural Practice, 1800–1900* (Berkeley: University of California Press, 1990), 191. See Freud's famous essay 'Mourning and Melancholia' (1917) in Sigmund Freud, *Complete Psychological Works: Standard Edition*, vol.XIV (London: Hogarth Press, 1957), 237–58. See also Freud's first published statement of his theory of melancholy and mourning, the short paper 'On Transience' (1916), which spins out from consideration of the melancholy of some walking companions to the realization that the beauties of nature inevitably decay and die: *Standard Edition*, vol.XIV, 303–7.

[130] See Daniel K. L. Chua, 'Adorno's Metaphysics of Mourning: Beethoven's Farewell to Adorno', *The Musical Quarterly* 87 (2004), 523–45.

[131] Theodor W. Adorno, *Aesthetic Theory*, trans, and ed. Robert Hullot-Kentor (Minneapolis: University of Minnesota Press, 1997), 152–3.

[132] Adorno, *Aesthetic Theory*, 32.

Example 2.8 Béla Bartók, *Elegy*, Op.8b No.1, opening

or organic moment which never existed. The play of mourning in a 'godforsaken' world is an elegiac vision which confirms the artistic legitimacy of modern melancholia and the saturnine temperament as a critical reflection.[133]

   These aesthetic-expressive aims and formal concerns are exemplified by Bartók's *Elegy*, Op.8b No.1 (1908). The opening exposes paradoxes of wholeness and brokenness, form and moment, regeneration and decadence. At its ending, drooping (*Trauer*) phrases and incomplete resolution suggest the fruitlessness of hope and the rejection of the comforts of closure. The harmonic diversity of the opening paragraph (Example 2.8), which includes chromatic symmetries, diatonic remnants, modal moments suggestive of the lost idyll and quasi-ecstatic whole-tone

---

[133] Max Pensky, *Melancholy Dialectics: Walter Benjamin and the Play of Mourning* (Amherst: University of Massachusetts Press, 1993), 19.

expansions, is bound within a disguised sentence structure (an idea and its immediate repetition in varied form, followed by development and expansion). The section ends with liquidation of the obligations of the motif to develop, in obliteration, dissolution, reduction and collapse, a gradual emptying-out towards a formal ending. Only residues are left, in a type of closure which Schoenberg identified as a 'letting-go', a clearing of space for the entry of a new subject.[134] Of course, many pieces begin in this way. Here the parallels between this musical subject and the process of mourning in the human subject – remembering and then relinquishing to allow fresh connections with the new – are clarified by aspects of the harmony and the ambiguous nature of the piece's ending. Augmented triads are embedded as structural pitch collections evoking dark descents, liquidations, incompleteness and unresolved tensions, all contributing to the articulation of a conflictual tonal strategy, a tragic descent from D♯ down to D♮, into a 'shadow' tonal structure. In the opening section the principal pitch D♯ and its associated augmented triad (D♯–B–G) are already shadowed by D♮ and its associated D–F♯–B♭ triad. In the final bars the large-scale descent to a structural D♮ appears complete, but the expected association with a D–F–A♯ augmented triad is missing, and the passage is nostalgically tinged with enharmonic echoes of the augmented triad built on D♯ (E♭). This suggests that the elegiac process is understood as potentially endless. Melancholic versions of the famous 'Stefi Geyer' seventh motif at the close also contribute to this effect. The augmented triads and the D♯–D relationship are aspects of an extremely complex tonal structure, but within such a complicated, often 'knotty' musical process, an elegiac thread connects the opening and ending of the piece.

Bartók explained to his muse Stefi Geyer that the first movement of his First String Quartet was a 'death song'.[135] In the opening movement, whose melodic gestures and chromatic counterpoint have been heard as modelled on the opening of *Tristan and Isolde*,[136] the collapse of expressive high-points contributes to the effect of modern, 'Lyotardian', sublime moments

---

[134] Arnold Schoenberg, *The Musical Idea and the Logic, Technique, and Art of its Presentation*, ed. Patricia Carpenter and Severine Neff (New York: Columbia University Press, 1995), 253.

[135] Quoted in János Kárpáti, 'A Typical *Jugendstil* Composition: Bartók's String Quartet No.1', *The Hungarian Quarterly* 36 (1995), 134.

[136] Dorothy Lamb Crawford writes of the 'Tristan-like anguish' of the 'deeply grieving fugal section'; see 'Love and Anguish: Bartók's Expressionism', in Elliott Antokoletz, Victoria Fischer and Benjamin Suchoff (eds.), *Bartók Perspectives* (Oxford University Press, 2000), 132. In later years Bartók acknowledged the Wagnerian recollections in the quartet; see Ferenc Bónis, 'Bartók and Wagner', in Todd Crow (ed.), *Bartók Studies* (Detroit: Information Coordinators, 1976), 84–93.

which approach the realization of the frightful truth. The movement has three main points of climax and dissolution (bb.14–16, 28–30, and 65–end). The first two are based on a fall from *forte* or *fortissimo* A major harmonies in 6–4 position (promising resolution as the dominant?) to A♭. The moment evokes the elegiac through a withdrawal of the desired closure and the post-Wagnerian 'shadow' tonal relationship in the semitonal descent. The last climax is based on a reinterpretation of the descending, quasi-octatonic bass of bars 29–31 and incorporates a strong allusion to the classical resolution of augmented sixth to 6–4 followed by 5–3 over a structural dominant of A flat. But again the promise of formal cohesion through closure is withdrawn. The moment is therefore expressive of the modernist crisis of faith in masterful, closing narratives of affirmation and liberation.

Bartók's model for opening a quartet with an elegiac slow fugue is obvious. Bartók recalled the profound impression that Beethoven's Op.131 had made on him as a fourteen-year-old in a letter to Geyer of July 1907.[137] He composed his own First Quartet just a year later. Beethoven's fugue is pervaded by elegiac ambiguity.[138] In part, Bartók's quartet is a monument to Beethoven's own monumental music. In this manner it is meta-elegiac, a characteristic strategy of the modern poetic elegy. The pervasiveness of the elegiac in modernism is often sustained through a distancing, meta-elegiac archaicizing mode, a remembering of earlier acts of remembrance in a mimesis of memorialization.[139] Op.131's obsession with C sharp and its Neapolitan D has its dark, inverted complement in Bartók's A and its shadow A♭. There are also significant parallels in the finales of the two quartets. In the last movement of Op.131 Joseph Kerman identifies critical echoes of the Beethovenian 'heroic' style in the disorientating retrieval of the opening fugue and in a sonata form dynamism which promises but fails to deliver the 'defiant apotheosis', leading rather to collapse at the final climax in the coda, in the enervation of the first theme. This is followed by the mourning

---

[137] Frigyesi, *Béla Bartók and Turn-of-the-Century Budapest*, 147. The importance of Beethoven for Bartók hardly needs reasserting; see for example ch.1 of János Kárpáti, *Bartók's Chamber Music* (Stuyvesant, NY: Pendragon Press, 1994), 'The Legacy of Beethoven', 21–30.

[138] See, for example, the reading by Amanda Glauert, 'The Double Perspective in Beethoven's Op.131', *19th-Century Music* 4 (1980), 118–20. On the ambiguity of the ending of the quartet see Nicholas Marston, '"The sense of an ending": Goal-Directedness in Beethoven's Music', in Glenn Stanley (ed.), *The Cambridge Companion to Beethoven* (Cambridge University Press, 2000), 94–5.

[139] See Jahan Ramazani, *Poetry of Mourning: The Modern Elegy from Hardy to Heaney* (Chicago University Press, 1994).

return of the sorrowful tone of the fugue.[140] The uncanny return of
material drawn from the fugue in Beethoven's finale has a parallel in
the climactic Adagio melody in Bartók's finale. The latter hints at monumental transformation, or an attempt at a redemptive recall of the
promise of the climaxes of the fugue, or an ecstatic retreat into a personal
inner world – into the metaphysical, the noumenal, a Schopenhauerian
Nirvana.[141] But its close relation, noted by Kárpáti, to the Transylvanian
folk song 'Romlott testem a bokorba' ('My Rotten Body in the Bush'),
which Bartók had collected in 1907, belies its decayed condition and
precarious position. Zoltán Kodály's assertion that the work's conclusion
represents a 'return to life'[142] is therefore too simplistically optimistic.
This resurrected body is a dancing cadaver. Wrenched back into somatic
reality, the recovered subject is then torn asunder by the restless Dionysian
frenzy of the Allegro.

Bartók's elegiac modernism frequently compares closely with Ady's
contradictory poetic voices of nihilism and affirmation. Ady's poems
express courageous heroic struggles pitted against pessimistic dejection,
the Nietzschean Will to power conflicting with tragic despair, where
'weird lamentations' coexist with 'vital passions', and sensual materialism
with intense psychological honesty.[143] In the poems which Bartók set in
his Op.16 (1916) nature is repeatedly characterized as alien and mocking,
as the source of anguished despondency as the mournful subject tearfully
expresses his sense of abject loneliness. This is no communion with
nature in the romantic manner. Whether the lonely ex-lover is in the
autumn gloom and echoes of the first two songs, or hearing the oceanic
moans in the fourth song, or bemoaning the cruelly unavailable beauty
of summer in the last, he and nature are in irrecoverable opposition.
Bartók insistently underlines this gloomy predicament through almost
unremitting tonal opposition. Triads are seldom heard without conflicting superimpositions or juxtapositions. The fourth song, for example,
opens with waves of F♯–F conflicts, and when the sea cruelly sings of the
absent beloved any hope of tranquil, simple and beautiful tonal effect is
undermined by the voice's bitingly dissonant opposition to the piano

[140] Joseph Kerman, 'Beethoven's Opus 131 and the Uncanny', *19th-Century Music* 25 (2001–2), 155–64.

[141] As Wagner heard in the deaf Beethoven's Op.131; see K. M Knittel, 'Wagner, Deafness, and the Reception of Beethoven's Late Style', *Journal of the American Musicological Society* 51 (1998), 49–82.

[142] Kárpáti, *Bartók's Chamber Music*, 264.

[143] Joseph Remenyi, 'Endre Ady: Hungary's Apocalyptic Poet (1877–1919)', *Slavonic and East European Review* 3 (1944), 84–105.

triads. 'Az ágyam hívogat' ('My Bed Calls', 1909), the poem which Bartók set as the third song, encapsulates in miniature the cyclic quality of loss and elegy. In an uncanny, persistent doubling, in a litany of inexorable repetition, each end is merely becomes another beginning, as the first stanza can only 'end' in a circular poetic retrograde:

Lefekszem, óh ágyam,
Óh ágyam, tavaly még,
Tavaly még más voltál.
Más voltál: álom-hely,
Álom-hely, erö-kút,
Erö-kút, csók-csárda,
Csók-csárda, vidámság,
Vidámság. Mi lettél?
Mi lettél? Koporsó,
Koporsó. Naponként,
Naponként jobban zársz,
Jobban zársz, Ledölni,
Ledölni rettegve,
Rettegve felkelni,
Felkelni rettegve,
Rettegve kelek fel.

I lie down. Oh my bed,
Oh my bed, last year still,
Last year still you were different.
You were different: dream world,
Dream world, well of strength,
Well of strength, kisses' pub,
Kisses' pub, happiness,
Happiness. And today?
And today? Burial,
Burial. Ever more,
Ever more you clasp me.
You clasp me. To lie down,
To lie down terrified,
Terrified to get up,
To get up terrified,
Terrified, I get up.[144]

---

[144] Trans. from Frigyesi, *Béla Bartók and Turn-of-the-Century Budapest*, 214.

The recalled dreams of the Bacchic pleasures of the kiss, expressed at a cadence in E which includes the Geyer seventh (bb.14–15), are heard as lost because they emerge a semitone down from the mournful F minor-major of the opening.[145] In the more turbulent middle section wave motifs lead to a further sinking to a B♭ pedal (suggesting a dominant function in E flat). This section's last explosion and collapse chromatically dissolve away from a bitonal clash between the white and black notes of E sharp major 6–4 harmony under F♯s and C♯s at the poem's height of the collision of desire and despair, at the moment when the greatest striving yields to despondency and unfulfilment. The final eleven bars of the song are a quasi-retrograde of the opening tonal structure. The opening gesture returns, now in E major-minor, which slips through chromatic slides and diatonic fifth progressions back to F minor-major, in a manner suggestive of palindromic symmetry. As Frigyesi puts it, Ady's poem 'depicts the circular movement from inertia to action and back to inertia'.[146] The cycle of rise and fall, which seems endless, is suggestive of the Nietzschean continuous need to 'overcome' as the struggles of life will always return – teaching a pessimism of strength, of the acceptance of eternal recurrence which is the true test of Nietzsche's 'formula for greatness in a human being', *amor fati*: 'not merely to endure that which happens of necessity, still less to dissemble it – all idealism is untruthfulness in the face of necessity – but to *love* it …'.[147] At its climax the song evokes a Nietzschean tone that eschews resignation and resentfulness through affirmation of the oppositional coexistence of the beautiful and the frightful, a modernist doubleness which replaces the Enlightenment's pairing of the beautiful and the sublime. In the musical idiom of romanticism the climactic 6–4 chord often functions as a marker of the sublime, which may be tragic or transcendent.[148] The

---

[145] On the romantic legacy of similar relationships and their reinterpretation in modernism see Patrick McCreless, 'An Evolutionary Perspective on Nineteenth-Century Semitonal Relationships', in William Kinderman and Harald Krebs (eds.), *The Second Practice of Nineteenth-Century Tonality* (Lincoln: University of Nebraska Press, 1996), 87–113. Crucial late nineteenth-century examples for Bartók, other than *Tristan* and Tchaikovsky's 'Manfred', are *Twilight of the Gods* (E flat as shadow to E) and Strauss's *Thus Spake Zarathustra* (B minor as shadow to C major).

[146] Frigyesi, *Béla Bartók and Turn-of-the-Century Budapest*, 215.

[147] Nietzsche, *Ecce homo*, 68. On Ady as the culmination of the early reception of Nietzsche in Hungary see Béla Egyed, 'Nietzsche's Early Reception in Hungary', in Alice Freifeld, Peter Bergmann and Bernice Glatzer Rosenthal (eds.), *East Europe Reads Nietzsche* (New York: Columbia University Press, 1998), 85–106.

[148] The 'tragic' 6–4 is the minor version, the 'evil twin in ironic opposition to the salvation and transcendence of its major-mode sister': Michael L. Klein, *Intertextuality in Western Art Music* (Bloomington: Indiana University Press, 2005), 66.

double harmonic clash of E♮ and F♯ at Bartók's climax may be a heightened version of the F–E relationship of the beginning and end of the song (and in this regard Bartók's 'awkward' spelling using E♯s and B♯s rather than Fs and Cs is telling), but the bitonality (it is hard to hear one as the neighbour to the other; a governing hierarchical relationship is difficult to assert) evokes the catastrophic undermining of the romantic sublime through expression of the experience of the oppositional coincidence of pleasure and loss.

This pessimistic crisis is the result of the experience of bleak isolation in the modern city that has separated man from nature. The doubts and anxieties, the destabilizing experience of the modern metropolis by contrast with the sublime experience of 'nature' in pre-urban societies, are expressed in what Lyotard called a 'constructed' sublime which releases the 'forces of scepticism and even of destruction'.[149] 'Natural', *gemeinschaftlich* relationships have dissolved into impersonal, contractual, *gesellschaftlich* relationships.[150] *The Miraculous Mandarin* explores the loss of 'natural' origins and relationships and the search for erotic renewal in the decayed modern city. This links Bartók's work to the 'Sunday Circle' group of intellectuals, including Karl Mannheim, Lukács and Balázs, who sought an affirmative alternative to Georg Simmel's pessimistic diagnosis of the decadent tragedy of modern urban culture. In the orchestral opening, depicting the 'horrible pandemonium' of the metropolis, Bartók distorts traditional musical symbols of the pastoral and natural creation. The first sound, an ostinato figure in the second violins, is a mechanical, obsessively repeated 'wave' pattern – non-developmental, and 'perverted' because it spans an augmented octave (G–G♯) rather than the interval of the natural overtone series. It is an unnatural figure churned out by the metropolitan machine.[151] This is a ferocious example of the 'constructed sublime', but also of the grotesque, of the deformation of 'natural' forms. It is an illumination of a mechanical rather than an organic world and builds to an apotheosis of

---

[149] Jean-François Lyotard, 'The Sublime and the Avant-Garde', in *The Inhuman: Reflections on Time*, trans. Geoffrey Bennington and Rachel Bowlby (Stanford University Press, 1991), 105. This new sublimity highlights the ideological construct of 'nature'; see Max Paddison, 'Nature and the Sublime: The Politics of Order and Disorder in Twentieth-Century Music', in Peter Dejans (ed.), *Order and Disorder: Music-Theoretical Strategies in 20th-Century Music* (Leuven: Rodopi, 2004), 108–9.

[150] See Peter Tregear, '"Stadtluft macht frei": Urban Consciousness in Weimar Opera', in Nikolaus Bacht (ed.), *Music, Theatre and Politics in Germany: 1848 to the Third Reich* (Aldershot: Ashgate, 2006), 237–54.

[151] For more, see my 'Eros in the Metropolis: Bartók's *The Miraculous Mandarin*', *Journal of the Royal Musical Association* 125 (2000), 41–61.

the grotesque, which for Mann, writing in 1924, was a 'parodic sublime' –
the only form of the sublime that remains available in a world of
pervasive categorical breakdown.[152] The vista is a brutally pessimistic
image which leads beyond the perils of the sublime into the realms of
the Nietzschean 'frightful'. It is a dawn of the dead.

Julie Brown has established the connections of the grotesque with
Bartók's interests in stylistic hybridity, primitivism (the 'barbaro'
idiom) and the body. In particular she identifies its associations with
invocations of dance, Nietzschean vitalism and mythic transformations
generated by the 'throbbing life' of folk music. She lists the finale of the
First Quartet as an 'upbeat' ending which evokes such bodily vitality.
But we have seen what kind of damaged body is recharged in that
movement. Its energies are the grotesque consequence of the dissolutions of the romantic sublime in the first movement's elegiac fugue.
Brown rightly points out that the grotesque encroaches on 'seemingly
contradictory aesthetic preoccupations' such as the realist, the expressionistic, the ironic and the fantastic. But she does not mention the
decadent. This is despite citing Beardsley's bizarre, sometimes monstrous figures and Baudelaire's essay on diabolic laughter as part of
the grotesque preoccupation with the violated body, the disfigured,
abnormal, distorted, exaggerated and hence inscrutable, ridiculous and
horrific. If the grotesque body is often formed through a decorative
excess or disturbing deformation which evokes the turmoil and anxiety
of the human figure *in extremis,* then the parallels with the typical
concerns of decadence are clear. Brown comes close to making this
link when she compares the 'bodily' functions of Bluebeard's castle in
the Balázs–Bartók opera with the house in Poe's *The Fall of the House of
Usher,* where in an atmosphere of decay, torpor and dilapidation
Usher's morbid sensitivity and sickness are connected with the crumbling state of the house. The pessimistic thread is maintained. In *The
Miraculous Mandarin* the joyous, carnivalesque, open and generative
grotesque celebrated in Bakhtin's famous study of Rabelais is resisted:
the grotesque figure of the Mandarin, as Brown proposes, is an embodiment of 'the optimism of progress gone wrong'. Brown compares the
mounting desperation as the girl dances a waltz in front of the strange
visitor with the increasingly extravagant and exaggerated gestures of
Ravel's *La Valse.*[153] The manic contrasts between apparently organic

---

[152] Quoted in Julie Brown, *Bartók and the Grotesque* (Aldershot: Ashgate, 2007), 13.
[153] Brown, *Bartók and the Grotesque,* 129.

generative process and grotesque distortion and mechanical breakdown in Ravel's grotesque apotheosis mark the degenerative, hysterical demise and final 'death rattle' of a decadent Viennese tradition. Decadent variants of the waltz topic are found elsewhere in Bartók: a melancholic type in the first Ady song, set as a sluggish and queasy waltz saturated with dissonant semitonal motions; a slow, 'erotic' version in the third of the Op.15 songs, 'Night of Desire', at the masochistic lines, 'painful torture, blissful torture'.[154] The decadent and the grotesque meet in the worlds of the melancholic, the masochistic and the misanthropic. Kárpáti has linked the grotesque with the more decadent aspects of *art nouveau* aesthetics. He cites the 1903 *Ver Sacrum* publication of Arthur Symons's essay on Beardsley, with its discussion of the distorted Pierrot figure in *The Scarlet Pastorale*, as significantly influential, and argues that Bartók arrived at the same theme in the grotesque waltz of the Bagatelle Op.8 No.14 (where 'She' rises from the dead as a dancing zombie) and also the finale of the First Quartet. On that last piece, Antal Molnár, viola player in the first performance of the quartet, perceptively commented that the 'fatal joke' is 'triggered by eternal misery'.[155]

Bartók's avid collection of peasant music in trips around many regions of south-eastern Europe and the incorporation of elements of this music in the generation of his modern 'organic' music remain the most prominent basis of his reputation. His music has attracted a legion of analysts who have exhaustively pursued the revelation of its unities. These images and preoccupations have deflected attention away from the significance of the inorganic and the 'unnatural' as driving forces towards these modern musical forms. Bartók's utopian hybrids and pastoral idylls coexist with their decadent and elegiac shadows.

---

[154] John C. Crawford and Dorothy L. Crawford, *Expressionism in Twentieth-Century Music* (Bloomington: Indiana University Press, 1993), 191.

[155] Kárpáti, 'A Typical *Jugendstil* Composition', 139; Molnár was writing in March 1911.

3 | Degeneration and regeneration

O death! O tender friend!
I don't understand at all:
Why don't all mortals and gods
Rush at once to your splendid halls?
Fyodor Sologub (St Petersburg, 1904)

As darkness descends over the land,
I feel my eyes becoming clearer
Richard Dehmel, 'Manche Nacht' (Berlin, 1907)

Introduction

In a famous letter of 25–6 January 1854 Wagner wrote to August Röckel: 'to be real, to live – what this means is to be created, to grow, to bloom, to wither and to die; without the necessity of death, there is no possibility of life'.[1] Here Wagner summarizes his belief in the necessary coexistence of degeneration and regeneration, in the opposing organic processes of development and decay which drive the natural cycle of life and death. At a fundamental level the enormous narrative of the *Ring* cycle is driven by the repercussions of interfering with the double forces of nature, which should continually operate in balanced opposition. When this equilibrium is broken or destabilized the deathly dangers of decay or degeneration must be held back through the imposition of unnatural powers. In *The Rhinegold*, the tragic end of the gods is foreshadowed in the section of scene ii in which the threatened loss of their source of eternal vigour, the golden apples, reaches its climax with the giants demanding possession of Freia, the keeper of these fruits, as the promised payment for the construction of Wotan's castle. Freia's apples possess symbolic associations with natural energy, naïvety and libidinal love.[2] The loss of this fruit of vitality would be a fatal blow to the gods. The predicament marks the

[1] Wagner, *Selected Letters*, 302–3.   [2] Donington, *Wagner's 'Ring'*, 86.

beginning of Wotan's tragedy (at least as presented in *Rhinegold* – we will later, in the Prologue to *Twilight of the Gods*, learn of his earlier attack on nature in his act of violence on the World Ash Tree). When Wotan and Loge subsequently descend into the Nibelungen world to steal the Rhinegold from Alberich, so that they can use it to pay a ransom for the captured Freia, they move further into the realms of decay. As Wagner wrote in his first prose summary of the *Ring* in 1848: 'From the womb of night and death, a race was begotten that lives in Nibelheim, i.e. in gloomy subterranean clefts and caves … with restless agility they burrow through the bowels of the earth, like worms in a dead body …'[3]

In the scene which Warren Darcy calls the 'premature twilight',[4] the treatment of Freia's motif and that of the golden apples alongside striking chromatic elements in the tonal structure are profoundly prophetic as degenerative processes imperil the gods (they turn pallid and aged) and Loge pronounces their doom. A pale mist descends and thickens as Loge turns his sights to the withering, anxious figures of the gods who surround the gloomy Wotan. E will emerge as the tonal centre of the scene, but it is approached via six bars of harmonic ambiguity (see Example 3.1). The transition from the F minor of the preceding section, during which the giants forcefully carried Freia away, is achieved by contrary semitonal motion away from its dominant, C. The bass falls to B, above which a D flat major arpeggio softly rises. D flat is of course the key associated with Valhalla, the newly built, fortified home of the gods, but here its security is undermined. At the end of the preceding section D♭ recurred motivically as the doomed flat sixth of F minor. Its potential function as a key in its own right is now weakened by the bass B, the dominant of the scene of decay which follows. As the D flat triad is altered to a diminished seventh over the pedal B, the rising part of Freia's motif peaks on the resolution of a plangently dissonant G♭ to F, an adumbration of the motif of grief. As the dominant function of the bass B is clarified the upper parts sink through a complete series of the three diminished sevenths. At the third statement of Freia's motif the semitonal anguish of the peak is altered into hopeful whole-tone G♯–F♯, a lightening transformation which dispels the diminished sevenths and introduces a statement of the golden apples motif in E major. But the image of regeneration quickly evaporates. Diminished seventh harmony returns. Freia's motif is heard again, but now it is coincident with not only with diminished seventh harmony but also with the even

---

[3] Quoted in Deryck Cooke, *I Saw the World End* (London: Faber, 1979), 132.

[4] Warren Darcy, *Wagner's 'Das Rheingold'* (Oxford: Clarendon Press, 1993), 159.

Example 3.1 Wagner, *The Rhinegold*, scene ii, Loge: 'Den sel'gen Göttern wie geht's?'

darker expressive tones of the Neapolitan F♮. It is overlaid with a new descending motif (C–A–G), and the bass slips away from the dominant B down to A. The bass then rises to B♭, and the diminished seventh is heard as a chromatic enrichment of the Neapolitan as Loge sings of the gods' sickness in one of Wagner's most alliterative poetic inventions ('Wie bang und bleich verblüht ihr so bald!'). The return to the dominant of E is achieved by

Example 3.1 (cont.)

Example 3.1 (cont.)

Example 3.1 (cont.)

turning the bass B♭ from neighbour-note to chromatic passing note, but the golden apples motif is now given in the tonic minor – its vital power is waning – and the chromatic alteration to the minor third, G♮, is a dark counterforce to the previously hopeful G♯s. The bass then sinks once more to B♭, and in a striking large-scale harmonic parallel to the sinking motif of

Example 3.1 (cont.)

grief the whole passage from the opening of the scene is repeated a semitone lower, thus locally centring on E♭, the lowered tonic. Alternatively, in retrospect, the preceding E is reinterpreted as the large-scale Neapolitan F♭ to E♭. At the local level the Neapolitan relationship is evoked again at

Example 3.1 (cont.)

another alliterative line: 'grämlichem Grau, das schier zum Greisen ihn
scafft?' (The alliterations poetically serve to heighten the importance of the
Neapolitan harmonies as symbol of degenerative decay.) The large-scale
repetition is curtailed to allow overt motivic statement of the semitonal
'Wehe!' motif, and the bass sticks on A (rather than rising to B♭ as expected,
given the preceding model). Froh and Donner express sinking powers and
failing hearts to the accompaniment of another series of falling diminished
sevenths over the pedal A. The golden apples motif returns to transform the
harmony to the dominant of G. The passage which follows is a harmonic
diversion on the minor mediant of E as Loge recognizes that the gods are
degenerating through lack of the fruit's vital powers. The motif of the apples
is now given full statement. But it is an image of life heard as doomed
because of the history of the minor mediant in this scene in the sinking from
brightly hopeful G♯ to darkened G♮. Its dissolution is caused by the introduction of its own Neapolitan (A♭), which is then prolonged in a remarkably
extended chromatic descent. Loge's flickering motifs now appear as he
reveals his semi-detached status and resistance to the degenerative condition. It allows him to declare the darkest prophecy: without the apples the
gods will wither and die. The harmonies here are piercing and pungent.
The apples' G major is mockingly asserted, and the hopefulness of their
motif is negated as the relationship to the motif of the downfall of the gods
is revealed over B flat minor and D flat minor chords. A flat minor then
functions as the minor Neapolitan, leading to Loge's ♭II–V–I cadence in
G minor. It is a desolate example of double mixture – ♭iii in E (E minor
returns at the end of the section). Bleakest of all are the B flat minor and
D flat minor chords. The former will come to possess associations with the
Nibelungen; the latter is an adumbration of the key in which Wotan's end
is foretold by Erda.

These forces of degeneration will be eventually be appeased by
Brünnhilde's ultimate understanding of Wotan's fate at the end of the

'real' *Twilight of the Gods*, knowledge that will allow the counteracting forces of regeneration to be released as she rides her horse to the ultimate sacrifice. She achieves this with two endings to her final monologue. In the first the dark force of the Neapolitan is pacified and a final transformation of woeful semitones to hopeful whole tones secured. In the second brightness illuminates reanimating vigour. These two endings are approached by different types of movement. The first is a sinking, slowing, shrinking of power, the second a rising, accelerating, energizing, expansive reinvigoration. The familiar romantic notion of 'doubleness' can be expanded into a way of analysing these musical and dramatic endings as part of an 'argument of doubleness' in which contradiction leads to ambiguous, open or multiple endings.[5] Doubleness is rife in Wagner.[6] As we saw, for Mann the double quality which characterized the nineteenth century – faith in progress overshadowed by pessimism and melancholy – was most powerfully expressed in the 'sorrows and grandeur' of Wagner's music. The potential productiveness of a double ending is also apparent, for the so-called 'second practice' of nineteenth-century tonality is characterized by the exploitation of ambiguity through double tonics and conflicts between diatonic structures and chromatic (symmetrical) 'counter-structures', both of which can set up processes which require completion or demand their own endings.[7] Doubleness is also central to Strauss's *Salome* and *Elektra*, in which the example of Brünnhilde's endings is a crucial model in dramatic conclusions evoking once more the polarity between the degenerative and regenerative. But first, Brünnhilde.

Brünnhilde's double end

The two endings of Brünnhilde's monologue in *Twilight of the Gods* have been analysed by Christopher Wintle. The first he describes as 'tenebral, grave and crepuscular', the second as 'jubilant, impetuous, luminous and

---

[5] See Lydia Goehr, *The Quest for Voice: Music, Politics, and the Limits of Philosophy* (Oxford University Press, 1998), 15 and elsewhere.

[6] For example, Jean-Jacques Nattiez points out that the fundamental duality in *Tannhäuser* is doubly complex, as in the overture each type of love contains its opposite in a 'double interplay': Wagner's notion of a 'higher love' capable of integrating the sensual into a replete sensuality was a way of coming to terms with this amorous duality. For Nattiez it is symptomatic of the torn state of the 'double' human. See his 'Memory and Forgetting: Wagner/Proust/Boulez', in *The Battle of Chronos and Orpheus: Essays in Applied Musical Semiology*, trans. Jonathan Dunsby (Oxford University Press, 2004), 187.

[7] See Kinderman and Krebs (eds.), *The Second Practice of Nineteenth-Century Tonality*.

replete with aspiration'. The first is preceded by the dark motivic shadow of Alberich, for Brünnhilde will not return the ring to the Rhinemaidens and thus absolve his curse. Its 'regressive' closure ends with a motif which rings with the falsity in the gods' attempt to withdraw behind the protective comforts of Valhalla's walls (heard at the end of *Rhinegold*), and recalls the perversion of nature's woodland paradise by Wotan's breaking of the World Ash Tree, as told by the first Norn in the Prologue to *Twilight*.[8] The second cadence, which for Wintle is a transformation of the first but also its polar opposite, is preceded by Brünnhilde's expressions of wonder at the prospect of rekindling her joyful union with Siegfried. Its final motivic gesture is one of animal vitality. What Brünnhilde presents, therefore, is a paradigmatic example of the double closing gesture required when regressive and progressive, degenerative and regenerative forces are held in tensed opposition. The two endings also play out different relationships between memory and forgetting. Wintle hears the melodic emphasis on the pitch E♭ in the statements of the motive of sublime wonder in the second cadence as nostalgically recalling the tonality of the opening of the cycle and the first Norn's telling of nature's perversion through Wotan's will to power. But this is the weakest part of Wintle's analysis. Brünnhilde's transformation of the first cadence's regressive, nostalgic tone is marked by the second cadence's performative immediacy and ecstatic forgetfulness.

The issue of memory in the *Ring* cycle has been much discussed. The same applies to the 'perpetual problem' of the future,[9] which is masked by the apparently endless motivic transformations through which the new is created in a retelling of the old. Through the reminiscence of material in different contexts fresh implications and new possible endings might proliferate, but 'the future' and its music remain an unrealized fantasy. This nexus of pastness, presentness and the desired future comes to a double head in *Twilight*'s final scene.[10] After Siegfried's funeral march,

---

[8] Christopher Wintle, 'The Questionable Lightness of Being: Brünnhilde's Peroration to *The Ring*', in Nicholas John (ed.), *Wagner: Götterdämmerung* (London: Calder, 1985), 39–48. See also Darcy, 'The Pessimism of the *Ring*', 37, 40–1.

[9] James Treadwell, *Interpreting Wagner* (New Haven: Yale University Press, 2003), 127.

[10] Robert Bailey notes that the dramatic structure of *Twilight of the Gods* has double significance: on the one hand it has a dramatic structure in parallel with *Rhinegold* (prologue followed by three scenes or acts), and on the other it parallels the form of the whole cycle (prologue and three dramas). See Bailey, 'The Structure of the "Ring" and its Evolution', *19th-Century Music* 1 (1977), 48–61. So two endings seem to be needed – one a reinterpreted return of the end of *Rhinegold*, and the second an end to the larger-scale dramatic and structural parallel.

the orchestral threnody, the sonorous monument to the hero's life which traces the process of memorialization through mourning, the end of the *Ring* cycle may primarily be cast as a looking back, with one exceptional moment. At her plunge into the fire Brünnhilde's exultation overwhelms this backwardness and we glimpse a possible future. She can only do this, however, once she has exorcised the tragic past of Wotan and rekindled her ecstatic past with Siegfried. Until the moment before his demise Siegfried has no sense of pastness or history; he has no memory, and hence no fear. (Bravery is true only if it overcomes the fear based on memory, not on the naïve fearlessness of the young Siegfried. The fear he experienced upon the awakening of his desire for Brünnhilde at the climactic end of *Siegfried* has long been forgotten.) As Steinberg notes, the 'belated nobility of Siegfried's death scene, on the other hand, is its focus on his sudden accrual of a past ... of recovered memory'.[11] This act of remembrance is reciprocated when, after the hero's death, Brünnhilde gains strength, knowledge and delight by recalling and lovingly meditating on the memory of Siegfried. Out of this memorializing process, the two endings emerge – one concerning Brünnhilde's relationship with Wotan, the other her relationship with Siegfried. Tracing the sources of these endings highlights the burdens they place on musical and dramatic memory, on the multiple recognitions demanded by the fact that they recall music and events often heard and seen long ago by the characters and/or the audience.

Brünnhilde's first ending has a double source, one in Erda's warning to Wotan from *Rhinegold*, scene iv, and the other in Waltraute's entreaties to Brünnhilde in *Twilight*, Act 1 scene iii. As Darcy says, the first of these sources 'simultaneously embraces the beginning and the end of the entire drama'.[12] It foretells the end of the cycle: the rest of the *Ring* is driven by Wotan's attempt to come to terms with Erda's words 'All that is must end', the knowledge of his own inevitable demise. Wagner explained to Röckel: 'fear of the end is the source of all lovelessness; and this fear is generated only when love begins to wane ... all that mankind did, ordered, and established, was conceived only in fear of the end! My poem sets this forth.'[13] Erda's command 'Hear me!' isolates a principal motif (the A–G♯ figure), a ♭6–5 traditional grief symbol which is also a chromatic distortion of the Rhinemaidens' 'Rhinegold!' call. It is symbolic, therefore, of woe

[11] Steinberg, *Listening to Reason*, 155–6.
[12] See Darcy's analysis of this passage and its sketches: *Wagner's 'Das Rheingold'*, 196–202.
[13] Wagner, *Selected Letters*, 306–7.

caused by corruption of natural order. In this dialogue the pitch A develops a double harmonic function, first as dominant of the dark Neapolitan D (symbolic of the gods' downfall) and then, at Wotan's plea for more information to help him understand, as part of an augmented sixth to the dominant of C sharp. Erda's reply moves Wotan into dreadful brooding over a dissonant G♯–A–C♯–E chord. This does not resolve but dissolves into chromatically descending sequences. Erda leaves Wotan fearfully pondering his end. The second source of Brünnhilde's first ending is what Waltraute tells her in *Twilight*, Act 1 scene iii.[14] The crucial passage begins at the image of Wotan surrounded by the gods in fear and dismay (see Example 3.2). This recalls the anxious assembly of the gods around Wotan at the beginning of the 'premature twilight' scene of *Rhinegold*. A G flat major cadence complete with rocking Valhalla figures (marked *etwas zurückhaltend*) sounds an appeasing tone. With his shattered spear in hand, Wotan is silent. The apparent security of the G flat closure is then undermined by fateful chromaticisms over the F♯ pedal. Tonal instability heightens as Waltraute reports that Wotan is no longer enlivened by the golden apples. The apples motif emphasizes the dissonant ninth G: its rising section (A–B–C–B–C–E–G) is a melancholy, degenerated variant of the closing section of the preceding Valhalla cadence (G♭–A♭–B♭–A♭–B♭–D♭). The degenerative process is then intensified in an extraordinary chromaticized version of the opening of the Valhalla

---

[14] As Bailey says, this monologue prepares melodic material for the beginning of Brünnhilde's immolation scene and the final subdominant cadence of the opera; see 'The Structure of the "Ring" and its Evolution', 59–60. On the ambiguous status of Waltraute's relationship to the absent Wotan's authority as she quotes his words see Sandra Corse, 'The Voice of Authority in Wagner's *Ring*', in Herbert Richardson (ed.), *New Studies in Richard Wagner's 'The Ring of the Nibelung'* (Lewiston: Edwin Mellen Press, 1991), 23–7. See also Dahlhaus's analysis of Waltraute's monologue in *Richard Wagner's Music Dramas*, trans. Mary Whittall (Cambridge University Press, 1979), 105–6. Brünnhilde's discerning hearing, which allows her to perceive false endings, has previously been crucial in her listening to Wotan's monologue in Act 2 of *The Valkyrie* (in which he confesses his fear of the end). For Abbate, Brünnhilde can hear the falseness of cadences which are not integrally connected to the material around them; see her *Unsung Voices*. By contrast, Wintle demonstrates that the cadences in Wotan's monologue do perform a structural role, as diatonic structures which are transformed by chromatic counter-structures – including ordered diminished sevenths and the 'sub-thematic' grief symbol of ♭6–5 – used to express Wotan's rhetorics of anguish: 'Wotan's Rhetoric of Anguish', *Journal of the Royal Musical Association* 118 (1993), 121–43. Whichever hearing one buys into, the crucial things are the ambiguous, layered functions of cadences and Brünnhilde's skill as a listener and learner. On the central importance of Wotan's monologue see also William McDonald, 'What does Wotan Know? Autobiography and Moral Vision in Wagner's *Ring*', *19th-Century Music* 15 (1991), 36–51, who says that Brünnhilde's hearing allows her to begin her journey to the end.

Example 3.2 Wagner, *Twilight of the Gods*, Act 1 scene iii, Waltraute: 'ihm zu Seiten ...'

theme. This is an extension of transformational processes previously applied to this part of the theme at its climactic statement in *The Valkyrie*, Act 2 scene ii. As David Lewin has pointed out, Wotan's bitter rage at this climax has its source in his gradual realization that his idea

Example 3.2 (cont.)

of Valhalla 'contains at its centre the source of its own corruption' (this is musically confirmed by the fact that the chromatic elements that are the basis of the corrupted transformation are already embedded in the modulations of first hearing of the complete Valhalla theme in

Example 3.2 (cont.)

Rhinegold, scene 2). As Lewin demonstrates, at this climax the diatonicism of the original opening of the Valhalla theme is transformed by
the substitution chords from the parallel minor and by applying
Riemannian *Leittonwechsel* (where the two notes of the minor third of

Example 3.2 (cont.)

a triad remain unchanged while the third note moves up a semitone to
generate a new triad of the opposing mode).[15] The extension of this
process to generate the chromatic Valhalla motifs in Waltraute's

[15] David Lewin, 'Some Notes on Analyzing Wagner: *The Ring* and *Parsifal*', *19th-Century Music* 16
(1992), 53–4.

Example 3.2 (cont.)

monologue is demonstrated in Example 3.3. The first level of the example shows the harmonies of the Valhalla opening presented in a diatonic minor form in C minor. The second and third levels show chromatic transformations, in the manner of Lewin's example from *The Valkyrie*, first through application of *Leittonwechsel* to the third, fourth and fifth chords and then through application of parallel transformation on the fourth and fifth chords. On the final level of transformation, the one going beyond Lewin's example, the second triad is altered to a diminished seventh and the third and fifth to half-diminished curse harmonies. Lewin turns to explicitly decadent imagery to provide a literary parallel to the chromatic corruption of Wotan's fortress from within, comparing Wagner's technique and its symbolism to how 'the progressive deformation of Dorian Gray's portrait merely log[s] the potential for corruption already implicit in the narcissism of the beautiful youth himself'.[16] The comparison is especially apposite, of course, as both Wilde's Gray and Wagner's Wotan are embroiled in ill-fated

[16] Lewin, 'Some Notes', 53.

Example 3.3 Chromatic corruption of the opening of the Valhalla theme

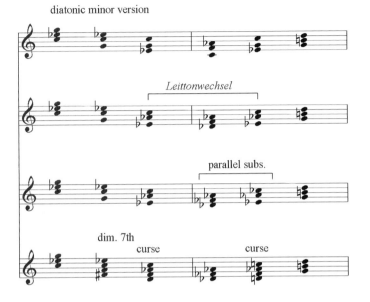

attempts to suspend the 'natural' aging process and retain the full flush and vigour of youth. The Valhalla transformation is stated twice. First it prolongs the top voice's G♮ through a chromatic motion in C minor which incorporates the local minor Neapolitan (D flat minor), precisely on the word 'bangen' – a poetic recollection of the text associated with the dark Neapolitan in the 'premature twilight' scene. It is then repeated a semitone lower, in B minor. This resolves the G♮ to F♯ in an expansion of the motif of grief and clarifies C's function as the local Neapolitan to B (confirmed by the internal use of that relationship in the second twisted Valhalla progression). Waltraute continues by describing Wotan's sending-out of his ravens and his sense of hopelessness, in lines supported by a motivic complex in which repeated variants of the grief motif are prominent. Only on remembering Brünnhilde can Wotan envisage an end to the curse, and he sinks into a semi-somnulent state of partial repose. The passage closes with the rocking Valhalla motif in the gods' 'home' key of D flat.

Before she appropriates and transforms Waltraute's music in the lead-up to her first D flat cadence, Brünnhilde sings through the music of the end of *Twilight*, Act 1 – the music of her betrayal – and the music of Erda's denunciation of the falsehood of Wotan (the Wanderer) from *Siegfried*, Act 3 scene i. That recalled, she can declare that she knows all, that all is clear to her (see Example 3.4). On proclaiming her acquistion of

Example 3.4 Wagner, *Twilight of the Gods*, Act 3 scene iii, Brünnhilde: 'Alles ward mir nun frei'

knowledge she sends the ravens 'home', adopting Waltraute's music, for she can now understand what Waltraute was saying to her (she was previously deaf to her pleas of 'Hear me, hear me' in F sharp minor,[17] which of course recall Erda's warning to Wotan in *Rhinegold*). The music now suggests the possible final transfiguration of the G–F♯ grief figure to a whole-tone G♯–F♯. Brünnhilde then significantly omits Waltraute's description of Wotan, with its tragic moves to D and C minor, and skips straight to Waltraute's music at the D flat cadence ('Rest, rest, O god'). Brünnhilde also appears simply to have exorcised, or forgotten, the golden apples, since Waltraute's music which incorporated the apple motif is absent. But a closer look at Brünnhilde's closing line reveals a more subtle resolution. Her D flat cadence is modelled on Waltraute's pronunciation of the same words but with two extensions so that Brünnhilde presents three closing gestures in one cadence. All these gestures are concerned with the resolution of the A/B♭♭ which is sounded in the motif of Alberich's curse on the ring. The first begins with the G flat minor chord, the enharmonic of Waltraute's principal key, F sharp minor, here functioning as the minor subdominant, a traditional harmonic symbol of melancholy close. The motif which elaborates this harmony in the bass recalls Waltraute's description of Wotan as a lonely figure mounted on his horse, restlessly wandering the world. (As we shall see, the elements in this tragic image – the horse, home-lessness and restlessness – are physically and symbolically transfigured in Brünnhilde's second, revitalizing D flat cadence.) Brünnhilde's vocal line over the subdominant minor chord, an A♭–G♭ suspension, is (enhar-monically) the redeeming whole-tone G♯–F♯, promising rest from fear of the end. It is the most poignant moment before closure because the dissonance is caused by the coexistence of the cursed A♮ and the resolving A♭/G♯.[18] A double move to D flat follows this subdominant signifier of imminent closure. The first, resounding and directly resolving the Neapolitan D, avoids the dominant, which is provided only in the second close with the statement of what Wintle describes as a 'comforting cadential figure'. This figure has a long history in the cycle, expressing Wotan's hopes of being 'safe from fear' – a false security heard at the end of *Rhinegold* and in the Norns' prologue to *Twilight*. Wintle argues that when Brünnhilde uses this at her cadence she does not merely purge the figure of its false security,

---

[17] Abbate, *Unsung Voices*, 233–4.

[18] Is it fantastical to hear the dissonance here as a new cadential version of the G♯–A–C♯–E dissonance which left Wotan so fearful after Erda's initial warning?

but restores its '"original" state of nature'.[19] But there is more. Its F–E♭ suspension echoes the preceding A♭–G♭ suspension and also supplies the next two pitches in the closing line. It recalls the F–E♭ 'Rhinegold!' motif: the intermediate minor subdominant is required to sustain the connection (or establish the reconnection) between restoration of the Rhinegold and appeasement of Wotan's restlessness. Furthermore, the 'comforting' figure is also a restful version of the flight motif originally attached to Freia, which in the 'premature twilight' scene of *Rhinegold* was associated with expressive duality of woeful semitonal descent versus hopeful whole tones. The golden apples motif is unheard, but its legacy lies imprinted on the cadential materials.

Brünnhilde's first cadence is associated with the Rhinegold out of which was fashioned the ring, Siegfried's token of his love for her. The second is associated with Grane, the horse that Brünnhilde gave to Siegfried in return. This second ending has its sources in *Valkyrie*, Act 2, and two actions involving the symbols of love and its faithful memory from the Prologue and Act 1 scene ii of *Twilight*. Siegfried's fate has been tied to Grane from before his birth. In *Valkyrie*, Act III scene i, the horse carries Brünnhilde and Sieglinde (pregnant with the unborn hero) in flight from Wotan. In exalted rapture Sieglinde sings the motif which, when Brünnhilde appropriates it at her immolation, reminds us of Grane's faithful and crucial role in saving the foetal hero and his mother. Grane later becomes symbolicaly linked to Brünnhilde's transformation into womanhood after her awakening by Siegfried (*Siegfried*, Act 3 scene iii.).[20]

---

[19] For discussion of this motif's significance see Wintle, 'The Questionable Lightness of Being', 46.

[20] James M. McGlathery provides an unusually sustained analysis of the horse's symbolic role. From the awakening of Grane and Brünnhilde by Siegfried, the steed is identified with Brünnhilde's body: in offering the horse to Siegfried in *Götterdämmerung* she offers her virginity and she is transformed from warrior-god to sexually active woman. Her words at the moment of plunging into the pyre suggests this identity, with the horse as her 'girlish mount'. Her desire for Siegfried is 'heavily physical, though modesty causes her at first to speak as if it were her horse … That is consumed by desire.' Brünnhilde's speaking to her horse 'suggests a degree of despair and madness'. 'In her romantic despair, she wishes to imagine herself transported back to the moment just before her surrender to desire for Siegfried, as though she were only now to become his bride, and the events just past were merely a horrible nightmare. Since the beloved is dead, the horse must stand in for him to test the ardor of her passion. Irrationally – or perhaps only rhetorically – she asks Grane to feel the beating of her heart to assure himself that her yearning to join Siegfried, his master and her husband, equals his': *Wagner's Operas and Desire* (New York: Peter Lang, 1998), 163–7. L. J. Rather suggests that Grane's role evokes a Schopenhauerian-Buddhist notion. Rather summarizes Schopenhauer (from *The World as Will and Representation*) thus: 'When Buddha – while still Bodhisattva and not yet having attained perfect knowledge – saddles his horse for the last time, he addresses it as follows: "O Kantanka, bear me away from here only this time again, and when I have attained the law

The sleeping horse is the first thing Siegfried sees on ascending to the mountain top. Siegfried's vocal line at that moment outlines a fragment of the motif of his heroic destiny which is closely related to the motif of the Valkyrie. Thus, before he has set eyes on his future bride, his fate is tied to hers at the moment of seeing the symbolic steed. In the middle of the love duet, with Siegfried in a state of confusion, increasing excitement and fearful arousal, Brünnhilde turns away from his fixed gaze and sees Grane, who was also awoken by Siegfried and now grazes nearby. The music accompanying Siegfried's statements of confused exhilaration becomes increasingly darkened by E flat minor and the A♭–C♭–E♭–F transposition of the curse harmony. The cadence on B♭ which follows is replete with darkened motivic fragments – of the Valkyries' augmented triad and the rising fourth of their motif, of the parallel thirds and trills of the lovers' devotion and of the accented turn of Wotan's dejection (see Example 3.5). The harmony over the B♭ is bitingly dissonant, emphasizing the Neapolitan darkness of the C♭–B♭ relationship by echoing the A♭–C♭–E♭–F curse chord.[21] The music remains plangent and yearning until Brünnhilde spots her awakened horse. A hesitant (*zögernd*) version of the motif of flight peaks on a darkening D♭–C before moving to a sustained dominant seventh ('I see there Grane'). Now the harmony brightens to Siegfried's heroic F, and the tone is transformed to suggest the bucolically pastoral. But on her noting that Grane has been woken by Siegfried there is a darkened allusion to the third-related chords of her awakening (the E flat minor, of course, here adumbrates the opening of *Twilight*). After this, the cadence on G♭ and *dolce* statement of the motif of love's passion are bittersweet (a character confirmed by the chromatic tail given to the motif) and the passage resolves G♭ as the flat submediant of B flat to usher in Siegfried's singing of his passion to the motif of vital delight. In the sequences which follow, Brünnhilde continues to explain her precarious position as her shield, helmet and sword have all been removed by Siegfried. Of her Valkyrie accessories only Grane remains. It is crucial that when she sang of her steed's awakening ('wie weidet er munter, der mit mir schlief!') her vocal line incorporated the motif of vital delight. This identifies Grane

---

(have become Buddha), I shall not forget you"': *The Dream of Self-Destruction: Wagner's 'Ring' and the Modern World* (Baton Rouge: Louisiana State University Press, 1979), 100–1. In Marc Weiner's discussion of animal metaphors (*Richard Wagner and the Anti-Semitic Imagination*) the horse is strangely absent.

[21] For a short discussion of this passage see Anthony Newcomb, '*Siegfried*: The Music', in Nicholas John (ed.), *Wagner: 'Siegfried'* (London: Calder, 1984), 38.

Example 3.5 Wagner, *Siegfried*, Act 3 scene iii, Brünnhilde: 'Dort seh' ich Grane …'

Example 3.5 (cont.)

SIEGFRIED

Auf won - ni - gem Mun - de_weid - et mein Au - ge:
On glad - den - ing lips my_glan - ces are feast - ing:

dolce

p

with the lover's passion. It also tells us that this is the prime factor in her predicament. And the darkened tones around it foretell that her lover's downfall will be linked to how he treats this symbolic beast.

In *Twilight*, Act 1 scene ii, Siegfried rather casually gives Grane away as Hagen offers to take the horse into his 'care'. At this moment the move from the dominant of Siegfried's virile, heroic F major to the curse harmony which opened the scene is repeated. A sensual, decadent Gibichung motif is also recalled, first to turn the harmony from F major to D minor and then, after a telling conjunction of Valkyrie and fate rhythms at the return of the dominant of F, at the harmonic twist onto the curse chord. As Hagen leads the horse away the recollection of Brünnhilde's and Siegfried's joyous B flat major turns (prophetically?) to a fleeting yet beautiful cadence in their amorous manner in D flat, but only in order to debase it through two minor third descents in the harmony – a move to B flat minor followed by the dominant of G minor. This minatory progression suggests an incomplete symmetrical counter-structure of minor-third-related keys: D flat–B flat–G and the withheld E or F flat. The loss of Grane is Siegfried's first fateful error, marking the beginning of his degeneration and of the drama's *dénouement*.[22] And he has yet to sip from any deceiver's goblet. The horse's associations with faithfulness and love's exchange, and therefore with fidelity through remembrance, are debased by Siegfried's careless, forgetful handing of Grane to Hagen, a relinquishing of the symbol of Brünnhilde's bodily prowess and faithful love for fame, fortune and ephemeral, furtive, decadent pleasures with Gutrune.

---

[22] On denouements see Grey, *Wagner's Musical Prose*, 363–74. On the problems or inadequacies in Wagner's untying of dramatic 'knots' see Nietzsche, *The Case of Wagner*, 175.

As her own end approaches, Brünnhilde's call to Grane to carry her into the fire (which he does, one presumes, without fear) restores that symbolic status. Furthermore, she does not wish to leave Grane and the impulses which he symbolizes behind.[23] The steed's function at this point is clarified by Donington's classic Jungian reading. Grane is symbol of 'the life of the instincts' of 'instinctual energy or animal vitality': his role in the immolation thus confirms that 'life can be transformed without becoming disembodied'.[24] The plunge into the flames is also preceded by recollection of the E major of the love duet in *Siegfried*, Act 3 scene iii, and Brünnhilde's sleep music in *Valkyrie* – thus of protecting fire, but also the lover's fiery passion, and therefore of the endings of the two preceding dramas in the cycle. The second D flat cadence (Example 3.6) is a revitalization of the regressive character of the first through the radically different function of the chromatic pitch A/B♭♭. In the first cadence it is a 'cursed' symbolic pitch, but the second emphasizes A's symbolic association with Grane.[25] At Brünnhilde's calling of Grane's name the harmony moves through a diminished seventh and a curse chord on A to shift to Siegfried's heroic F major, reversing the move which had marked Siegfried's debasing carelessness in handing the steed over to Hagen in Act 1 scene ii. The sequence is then modified to move through V/V of D flat and a different half-diminished curse chord (but one over a B♭♭, sustaining that pitch's emphasis) as the bass moves chromatically down to the dominant A♭. The diversion of the cadence onto a D♭–F–A augmented triad further sustains the crucial role of the pitch A, now as the climactic descant note. The augmented triad at the cadence's climax incorporates Grane's A, Siegfried's heroic F and the drama's final key of D flat. This D flat completes the 'counter-structures' which were left unresolved at Brünnhilde's giving of Grane to Siegfried in Act 1 scene i as a

---

[23] Adorno famously baulked: 'in the teeth of the cult of the prevention of cruelty to animals, she even insists that her horse should neigh with joy as it leaps into the flames': *In Search of Wagner* [1938], trans. Rodney Livingstone, with a foreword by Slavoj Žižek (London: Verso, 2005), 135. Abbate suggests that for most listeners it seems a 'tasteless miscalculation'. Her analysis of this passage invokes a Brünnhilde of 'double identity', one who is also 'double voiced': *Unsung Voices*, 242–9.

[24] Donington, *Wagner's 'Ring'*, 199, 272, 299.

[25] Grane also has associations with E flat major and B minor, the former, for example, in his joyful neigh through a descending octave and a half of E flat triads, and previously, when Brünnhilde requests that Grane be brought to her in order to accompany her to meet Siegfried, there is a restoration of E flat. We might equate this with the key of nature at the opening of the cycle. Grane is briefly associated with B minor when, after Siegfried's funeral music, Gutrune's sleep is disturbed by the horse's neighing. The key of B minor here has a double resonance: as the original key of the Valkyrie, and also that of the Gibichungs (the horse is presumably in Gibichung hands at this point).

Example 3.6 Wagner, *Twilight of the Gods*, Act 3 scene iii, Brünnhilde: 'Hei-a-ja-ho! Grane!'

love token in exchange for the ring, when the tonality moved from E minor, through G minor to B flat, and then from F to a pause on the dominant A, and closed with a long *crescendo* on an A triad as she asked that Siegfried often speak her name to the horse. These progressions – E through G to B flat, and then from F to A – both imply symmetrical completion on D♭/C♯ (the first to form a diminished seventh structure, the second an augmented triad).[26] The rhythmic patterns which articulate the augmented triad at Brünnhilde's climax confirm the return of animal vitality. The cadence's rekindling of the importance of augmented triads recalls the central role of E–A♭–C as chord and tonal structure in the *Siegfried* love duet.[27] As a 'fearless' plunge into magic fire it recalls the supreme image of Siegfried's blazing penetration.

The cadence, allied with physically energetic gestures, climaxes the achievements of the 'knowing' Brünnhilde and marks her highest moment of rapturous delight. Its vital energies seem, however, to be overburdened with memories.[28] In response we may return to Nietzsche, who characterizes the uncovering of knowledge as a recovery: metaphysics 'forgets' that the new is an illusion, that the perception of the new and the recollection of the old amount to the same thing, a recognizing, recollecting, return and homecoming.[29] But Nietzsche also asserts the necessity of forgetting, for an excess of memory leads to the decadence and melancholy of modern culture. His critique of metaphysics (in which concept formation is compared to constructing a tomb, where all sense of contingency and becoming is lost) sought a new emphasis on the body, for by contrast with the metaphysical, the physical emphasizes the here and now, not the beyond or the past. These concepts contributed to Nietzsche's developing notion of the Dionysian as the ecstatic forgetting of self and the intoxicating physical excitement which dissolves individual identity and opens up the sublime threat of incoherence. The rhythmic Valkyrie setting of the D♭–F–A augmented triad, confirming the return of Granian animal vitality, marks a transformed allusion to the ecstatic tone of the end of the love duet in

---

[26] On 'counter-structures' and their affective association with wildness and grief see Christopher Wintle, 'Kontra-Schenker: *Largo e mesto* from Beethoven's Op.10 No.3', *Music Analysis* 4 (1985), 145–82.

[27] See Mark Anson-Cartwright, 'Chord as Motive: The Augmented-Triad Matrix in Wagner's "Siegfried Idyll"', *Music Analysis* 15 (1996), 57–71.

[28] Hermann Danuser notes that 'the farther the tetralogy progresses, the more powerful becomes the force of memory, and the more significant the narration of past events. The linear course unrolls in the intensifying realization of the moment, but at the same time fans out both backward and forward – as "premonition" of events to come and "memory" of those past.' Danuser employs Wagner's three temporal categories outlined in *Opera and Drama: Ahnung* (premonition), *Vergegenwärtigung* (presentation) and *Erinnerung* (memory). See 'Musical Manifestations of the End in Wagner and in Post-Wagnerian "Weltanschauungsmusik"', *19th-Century Music* 18 (1994), 75.

[29] See Stephen Houlgate, *Hegel, Nietzsche and the Criticism of Metaphysics* (Cambridge University Press, 2004), 38–95.

Siegfried, Act 3 scene iii (which is where Nietzsche would probably have preferred the *Ring* to have ended). Through this ecstatic vitality the cadential interruption which is coincident with the D♭–F–A augmented triad, though commonplace as a Wagnerian harmonic event, is here marked as a moment of sublime wonder. The aesthetic of wonder – produced by instantaneous experience where presence is the primary category – is an aesthetic of delight which contrasts with the sublime aesthetic of fear; it is based on the pleasure of radical surprise, to which memory and narrative (necessary for fear) seem antagonistic.[30] This is the crowning moment, sustaining the augmented triad's association with the overcoming of fear which underpins the story of Siegfried's adventurous journey towards sexual union with Brünnhilde at the end of the previous drama in the cycle. The cadence may seem to be pervaded by memories, but it is also paradoxically a moment of Dionysian forgetfulness, especially heroic because the process of recovering memory has been the function of the music which leads up to it. The 'newness' of the cadence may be 'deceptive', but it is heard (immediately) as a deflection following sustained reflection, momentarily reinstating a 'lost immediacy'. This effect is a second immediacy 'mediated by reflection'.[31] We must also recognize it as an example of what Kramer calls a 'performative simulation of ecstatic immediacy'.[32] The burdens of memory are for one moment apparently forgotten; the metaphysical is replaced by the physical. Brünnhilde's first cadence offered multiple closural gestures in manifold recollection; her second, by contrast, performs the momentary obliteration of memory through restoration of physical vitality and the interruption of closure. Wagner, the master magician of the theatre, would want his audience to be as ecstatically forgetful as his heroine. But, though we may wish to forget, we know the effect is an illusion, because the conjunction of cadential interruption and augmented triad play on the surprise of deflection from the remembered cadential norm. This provides a type of symbolic meaning deviant from the stable

---

[30] The poetics of wonder inhabits a middle zone between the familiar and uninteresting and the unknowable and unthinkable; see Philip Fisher, *Wonder, the Rainbow, and the Aesthetics of Rare Experiences* (Cambridge, Mass.: Harvard University Press, 1998), 2, 10, 134, 180.

[31] Pieter van den Toorn writes that 'reflection serves immediacy … in an effort to capture and sustain immediacy': *Music, Politics, and the Academy* (Berkeley: University of California Press, 1995), 12, 54. For a response see Marianne Kielian-Gilbert, 'Invoking Motives and Immediacy: Foils and Contexts for Pieter C. van den Toorn's *Music, Politics, and the Academy*', *19th-Century Music* 20 (1997), 253–78.

[32] Lawrence Kramer, *Classical Music and Postmodern Knowledge* (Berkeley: University of California Press, 1995), 17.

order of the kind Wotan sought to restore and secure. In her doubleness of love Brünnhilde sings of the Wagnerian *ewig* which negates finitude.[33]

As Danuser says, after Brünnhilde's monologue the rest is a 'postlude'.[34] There are recollections of the two main harmonic features of Brünnhilde's cadences: the subdominant and Neapolitan inflection of the first and the transformation of symbols of fate and symmetrical structures in the second. Thus the double structural and symbolic importance of A continues to resonate. Magic fire music in F sharp (enharmonic G flat, the subdominant of D flat major) moves to its mediant A, after which A (once again) resolves as the flat sixth to the dominant A♭ of the home key (D flat). This A flat chord is prolonged by a move through the A♭–E–C augmented triad of the love duet and a prefiguring of the D 6–3 chord of the downfall of the gods. On the restatement of the A flat chord foreground motifs play on Brünnhilde's 'home' E♭–G–B augmented triad before moving to a diminished seventh on A, which functions as a chromatic pre-dominant chord in A flat. The complex legacy of the A is not resolved until the closing bars, for at Hagen's 'Zurück vom Ring!' the cadence to A flat is thwarted by the return of the F♯–A–C–E curse harmony. A flat returns as Flosshilde swims with the ring, but A, enharmonic B♭♭, turns the subdominant G flat major to minor with Siegfried's motif leading to another statement of the D major 6–3 harmony of the downfall of the gods. The latter reinstates the climactic descant A of the Grane-led cadence and in the last four bars the approach to the final resolution to D flat is A/B♭♭'s last musical mark.[35]

Salome's double end

Brünnhilde's double ending was a powerful model for Strauss, one ripe for recollection and deformation. Paul Banks describes Salome's monologue as

---

[33] Philip Kitcher and Richard Schacht, *Finding an Ending: Reflections on Wagner's* Ring (New York: Oxford University Press, 2004), 116, 120, 180. As Wintle concludes, the two cadences signify the 'extraordinary ambiguity' created by offering 'fantasy and tragedy together, and by asking us to respond to, and reflect upon both equivalently': 'The Questionable Lightness of Being', 48.

[34] Danuser, 'Musical Manifestations of the End', 76. Darcy has analysed the immolation scene as three 'rotations' leading to closure in the drama's final bars, the D flat cadence at the end of the third rotation achieving ultimate closure via arrival on the background structural dominant. Brünnhilde's 'endings' of the first and second 'rotations' are therefore in Darcy's reading not full closures: see 'The Metaphysics of Annihilation: Wagner, Schopenhauer and the Ending of "The Ring"', *Music Theory Spectrum* 16 (1994), 1–40.

[35] Darcy hears this as a rectification of the preceding 'aborted' D flat cadence: 'The Pessimism of the *Ring*', 48, n.49.

a 'pathological *Liebestod*',[36] but comparison of the final C sharp cadences of the monologue with Brünnhilde's D flat cadences at the end of *Twilight* is potentially more fruitful than one with Isolde's transfiguring end. It is a complex example of modelling, complicating and dismantling. The double forces of dissolution and regeneration are not separated out into polar opposite narrative and musical endings but are mixed in two climactic cadence points which offer powerful exemplifications of the symbolic possibilities inherent in Strauss's stylistic eclecticism. Salome's monologue offers a decadent reinterpretation of Brünnhilde's double ending, one in which the forces of decay and regeneration operate in knotted interactions rather than in separated polarity, and one where, similarly, the opposition of memory and forgetting is reforged into permanently tensed conflict, confusion and ambiguity.

Comparisons and contrasts can be made in precise musical details. Like Brünnhilde's D flat cadences, Salome's C sharp cadences are the final climactic element in a series of shifts through the music drama in the symbolic and harmonic status of the pitch A. Strauss's opera has two musical beginnings. At the opening the move from the dominant (G♯) to the pitch A initiates an upper-voice chromatic ascent. This rising line continues as the harmony moves through a circle of fifths of dominant chords (on D, G, C). The role of A is then central to the Page's invocations of the moon, projections of his images of Salome's body ('See the moon rises, she looks strangely eerie, she's like a woman who rises from her grave …'), whose harmonic shifts from F major to F minor and then A minor are contrapuntally fused by the A–A♭–A chromatic motion (an inversion of the neighbour-note relationship in Salome's motif). The opening musical paragraph ends with the Page's negation of Narraboth's image of the dancing Salome ('She's like a lifeless woman, still gliding slowly aloft') where the F minor–A minor chord succession proceeds to the dominant minor ninth of D, a series of chords in part contrapuntally motivated by a rising A♭–A–B♭ motion. As we shall see, the dissonant A–B♭ clash which occurs over this dominant of D minor (2 bars before fig.4) is darkly prophetic. This opening material is reworked in the 'second beginning', the music which immediately precedes Salome's bodily entrance at the start of scene ii. The music now cadences clearly in A major. As Salome looks at the moon (after fig.29) there is reworking of the contrapuntal textures and motifs from the opening, this time

---

[36] Paul Banks, 'Richard Strauss and the Unveiling of "Salome"', in Nicholas John (ed.), *Strauss: Salome/Elektra*, ENO Opera Guide 37 (London: Calder, 1988), 18.

intimating a resolution onto D flat. She then sings of the moon's virgin beauty as the music cadences back in A, but with elements of D flat still strongly heard – in a floating or potentially double tonality. The contrast between Salome's contemplation of the moon with the A minor and F major-minor of the Page's negative lunar imagery in the opening is especially marked. The dark A minor and F are replaced by strange light of A major and D flat (symmetrically 'opposite' F in its relationship to A). This association of A with Salome's somatic presence (at first imagined, then actual) is, of course, further confirmed by the opening of the 'Dance of the Seven Veils' in A minor. With these symbolic associations around the pitch A established, we can now turn to the opera's final climaxes.

Salome's first C sharp cadence ('Ah! Ah! Jochanaan, you were beautiful'; between figs.332 and 333) resolves the A pitch in two traditional, or 'normal', fashions, first as the root of an augmented sixth and then as the ninth over the dominant (Example 3.7). There is a sense of control, of momentary repose in an image of beauty. The cadence subsides to a gentle *pianissimo*. Salome then recalls the beauties of Jochanaan's body in an extended passage in C sharp whose *dolce* tone shifts only when there is an interrupted cadence onto A (fig.337) as her recollections turn from his body to his voice. The A harmony is prolonged for eighteen bars (up to fig.339). By contrast with the controlled resolution of A at the preceding cadence, the treatment of this symbolic pitch now takes a more disturbing turn. When she states that she heard strange music in his voice A's potential function as the dominant of the dark Neapolitan D is highlighted, but it still ultimately resolves as the flat submediant of C sharp to the dominant G♯ (1 bar after fig. 339). Recalling her experience of hearing, she has transposed Jochanaan's strange music into her own key (C sharp). But degeneration follows. The function of C♯ as tonic starts to break down as she gasps, 'Ah! And why did you never look at me?' (fig.340). Salome's 'Ah' recalls her affirmative vocal exclamations at the preceding C sharp cadence.[37] Now we hear this cry's enervation. The progression (or, perhaps better, regression) which initiates this degradation dissolves the C sharp key to an A minor version of her entrance music, reached via a hint of F minor. The move from the contemplation of a recalled physical beauty to the disembodied voice has undermined the Apollonian control of the preceding cadence. The association of A with F minor occurs again at the switch in mood between the lines 'all the surging waters cannot quench the fire of my desire

---

[37] Kramer describes this as her 'most uninhibited cry', where Salome's 'perversity becomes regenerative': *Opera and Modern Culture*, 160.

Example 3.7 Strauss, *Salome*, Salome: 'Ah! Ah! Jochanaan'

and longing' and 'Oh! But why did you not look at me?' (figs.346–7). There is a return to C sharp, but the aborted cadence of figs.349–50 represents a more drastic subversion, evoking the Freudian *Unheimliche* as the familiar is alienated, the homely defamiliarized in its association with the dismembered, reanimated or dead body and the disturbing function of memory. When Salome sings the famous line 'and the secret of love is greater than the secret of death' the second-inversion triads are illusory and conflictual.[38]

After Herod's statement of the recurring and portentous line 'Something terrible will happen' an A–B♭ trill, previously heard after the end of Salome's dance, signals the start of the move to the second structural cadence in C sharp. Initially (from fig.359) Salome's music seems to mark a return to relative security. Instead of dissonant A♮s the expressive melodic motions over the dominant emphasize ecstatic A♯s. The cadence is climactic, euphoric and rapturous (Example 3.8). But degeneration once again follows, foreshadowed by the A–A♯ clashes (formed by echoes of the A–B♭ trills) in the subdominant harmony which preceded the dominant. After the perfect cadence harmonic symbols of Salome's 'Dionysian' body are debased at their moment of apparent supremacy.[39] The infamous dissonance which follows the first tonic C sharp chord is an explosively concentrated mixture of recollections. It contains the A major triad which recalls Salome's erotic image of the moon and also, if we hear the B♯ missing in the piano reduction, the A minor associated with the darker lunar imagery long ago expressed by the Page and so crucial in the degradation of the earlier 'tonic' C sharp cadence. There is functional doubleness: the lower part of the chord has a potential function not only as an augmented sixth in C sharp, but also as dominant seventh to the Neapolitan D minor (associated in the opera with Jewishness). The top-voice parallel thirds outline the D sharp/E flat minor triad of Jochanaan's beheading, the triad of death, and, through their coexistence with A, recall the A–E♭ juxtapositions at the climax of Salome's dance. The abundant and concentrated symbolism of this cadence also operates on the motivic level. As Example 3.9 demonstrates, both of Salome's C sharp cadences incorporate three statements of a descending motif (and in both the third is, significantly, given not to Salome's voice, but to the orchestra). In the first ending the first two statements of the motif combine to form a chromatically elaborated arpeggiation of the A–F♯–D♯–B♯ diminished seventh which forms the upper parts of the dominant minor ninth in C sharp. In the third,

---

[38] See Richard Cohn's analysis in 'Uncanny Resemblances', 285–323.

[39] Salome's dance can be interpreted as a representation of Dionysian madness and possession, excess and transgression. In Gustave Flaubert's 'Hérodias' (1877) Salome danced 'like the bacchantese of Lydia'; as Linda and Michael Hutcheon write, this confirms that 'pathology' is directly linked to 'hysteria' in the 'Dionysian dancing body' of the 'adolescent nymphomaniac'. See *Bodily Charm: Living Opera* (Lincoln: University of Nebraska Press, 2000), 90, 97, 102.

Example 3.8 Strauss, *Salome*, Salome: 'Allein was tut's?'

orchestral statement the motif resolves the A and B♯ to G♯ and C♯. In the second ending the first two motivic statements outline a dominant major ninth: there is no chromatic elaboration and the voice is granted resolution to C♯. These contribute to the cadence's sense of exultant rapture. But

Example 3.8 (cont.)

Example 3.9 Strauss, *Salome*, cadential motifs

comparison of the two endings shows that this resolution is premature. The function of the third, orchestral motivic statement is to deny this resolution: it is abruptly curtailed at Herod's signal for her crushing destruction. The third motif is incomplete, crushed at the point of reaching the abjectly unresolved A♮, the biting alternative to the ecstatic A♯ which had begun the motivic sequence. Salome's motivic figure of completion is fatally disfigured.

Salome's final cadence is especially cruel for its combination of the high and low in one moment. The violent interruption of the D minor 6–4 chord which heralds Herod's order is confirmation of the shadowy, Neapolitan implications embedded in the lower part of the 'bitonal' chord. The position of this element at the bottom of the preceding harmonic complex is a parallel to the low and debased position of that which it symbolizes in the cultural order.[40] Herod's top B♭ sounds so vicious because, combined with the underlying D minor chord, it forms a final, screeching version of the A–A♯/B♭ dissonance and sounds as a debasement of the ecstatic A♯s of Salome's last C sharp cadence. The D minor chord and dissonant B♭ of Herod's interjection identify him as a Jew through its recollection of the music of the quarrelling Jews which had interrupted the Page's and Narraboth's contemplative comparison of Salome with the moon in the opening scene. The sickening bitonal chord degrades Salome's bodily ecstasy through its underpinning with the dominant of this dark, diseased, perverted, Semitic key.

In differing ways Wilde and Strauss both attempt to sustain the dichotomy of the beatific and the bestial, of the Apollonian symbolic image formed in the reflective mode of the imagination and the Dionysian ecstatic body celebrated in the physical moment.[41] In the characteristic doubleness of the *femme fatale*, carnality is doubled by the spiritual, the physically real by the aestheticized symbolic. Both C sharp cadences are driven towards their contrasting endings by Salome recollecting. In the first, Salome reflects upon the beauty of Jochanaan's absent body; at the second she recalls, in the darkness ordered by Herod, the experience of

---

[40] See Sander Gilman, 'Strauss and the Pervert', in Arthur Groos and Roger Parker (eds.), *Reading Opera* (Princeton University Press, 1988), 306–27. On Strauss's characterization of Herod see also Frisch, *German Modernism*, 82–6.

[41] In Wilde Salome's last speech is delivered in darkness, thus by her disembodied voice: she has moved from her initial 'silent physicality' to occupy Jochanaan's position as 'invisible voice'. On her return to physical visibility she is then crushed by Herod's guards: she must die because she has transgressed from the physical into the spiritual without relinquishing the place of the body. See Amy Koritz, *Gendering Bodies/Performing Art: Dance and Literature in Early Twentieth-Century British Culture* (Ann Arbor: University of Michigan Press, 1995), 75–85.

kissing his decapitated head. The two endings together represent a move from beautiful memories into a paradoxical moment of abundant recollection and sublime forgetting. In these terms an understanding of Salome's contrasting cadences is greatly enhanced through comparison with Brünnhilde's two endings in the *Ring*, in which the second similarly transforms the calming character of the first into a Dionysian, physical, sublime moment of forgetfulness. Brünnhilde's cadences were, successively, marked by descent (declining to rest) followed by ascent (a reinvigorating leap). At her sacrificial death the symbolic repossession of Grane allowed her to be carried by the vigorous libidinal energies of the 'natural', animal world. The sacrilegious Salome has no such 'natural' regeneration. What carried her to the second cadence, the moment of bliss, was her 'unnatural' possession of a dead head. Salome's first cadence achieved a beautiful stillness which was doomed from the start. The second cadence marked her ascent to the moment of highest bliss, but again degeneration was always inevitable and was signalled by the chromatic 'abnormalities' which preceded it.

As the power of this second cadence continues to resonate the focus turns to Salome's own, now moonlit body. Here the diverse decadent symbolisms of moonlight – reflected and therefore light but not light, somehow unreal and artificial, deceptive, occult, pale, enigmatic and symbolically associated with the narcissistic or sterile woman – are brought into focus, lethally so for Salome.[42] In *Salome*'s final bars the function of the orchestra (which Kramer calls Strauss's 'phallic eye', the instrument for observing the female neurotic exhibited on stage) is of course to provide not a 'Wagnerian' *Verklärung* but rather a brutal and horrific slaying. Deathridge describes this 'fatal conclusion' as 'so obviously alien to Wagner's affirmative religion of redemption that the peremptory killing of the female protagonist to the sound of clattering brass must have surely been consciously intended as a negative image of the famous closing soliloquies of Isolde and Brünnhilde'.[43] The C minor key of this vengeful bludgeoning is especially dark – is it the flat tonic or the inverted Neapolitan of Salome's C sharp? The semitonal rush after Herod's command to kill Salome resembles the musical gesture at Hagen's killing of Siegfried. We might also hear Herod's vocal exclamation after Salome's second cadence as a parallel to Hagen's desperate call 'Give me the ring', the last vocal statement in the *Ring*. The rising tonal relationship between the C minor of Siegfried's funeral march followed by the D flat of

[42] On the moon and decadent symbolism, see Pynsent, *Decadence and Innovation*, 205–6.
[43] John Deathridge, *Wagner: Beyond Good and Evil* (Berkeley: University of California Press, 2007), 225.

Brünnhilde's immolation is reversed at the end of *Salome*. There is no orchestral, disembodied 'voice' to sing Salome's glory. The curtain falls as quickly as the shields do upon her body. Salome's fate is the brutally dark double of transfiguration.

The double Elektra

In a well-known essay, Lawrence Kramer grounds an interpretation of *Elektra* in an analysis of the *fin-de-siècle* 'culture of supremacism' – the separation of 'high' and 'low' through obsessive, highly refined, yet brutal systems of classification. Underlying this formation was a 'dualistic, not to say phobic, contrast between cultural progress and cultural regression, evolution and degeneration'. This is exemplified by texts such as Weininger's notorious *Sex and Character* (1903). For Kramer, it is crucial to read *Elektra* in a manner which 'unsparingly' reveals the opera's 'participation … in the cultural logic of supremacism, while at the same time realizing that this participation may be critical, revisionist, and transformative as well as compliant'. This ambiguity is focused on the compellingly repellent Elektra, who 'embodies all the physical and emotional anarchy that the ancestral order of culture exists to suppress. But she does so only as a consequence of her absolute devotion to that order, which she asserts with ferocious cadential authority at crucial moments'; she 'resists what she embodies and embodies what she resists'.[44] The structure of *Elektra* has commonly been read as double-framed.[45] Kramer notes that the opera takes feminine excess 'not only as a force to be framed but also as a form that frames'. This collapses the distinction between 'excess' and 'frame' (to use McClary's well-known terms[46]), but only to demand an 'outer frame of exceptional violence', one which seeks to 'recapture the usurped boundary'. The outer frame of 'Agamemnon' carries the burden of the principle of cultural supremacy and the image of an idealized masculine virility, the symbolic order of the father whom Elektra so profoundly mourns. By contrast, the 'inner frame' which is formed by the maids' scene and the Chrysothemis–Elektra duet leading to the latter's maenadic dance has 'undifferentiated femininity' as its substance, released as 'polymorphic energy' and

---

[44] Kramer, *Opera and Modern Culture*, 203.

[45] Bryan Gilliam notes outer and inner 'arch relationships' between scenes i and vii, and ii and vi; see *Richard Strauss's 'Elektra'* (Oxford University Press, 1991), 78.

[46] Susan McClary, 'Excess and Frame: The Musical Representation of Madwomen', in *Feminine Endings: Music, Gender, and Sexuality* (Minneapolis: University of Minnesota Press, 1991), 80–111.

then as 'jouissance'.[47] Kramer associates consonant triads with the paternal law of culture, and high levels of dissonance with deviance, abjection and transgression. This categorization works well for many passages, but there are crucial moments where this binary logic is dismantled as triads sound as though they have a 'dissonant', destabilizing or degenerate quality.

Within Kramer's frames of reference it is possible to plot further musical details which are symbolically associated with somatic degeneration and reanimation. Of particular importance is the symbolic association of F minor harmonies with bodily deformation, an aspect of the work which has received only passing comment in the literature. Early in the opera B minor and F minor triads soon become associated with Elektra's animalistic bodily movements. These harmonies are then revealed to be the sources of her famous 'polymorphic' chord and motif (see the passage between figs.1 and 2). Elektra's B–F motif is transformed by the cadence at the end of the maids' scene. The B minor triads become 6–4 of D, first major, then minor, resolving to V^7 of D. The F minor here sounds like a degrading intrusion in the D cadential progression, a hearing confirmed when the fifth maid subsequently sings 'They beat me' to a motif recalling F minor. Thus, in two ways, F minor subverts the cadence of the inner frame.[48] This harmony's moment of greatest symbolic import will come in the inner frame's corresponding sixth scene. But it also maintains a crucial role in the music between these two framing points.

Before continuing the degrading story of F minor, one important motivic association with Elektra's body needs recalling. When her groans and prostration are described we hear a chromatic version of the Agamemnon motif. Thus, as Wintle notes, psychological suffering – the trauma caused by her father's death – is related to the physical.[49] Thus, also, the paternal diatonic frame is weakened. This motivic version returns at a crucial moment in Elektra's monologue. As Kramer analyses it, the fulcrum of the monologue's own frame structure can be found between Elektra's cries of 'Agamemnon! Vater!' and 'Vater! Agamemnon!' Her

---

[47] Kramer, *Opera and Modern Culture*, 217.

[48] These symbolic harmonies form part of a symmetrical tonal structure: the B–F tritone and the D–Ab/G♯, which, from fig.32, becomes increasingly prominent and leads to the A flat of the return of the Elektra motif at her entrance (3 bars before fig.35).

[49] Wintle, 'Elektra and the "Elektra Complex"', in John (ed.), *Richard Strauss: Salome/Elektra*, 64–5. Abbate, for whom the significance of the opera's opening gesture is tied to Elektra's psychological state, writes: 'The thing for which the motive stands, in the classic semiotic sense, is not Agamemnon at all, but rather Elektra's voice; more specifically, the mourning lament that so strongly marks her existence': 'Elektra's Voice: Music and Language in Strauss's Opera', in Derrick Puffett (ed.), *Richard Strauss*: Elektra (Cambridge University Press, 1989), 111.

Example 3.10 Strauss, *Elektra*, Elektra: 'Allein! Weh, ganz allein'

second cry of the name (2 bars after fig.46) 'slips chromatically out of focus, marking Elektra's always implicit expulsion from the closed moral and mental order to which she is so compellingly devoted'.[50] This unfocusing is generated by the chromatic version of the Agamemnon motif which was previously heard at her moaning and physical prostration. The recurrence confirms the association of her expulsion with her bodily degradation. These symbolic harmonies and motifs inform musical expressions of degradation in other parts of Elektra's monologue. The music at Elektra's entrance is based on motivic inversion and tonal polymorphism. The character of the 'Elektra chord' has been much analysed, but it is also significant that the ascending G♭–G–A♭ which ends her motif is inverted by the *fortissimo* G♭–F–E which forms the end of the somatic, degraded, moaning version of the Agamemnon motif in the bass (2 bars after fig.35) – a motivic statement whose first three notes form the deathly E flat minor triad (see Example 3.10). B flat minor becomes firmly established with Elektra's first vocal statement of the Agamemnon motif, leading to a statement of the motif of her royal descent on the dominant, F. What follows is enormously subtle. The similarity between the motif of royal descent and that of Elektra's body is confirmed through its restatement in a phrase (3 bars before fig.38) which renews the association of B and F (see Example 3.11). The F major triads at this point have a clear tonal function as dominant of B flat minor. But this function is then degraded. Any potential Neapolitan function of B as enharmonic C♭ in B flat minor is also enfeebled. The motif of Agamemnon as father that emerges from this B minor (2 bars after fig.38) moves to F minor through a series of chords generating a top-voice statement of the F♯/G♭–G–A♭ motivic tag which had opened the monologue (recall Example 3.10). This

---

[50] Kramer, *Opera and Modern Culture*, 212–3.

Example 3.11 Strauss, *Elektra*, Elektra: 'Hast du nicht die Kraft ...'

F minor, following the tonally disruptive B minor, no longer carries a clear diatonic relationship to B flat minor. It is sustained, *ppp*, doom-laden and minatory. The symbolic status of F minor is thereby magnified. Later in the monologue the fateful progression at Elektra's blood-curdling 'And perish' ('und sterben') (2 bars before fig.52) also alludes to F minor through its dominant. A transposed Elektra chord is combined with the chromatically rising end of Elektra's motif at the original pitch (Gb–G–Ab) in the upper part, while its inversion, the chromatic tail of the degraded Agamemnon motif, forms the bass (D–Db–C; see Example 3.12). Elektra's

Example 3.12 Strauss, *Elektra*, Elektra: 'und sterben'

vocal line here is a chromatic degeneration of the C minor triads to which she twice has sung her father's name earlier in the monologue. The moment is extraordinary in its symbolic concentration. (The twisted echo of the fate motif from Wagner's *Ring* adds to its resonance.) There is also, through the passing augmented triads in the progression, a hint of the harmonies associated with Klytämnestra's sacrifices. Thus the dreadful familial tensions are finely embedded in a two-chord progression which, through the symbolism by now firmly attached to its primary diatonic function (V of F minor), focuses the whole horrible scenario on Elektra's degraded body.

B minor and F minor harmonies subsequently become associated with Klytämnestra's frenzy and terrible dreams. At Elektra's declaration that Klytämnestra must die (2 bars after fig.241) F minor harmony is sustained, in a moment of clarification and stasis, before the long lead-up to the climactic cadence of figs.258–9. As this famous climax is reached the dominant of C is not resolved but moves to the dominant of B, then sinks further to cadence in B flat (the key of Elektra's preceding description of her dance). Towards the end of the opera this cadence twice returns in significantly transformed versions. These will be considered shortly. For now it is important to note that the semitonal motifs G–F♯–F in the top part and (augmented and broken by rests) in the bass are curtailed versions of the chromatic tail of the 'debased' Agamemnon motif (see Example 3.13).[51]

The sixth scene further confirms the association of F minor with Elektra's degraded body, first at fig.70a at the setting of the line 'with my sad withered

---

[51] Gilliam notes that the 'double climax' reverses the move from B flat to C in the monologue – the 'apparent victory over her mother in this scene is short-lived': *Richard Strauss's 'Elektra'*, 92. For Arnold Whittall 'there could hardly be a more arresting image of the supreme confidence inseparable from intense instability': 'Dramatic Structure and Tonal Organisation', in Puffett (ed.), *Richard Strauss*: Elektra, 66.

Example 3.13 Strauss, *Elektra*, Elektra: 'jauchzt und kann sich seines Lebens freun!'

arms', which she sings to the chromatic moaning Agamemnon motif as she
moves to embrace a resistant Chrysothemis. Four bars after fig.136a, when
Orest questions Elektra's identity, the music turns to E major as he repeats
her name and gradually recognizes her, realizing that her terrible physical
state has deceived him. This prefigures the E major of her maenadic dance –
the revitalization of her withered body – but F minor returns as Elektra
implores him to 'leave my dress! Don't pierce me with your curious look'
(2 bars after 138a), the shift suggesting a symbolic opposition of F minor and
E major. At fig.144a, when Elektra cries out Orest's name in recognition,
dissonant new versions of the association of F and B harmonies usher in the
long orchestral passage towards the A flat major theme of familial belonging.
At 2 bars before fig.172a Elektra notices that Orest's body is quaking. Orest
answers that his limbs shake because he knows the path they must take. The
association of F and B minor is once more embedded here: Elektra sings of
her brother's quaking body in an enharmonically notated F minor, picking

out chromaticisms over the orchestra's V/V chord in B minor. Orest answers over B minor 6–4 hamony. But the expected B minor cadence is deflected. The passage leads to a return of the cadence of figs.258–9 (where Elektra predicted or demanded Klytämnestra's demise), and again the dominant of B deflects the prepared C to B flat (this time minor) as we move towards Klytämnestra's murder. After this confirmation of the symbolic attachment of F minor to bodily malfunction or degradation it is no surprise that although Aegisth's music is in F major (2 bars before fig.199a) and is marked 'comfortable' and 'strolling' (*behaglich schlendernd*) it is from the start imbued with F minor elements, reflecting his status in the symbolic order as the bodily degenerate homosexual. Significantly, the A♭ (the minor third of F) is shown to originate in Elektra's chord, which is played in a rhythmic version of her animal movements; thus she is once more somatically related to the degenerate contagion within the cultural order. (The expected B minor occurs at 1 bar after fig.200a. At Aegisth's murder, at fig. 213a, F minor is, inevitably, brutally reinforced.)

Chrysothemis's motif of greeting to Orest (4 bars before fig.221a) in E major is embellished in Elektra's famous and much analysed statement 'how should I not hear the music?' (3 bars after fig. 229a).[52] This leads to the first statement of the music which will accompany the maenadic dance. It is Elektra who must lead the dance, but she cries that she cannot, for the weight of the ocean presses on her limbs. E major has moved to the dominant of C, but this resolution is denied as the motif of greeting is transformed into a dissonant F minor setting (3 bars after fig.232a). Once more, then, this key is associated with Elektra's degraded body (here specifically described as heavy and graceless), and the music mirrors the motivic inversions heard in her entrance music as the motif of greeting is inverted in the bass (at fig.233a; see Example 3.14). Chrysothemis leads the music back through the principal keys of E and C, which will dominate the rest of the opera. F minor seems dismissed, but it returns as a passing shadow when Elektra declares, 'I was a blackened corpse among the living' (fig.240a). The dance in E major – the symbolic opposite of degenerate F minor – marks the moment of her reanimation, and the relationship of E and C, symbols of the 'bacchic and the victorious', is worked out in the rest of the final scene.[53]

---

[52] The most subtle analysis of the meaning of this moment comes from Abbate, 'Elektra's Voice', 107–27. Abbate demonstrates that this is music which Elektra not only hears, but also creates: it is 'a sonorous world which is her thought, loosed upon us' (109).

[53] Gilliam, *Richard Strauss's 'Elektra'*, 86, 102. For Gilliam the E major of the final scene symbolizes the 'bacchic impulse of cathartic celebration'. Gilliam sees the two-key scheme as identifying

Example 3.14 Strauss, *Elektra*, Elektra: 'Und ich kann nicht ...'

During the cadence of the inner 'feminine' frame there is another shock shift, this time to four bars of a *fortissimo* D major triad in second inversion (fig.254a). At first it is hard to make harmonic sense of this. Two bars before fig.253a E major had returned after a sustained stretch of tonal instability. After the D chords Chrysothemis cries out Elektra's name over the dominant of E (an act of naming which seeks to end or

two types of dance in the scene, the round dance and the maenadic: the first is one of social harmony, the second one of soloistic release or transcendence. Elektra sings of the round dance but this only takes place in her imagination; she is dancing the solo maenadic dance. Reflecting Elektra's 'Dionysian, passionate, or even erotic sensations', Strauss uses themes which share a 'rapid, upward surge' (68–9), but when it rises towards an expected peak it leads only to the downward plunges of her motif as a wild animal (fig.249a). This proceeds to music recalling the unstable passage from her monologue which led to the premonition of the dance (fig.57 onwards). At 2 bars before fig.253a E major returns with motifs from the monologue's dance of victory but this is short-lived. For Gilliam, the dance's final move away from E to C (the key which Gilliam identifies with the round dance) is the ultimate dissolution of the individual (226–7).

control the 'nameless' dance), but this apparent restoration lasts just two bars. The harmony now turns to the dominant seventh of D – which can be heard as a delayed resolution of the 'shock' 6–4 D major chord. Elektra now becomes motionless, staring at Chrysothemis; the seizures of her body are transferred to her psyche, and the moaning chromatic version of the Agamemnon motif is stretched out across three bars of this dominant. The dominant of D does not resolve, as Elektra tells her sister to dance, not speak, but moves to the dominant of C. The D cadence may, however, be a distant recollection of the cadence in the same key at the end of the maids' scene (the equivalent moment in the symmetrical inner frame), with the F minor interruption of that scene now replaced by the interruption of the dominant of E: the rapture of the Dionysian dance has momentarily usurped the place of the debased body in relation to the diatonic frame.

The opera's double frame structure demands two endings. The final cadence in the key of C is the second return of the cadence of figs.258–9 which reversed the process of deflecting from B flat to C in the monologue (from fig.60). In this final return there is also motivic inversion and retrograde (recalling the processes of the opening of the monologue). Chrysothemis's 'Orest!' (E♭–G–F♯) is an irregular retrograde of her 'Elektra!' at the cadence of figs.254a–255a; the emphasized G–F♯ is then reversed in the bass motion to the dominant of C (see Example 3.15). The close juxtaposition of the abbreviated Agamemnon motif (C–G–E♭) and the chromatic descending line is a broken reminder of this motif's moaning, somatic chromatic version. The association with bodily brokenness is further reflected by the cadence's recollection of the moment where Orest described his quaking limbs at the thought of the murderous deed ahead of him (5 bars after fig.172a), where the dominant of C was again deflected to B flat. But the main significant difference is the terrifyingly violent force of the final closure in C minor. Instead of the chromatic shift from the dominant of B to the dominant of B flat, the bass move from F♯ to G produces a quadruple suspension whose dissonant effect can be heard as a distant relative of the Elektra chord (both are types of dominant seventh formation over an alien bass note). Thus the cadence is replete with symbols of debasement. The degraded F minor does not return, for Elektra's body is now finally still. In its symbolic place lie the E flat minor chords, the dark and deathly sinking of her Dionysian E major. Finally, we recognize that the E flat minor and C chords at the end together form the shadow of the E and D♭ embedded in the Elektra chord. As with Salome's, Elektra's ending has been appointed to her from the opera's beginning.

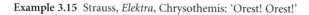

Example 3.15 Strauss, *Elektra*, Chrysothemis: 'Orest! Orest!'

Mann dismissed Strauss as a Wagnerian epigone. In the incomplete essay 'Mind and Art', whose notes were compiled in the year of the *Elektra* premiere (the opera was first performed in Dresden on 25 January 1909), Mann wrote: 'Wagner is still a burningly topical issue, a problem, the problem of modernism itself – and everything that has followed, including *Elektra*, seems uninteresting by comparison.'[54] In a letter of the same year he declared that 'Wagner's music is the ultimate in modernism. Nobody has ever gone beyond it. Strauss's so-called "progress" is all twaddle.'[55] But Mann's judgement can be countered by hearing the endings of *Salome* and *Elektra* as creatively ambivalent, redoubtably modern rewritings of Brünnhilde's double ending. And in them the forces of decay and degeneration play vitally stimulating roles. Towards the end of his famous 1933 essay 'The Sorrows and Grandeur of Richard Wagner' Mann contrasts Schiller drawing inspiration from the smell of rotten apples wafting from

[54] Mann, 'Mind and Art' [1909], in *Pro and Contra Wagner*, 41.
[55] Mann, letter to Walter Opitz, 26 August 1909, in *Pro and Contra Wagner*, 45.

the drawer of his writing desk with Wagner's preferred composing garb of 'silk dressing gowns'. Both are, Mann states, examples of 'standard artistic pathology, bizarre but innocuous'. For Mann, the difference lies in the fact that Schiller's work 'contains no hint of the rotten apples whose odour of decay so stimulated him. But who can fail to see that Wagner's satins are in some way still there in the finished work?'[56] But there can also be no doubt that in Wagner's work the voluptuous and sensuous musical 'fabric' can reek of the putrid aroma of golden apples gone bad. Strauss pursued this paradox into decadent territories only partially imagined by Wagner.

[56] Mann, 'The Sorrows and Grandeur of Richard Wagner', 136–7.

4 | Deformation and dissolution

> a tidal wave of intoxicating, poisonous colour and drunken, sucking
> perfume overwhelmed him ...
>
> Stanisław Przybyszewski, *Androgyne* (Berlin, 1906)

> To sink – first everything had to sink, to flicker out, to be extinguished.
>
> Hermann Bahr, *The School of Love* (Berlin, 1890)

Introduction

In *The Joyful Wisdom* Nietzsche established the difference between
Dionysian and romantic suffering:

What is romanticism? Every art, every philosophy may be viewed as a healing and a
helping application in the service of growing, struggling life: they always presup-
pose suffering and sufferers. But there are two kinds of sufferers: on the one hand,
those who suffer from overflowing *vitality*, who need Dionysian art, and require a
tragic view and insight into life; and on the other hand those who suffer from
reduced vitality, who seek repose, quietness, calm seas, and deliverance from
themselves through art or knowledge, or else intoxication, spasm, bewilderment
and madness. All romanticism in art and knowledge responds to the twofold
craving of the *latter*; to them both Schopenhauer as well as Wagner responded
(and responds) ...[1]

As he later explained in *The Case of Wagner*, though Wagner initially
pursued a revolutionary course, 'his ship struck a reef; Wagner was stuck.
The reef was Schopenhauer's philosophy.' Wagner became 'ashamed' of
the 'optimism' that he had 'transposed into music'. Schopenhauer, the
'philosopher of decadence', became Wagner's redemption.[2] Brünnhilde's
double ending to the *Ring* cycle was based on degenerating and regenerating forces, on a polarity comparable with those described by Nietzsche
in the passage in *The Joyful Wisdom*. Nietzsche might have heard the rest

---

[1] Friedrich Nietzsche, *The Joyful Wisdom*, trans. Thomas Common (New York: Frederick Ungar,
1960), section 370, 332–3.
[2] Nietzsche, *The Case of Wagner*, 160, 163–4.

which Brünnhilde grants the gods in her first ending as correlating with the 'deliverance' found in 'calm seas', and her second ending – one of vitality and wonder, with its performative sense of immediacy and forgetting at the moment of plunging into the fire to reunite with Siegfried – as evoking 'intoxication, spasm, bewilderment and madness'. Nietzsche's metaphors – the contrast between overflowing and tranquil waters, Wagner's creative development as a voyage across perilous seas – are striking. This chapter takes these images as the spur for considering how, in a context of cultural preoccupation with 'endings', in a post-Darwinian evolutionary world and in the age of a theory of musical 'energetics', the developmental dynamism imputed to the romantic metaphor of the musical 'wave' is subjected to formal interrogation driven by the counterforce of decadent devitalization. The musical wave form assumed special significance at Austro-German music's highest 'moment' (of immanent apparent decline) and has a clear relationship with the structural importance placed on the *Höhepunkt*, the moment of greatest intensification (*Steigerung*) which also marks the beginning of inevitable weakening. Recall Barrès: 'At the height of the waves to which *Tristan* bears us let us recognise that pestilence which rises from the lagoons at night.'[3] Wave 'deformations' were powerful strategies and metaphors as cultural anxieties became manifest in the resistance or desired countering to perceived forces of degeneration and stagnation, or, by contrast, in the exploration of the attractions of decay and dissolution.[4]

Romantic wave form and energetics

Karol Berger has noted that through the cultural impact of European industrial progress and the political repercussions of the French Revolution a radical temporalization in all domains of knowledge occurred around 1800. Progressive or revolutionary narratives of secular universal history became definitive of modernity.[5] The corollary of this progressive

---

[3] Barrès, *Amori et dolori sacrum* (1902), trans. in Furness, *Wagner and Literature*, 49.

[4] I also explore this topic in 'Modern Maritime Pastoral: Wave Deformations in the Music of Frank Bridge', in Matthew Riley and Paul Rodmell (eds.), *British Music and Modernism 1895–1960* (Aldershot: Ashgate, forthcoming).

[5] Karol Berger, 'Time's Arrow and the Advent of Musical Modernity', in Karol Berger and Anthony Newcomb (eds.), *Music and the Aesthetics of Modernity* (Cambridge, Mass.: Harvard University Press, 2005), 3–22. This is of course not to deny that temporal order and signs of beginning, middle and end were not crucial in eighteenth-century music. Kofi Agawu's 'introversive semiosis' of the 'dynamic quality of Classic music', of its 'sense of directed motion', reminds us of the Kapellmeister of Mattheson's *Der vollkommene Capellmeister* (1739) who

view was the fear of decay or decline. In this cultural context, and given
E. T. A. Hoffmann's famous and influential proclamation that music's only
subject is 'infinity', it is unsurprising that 'endings' are frequently problematic in romantic and post-romantic music.[6] The burden placed on the 'end'
was intensified by romantic preoccupations with becoming and 'endless
longing', the Hegelian dialectic, dynamic historical progress and utopian
fantasies of revolutionary transformations. The problem was further compounded by an aesthetic in which the demands of teleology and nostalgia
pull in opposite directions, where completion and fulfilment are therefore
repeatedly deferred, and the meaning of events is apparently defined only
by self-fulfilling, goal-directed impulses, or (as in Goethe's organic view of
form) where polarities and intensification (*Steigerung*) engage in a restless
striving toward higher synthetic levels. The romantic obsession with tragic,
fateful destinies, recovered memories or the yearning for blissful or restful
redemption (*Erlösung*), which Nietzsche famously saw as the decadent basis
of all Wagner's work,[7] seem immanently ripe for their own undoing.

Writing in 1810 on the effect of the coda to the first movement of
Beethoven's Fifth Symphony, E. T. A. Hoffmann described an 'irresistible
surge – a swelling torrent whose waves break higher and higher'.[8] Wagner,
in *The Art-Work of the Future* (1849), described Beethoven's music as based
on processes of continuous intensification. Writing of the 'Bacchanalian'
Seventh Symphony he described the composer as embarking on a stormy
voyage with his direction navigated not homewards but towards the
beyond, in a testing of limits on the sea of insatiable longing. Scriabin
conceived his large-scale works in terms of waves. As Boris de Schloezer
recollected, Scriabin's works 'represented to him a series of gradual expansions, systematically and logically evolving in the direction of a final

considered rhetorical power to be determined by the order of presenting ideas; tellingly, in his
own compositional process, Mattheson worries most about the end, and in fact he says he
'usually begins at the end': V. Kofi Agawu, *Playing with Signs: A Semiotic Investigation of Classic
Music* (Princeton University Press, 1991), 51–2, 68. The difference lies in nineteenth-century
music's heightened questioning of closure, manifest, for example, in the romantic fragment, in
the aesthetic of incompleteness and in the pervading expression of endless yearning (*Sehnsucht*).

[6] It is important to remember that closure, or the 'sense of an ending', is a process or effect which
may be repeatedly invoked, subverted, interrupted, intermittent or perpetuated, and a structure
is typically based on closing gestures which exist in hierarchic relationships; see for example
V. Kofi Agawu, 'Concepts of Closure and Chopin's Op.28', *Music Theory Spectrum* 9 (1987),
1–17. In most scenarios closural gestures at or towards the 'end' are likely to bear the most
profound structural and expressive burden.

[7] See Nietzsche, *The Case of Wagner*, 160.

[8] E. T. A. Hoffmann, review of Beethoven, Symphony No.5, *Allgemeine Musikalische Zeitung*, 4 and
11 July 1810, trans. in Ian Bent (ed.), *Music Analysis in the Nineteenth Century*, vol.II:
Hermeneutic Approaches (Cambridge University Press, 1994), 152.

ecstasy … This outline is basically simple; it is built on a series of upswings, with each successive wave rising higher and higher toward a final effort, liberation and ecstasy.'[9] These famous and influential descriptions allow us to invoke wave forms as a paradigmatic metaphor in musical romanticism's aesthetics of the sublime. In musical waves the height of expression is followed by an end which might be felt as a decline or disintegration as much as a resolution of tension.[10] In romantic musical forms the wave is one of several familiar models where the emphasis on the end often coexists with its potential unravelling. Its relationship to Beethovenian and post-Beethovenian end-weighted form, with the coda marked as culmination or apotheosis, after the example of the *Eroica*, the Fifth Symphony and several late works,[11] and to narratives of redemption, erotic union or transfiguration figured in gendered terms,[12] is clear. The legacy of both these models for Wagner's conception of music and drama is, of course, crucial. Wagner also employed the wave as a metaphorical figure for the inspirational source of sublime musical creation. In his famous description of the dream inspiration for the depiction of the waves in the opening of *Rhinegold* Wagner transforms the natural image into a metaphor for the creation of the world and the process of evolution.

I sank into a kind of somnambulistic state, in which I suddenly had the feeling of being immersed in rapidly flowing water … I awoke in sudden terror from this trance, feeling as though the waves were crashing high above my head. I recognized at once that the orchestral prelude to *Das Rheingold* … had at last been revealed; and I also saw immediately precisely how it was with me: the vital flood would come from within me, and not from without.[13]

[9] Schloezer, *Scriabin: Artist and Mystic*, 97.

[10] For Wagner, Beethoven's anchor, of course, was the word in the finale of the Ninth Symphony, and in *Opera and Drama* Wagner pursued metaphorical descriptions in which fluid, feminine musical formlessness is redeemed by logical, masculine poetic order.

[11] As Maynard Solomon reminds us, Beethoven was often obsessively preoccupied with revising endings, a creative predicament that reflected his scepticism of monumental, affirmative closure, exposing a contra-teleological impulse, an acknowledgment of non-inevitablilty, of the existence of multiple possible 'solutions', some unrealized, of perpetual openness. In certain late works there is an especially intense elaboration of multiple images of endings, without the fear of disintegration being permanently assuaged; see Solomon, 'Beethoven's Ninth Symphony: The Sense of an Ending', *Critical Inquiry* 17 (1991), 289–305.

[12] See James Hepokoski's discussion of what he calls the 'Dutchman model', after the structure and expressive content of Wagner's *Flying Dutchman* overture: 'Masculine–Feminine', 494–9.

[13] Richard Wagner, *My Life*, trans. Andrew Gray, ed. Mary Whittall (Cambridge University Press, 1983), 499. The account was dictated in 1869. On the problems and interpretative issues raised by Wagner's description see Warren Darcy, '*Creatio ex nihilo*: The Genesis, Structure, and Meaning of the *Rheingold* Prelude', *19th-Century Music* 13 (1989), 79–100.

The wave's decline, the falling motif predicting the end of the gods, stands for the corruption of this generative form and process.

Form primarily conceived as the product of becoming, dynamic process and teleology led Ernst Kurth in his writings on Wagner and Bruckner to consider 'intensifying waves' as the 'basic formal principle'. These waves were generated by dynamic impulses of the will towards motion, the 'internal energetic will of surging undercurrent'.[14] Kurth's ideas were part of a wider discourse of dynamism and musical 'energetics' in the early twentieth century. This discourse turned against positivism towards neo-romantic psychologism and considered sensual material as moving into spiritual content, with cultural meaning imparted to 'natural' forms as part of the mediation between inner and outer worlds.[15] In his *Musical Form* (begun in 1911) Hugo Leichtentritt stated that in the Prelude to Act 1 of *Tristan and Isolde* 'surging and ebbing motion … is the real dominating motif of the entire structure'. Leichtentritt represented this by drawing a 'curve of intensity', a formal chart for the Prelude constructed as a visualization in waves.[16] This wave-like intensification and subsidence can be heard not only in Wagner's music, but also in the prose style in Wagner's programme for the concert version. After a summary of the dramatic theme, Wagner presents his characterization of the compositional response:

Here in music's own unrestricted element, the musician who chose this theme for the introduction to his drama of love, could have but one care: how to impose restraint upon himself since exhaustion of the subject is impossible. So just once, in one long-articulated impulse, he let that insatiable longing swell up from the timidest avowal of the most delicate attraction, through anxious sighs, hopes and fears, laments and wishes, raptures and torments, to the mightiest onset and to the most powerful effort to find the breach that will reveal to the infinitely craving heart the path into the sea of love's endless rapture. In vain! Its power spent, the heart sinks back to languish in longing …[17]

---

[14] Ernst Kurth, *Romantische Harmonik und ihre Krise in Wagners 'Tristan'* (1920); *Bruckner* (1925). For translations of passages from these two works see Lee A. Rothfarb (ed. and trans.), *Ernst Kurth: Selected Writings* (Cambridge University Press, 1991), 99–147 (*Romantische Harmonik*) and 151–207 (*Bruckner*).

[15] See Lee A. Rothfarb, 'Hermeneutics and Energetics: Analytical Alternatives in the Early 1900s', *Journal of Music Theory* 36 (1992), 43–68; and 'Energetics', in Thomas Christensen (ed.), *The Cambridge History of Western Music Theory* (Cambridge University Press, 2002), 927–55.

[16] Hugo Leichtentritt, *Musical Form* (Cambridge, Mass.: Harvard University Press, 1951), 357. Robert P. Morgan identifies cycles of material which generate an 'initial build-up', 'climactic plateau' and 'dissolution' through processes of intensification and overlaps of units: 'Circular Form in the "Tristan" Prelude', *Journal of the American Musicological Society* 53 (2000), 69–103.

[17] Wagner, programme note for the Prelude (with concert ending), trans. in Robert Bailey (ed.), *Wagner: Prelude and Transfiguration from 'Tristan and Isolde'* (New York: Norton, 1985), 47.

The length of sentences is carefully controlled to generate a curve of intensity building a single sentence from 'one long-articulated impulse' to the moment of 'endless rapture', only to collapse, 'its power spent', into short, fragmented statements.

Waves play a number of symbolic roles in *Tristan and Isolde*. In her first long solo passage in the drama, 'Entartet Geschlecht' (Act 1 scene i), Isolde rails against the degeneration of her mother's powers to control and move the waves. The scene begins with the G–A♭ motif in C minor, recalling the 5–♭6 chromatic relationship which controlled the Prelude's final decay into C minor. With a wild gaze she cries out for the regeneration of the power to stir the dreaming sea, so as to destroy the boat on which she travels to her unhappy destiny.[18] The 'waves' which engulf Isolde at the climactic end of her Transfiguration contrast with the preceding unfulfilled state of sinking into deeper yearning, which seem to confirm the 'fluidity' of libinal desire.[19] These final waves evoke a musical expression of drowning into the absolute, in 'an intoxicating sea of melody' which submerges Isolde's voice.[20] When heard in succession with the concert version of the Act 1 Prelude, the Transfiguration is heard as an ecstatic countering of the Prelude's last declining wave. Inevitably, the 'oceanic' effect of this music recalls Nietzsche's critique of the aims of 'endless melody', where, he said, 'one walks into the sea, gradually loses one's secure footing, and finally surrenders oneself to the elements without reservation: one must *swim*'. In the kind of movement evoked by these waves Nietzsche argued that Wagner 'overthrew the physiological presupposition of previous music. Swimming, floating – no longer walking and dancing.'[21] Postmortem, Isolde's body floats into an oceanic abyss, on waves of nervous intoxication. On hearing this music, even only in piano reduction, Ferdinand van Saar wrote of its cruel seas: 'The most violent attack on human nerves known to music developed out of vivid, trembling waves of sound, in gradual intensifications that are cruelly lustful, continually rising and retreating.'[22]

The Kurthian wave model focuses on melodic shape. As Christopher Wintle has demonstrated, a note by Schoenberg on processes of *Steigerung* promises application of the principle to all musical dimensions. The curve of

---

[18] For further commentary on this passage see Grey, 'Wagner the Degenerate', 73–92.
[19] See the analysis of the Act 2 love duet in Kramer, 'Musical Form and *Fin-de-Siècle* Sexuality', in *Music as Cultural Practice*, 135–75.
[20] See Deathridge, *Wagner*, 133–55.   [21] Nietzsche, *Nietzsche contra Wagner*, 666.
[22] Ferdinand van Saar, *Geschichte eines Wiener Kindes* [1879], quoted in Karen Painter, 'The Sensuality of Timbre: Responses to Mahler and Modernity at the *Fin de Siècle*', *19th-Century Music* 18 (1995), 238, n.9.

the melodic arch works with other pulsations and dynamics. Analysis of multiple parameters operating within the basic wave morphology of *Steigerung*, *Höhepunkt* and *Auflösung* leads to fuller understanding of the complexity of forces simultaneously working, in a sort of dynamic counterpoint, towards intensification or liquidation.[23] The interaction of wave forms with traditional formal models also requires consideration. When wave form is placed in the context of traditional *Formenlehre* models, sonata form seems to offer the most powerful example. There have been discussions of nineteenth-century sonata first movements which suggest the confluence of these two formal models. Leonard B. Meyer's well-known discussion of 'emergent structures' based on 'statistical processes' which override the 'syntactic structure' leading to changes in the structure of sonata form movements also suggests the workings of wave form and energetics.[24] Nonetheless, the significance of wave forms and deformations in sonata forms of the modernist period remains little discussed.

In a Wagnerian or post-Wagnerian context the notion of wave dynamics immediately brings to mind Alfred Lorenz's discussion of bar forms, with the *Abgesang* as an intensification dynamically generated from the preceding *Stollen*, and a climax positioned within the form at the turning from *Stollen* into *Abgesang*, whose close represents a decline in dynamic energy.[25] In his description of the bar form at the start of *Tannhäuser*, Act 2 scene ii, Adorno noted that the 'expansive gesture' of the *Abgesang* has a subsidence 'like the collapse of a wave'. Adorno, of course, considered Wagner's use of wave forms to be failed attempts at resolution or synthesis, as a simulated unity of the internally expressive and externally gestural and a negation of the flow of 'symphonic' musical time. Adorno, furthermore, denounced Wagner's music as based upon static repetitions of immutable gestures, as abandoning the masterful struggle with the temporal framework which he heard in musical 'symphonic' process. It also therefore inadequately dealt with the 'end': Wagner's music 'acts as if

[23] Christopher Wintle, 'On Intensification ("Was ist Steigerung")', in *All the Gods: Benjamin Britten's 'Night-Piece' in Context* (London: Plumbago, 2006), 103–5.

[24] Leonard B. Meyer, *Style and Music: Theory, History and Ideology* (Philadelphia: University of Pennsylvania Press, 1989), 198.

[25] Alfred Lorenz, *Das Geheimnis der Form bei Richard Wagner* (Berlin: Max Hesse, 1924–33). Criticisms of Lorenz have of course been legion, but some are rather telling in the context of this chapter: for Rudolf von Tobel, for example, bar form was the 'principal type of dynamic process' and Lorenz's theory was not sufficiently dynamic; see *Die Formwelt der klassischen Instrumentalmusik* (Bern and Leipzig: Paul Haupt, 1935), quoted and discussed by Stephen McClatchie, *Analyzing Wagner's Operas: Alfred Lorenz and German Nationalist Ideology* (University of Rochester Press, 1998), 170.

time had no end', in a 'negation of the flow of time'.[26] But as will become clear, the 'wave' becomes a primary feature of 'symphonic' process in the Wagnerian and post-Wagnerian style precisely because of its expressive and structural potential to generate development towards a long-postponed but long-anticipated 'end'. For Wagner the 'symphonic' suggested both an endless spinning-out of motifs and organic interconnection where everything evolves towards the final moment.[27] So the double character of the 'symphonic' (endless process, end-directed cohesiveness) redoubles the problem of the convincing ending. Impossibly utopian longing places an impossibly heavy structural and affective burden on supposedly 'symphonic' endings.

The most recent analysis of Wagnerian bar form has come from Matthew BaileyShea, who analyses its relationship to the similarly structured sentence. As he notes, there are subtle differences between the sentence's liquidation or dissolution and the *Abgesang*'s characteristic intensification and 'emotional discharge', but he identifies a common 'wave-like contour' as the first 'notable characteristic' of the Wagnerian *Satz*. His hermeneutic reading of the Prelude to *Tristan* Act 3 is especially provocative. The Prelude's presentation of a diatonic version of the desire motif from the Prelude to Act 1 'exudes both physical and emotional despair, an exhausted attempt to ascend out of the realm of "der Welten Nacht"' (see Example 4.1). As a musical parallel to the enfeebled physical condition of the wounded Tristan, this material is repeated exactly 'before being released into its weak, fading ascent', a treatment in marked contrast with the chromatic energetics and the upward sequences of the opening section of the Prelude to Act 1. BaileyShea also hears the gesture as an 'ironic antithesis' of the Beethovenian sentence, one where 'the strength of assertion … is displaced with desperation and weakness'.[28] The 'source' of this motif is of course the Wesendonck song 'Im Treibhaus'. Through its poetic content and musical continuation, this song presents an even clearer image of the final decadent fate of wave form as the waters vaporize in the debilitating heat and condense into precariously heavy drops about to meet their demise:

---

[26] Adorno, *In Search of Wagner*, 29–33.

[27] See Carolyn Abbate, 'Opera as Symphony: A Wagnerian Myth', in Carolyn Abbate and Roger Parker (eds.), *Analyzing Opera: Verdi and Wagner* (Berkeley: University of California Press, 1989), 115.

[28] Matthew BaileyShea, 'The Wagnerian *Satz*: The Rhetoric of the Sentence in Wagner's Post-*Lohengrin* Operas', unpublished PhD thesis, Yale University, 2003, 77, 88, 91–7.

Example 4.1 Wagner, *Tristan and Isolde*, Prelude to Act 3, bars 1–15

Stille wird's, ein säuselnd Weben
füllet bang den dunklen Raum:
schwere Tropfen seh' ich schweben
an der Blätter grünem Saum.

It still grows, a rustling movement
timidly fills the dark room.
I see heavy drops hanging
on the green fringe of the leaves.

Wagner's microscopic musical drips towards the end of the song (D–E♭ semitone moving to D–E♮) are the chromatic surges of the intensive style reduced to the most condensed miniature residue, drained of all their energies in the artificial heat of the greenhouse (Example 4.2).

Recognition of wave forms has not, of course, been confined to the music of Wagner and Bruckner. Kofi Agawu, writing on Schumann, considered a narrative or dynamic curve structured around a highpoint to be an archetypal pattern, 'the most consistent principle of formal structure in nineteenth-century music'. Agawu describes modifications of the basic model in terms of withholdings, truncations and extensions of the normative curve, which he posits as a 'biological or Darwinian model'.[29] But the works of Schumann and Bruckner also exemplify the imminent and immanent tendency of waves to collapse, dissolve, degenerate or

---

[29] Kofi Agawu, 'Structural Highpoints in Schumann's *Dichterliebe*', *Music Analysis* 3 (1984), 159.

Example 4.2 Wagner, 'Im Treibhaus' (Wesendonck), ending

disintegrate.[30] For Charles Rosen, 'the music of Schumann in particular …
comes in a series of waves, and the climax is generally reserved for the
moment before exhaustion'.[31] Elsewhere Rosen writes: 'Schumann's radical innovation was a new large sense of rhythm conceived as a series of
waves of energy, crucial to later composers like Wagner and Strauss'.[32]
Writing of the *Fantasie*, Op.17, Rosen pinpoints the difference from
classical sonata forms:

the structure is like a series of waves, starting with the climax, losing momentum each
time, and then beginning again. Except in the slower middle section, the music does
not build to a climax; on the contrary, it continually threatens to collapse, to split into
pieces – and does in fact break down gradually starting at bar 70, into a series of
fragments … It is only with difficulty that the movement recovers its life in the
extraordinary syncopations that follow and that destroy the clarity of the beat.[33]

---

[30] We can also hear this in Timothy Jackson's identifications of 'crystallization' and its
catastrophic double, entropy, in nineteenth-century formal structures with their build-up to the
highpoint, the sublime, awesome moment succeeded by an attempt at restoring formal
equilibrium and ordered representation at the cadence, an ending which may sound either
replete or empty: 'Observations on Crystallization and Entropy in the Music of Sibelius and
Other Composers', in Timothy Jackson and Viejo Murtomäki (eds.), *Sibelius Studies*
(Cambridge University Press, 2001), 176–9.

[31] Charles Rosen, *The Classical Style* (London: Faber, 1971), 453.

[32] Charles Rosen, *The Romantic Generation* (London: HarperCollins, 1995), 110.

[33] Rosen, *The Romantic Generation*, 109.

The processes of wave decline and dissolution may have been a crucial source of the 'unhealthiness' which informs parts of the reception of Schumann. Adorno, for example, wrote that 'the way end of the C Major Fantasy opens into infinity, yet without transfiguring itself to the point of redemption … anticipates the innermost essence of Berg's tone', that which is *contra* the affirmative and healthy, expressing a 'partiality for the weaker, the defeated'.[34]

The energetic highpoint is the moment which precedes inevitable demise, weakening or structural crumbling. Romantic utopianism is heard riding the wave towards self-destruction. In the Adagio of Bruckner's Seventh Symphony wave forms promise redemption (*Erlösung*) through elegiac expression in the 'afterwave' of the composer's foreboding of Wagner's imminent death.[35] These waves are features generated by *Steigerung*, which critics heard as a feature of the 'echt symphonisch'. Paul Marsop, for example, in his review of Bruckner's Seventh considered the work to be a public, 'manly', monumental post-Beethovenian sublime statement, by contrast with Schumannian aphoristic beauty, which was expressed in the piano or chamber sensibility of private sorrows (a sensibility which he also attached to Brahms).[36] However, Bruckner's Adagio is an example of the romantic or modern form of elegy, which, as we saw in Chapter 2, while characteristically seeking a 'breakthrough' rather than wave-like 'breakdown', is an approach towards silence, absence and the unspeakable.[37] The sinking of the modern wave confirms the fatal problematization of monumental apotheosis. The many post-1840 statements concerning melancholy in connection with frustrated experiences of the sublime are manifestly related to the susceptibility to crisis or resignation expressed in the wave forms found in late romantic symphonic Adagios and finales.[38]

---

[34] Theodor Adorno, *Alban Berg: Master of the Smallest Link*, trans. Juliane Brand and Christopher Hailey (Cambridge University Press, 1991), 5.

[35] Stephen Parkany, 'Kurth's *Bruckner* and the Adagio of the Seventh Symphony', *19th-Century Music* 11 (1988), 262–81.

[36] See Margaret Notley, '"Volksconcerte" in Vienna and the Late Nineteenth-Century Ideology of the Symphony', *Journal of the American Musicological Society* 50 (1997), 421–53.

[37] See Shaw, *Elegy and Paradox*.

[38] The fourth movement of Brahms's Third Symphony is a much discussed example. See Andreas Eichhorn, 'Melancholie und das Monumentale: Zur Krise des symphonischen Finaldenkens im 19. Jahrhundert', *Musica* 46/1 (1992), 9–12. On the ambiguities in the critique of Beethovenian heroism which the symphony invokes see Susan McClary, 'Narrative Agendas in "Absolute Music": Identity and Difference in Brahms's Third Symphony', in Ruth Solie (ed.), *Musicology and Difference* (Berkeley: University of California Press, 1993), 326–44.

As James Hepokoski states, a compositional response of the modern generation born around 1860 to the 'recently reified or crystallized' Wagnerian musical idiom was the exploration of 'deformations' of traditional formal structures and narrative processes, some of which are already found in the late works of the previous generation.[39] Deformations of wave forms are an important category within this modern project, but one that, by comparison with analyses of deformations of sonata, rondo or periodic forms, has been little discussed. In Hepokoski and Darcy's definition 'deformation' is 'the stretching of a normative procedure to its maximally expected limits or even beyond them – or the overriding of that norm altogether in order to produce a calculated expressive effect. It is precisely the strain, the distortion of the norm (elegantly? beautifully? wittily? cleverly? stormily? despairingly? shockingly?) for which the composer strives at the deformational moment.' These authors are very concerned to distance 'deformation' from the negative associations of the term 'deformed', and as they rightly clarify, deformation as departure from the established formal norm is an expected dimension of the 'art' work. It is a sign of an 'aesthetic health and integrity'.[40] But in an decadent aesthetic such negativity becomes pervasively and perversely attractive as a critique of bourgeois aesthetics of Ideal or stellar aspiration. The mid-nineteenth-century rise of the wave form as a 'norm' or archetype was coincident with the 'upsurge' of *Formenlehre*, which, as Joseph Straus has recently highlighted, was itself contemporaneous with the 'invention' of a modern language for the discussion and definition of norm and abnorm, for example, of physical and psychological health and their opposites, disability and deviance. The reified musical formal norms were described in terms of 'containment', 'balance', organic growth and vital energy in a theory often derived from illustrations of the 'heroic' music of Beethoven.[41] Decadence, with its delight in derangement, atrophy and abandon, offered a potent challenge to these formal traditions. Similarly, the dynamics, energetics and proportions of 'normal' wave forms emerged in the formal theories of the modernist period, with emphasis on post-Darwinian evolutionary notions, on musical form as a metaphor for, or expression of life's struggles to, higher, stronger forms. The 'abnormal'

---

[39] James Hepokoski, 'Introduction: Sibelius and the Problem of "Modernism"', in *Sibelius: Symphony No.5* (Cambridge University Press, 1993), 1–18. See also Warren Darcy, 'Bruckner's Sonata Deformations', in Timothy L. Jackson and Paul Hawkshaw (eds.), *Bruckner Studies* (Cambridge University Press, 1997), 256–77.

[40] James Hepokoski and Warren Darcy, *Elements of Sonata Theory: Norms, Types, and Deformations in the Late-Eighteenth-Century Sonata* (Oxford University Press, 2006), 617.

[41] Joseph Straus, 'Normalizing the Abnorm: Disability in Music and Music Theory', *Journal of the American Musicological Society* 59 (2006), 126–36.

converse, equally reified, evoked physical degeneration and psychological derangement. This was codified by modern sexual science (e.g. in the work of Krafft-Ebing), contextualized by the rise of cultural pessimism and internalized by the modern sciences of the mind, especially, of course, as formulated by Morel in the mid-nineteenth century and Freudian psychoanalysis at the beginning of the twentieth. In all these dimensions, wave deformations can express the trauma and tragedy of the modern existential crisis.

The following sections describe how hierarchically organized, multiparametric wave deformations, those musical structures and expressive strategies which evoke decadent preoccupations, can be heard in Austrian and German music from the first decade of the twentieth century. In Strauss's *Salome* (1903–5), the finale of Mahler's Sixth Symphony (1903–4), Berg's Piano Sonata, Op.1 (1907–8), and the Count's ballad from Act 2 scene vi of Schreker's *Der ferne Klang* (completed in 1910) manipulations, transformations, obliterations and imitations of wave deformation reveal defining aspects of style and aesthetic. (In Chapter 5 Schoenberg's *Herzgewächse*, Op.20 (1911), will be seen to trace an inversion of the wave form, beginning with decadent descent and, at its mid-point, turning to regenerative ascent.)

Intensification and dissolution: a wave deformation in Strauss's *Salome*

Salome is famous for its provocative stylistic conflict. This has been identified, for example, in the apparent opposition between Strauss's vivid, realistic musical revelation and Wilde's veiled, symbolist, poetic concealment. This complex and unresolved paradox of tone is surely a factor in the disparate aesthetic responses to the opera.[42] Vivid depictions and complex characterization within this aesthetic diversity raise ambivalent reactions towards the central figure of Salome, the embodiment and voice of the most favoured *femme fatale* of the *fin de siècle*. Much of the recent critical and hermeneutic work on the opera has invoked 'decadence' or related terms.[43] Decadence

---

[42] Banks, 'Richard Strauss and the Unveiling of "Salome"', 21. Strauss's strategies of stylistic veiling and musical fancy dress have received much comment. On the adoption of multiple Bavarian and Viennese stylistic guises see Robin Holloway, '*Salome*: Art or Kitsch?', in Derrick Puffett (ed.), *Richard Strauss*: Salome (Cambridge University Press, 1989), 145–60; see also Leon Botstein, 'The Enigmas of Richard Strauss: A Revisionist View', in Bryan Gilliam (ed.), *Richard Strauss and his World* (Princeton University Press, 1992), 6–7.

[43] See, for example, Hutcheon and Hutcheon, *Bodily Charm*; Gilman, 'Strauss and the Pervert'; Kramer, *Opera and Modern Culture*; Stefan Wurz, *Kundry, Salome, Lulu: Femmes fatales im Musikdrama* (Frankfurt am Main: Peter Lang, 2000).

clearly plays a crucial role in the stylistic *smorgasbord* which Strauss lays out for the modern operatic epicurean. There remains scope, however, for making this association with decadence more precise. This section aims to identify decadent tone in specific musical processes and effects. Comments from early critics raise descriptive terms which are useful for this purpose. Romain Rolland wrote to Strauss concerning the Paris premiere of *Salome*: 'I fear (forgive me if I am wrong) that you have been caught by the mirage of German decadent literature … There is in Europe today an unbridled force of decadence, of suicide … beware of joining forces with it. Let that which must die, die – and live yourself.' In spite of his misgivings over Strauss's potential fall into decadence, Rolland had evaluated Wilde's text as 'admirably suited to the stage; it is at the same time picturesque, and compact, concentrated: it is a dramatic crescendo from beginning to end'.[44] Thus Rolland viewed the drama as a single process of intensification. Max Kalbeck, writing in the *Neues Wiener Tageblatt* (28 May 1907), condemned Wilde's text: 'Adultery, incest, and sexual madness are the motives; suicide, execution, and necrophilia the consequences of this drama, which sends itself in brutal effects and is so drastic that it seems to demand a palliative.' Kalbeck suggests that Strauss's music promises this 'relief', a 'purging' and 'cleansing' 'by means of colossal exaggeration, which, admittedly against the will of the composer, turns into parody' and descends into the 'artificial', into 'heartless jumble' with 'dazzling and deceiving inessentials, which glitter with a thousand nuances'. For Kalbeck Strauss's 'intoxicated' muse is made most productive in the Dance of the Seven Veils, 'the high point of the musical drama, surpassing two other high points of the work – the terrible illustration of the execution of John the Baptist and Salome's infatuation with the *caput mortuum*'. In such passages,

the purple sound ocean of the painter of musical colours makes its proudest waves, and when they close over our heads we are made blind and seeing at the same time – seeing its advantages, blind to its shortcomings. But the marvels of the palette do not last … and we leave the poisonous plant that has been cultivated in the greenhouse of modern hyperculture …[45]

In this passage Kalbeck extravagantly strings together a series of decadent metaphors and images – evoking the waning of creative powers, the ephemeral pleasures of the art of musical colours, the unhealthy artificiality of modernity. For Kalbeck the musical 'wave' at the dramatic highpoints is

---

[44] Rollo H. Myers (ed.), *Richard Strauss and Romain Rolland: Correspondence* (London: Calder, 1970).

[45] Kalbeck, trans. from Gilliam (ed.), *Richard Strauss and his World*, 341–2.

paradoxically double in character – insightful yet deceptive, productive yet inadequate.

Rolland's and Kalbeck's descriptions explictly raise decadent topics. But Gary Schmidgall has argued that, by the time of *Salome*'s performance, decadence was already largely a dead idea, so that Strauss's decision to set Wilde's play was a 'decadent' choice in itself: *Salome* is therefore a sort of posthumous addition to the German decadent tradition, which Schmidgall (controversially) identifies with *Jugendstil* and the Viennese Secession, whose 'climax' was felt around 1902. When he poses the question 'is the music of Strauss "decadent"?' Schmidgall states that 'the answer lies in the fact that decadence is in the ear of the beholder. If history is an indication, musical decadence is largely a function of time, place, and personality.' The usefulness of the term in music, he decides, is usually merely abusive. And yet Schmidgall goes on to write: 'The last pages of the opera are surely the apotheosis in music of the Decadent malaise', and that the 'two bars following [Salome's] last words are the quintessence of Decadence: here is ecstasy falling in upon itself, crumbling into the abyss at the sound of that most sickening chord in all opera in the second bar'.[46] The music which immediately follows this moment – the peak of the 'dramatic crescendo' noted by Rolland – is the final version of material which first appears as part of a wave dissolution and represents one of the opera's most distinctively decadent moments. Within this broad dynamic trajectory in Strauss's operatic treatment, processes of *Steigerung* operate in a number of situations and in a variety of ways, reflecting the polystylistic character of the work. In certain crucial passages these processes move to musical material of decay and degeneration which mark the most perverted, decadent moments of the drama.

It is interesting to note that the term *Steigerung* is found only twice in the score of *Salome* as a performance instruction.[47] In both cases the word heads a section leading to a moment where the music can be heard to exude a notably decadent tone, precisely in the manner by which the intensification in the wave form is dissolved.[48] The first use of the indication, *mit*

---

[46] Gary Schmidgall, *Literature as Opera* (Oxford University Press, 1977), 266–8, 283.

[47] James Hepokoski has discussed processes of *Steigerung* in the tone poems of Strauss in several essays, most recently in his 'Framing *Till Eulenspiegel*', *19th-Century Music* 30 (2006), 4–43.

[48] Edward F. Kravitt cites Strauss's setting of Heine's 'Frühlingsfeier', Op.56 No.5, as 'a remarkable expression in the *lied* of decadence, close in style and time of composition to *Salome*': *The Lied: Mirror of Late Romanticism* (New Haven: Yale University Press, 1996), 171. However, the turbulent passion of the setting, though it certainly has correspondences with passages in *Salome*, and is also in C sharp minor, *Salome*'s principal key, does not parallel the 'decadent' features of the opera, in spite of the decadent possibilities in the poem's image of hyper-emotional, bare-breasted, blossoming girls. Only the music at the image of the dead Adonis evokes a process which

grosser Steigerung, occurs when Salome sings, 'Thy mouth is like a bunch of coral found in the twilight of the sea' ('Dein Mund is wie ein Korallenzweig in der Dämm'rung des Meers'; 2 bars after fig.119). This marks the start of the closing part of the E major formal section devoted to Salome's infatuated descriptions of Jochanaan's mouth (which begins at fig.114), a function signalled by the return to the section's tonic, E, and the opening motif at its primary pitch level. In response to Wilde's poetic image of the red coral in a twilight ocean, Strauss initiates a sequential intensification forming two four-bar *Stollen* of a 'bar' form (Example 4.3). This can be called a bar form, rather than a sentence, because not only is this (obviously) a vocal work, but this section is (perhaps less obviously) part of a 'song'. Within a passage in Strauss's more diatonic style the sensual dissonances catch the ear (the first is emphasized *fortepiano*). They are characterized by coincident rising and falling chromatic passing motions which generate piquant sevenths and diminished octaves. They also form part of the rising inner line (from B through to D; shown on the second stave of the example) which drives the melodic ascent. In the *Abgesang* the 'kingly' move to G major is a chromatic enrichment which prolongs the E major, functioning as the minor mediant leading towards the dominant and as the dynamic peak of harmonic intensification, as musical correlative to the poetic image of lordly power. The *Höhepunkt* is achieved at fig.121 – the height of Salome's psychological excitement being indicated by the phrase 'ausser sich' ('beside herself'), which is less a performance instruction than a piece of psychoanalysis, suggesting doubleness and revealing that her mounting ecstasy also includes a growing tendency to distress. It is also the moment when the highest point of the inner line (D♯) sinks to D♮: at the diatonic peak chromatic descent is already in chain.

The closure on E which follows is superficially strong, with the dominant chord coloured by dissonances which recall the chromatic effects in the *Stollen* in order to resolve them. But the impact of the D♮ at the highpoint is insufficiently resolved by the cadence: this poetic and musical image of strength and cohesion is now turned to decadent collapse and perversion. It is the music after the close back in E, what we might call an extension of the *Abgesang* of this section, which changes the tone to decadent decline in excessive, supplementary dissolution. It is telling that the decadent image is placed outside the boundary of 'normal' form, thus banished and abjected. But it is even more telling that the sources of that image lie at the highpoint of that 'normal' form. Salome for the first time asks the fatal question 'Let

might be heard as decadent, where the pure E major diatonicism which represents Adonis's beautiful form collapses into ambiguous chromaticism.

Example 4.3 Strauss, *Salome*, Salome: 'Dein Mund ist wie ein Korallenzweig …'

me kiss thy mouth' ('Lass mich ihn küssen deinen Mund'). A harmonic move, based on the unfulfilled resolution potential of the D♮ from the *Abgesang* and on a recollection of the G♯–A neighbour note prominent in the *Stollen*, suggests the subdominant A – which some commentators identify as Salome's key of desire. This is a traditional post-closural harmonic signal. However, decorated by elements derived from the dissonant moments in the preceding sequences of *Steigerung* (B♯ and E♯ in rising lines and an upper voice accented passing motion in double thirds, here G♯–B to F♯–A), this goes 'too far' to suggest D major – the subdominant of the

Example 4.3 (cont.)

subdominant. Furthermore, the movement of contrapuntal lines whose resolutions do not coincide, and false relations with the motivic statement in
Salome's vocal line (E versus E♯), make this traditional closural harmonic
move sound queasy and queer. To recall Taruskin's image of decadent form,
we might say that this is when Salome imagines sticking the piece in a place her

Example 4.3 (cont.)

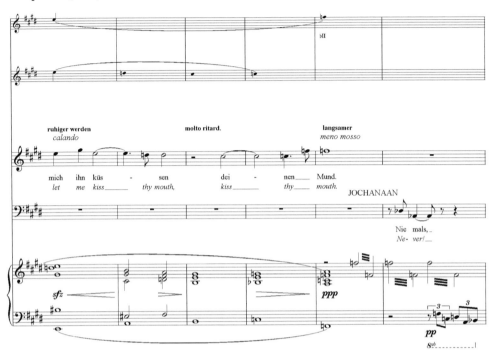

mother might prefer not to know about. The tonic E then shifts to the Neapolitan F – traditionally a doomed and dark tonal relationship – for a final dissipation (*Langsamer* and triple *piano*) of all the energies of the preceding passage before Jochanaan's horrified interjection ('Never!') signals the religious man's abhorrence at Salome's decadent expression of desire. By contrast with the degenerate transformations of the images of Jochanaan's body and hair which preceded this passage, at Jochanaan's refusal (expressed 'in soundless horror') Salome does not then turn her unfulfilment into degradations of what she previously described as exquisitely beautiful. Instead, she obsessively repeats the demand, her desire is maintained, and the mouth retains its beauty in her erotic imagination. But the seeds of its degradation lie in the music which accompanies her first demand to kiss those lips.

The harmonic motif from fig.122 – static, de-energized, decadent material derived from the dissolution of previously dynamic intensifications – reappears twice in the opera as a kind of *Leitsektion*. The first reappearance is at the moment in Salome's final monologue where she has been recalling the beauty of his body, hair and mouth in a musical and poetic recapitulation offered after the dramatic decapitation. As we saw in Chapter 3, previously, at fig.335, the music cadenced in C sharp major.

Example 4.4 Strauss, *Salome*, Salome: 'Und das Geheimnis der Liebe ist grösser als das Geheimnis des Todes'

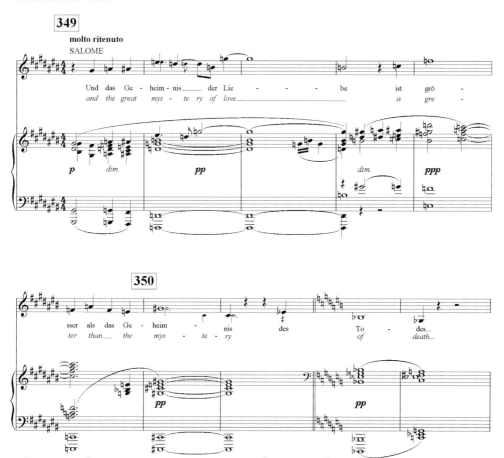

Salome recalls the magical music evoked by Jochanaan's voice: there is a local move to A, which here functions as the flat submediant. When she asks the severed head, 'Ah! Why did you never look at me?' the decadent *Leitsektion* is stated in 'her' C sharp major (fig.340). The subsequent allusion to F with dissonant D♭ recalls Jochanaan's refusal to allow her to kiss his mouth, but perhaps more importantly, the upper-voice 6–5 resolution (D♯–C♯) is heard as an echo of the similar motion (B–A) over the move to the pedal A at the line 'geheimnis-volle Musik'. The motif of which this is part (F♯–G♮–G♯–B–A, paralleled in thirds) returns, in a musical-poetic parallel, in two transformed versions at the famous line 'And the great mystery of love is greater than the mystery of death' ('Und das Geheimnis der Liebe ist grösser als das Geheimnis des Todes', figs.349–50: Example 4.4). Preceding this moment the instruction *Mit*

grösser Steigerung makes its second appearance, as Salome sings 'Not by floods, not by great waters can ever the heat of my strong passion be quenched' (fig.347), again associating the intensification instruction with one of Wilde's oceanic poetic images. There is an interruption to F (although this has a very different function and expressive character from the parallel move to G in the preceding passage of *Steigerung* it has a similar intensifying effect). Salome implores once more, 'Why did you not look at me?' – if he had, she speculates in a promised cadence in 'her' key of C sharp, he would have loved her. The 'Geheimnis' music occurs just as the anticipated closure in C sharp seems imminent. The motivic parallel with Jochanaan's mysterious music is overt. More subtle are the harmonic reminiscences of the 'decadent' *Leitsektion*. These are clearest at the move to the F 6–4 chord, where chromatic motions underlie the upper part's 6–5 resolution. Again, it is at a moment which follows the promise of closure that we hear the most overtly decadent music.

The third and final statement of this music, which has by now accrued layers of meaning suggesting unfulfilled desire, fetishization of Jochanaan's mouth, secret connections between love and death and indeed the *Geheimnis*-like character of music itself (as it is heard emerging from that desired mouth), occurs at the climactic moment before Salome's brutal slaying. Again it is placed as part of traditional coda material, Salome's last, ecstatically intensifying passage, here after the second C sharp cadence of her monologue. 'I have now kissed your mouth,' she deliriously declares, after which we hear the opera's most infamous, 'sickening' dissonance. The multiple symbolic reverberations in this notorious chord (which were traced in Chapter 3 and to which we will return in Chapter 5) include an excruciating version of the more seductive dissonances around fig.120, which previously led to the first statement of the 'decadent' progression. Dissolutions of *Steigerung* within wave deformations thus perform a central symbolic role in the opera and generate the formal context for particularly decadent tones and processes.

Resisting decadence: the finale of Mahler's Sixth Symphony

Mahler did not share the enthusiasm held by many of his Viennese contemporaries for symbolist or decadent writing and aesthetics. He preferred instead the work of romantic authors (Goethe, Rückert, Jean Paul, etc.) and considered the struggle to Ideal redemption that he heard in the music of Beethoven and Wagner to be still relevant as a basis for asking and answering profoundly modern questions. But the sustaining of a redemptive romantic element within his creative project in the *fin-de-siècle* cultural milieu generated uneasiness and doubt. Morten Solvik argues that this led Mahler to harbour a 'tortured soul that maintained a tenuous balance between idealism and nihilism', manifest in the contrast between redemptive symphonic conclusions such as those of the Second, Third and Eighth Symphonies and the 'anti-heroic' endings of the Sixth and Ninth.[49] But the Sixth is a work whose complex tone moves between opposing world views. It presents a conflict between redemptive and pessimistic narratives, manifest in polarized affects and contradiction between two possible endings, until the final section of the finale crushes any lingering hope that the vigorous closure of the first movement might return to save the day. It is often associated with Mahler's enthusiasm for the romantic pessimism of Schopenhauer, but can also be related to his interest in the work of Nietzsche. (Mahler's relationship to Nietzsche's writings was crucial, if profoundly ambivalent.) In the extensive critical literature a notion of decadence has hardly attached itself to this work, whose overriding impression is of bitter and often violent conflict leading to a brutally tragic demise. Indeed, Mahler's lack of interest in decadent literature seems to discourage any attempt to make such associations. Examination of deformed 'waves' in the finale and the expressive qualities of the Andante, however, reveals that the perils and pleasures associated with decadence are part of the symphony's narrative and aesthetic terms of reference. Through these processes and effects the symphony evokes and then resists decadence.

Before examining the Sixth in detail, it is useful to consider whether resonances of decadence are manifest in other Mahler symphonic movements. In an analysis of the narrative of the Third Symphony Vera Micznik identifies productive relationships between Mahler's musical response to the pessimistic humour of *Wunderhorn* poetry and Nietzsche's notion of light-hearted, irreverent emergence out of suffering. She cites the preface to *The Joyful Wisdom*: 'if we convalescents still need art, it is another kind of art – a mocking, light, fleeting, divinely troubled, divinely artificial art that, like a pure flame, licks into unclouded skies …'. Micznik is convinced of the coherence of 'interpenetrations of Nietzschean and *Wunderhorn* aesthetics' in the symphony. In its gigantic opening movement she describes how the 'saturnalia' of the movement's tragic narrative moves to Nietzschean 'hope for health, and the intoxication of convalescence' (once more a quotation from *The Joyful Wisdom*).[50] If we buy into Micznik's reading of the

[49] Morten Solvik, 'Mahler's Untimely Modernism', in Jeremy Barham (ed.), *Perspectives on Gustav Mahler* (Aldershot: Ashgate, 2005), 153–71.
[50] Vera Micznik, '"Ways of Telling" in Mahler's Music: The Third Symphony as Narrative Text', in Barham (ed.), *Perspectives on Gustav Mahler*, 305–16.

movement as an unfolding of Nietzschean convalescence then the familiar associations with Dionysus (and his close mythological relations, Bacchus and Pan) become freshly relevant as figures of provocative revitalization. The move from decadent lifelessness to recuperation is revealed as a parallel to the more familiar reading of the symphony as tracing a trajectory from death to evolutionary higher forms of life, and the awakening of conscious-ness from sleep.[51] In fact, decadence's defining fragmentations, dissolu-tions and aesthetics of the (last) moment can be related to the challenges to the processes of integration and telos which inform much of Mahler's music. On the Scherzo of the Fifth Symphony the composer anticipated problems for the audience because of 'this chaos which is constantly giving birth to new worlds and promptly destroying them again … this rushing, roaring, raging sea, these dancing stars, these ebbing, shimmering, gleam-ing waves'.[52] What the waves tell us here is that in the oceanic musical tone the destructive and constructive, the degenerative and regenerative, like the motions of the sea, are forces in constant battle. But the Fifth moves towards a tone of apparent health, vigour and formal affirmation through allusion to Mahler's 'reverential attitude to Bach', which he confirmed around the time of the composition of the Fifth (1901–3). Walter Frisch has suggested that the 'Bachian' polyphony in the finale of the Fifth is an effect different from related procedures in the music of other German modernists (e.g. in Reger's 'historicist modernism') because of its comic (Nietzschean?) manner, a 'new, more detached attitude toward the music of the past'.[53] For many artists working at the turn of the century Bach was a symbol of regeneration, healing and the medicinal. His music was heard as a 'cultural balm'. Recourse to the 'Bachian' idiom established a distance from late romantic unhealthiness by evoking, in an earnest not parodic manner, a more distant past.[54] In the finale of Mahler's Fifth the energetic contrapuntal passages contribute to the evocation of a Nietzschean comic sublime as an antidote to decadence and demise. As I have shown

---

[51] According to Peter Franklin, the Third can be heard as 'seeking to frame dynamic Darwinian evolution (both in Nature and Society) as an eternal or inevitable organic structure', what Mahler called the 'moans of the youth, of captive life struggling for release from the clutches of lifeless, rigid Nature'. In the Panic or Bacchic mood the rough humour emerges out of summer sleepiness, dispelling Schopenhauerian pessimism, and releases the destabilizing Dionysian forces. See Franklin, *Mahler: Symphony No.3* (Cambridge University Press, 1991), 38, 50–1, 77.

[52] Gustav Mahler, *Letters to his Wife*, ed. Henry-Louis de La Grange and Günther Weiss in collaboration with Knud Martner, trans. Antony Beaumont (London: Faber, 2004), 179.

[53] Frisch, *German Modernism*, 182–5.

[54] See Reger and Riemann's 1907 exchange on 'degeneration' and 'regeneration'. Reger's response is available in Daniel Albright (ed.), *Modernism and Music: An Anthology of Sources* (Chicago University Press, 2004), 148–54.

Example 4.5 Gustav Mahler, Symphony No.6, Andante, opening theme

elsewhere, the dangers and seductions of de-energizing, sensuous beauty in the transformed return of material from the Adagietto are real but resisted. In Mahler's pun the 'Bachic' music evokes both Johann Sebastian's control through contrapuntal mastery (or through the redemptive chorale's monumentalism) and the intoxicating abandon of the Bacchic/Dionysian – two strategies for overcoming decadence, in a 'doubleness' reflected in the symphony's kaleidoscopic, frenzied final bars.[55] In many ways the Sixth Symphony is the negative image of the narrative of the Fifth. If the Fifth can be heard as a Nietzschean comedy, then the Sixth can be heard in part as a Nietzschean tragedy. In its relation to decadence there is no 'Bachic' revitalization or redemption, nor in its finale is there an attempt at convalescence of the kind Micznik hears in the first movement of the Third. In the end there is only obliteration, which is arrived at through a brutal crushing of romantic wave form and an eschewing of the decadent pleasures of a lingering end.

A decadent tone can be located in the Sixth Symphony in the last part of the main theme of the Andante movement, in the treatment of the sighing or sobbing motifs that follow what Warren Darcy has called the 'anguish chord'[56] (Example 4.5). This motif of sorrow becomes transformed into the

---

[55] See my *The Muse as Eros*, 119–34.
[56] Warren Darcy, 'Rotational Form, Teleological Genesis, and Fantasy Projection in the Slow Movement of Mahler's Sixth Symphony', *19th-Century Music* 25 (2001), 49–74.

rocking motif which forms the principal content of the *Abgesang* (from
b.42). Crucially, as James Buhler explains, an *Abgesang* is characteristically
the site of new material which responds to a theme – an area of freedom as
much as closure, an area of 'surplus'. Tellingly, the movement 'pushes its
most distinctive elements into the *Abgesang*-like passages'. Their position-
ing with regard to climax points is even more important. The rocking motif
dissipates the energy of the first highpoint (bb.79–81) and then emerges out
of the later highpoint of bars 179–80 to initiate and prolong the final
cadential dominant. According to Buhler, across the movement the motif
is increasingly 'embraced as something beautiful' – the 'rhetorical emphasis
on the *Abgesang* rather than the theme, cherishes non-identity. Savouring
the beauty of the fleeting sunset …' it thus leaves 'itself open and vulnerable'.[57] The emphasis is placed on material which has formal functions of
ending and decay. Here lie the signs of decadence: characteristically placed
in the *Abgesang* or as material in the dissolution of climax, the rocking
motif evokes and savours the regressive ending, the repetitive and the
melancholic recollection of suffering. Through the Andante, then, formal
and expressive functions characteristic of a decadent tone are established.
In the last movement this decadent function and effect is annulled. (This
contributes a neglected dimension to the negative tone in a movement
often heard as a negation of the first.)

The finale profoundly problematizes progression, integration, closure
and teleology. Adorno's famous reading of the movement characterizes it
as based upon conflicting powers of life and death, of intensification and
decay.[58] This conflict has an important focus on the deformation, dissolution and destruction of wave forms in the second subject group, manifest in
a brutally anti-decadent gesture. Marked *Fliessend* (which we might translate as 'flowing'), the second thematic group begins, to use Adorno's
imagery, by 'dancing like an imperilled boat in choppy water' and contains
an iridescent shift from an effect of 'careless joy' to a tone of 'surging
intoxication'.[59] Adorno is here alluding to a passage from Schopenhauer's
The World as Will and Representation which Nietzsche famously quotes
near the beginning of *The Birth of Tragedy*: 'Just as the boat man sits in his
little boat, trusting to his fragile craft in a stormy sea which, boundless in
every direction, rises and falls in howling, mountainous waves, so in the

[57] James Buhler, 'Theme and Form in the Andante of the Sixth Symphony', in Barham (ed.), *Perspectives on Gustav Mahler*, 291–3.
[58] Theodor W. Adorno, *Mahler: A Musical Physiognomy*, trans. Edmund Jephcott (Chicago University Press, 1992).
[59] Adorno, *Mahler*, 98.

midst of a world full of suffering the individual man calmly sits, supported by and trusting the *principium individuationis*.'[60] Out of this image of the hero's experience of the sublime emerges the famous dualism of the Apollonion and the Dionysian. For Nietzsche, of course, Apollo is the divine image of the beautiful dream illusion, the sculptured form of individual unity which is fragmented as man's reason 'seems suspended' when he is gripped by 'dread' and 'blissful ecstasy' in a glimpse of the 'intoxication' of the Dionysian oceanic.[61] Schopenhauer's and Nietzsche's images are strikingly recalled in Mahler's characterization of his relationship with Alma. As he wrote to her on 14 December 1901: 'your sweet breath again convinces me that my ship has weathered every storm and safely reached its haven'.[62] In the finale of Mahler's Sixth the figure of the redeeming muse lies behind both the graceful dancing figure and the passionate surging swell of the second subject – through Her he seeks to ride the waves towards reconciliation, via the erotic union of Apollonian illusion and Dionysian intoxication.[63] But this oceanic thematic section occurs within a movement whose overriding tone is one of crushing loss and absence. This character is hinted at in the problematic way in which the exposition of the finale closes after the second theme.

The wave deformations in the treatment of the second subject of the finale are summarized, in Leichtentrittian fashion, in Figure 4.1. (As in the wave diagrams of Leichtentritt and others, the shape of the wave is drawn rather impressionistically. The vertical dimension – rates of ascent and descent – can only be an approximate visualization of the musical effects of intensification, highpoint and dissolution. The horizontal 'axis' is also drawn to match duration only approximately, and thus also the size of the formal sections.) Adorno notes that in the finale's exposition 'what is foregone, after the graphic dualism of the first and second themes, is a more extensive closing section or third theme'.[64] It is important at this point to recall the crucial symbolic and structural functions of the *Abgesang* in the Andante and also the tone and function of the *Abgesang* to the second subject in the first movement, which suggested the closing, resolving calm of an idyllic F major realm, the key of pastoral pleasures (but also, in an

[60] Arthur Schopenhauer, *The World as Will and Representation*, trans. E. F. Payne (New York: Dover, 1968), vol.I, 352.
[61] Friedrich Nietzsche, *The Birth of Tragedy out of the Spirit of Music*, trans. Shaun Whiteside, ed. Michael Tanner (Harmondsworth: Penguin, 1993), 14–17.
[62] Mahler, *Letters to his Wife*, 66.
[63] For more on the function of the muse figure in this symphony see my *The Muse as Eros*, 134–44.
[64] Adorno, *Mahler*, 98.

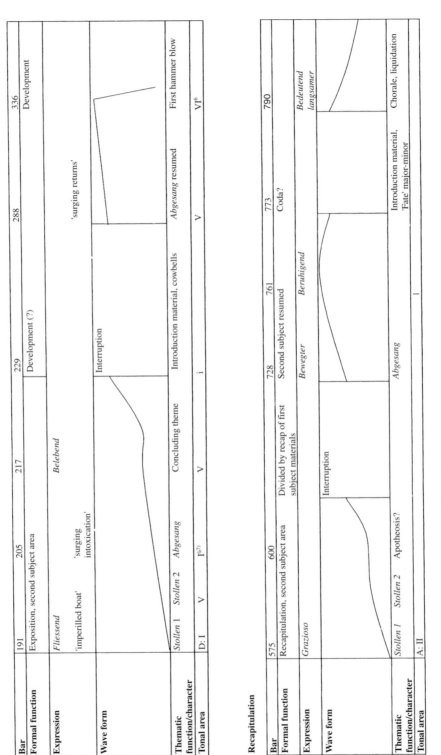

Figure 4.1 Mahler, Symphony No.6, finale: wave deformations

A minor-major movement, on the unstable flat submediant). In the finale these realms of precarious beauty, nostalgia and ending are absent. *Contra* Adorno, Bernd Sponheuer considers that an *Abgesang* of the finale's second subject does move into a 'concluding theme',[65] one which (marked *Belebend*, 'revivifying'; b.217) suggests the potential for revitalization or redemption. This theme is, however, interrupted by the return of music from the introduction (fig.120; b.229), with cowbells, which can be heard as a 'fantasy projection' dividing the second subject group, for after it the intoxicating, surging second part of the theme returns (fig.124; b.288).[66] This static image of nature breaks the 'natural', dynamic wave form. One image of nature works against another. The music evokes an Adornian suspension, establishing stasis rather than intensifying kinetic energy, elaborate patterning rather than developmental process.[67] The principal parameters generating the process of *Steigerung* to the wave peak are textural (achieved by orchestral thickening rather than the addition of contrapuntal lines), melodic (the ascendant striving profile and energetic *Schwung* of the upper melodic line), dynamic (a broad, controlling *crescendo*) and harmonic (the move to a dominant pedal). The 'space' which opens up at the wave's interruption is a premature mirage of the mountain top, whose territory is invaded by troubling echoes of previous struggles and torments. After this interruption the second subject's wave form returns in a more intense and ecstatic build-up over a prolongation of the dominant of D. Expectations of a redemptive wave climax are thus raised, only for this hoped-for field of fulfilment to be crushed by the first hammer blow and the subsequent cruel and fatalistic tone. The power of the effect is generated by the sudden deviation from the anticipated continuations of romantic wave form, from the dynamics of the bar form which structures the thematic material and from the formal obligations of

---

[65] Bernd Sponheuer, *Logik des Zerfalls: Untersuchungen zum Finalproblem in den Symphonien Gustav Mahlers* (Tutzing: Hans Schneider, 1978), 312.

[66] I borrow the term 'fantasy projection' from Darcy's analysis 'Rotational Form, Teleological Genesis'. As La Grange recounts, there has been dispute over formal functions in the finale, a debate focused on the issue of identifying the start of the development (*Durchführung*) section. Sponheuer argues that the passage from bar 288, the return of the surge of the *Abgesang*, is the true conclusion of the exposition. See Henry-Louis de La Grange, *Gustav Mahler*, vol.III: *Vienna: Triumph and Disillusion (1904–1907)* (Oxford University Press, 1999), 829–35.

[67] The use of 'spatial' effect of distance in the material which interrupts the wave form contrasts with the use of a similar effect in the first movement of the First Symphony, in which, as Paul Banks has noted, the off-stage fanfares are at first isolated but subsequently become structurally incorporated as heralds of the main climax, where the peak of the second of two waves is formed by intensifications of dynamics and tempo: 'Mahler and Viennese Modernism', in Philip Reed (ed.), *On Mahler and Britten* (Woodbridge: Boydell, 1995), 16–19.

the climactic closing dynamics of the sonata exposition.[68] The liquidation or dissolution of the wave form (in which we may find resolution or, if not, then lingering expression of decline) is absent in the exposition.

In the recapitulation the second subject is again divided. The first part, Grazioso in B flat, moves to a suggestion of apotheosis (bb.575–610). The *Abgesang* is not recapitulated until bar 728, after the delayed return of first subject material. When it does return the *Abgesang* is marked *Bewegter* ('turbulent'), and where the wave peaks and leads to the promise of affirmation and resolution the marking is *Beruhigend* ('pacifying'; b.761). However, this in turn is interrupted, by a return of the movement's introductory material, but now without the pastoral-idyllic cowbells (b.773). By contrast with the exposition's succeeding surge to higher peaks, this return of the introduction is now followed by material evoking a mournful chorale (the dark alternative to the 'redemptive' chorale of the finale of the Fifth?) and a section of liquidation (absent from the exposition) of motivic developmental drives. In this formal-expressive position after an unfulfilled wave form the liquidation expresses obliteration, dissolution, reduction and collapse. It is a gradual draining-away towards the inevitable tragic ending, in the *morendo* which is so prevalent in Mahler's music and which raises liquidation as a primary formal principle.[69] If this is Mahler's 'Tragic' Symphony then it is in part because the finale is based on the failure of, or loss of faith in, the romantic wave form and on the failure to assimilate the decadent consolations so beautifully prominent in the Andante movement. In an alternative to the usual Schopenhauerian interpretation, this symphony is thus read as Nietzschean and anti-romantic because, to recall the characterization of romanticism from *The Joyful Wisdom*, it destroys the attempt to 'seek repose, quietness, calm seas, and deliverance' as well as denying the escape 'through intoxication, spasm, bewilderment and madness'. As an ultimately anti-decadent symphony it can, furthermore, be heard to express a pessimism of strength, which Nietzsche raised as the counter to the romantic and decadent pessimism of weakness.[70]

---

[68] On 'dynamic curves' in the 'subordinate' and closing themes of classical sonata forms see William E. Caplin, *Classical Form: A Theory of Formal Functions for the Instrumental Music of Haydn, Mozart, and Beethoven* (New York: Oxford University Press, 1998), 123.

[69] See the work of Peter Revers: 'Liquidation als Formprinzip: Die formprägende Bedeutung des Rhythmus für das Adagio des 9. Symphonie von Gustav Mahler', *Österreichische Musikzeitschrift* 33/10 (October 1978), 527–33, and *Gustav Mahler: Untersuchungen zu den späten Sinfonien* (Hamburg: Wagner, 1985).

[70] In this regard the description of the finale by Maximilian Muntz, the critic of *Deutsche Zeitung*, as 'a monument to the impertinent weakness of decadence' and an 'orgy of the empty phrase, great wanton illusion, and artistic lie' seems especially perverse: *Deutsche Zeitung*, 6 January 1907, trans. from Painter, 'The Sensuality of Timbre', 245.

Berg's Op.1 and the emaciation of dissonance

Adorno's 1955 essay on Berg's 'Tone' is replete with language suggesting the aesthetics and topics of decadence. Adorno writes of Berg's 'complicity with death, an urbane cordiality toward his own extinction', reflected in the 'profoundly melancholy dissolution of the music, which is granted no affirming finality', but only its 'evanescence, the revocation of one's own existence'. Berg's music exhibits 'atomization', based on 'minuscule motives' which 'do not really possess the ambition to establish themselves and unite into a massive and powerful whole'. Berg's is a Wagnerian art of transition pushed to an exaggerated stage of 'mannerism'; 'Berg assumes a position in extreme antithesis to that which musical tradition calls healthy', and his music is 'radical and shocking in its partiality for the weaker, the defeated'. Thus Adorno raises a number of defining characteristics of the decadent: pessimism, miniaturism, mannerism (on which see Chapter 5) and unhealthiness (explored more fully in Chapter 6). In summary, to employ Adorno's image most closely recalling musical waves, Berg characteristically creates 'an elaborate musical structure that springs from nothingness and trickles away into nothingness'.[71]

Compare the anguished climax and dissolution of the main theme of the Andante of Mahler's Sixth Symphony – which is isolated, as a sort of decadent thematic fragment, in Example 4.6 – with the opening theme of Berg's Piano Sonata, Op.1. The comparison may seem to be based on a perverse decapitation of Mahler's tune, but it confirms that what Berg presents at the beginning of his sonata is an ending. It is thematic subsidence from a dissonant highpoint which is almost immediately presented, with no preamble, by the opening gesture. Intensification is reduced; dissolution is the prime effect. The sonata opens with thematic material which emphasizes the processes of decay away from the moment of expressive and harmonic intensification. Berg's sonata is of course in many ways formally conservative, displaying an arrangement of functional materials and tonal relationships conforming to the 'normal', first-movement sonata requirements as codified by the *Formenlehre* of A. B. Marx. These materials are saturated with processes which suggest Schoenbergian 'developing variation', with its supposedly 'evolutionary' subjective connections emerging from a *Grundgestalt*.[72] But, as Adorno famously

---

[71] Adorno, *Alban Berg*, 3–5.

[72] Although Schoenberg was yet to coin this term, as Janet Schmalfeldt points out, the sonata suggests that Berg and his teacher 'fully comprehended' this compositional issue in 1907: 'Berg's

Example 4.6 (a) Mahler, Symphony No.6, Andante, theme (part); (b) Alban Berg, Piano Sonata, Op.1, opening

stated, the abundance so generated coexists in a dialectic with disintegra-tion, with 'permanent dissolution' (*Auflösung*).[73] This leads to a reinter-pretation of the dynamics of sonata form. In Berg's sonata we can hear these pervasive liquidation processes coexisting with reminiscences of the oceanic erotics of Wagner's *Tristan*. Max Paddison has related Berg's dissolutions to *Tristan*'s model of transition, dissolution and motivic remnants – a model acknowledged in the work's climactic allusions to the Tristan chord and also revealed by the peak of the wave of the develop-ment being rather overtly modelled on the *Tristan* Prelude's waves of libidinal desire[74] – Lawrence Kramer's *Lust* trope – where the peak is an overlap of contradictory forces of fulfilment and unfulfilment.[75] However, by contrast with Isolde's B major *Verklärung*, the sonata closes with a long elegiac decline in B minor.

Schmalfeldt identifies the opening phrase as the sonata's *Grundgestalt*, but also notes that this is a closing gesture, a lead down to an end, rather

Path to Atonality: The Piano Sonata, Op.1', in David Gable and Robert P. Morgan (eds.), *Alban Berg: Historical and Analytical Perspectives* (Oxford: Clarendon Press, 1991), 90.

[73] Adorno, *Alban Berg*, 38.

[74] Max Paddison, *Adorno's Aesthetics of Music* (Cambridge University Press, 1993), 171–3.

[75] Kramer, *Music as Cultural Practice*, 149.

than up or away from an originating beginning. (As such, she suggests, it may be heard as an epigraph or motto lying outside the movement proper.) Its 'proper' function as a closing phrase is confirmed in bars 9–11 at the decline of the wave-form processes of intensification which shape the rest of the first subject area.[76] By contrast with *Tristan*'s open-ended *Grundgestalt*, which in the opening paragraph rises in waves to peak at the well-known interrupted cadence, Berg's basic shape or idea is modelled on the decline or dissolution of the wave, with the initial ascent or *Ursprung* proto-expressionistically compressed. Within this opening shape the *accelerando*, marked to begin at the melodic highpoint (G♮), might be heard energetically to counteract the melodic wave's descent, but it only serves to speed up the plunge, with the ensuing *rit.* poignantly positioned to emphasize expressively the reversal of the ascendant F♯–G semitonal motif into the grief-ridden descending ♭6–5 (G–F♯) at the cadence. Indeed, there is much complexity in the dialectic between declining and intensifying forces within the overall shape of decay. The dynamic markings (which curiously only indicate a basic *piano* level at the third note) indicate a small *crescendo* over the middle part of the *Ursprung*; the mirroring *decrescendo* is placed over the recurrence of the dotted-crotchet–quaver rhythm in the melody, which articulates the reversal of the ascending semitonal motion of the *Ursprung*. This dynamic and motivic reversal immediately precedes the temporal reversal of *accel.* into *rit.* The counterpoint is subtly woven into the wave patterning. The lines in the upper voices emphasize the central role of F♯–G in upper and 'alto' voice; the pervasive semitonal descent of the lower parts (the 'creeping chromaticism' which 'weakens' or 'subverts' harmonic progression[77]) leads the upper-voice move from E♭ through D to C♯ as an incomplete melodic fragment, which is especially poignant as the line is unclosed on the second scale degree. This enfeebles the cadence, which is also weakened by metrical ambiguity: the notated three in a bar is illusory, for the tonic chord is more likely to be heard as falling on the fourth beat of a second bar in 4/4. The slurring of the 'tenor' E to the bass F♯ at the dominant seventh is also a telling detail: the falling minor seventh which it spans becomes a prime melodic and motivic carrier of the elegiac close of the exposition (bb.45ff.). Finally, Berg controls the dissonance-consonance relationship with great precision to produce a sort of evolutionary regression. The peak of the wave is coincident with the most dissonant chord; the

---

[76] Schmalfeldt, 'Berg's Path to Atonality', 90.
[77] Mark DeVoto, 'Alban Berg and Creeping Chromaticism', in Gable and Morgan (eds.), *Alban Berg*, 57–78.

less characteristic or 'advanced' passing seventh chord on C is the first to be subject to acceleration, to move the passage quickly to the locally embellished whole-tone harmony (there is a move between the two whole-tone collections generated by the inner part dotted articulation of the resolution of the neighbouring G♯ to G). Thus the tension at the peak is discharged through the acceleration into and through the whole-tone harmony. The *rit.* and motivic inversion and reversal coincide with diatonic clarification, which is heard as a decline into the moribund, into old and tired harmonic forms. The bass ascending B–F♯–B at the close of the cadence is a formulaic echo of the initial motivic *Ursprung*. Harmonically, then, we move from complex to simple, from the highest, most advanced form to the lowest. Once again comparison with the opening gesture of the *Tristan* Prelude is revealing, for Wagner's opening is similarly controlled in its disposition of dissonance. As in Berg's phrase, the first chord is the most advanced and dissonant; it is discharged through 'less advanced' whole-tone harmonies to move to a chromatically altered dominant, the least 'advanced' species. But in the Wagner this process of dissonant regression is counterpointed by melodic intensification generated by the rising chromatic motive. Berg's chromatic counterpoint contains no such aspiring shape. This emphasizes that dissonance is not emancipated: it is emaciated in a creeping motion which slides down from under the peak of the wave. This opening can also be heard as a negation of Wagnerian 'endless melody', the principle of 'eloquence' (*das redende Prinzip*), which Dahlhaus summarizes thus:

the primary meaning … is not that the parts of a work flow into each other without caesuras but that every note has meaning, that the melody is language and not empty sound. The technical characteristic, the absence of formal cadences, is merely a consequence of the aesthetic factor: cadences are to be regarded as formulas, syntactic but not semantic components – in short, they express nothing and are therefore to be avoided or concealed.[78]

Berg's negation of this aesthetic principle is itself profoundly eloquent: placing the 'old', outworn, supposedly empty melodic close four bars after an initial three-note motivic particle of intensely condensed expressive content is a tactic that speaks of pessimism and decay. It is not restorative, nor is it primarily nostalgic (though the end of the phrase has elements of that tone). It is a sonorous image of the approach to nihilism.

It is instructive to compare the sonata with Schoenberg's setting of Stefan George's Baudelaire paraphrase 'Ich darf nicht dankend' (written in

---

[78] Dahlhaus, *Between Romanticism and Modernism*, 55–6.

Example 4.7 Schoenberg, 'Ich darf nicht dankend', Op.14 No.1 (George), bars 1–5

December 1907 and thus contemporaneous with Berg's sonata). Schoenberg declared this song to be 'distinctly a product of evolution'.[79] The opening phrase begins with a pair of symbolic chords, one of which is identical to the 'advanced' trichord *Ursprung* of Berg's sonata, and the motivic and contrapuntal treatment shares many similarities with Berg's theme (Example 4.7). As Ethan Haimo writes in his Darwinianly titled essay 'Schoenberg and the Origins of Atonality', 'the concept of organicism dictated that this harmonic succession become the structural foundation of the entire composition. The consequences of this for the destabilization of tonality are clear.'[80] The opening chords are the origin of an advanced species of chromatic counterpoint, and the song's 'syntactic foundation' lies in their 'sound and the characteristic succession'.[81] In Dahlhaus's reading the dissonant fourth chord functions as a motif and 'symbolic entity', on the edge of 'renunciation' or 'emancipation'; it 'articulates the tonal and atonal implications that express its moment in history, an unreduplicatable instant in the evolution of compositional technique and the history of ideas'.[82] This illustrates both the combination of advanced aesthetic totality and social timeliness which Adorno sought in the authentically modern artwork, and also a dynamic organic whole which deprives the fetishized objects of their self-evidence. This is the Schoenbergian,

[79] Schoenberg, 'My Evolution' [1949], in *Style and Idea: Selected Writings*, ed. Leonard Stein, trans. Leo Black (London: Faber, 1984), 86. The song may have been composed as a reflection upon the debt Schoenberg felt to Mahler.

[80] Ethan Haimo, 'Schoenberg and the Origins of Atonality', in Juliane Brand and Christopher Hailey (eds.), *Constructive Dissonance: Arnold Schoenberg and the Transformations of Twentieth-Century Culture* (Berkeley: University of California Press, 1997), 84.

[81] Edward T. Cone, 'Sound and Syntax: An Introduction to Schoenberg's Harmony', *Perspectives of New Music* 13 (1974), 32.

[82] Dahlhaus, *Nineteenth-Century Music*, 378–9.

arguably post-Wagnerian, modernist solution to the relation of particular and whole. The end of the song supplies the tonic B minor triad, but there is no perfect cadence. Neither is there a clear perfect cadence at the end of Berg's sonata (there are two greatly weakened points of cadence, bb.174–5 and 176–8, on which more later), for this moribund ending has been supplied at the very beginning. Schoenberg's song is a tonal structure which emerges from an advanced and implicative position. Berg's sonata emerges from a position of deathly closure.

It is also instructive to compare the Berg sonata with the 'normative' or 'ideal' sonata opening of Beethoven's Piano Sonata Op.2 No.1, often raised in formal theory as an example of how 'forward-striving' energies to a climactic highpoint operate within the sentence,[83] with intensification generated through condensation ('Kontraction') in all dimensions.[84] Schoenberg states that in the continuation of a sentence development may be of a kind 'comparable in some respects to the condensation technique of "liquidation". Development implies not only growth, augmentation, extension and expansion, but also condensation and intensification.'[85] But Beethoven's opening gesture is primarily heard as open-ended and implicative: as Nicholas Marston argues, the ending of the sonata 'responds directly to an initial premise' which has 'gaps' and implications requiring completion and resolution.[86] By contrast, Berg begins his sonata by emphasizing the liquidation to the cadence, the decline and close of the wave. Only after the opening closed phrase (the apparent paradox here is characteristic of *fin-de-siècle* pessimism or apocalypticism) do we hear a sentence-type thematic structure behind the wave form (bb.3–10), with the peak achieved, as in Beethoven, by sequentially ascending and accelerating abbreviations of the initial idea (which, of course, by contrast with Beethoven's ascendant rockets, is a dying fall into a black hole).

From the sonata's opening phrase we already know the end. Berg's sonata is a dark critical commentary on the predestinations of teleology, or a bleak reversal of the evolution to higher forms. To compensate, organicism turns to obsessively dense developing variation, to the kind of complex 'motivic evolution' Schoenberg discussed, for example, in the

---

[83] See Matthew BaileyShea, 'Beyond the Beethoven Model: Sentence Types and Limits', *Current Musicology* 77 (2004), 5–33. The 'normative' status of the opening of Beethoven's Op.2 No.1 as archetype of the sentence is familiar from Arnold Schoenberg, *Fundamentals of Musical Composition* (London: Faber, 1967), 63, and maintained through Erwin Ratz to Caplin, *Classical Form*, 10.

[84] Schoenberg, *The Musical Idea*, 250–1.

[85] Schoenberg, *Fundamentals of Musical Composition*, 58.

[86] Marston, '"The sense of an ending"', 86–9.

Example 4.8 Berg, Piano Sonata, analysis of second subject

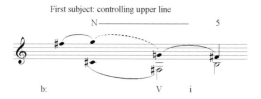

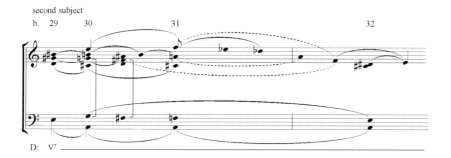

Cello Sonata Op.99 of the 'progressive' Brahms.[87] It is possible, in this spirit, to hear Berg's second subject as a developed variant of the first, transforming the 5–6–5 controlling upper line and sharing similar parallel descending chromatic inner parts (demonstrated analytically in Example 4.8). But this kind of subjective unity was already beginning to break down in certain pieces by Brahms. The recent debate on unity and hetero-geneity, sparked by Robert P. Morgan's article 'The Concept of Unity and Musical Analysis', is helpful here, in particular the historical and cultural contextualization of the concept of unity which lies at the heart of the issue. Aesthetics from the mid-eighteenth century related the unity of the artwork to the supposed unity of the bourgeois subject, an idealized image of synthesis. Kevin Korsyn's discussion of Lewin's and Morgan's analyses of the opening of Brahms's String Quartet Op.51 No.1 illustrates this historical contextualization of formal notions of subjective unity, when he hears it as invoking the sentence – a form associated with Beethovenian, 'heroic' statements – but only in order to subject it to historical contra-dictions and contextual critiques, through the music's shift of tone into lyrical nostalgia.[88] In one respect this confirms Brahms as a figure of 'lateness', as the last in a line composing in 'aged' forms and genres, a

---

[87] Arnold Schoenberg, 'The Orchestral Variations, Op.31: A Radio Talk', *The Score* 27 (1960), 28–30.
[88] Kevin Korsyn, 'The Death of Musical Analysis? The Concept of Unity Revisited', *Music Analysis* 23 (2004), 338, 340–2. This article is a response to Robert P. Morgan's 'The Concept of Unity and Musical Analysis', *Music Anaylsis* 22 (2003), 7–50.

Example 4.9 Berg, Piano Sonata, closing bars

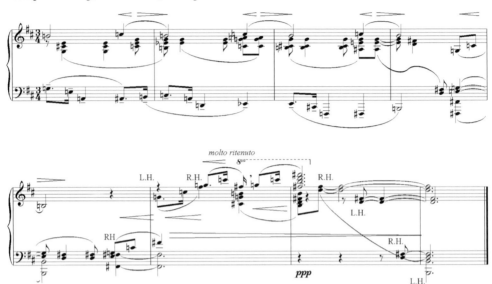

composer identified with the 'twilight' of Viennese middle-class liberalism, by contrast, of course, with Wagnerian radical 'progressiveness'.[89] In a note published in *The Will to Power* Nietzsche declared Brahms as typical 'epigone', associating him with 'borrowed forms', where 'an earlier soul is *recaptured poetically*'.[90] Berg's and Schoenberg's allegiance to, and rehabilitation of, a Brahmsian 'logical', 'potent', developmental style is well known and much discussed, but also it is possible to hear in Berg's Piano Sonata this 'late' or 'decadent' image of Brahms. After the sonata's *Tristan* climactic allusions, post-Brahmsian echoes can be heard in the closing bars. Compare Berg's ending (Example 4.9) with the end of Brahms's Intermezzo Op.119 No.1 (1893) (Example 4.10), where the cadence is coloured by the opening motif, a process whereby motivic closure becomes more potent in the move to the final tonic than the resolution of the dominant: the *closural* potential of the opening motif is thus revealed. In the last bars of Berg's sonata the *Ursprung* is exposed as a coloured version or alternative to the dominant; the weakened cadences are 'borrowed forms' of closure which are the decadent polarity to the 'advanced' quartal motifs which bring about the end.[91]

---

[89] Margaret Notley, *Lateness and Brahms: Music and Culture in the Twilight of Viennese Liberalism* (Oxford University Press, 2007).

[90] Nietzsche, *The Will to Power*, 66.

[91] There are also symbolic repercussions from establishing the key of the sonata so early – raising the question, why B minor? In the Austrian tradition it recalls Schubert's 'black' key of 'Die liebe Farbe' (*Die schöne Müllerin*) – referring to the green which, ironically and painfully, is not of

Example 4.10 Johannes Brahms, Intermezzo Op.119 No.1, closing bars

The work is haunted by the wave form which dies in its opening bars, confirming, as Adorno argued, that by contrast with Wagnerian 'highest joy' ('höchste Lust') there is no ecstatic, glorifying self-extinction, only self-negation.[92] Elegiac wave form operates at large structural level in the sonata. The exposition is structured around a series of highpoints ('Höhepunkte'), with the dissolution of the highest peak followed by an expansive and elegiac *Abgesang*. The peak of the exposition's overarching wave occurs at the tonal clarification of the supertonic seventh chord (b.45), which, in chromatically altered form, was the opening sonority of the piece. The moment of decline from this peak is also marked by motivic clarification of the tragic ♭6–5 (G–F♯) as a signal of closure (recalling its position and function in the descending wave of the opening theme). This then forms the motivic basis of the *Abgesang*, the long, slow, melancholic dissolution of the wave in the exposition's final section. When the opening *Grundgesalt* returns at the repeat of the exposition it sounds more as an end to the *Abgesang* than as a restart. The *Abgesang* material is not used in the development; it is 'held over until the recapitulation, where it brings the Sonata to a close with the movement's most distant recollection, underlying the nostalgic sense of the whole work. This lingering impression is actually enhanced by the absence of any following movements.'[93] The energetics of the wave form are drained

nature's new growth, but of the material covering of the grave. Berg's repetitions of the C–B motif might also evoke the B minor Prelude of Chopin's Op.28.

[92] Adorno, *Alban Berg*, 5.

[93] Anthony Pople, 'Early Works: Tonality and Beyond', in Pople (ed.), *The Cambridge Companion to Berg* (Cambridge University Press, 1997), 61.

away leaving an elegiac tone. Originally conceived as the first movement of a multi-movement work, the piece functions in its solitude because it is so obsessed with ending. At the recapitulation the close of the B minor cadence is avoided: this would be one closure too many. Climax is positioned not at the coda, as is common in romantic form, or at the moment of thematic recapitulation and tonal resolution, as is typical of classical form, but at bar 92 out of 179, almost exactly halfway through the piece, at the peak of the second, greatest process of *Steigerung* in the first half of the development (the first wave is in bb.57–71, with peak at b.68; the second wave is in bb.72–100, with peak at b.92). This suggests decadent form because the recapitulation is weakened not, as in many examples from Brahms, in order to sustain developmental process over this point to the later teleological goal. Although the *Abgesang* is absent from the development section the music from the dissolution of the climax through to the recapitulation is hardly a revitalization. In this transitional-decadent passage the second subject appears in compressed fragments, and although there is an *accelerando* into the recapitulation and a 'resolution' or completing function as it moves to the 'home' augmented triad of the symmetrical counter-structure,[94] there is no strong sense of a new beginning.

While Berg did not discard the 'old' language of Romanticism and sought similar effects to Mahlerian 'nostalgia' and Straussian 'intensifica-tion' he recognized the limitations of such expressions.[95] He also saw the limitations of Schoenberg's view of generative, post-Brahmsian organicism and expressed his opinion in musical structures and process which empha-size a sense of decay and dissolution – those forces contrary to, or compet-ing with, the forces of development and intensification. In this way the tone of his music resonates with cultural pessimism. Berg's Piano Sonata, unlike Mahler's Sixth, with its double Schopenhauerian-Nietzschean character, presents a uniformly Schopenhauerian impression. In a letter dated 30 July 1908 (a few months before he started work on the sonata) he wrote: 'for the last week or so I've been deep in Schopenhauer, who has a great deal to say that's fine and true ... I'm impressed by his pessimism, of course, because of its link with Wagner.' However, Berg continues that, unlike Schopenhauer, Wagner was not 'obsessed' with pessimism but envisaged an optimistic future: 'emancipated' from his Schopenhauerian pessimistic model, 'he's much more modern than Schopenhauer because, like Ibsen

---

94 See Wintle, 'Kontra-Schenker', 175.

95 See J. Peter Burkholder, 'Berg and the Possibility of Popularity', in Gable and Morgan (eds.), *Alban Berg*, 33.

and Nieztsche, he "says yes to life".' Thus in a letter of 23 August 1909 he writes of our 'goal' or 'destination':

a way that leads past the external worldly goals up to the perfection of each human soul. The nearer to this I feel that I am approaching, the more I recognize how long the road still is before we arrive at the mountain top, which from the valley of our lowly existence looked so easy to reach … (a summit which, among other works, includes Mahler's 9th).

Berg then turns to the now familiar oceanic imagery: 'Nietzsche uses the image of "new seas" towards which his ship is irresistibly heading.'[96] Berg's move through decadent pessimism in part may reflect the contemporaneous 'Young Viennese' fascination with Baudelairean morbid and pathological states and (*contra* Loosian anti-ornament and Kraussian cutting clarity) stylized degeneration.[97] The subsequent, Nietzschean embarkment to 'new seas' seems to contrast with Baudelaire's voyage under the sign of death in the last poem of *Les Fleurs du mal*, until the telling last line's evocation of the desire for the new. As Nietzsche proclaimed, in the decadence of modern culture there is no turning back, only moving forward through decadence.

Death, old admiral, up anchor now,
this country wearies us. Put out to sea!
What if the waves and winds are black as ink,
our hearts are filled with light. You know our hearts!
Pour us your poison, let us be comforted!
Once we have burned our brains out, we can plunge
to Hell or Heaven – any abyss will do –
deep in the unknown to find the *new*![98]

Artificial waves: the Count's ballad from Schreker's *Der ferne Klang*

'Artifice is the distinctive mark of human genius.' Thus declares Des Esseintes. He continues by announcing that nature

---

[96] Alban Berg, *Letters to his Wife*, ed. and trans. Bernard Grun (London: Faber, 1971), 37–8.
[97] Andrew Barker, 'Battles of the Mind: Berg and the Cultural Politics of "Vienna 1900"', in Pople (ed.) *The Cambridge Companion to Berg*, 24–37.
[98] 'O Mort, vieux capitaine, il est temps! Levons l'ancre. / Ce pays nous ennuie, ô Mort! Appareillons! / Si le ciel et la mer sont noirs comme de l'encre, / Nos coeurs que tu connais sont remplis de rayons! / Verse-nous ton poison pour qu'il nous réconforte! / Nous voulons, tant ce feu nous brûle le cerveau, / Plonger au fond du gouffre, Enfer ou Cile, qu'importe? / Au fond de l'Inconnu pour trouver du *nouveau*!': Baudelaire, 'Le Voyage', in *Les Fleurs du mal*, trans. Richard Howard (Brighton: Harvester Press, 1982), 156–7 (English version), 334–5 (French original). See Raymond Geuss, 'Berg and Adorno', in Pople (ed.), *The Cambridge Companion to Berg*, 39–41.

has had her day; she has finally and utterly exhausted the patience of sensitive
observers by the revolting uniformity of her landscapes and skyscapes … In fact,
there is not a single one of her inventions, deemed so subtle and sublime, that
human ingenuity cannot manufacture … There can be no shadow of doubt that
with her never-ending platitudes the old crone has by now exhausted the good-
humoured admiration of all true artists, and the time has surely come for artifice to
take her place whenever possible.[99]

Des Esseintes rejects the healthy outdoor pursuit of nature's offerings. He
finds them faded, boring and even abhorrent. Instead, he creates a private,
interior, multi-sensual experience of the sea from the secret chemical
combination of the Pharmacopoeia, so that he can enjoy the sensation of
being 'lulled by the waves created in your bath'. In place of experiencing the
worn-out sublime of nature's waves he sinks into simulated pleasures. The
final section of this chapter explores the concept of artificial waves in a
crucially symbolic section of Schreker's *Der ferne Klang*.

The reputation of Schreker's music has suffered from criticism which
sustains the employment of the term 'decadent' to denote tasteless excess,
sensuality, stylistic licentiousness or aesthetic incoherence. Recently, however, the decadence of his music has been reassessed. A leading voice has
been that of Peter Franklin, who has urged that we get beyond 'culturally
inherited Nordauism' and the more unsophisticated polemics which can
characterize discourses of the 'anxiety of decadence'. Franklin states that we
need to develop a critical discourse which can begin to unravel the way in
which Schreker's *Die Gezeichneten* (1918), for example, 'is itself not only a
symptom but is also in its own way a contribution to discourse *about* art
and degeneracy in the spirit of the times in which it was written'.[100] *Der
ferne Klang* is obviously also about such things. The early critical discussion
of the opera opens up ideas that can form the basis of an example of the
kind of discourse on decadence that Franklin desires. Christopher Hailey's
discussion of the reception of *Der ferne Klang* in his 'cultural biography' of
Schreker focuses on concepts of psychological 'impressionism'. Walter
Niemann, for example, in his *Die Musik seit Richard Wagner* (1913),
described Schreker's as external and superficial music, as an art of the
nerves and senses, whose colour and sound (*Klang*) embodied a style

[99] Huysmans, *Against Nature*, 36–7.
[100] Peter Franklin, '"Wer weiss, Vater, ob das nicht Engel sind?" Reflections on the Pre-Fascist
Discourse of Degeneracy in Schreker's *Die Gezeichneten*', in Nikolas Bacht (ed.), *Music, Theatre
and Politics in Germany: 1848 to the Third Reich* (Aldershot: Ashgate, 2006), 174–8. See also
Franklin's earlier essay 'Style, Structure and Taste: Three Aspects of the Problem of Franz
Schreker', *Proceedings of the Royal Musical Association* 109 (1982–3), 134–46.

liberated from linear and temporal obligations to allow the generation of momentarily stimulating impressions. For Niemann, Schreker's music was radical in its freedoms, and decadent in its effect. Richard Specht, in his review of the premiere of the *Nachstück* section of the opera (1910), wrote of 'hallucinatory, mysterious, mystical sounds of haunting fascination, confused whisperings, beseeching voices, whose glimmering murmurs ultimately dissolve into resplendent, transfigured rapture'.[101] Both Specht's identification of musical hallucinations producing new forms of transfiguration and Niemann's description of a quality of external musical colours pinpoint a crucial aspect of the music's characteristic effect, and in particular one strategy for dealing with the legacy of Wagner's 'oceanic' erotics: namely, Schreker's technique of reproducing in new light the characteristic harmonic and motivic content of Wagner's waves to create artificial and illusory impressions of critical symbolic importance.

Adorno's 1959 essay 'Schreker' remains a central critical text in Schreker reception. His observation that Schreker made reproductions of the technical effects of Wagner's 'phantasmagoria' and placed them at the 'centrepiece of his own work' has in particular generated an important strand in recent criticism.[102] The phantasmagoric is a mirage of timelessness and naturalness in which the technique of its construction – its artifice – is concealed. In *Der ferne Klang* the concept of phantasmagoria rises to special symbolic prominence. Adorno described the *Klang*, which is the opera's most famous musical-symbolic entity, as an 'auditory *Fata Morgana*': it 'hangs in the air, colourful, transparent and denatured'.[103] It is possible to read Schreker's operas against Adorno and view the illusory, deceptive characteristics of the phantasmagoric in more positive critical light. Two recent essays have explored such an approach. Sherry D. Lee has identified 'multiple instances in which musical gesture that seems regressive or phantasmagorical on first hearing sounds much more authentically critical after the significance of its dramatic context is examined'.[104] Adrian Daub writes of the self-consciousness of phantasmagoric production through which 'Schreker constitutes an alternate modernity to that of the "new music" – an alternative that does not break phantasmagoria by allowing for rupture and alienation within

[101] *Der Merker*, 1–8 January 1910, trans. in Christopher Hailey, *Franz Schreker 1878–1934: A Cultural Biography* (Cambridge University Press, 1993), 51.

[102] Adorno, *Quasi una fantasia*, 132.

[103] *Quasi una fantasia*, 134; *In Search of Wagner*, 86. For wider cultural manifestations of *fata morgana* see Marina Warner, *Phantasmagoria: Spirit Visions, Metaphors, and Media into the Twenty-First Century* (Oxford University Press, 2006), especially 95–103.

[104] Sherry D. Lee, 'A Minstrel in a World without Minstrels: Adorno and the Case of Schreker', *Journal of the American Musicological Society* 58 (2005), 661, 687.

the audience's experience, but one that overburdens and over-invests phantasmagoria to its breaking point'. Daub concludes that the 'relationship of the Schreker-sound to phantasmagoric identity is thus an ambivalent one'.[105] With Lee's and Daub's comments in mind we can turn to a crucial moment in the opera, the Count's ballad in Act 2, where counterfeit waves of 'Wagnerian' sound rise to symbolic prominence.

The act is set in the Casa di Maschere, on an island in the Gulf of Venice. The Count arrives on a gondola and looks for Greta, who has previously rejected his amorous advances. His ballad is the first contribution in a story-telling contest for Greta's affections. It tells of a king who, whenever he falls in love, is tormented by a burning crown. When the crown is thrown into the waves the figure of a pale woman rises and drags the king down into the waters. Ulrike Kienzle analyses Schreker's music for the ballad as a three-part exposition (matching the first three strophes – the presentation, explanation and fixation of the situation), followed by *Steigerung*, the musical and dramatic turning point (*Einschnitt*), building to the *Höhepunkt* (when the king throws the crown into the sea), *Peripetie* and *Katastrophe* (the rise of the female figure and the death of the king), with a concluding instrumental *Nachspiel*. Kienzle's formal intepretation is based on a controlling tonal progression of E flat minor (expositions) to D major (at the *Steigerung*), closing in E flat major.[106] The formal functions outline the contents and characteristics of the romantic wave form through presentation, intensification, highpoint, moment of crisis and instability and dissolving resolution. But Schreker undermines the wave form by placing the intensification in the key a semitone lower than the opening and close. Tonal 'sinking' is coincident with rising processes of *Steigerung* in other musical parameters. Furthermore, the D major is not a tonic as Kienzle hears it, but acts as a subdominant to an unachieved A (which would be tritonally distant from the local tonic E flat), and is always shadowed by allusions to B minor (enharmonic C flat), the tragic flat submediant minor of the tonic E flat. Thus in this relationship of formal and harmonic design Schreker invokes the wave form, but in a manner which lends it a distanced and denuded form. The ascent to the *Höhepunkt* seems artificial as it is not organically unified with the expressive effect of the tonal process. This strategic subterfuge is further concentrated in the music of

---

[105] Adrian Daub, 'Adorno's Schreker: Charting the Self-Dissolution of the Distant Sound', *Cambridge Opera Journal* 18 (2006), 261, 271.

[106] Ulrike Kienzle, *Das Trauma hinter dem Traum: Franz Schrekers Oper 'Der ferne Klang' und die Wiener Moderne* (Schliengen: Edition Argus, 1998), 380.

the *Peripetie* and *Katastrophe*. As Lee describes it, 'from the waves come the muffled strains of music (tellingly, polytriadic chords and arpeggios in harp and celesta); a pale woman "with a mad look" rises, reaches for [the king] and pulls him under with her. This woman, who appears on the ocean surface like the *Fata Morgana* invoked by Adorno, is both the visual and musical manifestation of phantasmagoria.'[107] Lee notes that the ballad has multiple Wagnerian resonances, citing the ballads in *The Flying Dutchman* and the song contests in *Tannhäuser* and *Mastersingers*. When the wave form of the ballad is scrutinized on the level of harmony and motif, symbolic relationships also emerge with *Tristan and Isolde*.

The *Tristan* allusion is especially marked in the materials through which the ballad's illusory 'waves' end. Danuser has demonstrated that Wagner developed a 'structural harmonic formula' for endings which was often combined with versions of an *Erlösungsmotiv*. Only after composing the ideal type of this ending in *Tristan and Isolde* did Wagner feel that he could write the correct ending for *The Flying Dutchman* – the oceanic-redemptive moment, achieved by the sacrifice of the woman, where the final tonic is approached by the move from the minor subdominant under a rising 5–6 melodic line to the third over the tonic. In Isolde's Transfiguration, as she sings, 'In the delicious sea of the surging swell, in the reverberating sound of scented waves, in the billowing, all-embracing vastness of the world-breath, to drown – sink down – unconscious – highest bliss!', the same formula is 'individualized' by the chromatic rising line of the *Sehnsuchtmotiv* (Example 4.11).[108] In the closing paragraphs of the Count's ballad Schreker turns to Wagner's device, as an experimentally tested formula, a kind of alchemical musical compound in a symbolic solution. When the king throws the crown into the sea and the pale woman rises from the waves to claim him, unstable chromaticism moves towards functional clarification in the form of an embellished dominant ninth chord on E. As the female figure rises the harmony shifts to D major, whose harmonic implication in this context is the subdominant of an unheard A major. This turns to D minor (3 bars after fig.60) and the orchestral upper line rises to A, then B. The music is by now beginning to evoke Wagner's formula by the implied modal shift from major to minor subdominant supporting a rising 5–6. But at the wave climax (fig.61) there is an unexpected shift as the anticipated A major is replaced by an altered dominant on F♯ (V of B). The

[107] Lee, 'A Minstrel in a World without Minstrels', 679.
[108] Danuser, 'Musical Manifestations of the End'.

Example 4.11 Wagner, *Tristan and Isolde*, closing bars

orchestral melodic line continues with D–C♯, to complete a version of Wagner's *Erlösungsmotiv* (A–B–D–C♯). This dominant now behaves exactly as did the preceding dominant of A: it moves to the subdominant of the implied key, which is now B major, the *Tristan* key of transfiguration. Once again the subdominant chord, E, turns to minor. Over this chord the waves repeatedly articulate further 5–6 motifs up to the resolution to B major, at which 7–6 (A♯–G♯) moves echo the falling dyad at the end of Wagner's *Erlösungsmotiv* (Example 4.12). Thus not only is Wagner's wave-like model of *Erlösung* ending overtly copied, but its defining harmonic move to the minor subdominant is also mimicked, twice. It reveals the compulsion to imitate and artificially reproduce, to repeat the famous, formulaic ending.

But there are significant symbolic differences. In the closing bars of *Tristan* Wagner's chromatic harmony suggests that 'transfiguration' includes the final satisfaction of desire through a mythical, androgynous union. As Wagner knew, Plato's theory of Eros as described in *Symposium* sees the arousal of erotic desire as driven by the urge to reunite male and female to re-form the primary androgynous being. Wagner's music suggests a musical correlative to this by drawing together materials with dominant and subdominant functions. The final resolution to B major is achieved through a last recollection of the famous chromatic motifs and chord which opened the work, with the A♯–B now functioning not as an alteration or decoration of a dominant chord, but as chromatic embellishment of the 'feminine' subdominant. The Tristan chord now has a pre-subdominant, rather than the pre-dominant function it served in the Prelude. In the transfigured chromaticism of the final cadence the A♯ also serves to recall the immediately preceding chromatic alterations of the dominant of B which earlier generated a passing dominant minor ninth, including the same diminished seventh that is now produced above the minor subdominant chord. Furthermore, the A♯–B over the subdominant is, of course, a motivic statement of the motion from leading note to tonic. Dominant and subdominant figures are in this way tied together in a complex, chromatic fusion. This symbolic union of function is absent in Schreker's ballad. Its waves lead only to a return of the Count's fateful refrain. In this doubled Wagnerian phantasmagoria the satisfaction of desire in mythic union is denied: *Erlösung* is revealed as an illusion, now manifestly available only in highly wrought simulation. This characteristic is also suggested by the orchestral timbre, which, by contrast with the surging, throbbing, pulsating depths of Wagner's waves of transfiguration, is febrile yet fragile, a complex filigree of surface patterns.

Schreker's 'Wagnerian' waves have a well-known literary parallel in Mann's *Buddenbrooks*. The young Hanno's composition is tacitly modelled on the conclusion of *Tristan*. It is severely criticized by his teacher:

Example 4.12 Franz Schreker, *Der ferne Klang*, Act 2 scene vi, the Count's ballad, Count: '(und) nassem Haar …'

Example 4.12 (cont.)

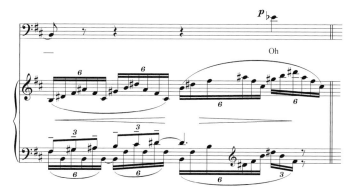

why do you suddenly fall from B major into the six-four chord on the fourth note with a minor third? These are tricks; and you tremolo here, too – where did you pick that up? I know, of course: you have been listening when I played certain things for your mother. Change the end, child: then it will be quite a clean little piece of work.[109]

In spite of his teacher's dissatisfaction with this artifice its closing formula was the boy's favourite effect. On his playing it again, with his mother joining in on the violin, its effects on the boy, as Danuser notes, are described 'in scarcely veiled terms as an orgasm'. What Danuser fails to note is that this obsession with the formula continues in a later performance. 'Then he went to the piano. He stood for a while, and his gaze, directed fixed and unseeing upon a distant point, altered slowly, grew blurred and vague and shadowy. He sat down at the instrument and began to improvise.' The improvisation's ending was based on the working over of a motivic particle 'of a bar and half in length'. Hanno's fervent focus on a Wagnerian miniature formula is then described:

There was a quality of the perverse in the insatiability with which it was produced and reveled in: there was a sort of cynical despair; there was a longing for joy, a yielding to desire, in the way the last drop of sweetness was, as it were, extracted from the melody, till exhaustion, disgust, and satiety supervened. Then, at last; at last, in the weariness after excess, a long, soft arpeggio in the minor trickled through, mounted a tone, resolved itself in the major, and died in mournful lingering away.[110]

The repetition 'at last; at last …' expresses the gasping relief at reaching the desired expression, the magical formula of the end, after the exhaustions of

---

[109] Mann, *Buddenbrooks*, 412.   [110] Mann, *Buddenbrooks*, 595, 597.

squeezing the 'last drops' of exquisite effect from the musical particles. But the hyperbole of the repetition of 'at last' not only speaks of the great expressive burdens invested in that ending, but also reveals its mannered, overwrought character. The ironic use of a tawdry expression speaks of Hanno's post-Wagnerian musical artifice.[111]

The Count's ballad ends with waves in the tonic major, E flat, and thus evokes the paradigmatic wave forms of Wagner's magical musical image of the 'natural', the opening of *The Rhinegold*, whose special, 'authentic' waves were, Wagner said, dream-revealed while he was in Venice.[112] The Count's imaginary recreations of these waves remind us that Venice is the setting of Act 2 of Schreker's opera, where waves are reclaiming the beautiful, decaying fabric of human endeavour, the city of the venerable and the venereal. As Aschenbach puts it: 'Yes this was Venice, this the fair frailty that fawned and that betrayed, half fairy-tale, half snare; the city in whose stagnating air the art of painting once put forth so lusty a growth, and where musicians were moved to accords so weirdly lulling and lascivious.'[113] The symbolic status of Venice is heightened by Wagner's stay at the Palazzo Giustiniani in August 1858 with *Tristan* as yet unfinished, and by his death celebrated by D'Annunzio's inscription on the wall of the Palazzo Vendramin, where Wagner's final exhalation eternally returns in the incoming waves:

In this palace the souls hear
the last breath of Richard Wagner
perpetuating itself like the tide
which washes the marble beneath.[114]

The E flat of the ballad's conclusion foreshadows the end of the opera. (Parallels between the ballad's narrative of the king's predicament and Fritz's story across the opera have been noted by Paul Bekker and Kienzle.) But at this end the waves are annihilated. Again the Wagnerian resemblances are crucial. For Lee, the end of *Der ferne Klang* is 'almost like a

---

[111] Hanno's father, Thomas Buddenbrook, had earlier compared the relative health of those who contemplate the mountains and the sea. 'It is a strong, challenging gaze, full of enterprise, that can soar from peak to peak; but the eyes that rest on the wide ocean and are soothed by the sight of its waves rolling on forever, mystically, relentlessly, are those that are already wearied by looking too deep into the solemn perplexities of life. – Health and illness, that is the difference': Mann, *Buddenbrooks*, 538.

[112] On the *Rhinegold* waves as illusion see Richard Leppert, 'Paradise, Nature and Reconciliation, or, A Tentative Conversation with Wagner, Puccini, Adorno and The Ronettes', *Echo: A Music-Centered Journal*, 4/1 (2002), http://www.echo.ucla.edu/Volume4-Issue1/leppert/index.html, accessed 12 December 2008.

[113] Mann, *Death in Venice*, 59.   [114] Trans. from Furness, *Wagner and Literature*, 45.

Liebestod', but a 'seemingly Wagnerian moment of transcendence in music and in death ... is somehow thwarted'.[115] The *fortissimo* E flat minor chord at the very end sounds a pessimistic and dystopian conclusion. For Daub, what appears to be a '*Liebestod*-pastiche is disrupted by a final, violent blow, which seems to achieve the opposite of transfiguration'.[116] This ending is the final confirmation of the opera's complex relationship with *Tristan*'s erotics and Schopenhauerian metaphysics, and of Schreker's self-consciously ambiguous position with regard to Wagner – seeking to break away from him, yet always overshadowed by him.[117] This defining position is encapsulated in the artificial wave, where the dangers of pale imitation are turned to exquisitely colourful products.

[115] Lee, 'A Minstrel in a World without Minstrels', 684.　　[116] Daub, 'Adorno's Schreker', 268.
[117] Carl Dahlhaus, 'Schreker and Modernism: On the Dramaturgy of *Der ferne Klang*', in *Schoenberg and the New Music*, trans. Derrick Puffett and Alfred Clayton (Cambridge University Press, 1987), 199–200.

5 | Mannerism and avant-garde

Art will produce in [her votaries] a fastidiousness, an over-refinement,
a nervous fever and exhaustion, such as a career of extravagant passions
and pleasures can hardly know.

Thomas Mann, *Death in Venice* (1911)

Palms with sharp fingers stab me, crumbling leaves in hissing throngs…

Stefan George, *The Book of the Hanging Gardens* (1895)

Introduction

'Mannerism' and 'decadence' are terms frequently tainted by associations
with deterioration of stylistic quality. Both are commonly understood as
signs of enfeeblement and the moribund. The *Oxford English Dictionary*
defines mannerism as 'excessive addiction to a distinctive manner' and as
a 'trick of style'. It is, by this definition, obsessively dependent, meretricious
and mendacious. In eighteenth- and nineteenth-century art criticism 'mannerism' was a term which denoted 'fatal' decline. It was employed, for
example, by Burckhardt in 1855 (*Der Cicerone: Eine Anleitung zum Genuss
der Kunstwerke Italiens*) to describe the period of decadence following
the immense artistic achievements of the Renaissance. 'Mannerism' was
later used to denote the period of sickly 'disintegration' of *art nouveau*
which followed the heroically integrative aspirations of romanticism. In
these and other contexts 'mannerism' was characteristically invoked to
'connote negative criteria of extravagance, preciosity and abnormality' –
'in short', as Maria Rika Maniates put it, to identify 'stylistic "effeteness".
"Virility" … is rarely imputed to "mannerism".' The term was, however,
granted some degree of rehabilitation in twentieth-century scholarship. Its
associated qualities of distortion, morbidity, obsolescence or artificiality
could be justified, and even lauded, through their relationship with more
widely valued notions of artistic style, such as expressionism. In other
contexts it was invoked as 'neomannerism', a term designed to denote a
supposedly healthy distance from old forms of mannerism, in a strategic

labelling aimed at indicating a 'newness' or fresh relevance. This new validity was based on viewing the trend as a crucial artistic response to periods of intense social stress, as a 'mirror of a spirit of alienation, hypersensitivity and nervous refinement', for example, as particularly strongly manifest at the *fin de siècle*. Thus, as Maniates concludes, 'rather than dismiss these [mannerist] elements as illustrations of sterile decadence, we should examine them as the vital expression of a period, a group, or an individual', consider their 'affections as cultural symptom'. Mannerism in particular should be revalued as a 'virile tendency to anticlassical and anti-natural style'.[1] These oppositions – classical versus anti-classical, and natural versus artificial – will emerge as crucial in this chapter. This revaluation of mannerism also further reveals that decadence is far from simply an indicator of senility or sterility.

Decadence's association with ideas of mannerism arises from a shared sense of lateness. Both seem to pursue a style beyond its 'natural' lifespan and functional purpose. But apparently non-functional formal complexity and stylistic excess have also been observed in nature, sometimes obsessively so. Early in Mann's *Doctor Faustus* we learn that the young Adrian Leverkühn was absorbed by the illustrations he saw in his father's books of 'exotic lepidoptera and sea creatures' and tropical insects of 'fantastically exaggerated beauty'. On the surfaces of such 'freaks' of nature kaleidoscopic colourings, optical illusions and 'tricks' were produced in 'miniature construction'. Leverkühn observed with wonder the 'hieroglyphs' on the shells of sea-snails and mussels, ornamental figures of indecipherable meaning, and the 'windings and vaultings, executed in splendid perfection, with a sense of form as bold as it was delicate, these rosy openings, these iridescent faience splendours …'. This exquisite, surface beauty was 'sometimes even malignant', reflecting the potential employment of these bizarre curiosities in the black magic of the 'witch's kitchen and alchemist's vault'. And yet 'they had served as shrines and reliquaries and even for the Eucharist. What a confrontation there! – poison and beauty, poison and magic, even magic and ritual.' Imitations of the complex organic forms of nature were also of great interest, including the 'phantasmagoria' of ice crystals and chemical gardens.[2] This detailed reporting of Leverkühn's youthful enthusiasm for these phenomena is clearly intended to throw light on an important

---

[1] Maria Rika Maniates, 'Musical Mannerism: Effeteness or Virility?', *The Musical Quarterly* 57 (1971), 270–93.

[2] Thomas Mann, *Doctor Faustus*, trans. H. T. Lowe-Porter (Harmondsworth: Penguin, 1968), 19–25.

formative stage in the development of his creative imagination. His early preoccupation with late or artificial extravagance is a vital aspect of his character. Miniaturized, excessive complexities, which push their forms beyond 'natural' norms into the realms of arabesque over-abundance, represent a key inspirational idea in his art.

Leverkühn's example is instructive. His fascination with over-developed microscopic complexity offers a compelling case for reconsidering the artistic productivity of mannerism. In the next two sections mannerism will be explored by considering its relationship with other important ideas associated with the decadent. Miniaturism, like mannerism, is often identified as a characteristic aspect of decadence.[3] Mann considered a 'love of the very small' to be the obverse of nineteenth-century monumental grandeur.[4] In the decadent pantheon miniaturism is familiar from Des Esseintes's infatuation with Fabergé jewellery in Huysmans's *À Rebours* and Bourget's study of Baudelaire, which so heavily influenced the discussion of miniaturism in Nietzsche's coruscating diagnosis of modern musical decadence in *The Case of Wagner*. Nietzsche declared that 'What can be done well today, what can be masterly, is only what is small.'[5] Manifestations of miniaturism in *fin-de-siècle* Russian music provide a particularly fruitful context for reassessing the relationship of mannerism and decadence.

Russian miniaturism: Scriabin, Lyadov and the Chopinesque

Miniaturism is an especially intriguing aspect of the Chopinesque in Russian music. As a creative response to the Polish composer's mastery of small forms and art of exquisite detail and ornament, it forms part of Russian composers' strategic, 'metonymic' selection of technical and aesthetic aspects of Chopin's style.[6] The epigonal indictment implied by certain uses of the term 'mannerism' is encapsulated by labelling

---

[3] Recall that Taruskin turns to 'tiny pieces' for his examples of musical decadence; see *The Oxford History*, 30.

[4] Mann, 'The Sorrows and Grandeur of Richard Wagner', 92.

[5] Nietzsche, *The Case of Wagner*, 188.

[6] See Jim Samson, 'Chopin Reception: Theory, History, Analysis', in John Rink and Jim Samson (eds.), *Chopin Studies 2* (Cambridge University Press, 1994), 9. At this point, a caveat. Murray Perahia once called the description of Chopin as a miniaturist 'repulsive' and 'dishonest'; see John Rink, 'Chopin in Performance: Perahia's Musical Dialogue', *The Musical Times* 142 (2001), 9–15. My comments do not seek to sustain the cliché of limiting Chopin's achievements to the small scale; they are motivated by the concern, which Jeffrey Kallberg raised some years ago, that 'we finally move the veil of aesthetic suspicion from smallness': Kallberg, 'Small "Forms":

something with the suffix '-esque'. Terms such as 'Chopinesque' are ambiguous, suggesting either stylish evocation of a prestigious predecessor or the perilous dangers of pale imitation. This indicates stylistic borrowing or emulation which may, explicitly or implicitly, be homage or compliment, but at worst may be viewed as parasitical, a weak imitation which actually drains the artistic life out of the revered source of inspiration.[7] For some composers, the coincidence of the *fin de siècle* with the fiftieth anniversary of Chopin's death further intensified the burden of 'timeliness', which, as Edward Said has demonstrated, characteristically implies a creative healthiness dependent on appropriateness. By contrast, 'lateness' accrues associations with 'the decay of the body, the onset of ill health or other factors which even in a younger person bring on the possibility of an untimely end'.[8] Decadence can be viewed, on the one withered hand, as mannerism inappropriately or unnaturally come too soon, *à rebours*. In this sense it is identified in prematurely aged works of untimely over-ripeness, showing too early those 'wrinkles' or 'fissures' and 'more traces of history than of growth', all of which Adorno identified as features of the authentic 'late work'.[9] Or, on the other emaciated hand, decadence can be viewed as belatedness, the far too late, as the necrophiliac resuscitation of the decaying cadaver of a previously vital style, as might be implied by the term 'late romantic', let alone by the 'posthumous'

In Defense of the Prelude', in *Chopin at the Boundaries: Sex, History and Musical Genre* (Cambridge, Mass.: Harvard University Press, 1996), 158.

[7] Here one might invoke Harold Bloom's famous theory of the modern poet who, in his position of anxious belatedness, employs strategies to resist incestuous dependence on his predecessors, thereby gaining creative health and strength. In a famous musicological appropriation of Bloom's theories Kevin Korsyn raises No.12 of Max Reger's *Träume am Kamin*, Op.143, as an example of creative feebleness, hearing its arabesques as 'flaccid' and 'meandering' because, by contrast with the 'dialectical tension' between periodicity and 'endless melody' in its all-too-obvious model, Chopin's *Berceuse*, there is nothing to resist or 'overcome': Kevin Korsyn, 'Towards a New Poetics of Musical Influence', *Music Analysis* 10 (1991), 46, 49. Bloom is now much criticized, of course, but in my context his problematic image of masculine creativity raises important questions. Lloyd Whitesell's devastating critique highlighted the symptomatic crisis of masculine virile identity, the image of the weak artist as degenerate last of the line, which is magnified by the anxieties and gender challenges in *fin-de-siècle* cultural discourse. Indeed, tellingly, at the opening of *The Anxiety of Influence* Bloom raises Oscar Wilde as exemplar of the 'failed' poet: here he turns to the decadent effete as a paradigm of the creatively feeble figure of shame. See Lloyd Whitesell, 'Men with a Past: Music and the "Anxiety of Influence"', *19th-Century Music* 18 (1994), 152–67.

[8] Edward W. Said, *On Late Style: Music and Literature Against the Grain* (London: Bloomsbury, 2006).

[9] Theodor W. Adorno, *Beethoven: The Philosophy of Music*, ed. Rolf Tiedermann, trans. Edmund Jephcott (Stanford University Press, 1998), 123. It could also be seen as creative response to late 'non-normative bodily or mental functions, of impairment or disability': Joseph Straus, 'Disability and "Late Style" in Music', *Journal of Musicology* 25 (2008), 3–45.

connotations of 'post-romantic'. As Dahlhaus noted, the decades between Wagner's death and the 'New Music' of around 1910 are often labelled 'late Romantic' or 'post-Romantic' and thus too often either dismissed as 'nothing but an end and a decline' or considered to be merely a transition towards something healthier and stronger.[10] Dahlhaus raised Scriabin as a representative of this problematic period. As we shall see, in Scriabin, out of mannerism and decadence emerge miniature documents of the New Music, compressed expressions of the avant-garde. Scriabin's critical reputation as visionary modernist or hero of the avant-garde seems to be the very opposite to the status granted to Lyadov, who is usually dismissed as an indolent epigone or incurable romantic, as an anachronistic figure ignoring the turbulent events around him.[11] These composers are, however, closely linked through their turn to the Chopinesque.[12] Analysis of their creative responses to Chopin enhances understanding of their relationship and clarifies the significance of miniaturism and mannerism in Russian *fin-de-siècle* music.

Chopin's reputation in Russia, built on an image of him as 'modernist' (*noveishii*) nationalist in the 1850s and also as 'Slavic' composer, suffered something of a decline in subsequent decades as projects of realism, positivistic nationalism and Russification saw him reassessed as belonging to an apparently irrelevant Polish romantic past.[13] In the Russian reaction against Chopin familiar tropes of femininity and sickness emerged. Anton Rubinstein, who in his memoirs stated that Chopin had written the last note in the history of genuine music, in 1861 nevertheless warned his pupils against imitating Chopin's *rubato* because it was a product of

---

[10] Dahlhaus, 'Structure and Expression in the Music of Scriabin' [1972], in *Schoenberg and the New Music*, 201–9.

[11] The first verse of Verlaine's 'Langueur' (1883) seems especially appropriate: 'Je suis l'Empire à la fin de la décadence, / Qui regarde passer les grands Barbares blancs / En composant des acrostiches indolents / D'un style d'or où la langueur du soleil danse.' ('I am the empire at the end of the decadence, / Watching the white Barbarians as they pass, / Making acrostics up in my idleness / In a golden style of sunlit languor.') For commentary see Philip Stephan, *Paul Verlaine and the Decadence, 1882–90* (Manchester University Press, 1974).

[12] See Seong Ae Lim, 'The Influence of Chopin's Piano Music on the Twenty-Four Preludes for Piano, Op.11 of Alexander Scriabin', unpublished PhD thesis, Ohio State University, 2002. On Chopin's influence on Lyadov see Zofia Lissa, *Studia nad twórczości Fryderyka Chopina* (Cracow: PWM, 1970).

[13] Anne Swartz, 'Chopin as Modernist in Nineteenth-Century Russia', in Rink and Samson (eds.), *Chopin Studies 2*, 35–49; and 'Chopin, Politics, and Musical Meaning in Russia during the Reign of Nicholas 1', in James S. Pula and M. B. Biskupski (eds.), *Selected Essays from the Fiftieth Anniversary International Congress of the Polish Institute of Arts and Sciences of America*, vol.III: *Heart of the Nation: Polish Literature and Culture* (New York: Columbia University Press, 1993), 203–9.

the composer's sickness. Balakirev publicly sustained the memory and celebration of Chopin beyond the break-up of the Kuchkists, but Rimsky-Korsakov recalls him characterizing Chopin as 'a nervous society lady', producing 'pretty lacework' and cautioning against the emulation of Chopin's 'sweet and womanish' melodic style.[14] In Rimsky-Korsakov's verdict Chopin emerges with more 'healthy' artistic credit. Rimsky was obsessively concerned with avoiding the 'decadence' he heard in the music of Debussy and Strauss and the trappings of what, in a terrible pun, he called 'D'Indyism' (Dandyism). He pursued this through polyphonic and systematic harmonic rigour and a retreat into fantasy, the recherché and the recondite.[15] He shared with Lyadov a fascination with the controlled complexity of octatonic pitch structures, as revealed in the harmonic procedures of many of his works and in Lyadov's 'fantasy miniatures' for orchestra.[16] The Lisztian legacy here is well known – but in other respects Chopin was acknowledged as a crucial model. Rimsky wrote in his memoirs: 'Chopin's influence on me was indubitable, in the melodic turns of my music as well as in many of my harmonic devices; but this fact the gimlet-eyed critics had never observed, to be sure.'[17] Though not often sounding much like Chopin, Rimsky's opera *Pan Voyevoda* (1902–3) was composed as a celebration of Chopin's sustained significance.

And yet in seeking to resist one species of apparent decadence, Rimsky, his colleagues and his successors spawned it in another form. In their music Chopinesque techniques were extended into the mannerist and the fastidious. The Belyayev group – of which Lyadov was a leading figure – might have been a 'safe harbour' for conformist and minor talent against the perceived threat of 'Silver Age' decadence, but it also functioned as an artistic 'hothouse' through its 'isolationism', its closed, inward-looking perspective which sought to protect growth from contamination. As such the group appears closeted, artificial, incestuous. Indeed, Taruskin sees the 'Belyayevets' generation as exhibiting 'symptoms of genetic decay' as the once vital and energetic New Russian School sank into 'eclecticism and epigonism'.[18] Scriabin spent his formative years in this Belyayev 'incubator', and 'retained to the end of his career a fastidious, not to say pedantic concern

[14] Nikolay Andreyevich Rimsky-Korsakov, *My Musical Life*, trans. from the 5th rev. Russian edn by Judah A. Joffe, ed. with an introduction by Carl van Vechten (London: Eulenburg, 1974), 20–1, 28. On feminine tropes in Chopin reception see Kallberg, *Chopin at the Boundaries*, Part I, 'Ideology, Sex, and the Piano Miniature', 3–86.
[15] Taruskin, *Defining Russia Musically*, 83–4.
[16] Taruskin, *Stravinsky and the Russian Traditions*, vol.I (Oxford University Press, 1996), 298.
[17] Rimsky-Korsakov, *My Musical Life*, 397.
[18] Taruskin, *Stravinsky and the Russian Traditions*, 56, 65, 73.

for polish and finish'. In the music composed by members of this closed circle, particularly that composed after Rimsky's death in 1908, Taruskin sees 'maximilization', an 'intensifying of means' and extension of traditional techniques and forms, pursued 'to the point of so-called decadence'.[19] Contemporaneous criticism helps us to unpick this tendency, particularly the confluence of 'maximilization' and Chopinesque miniaturism.

Vyacheslav Karatïgin's 1914 obituary for Lyadov describes the composer as an 'intermediate' figure between the Kuchkists and Belyayevites, especially because of his 'Schumannism and Chopinism', which were parts of his 'cult of technique, the perfection of a composition's technical finish'.[20] The obituary is an apologia. Lyadov's works are 'slight', 'intimate', 'domestic', expressive of 'indoor comforts' in the form of 'musical jewelry', but they are miniatures which represent the 'highest achievements of Russian creativity in music' and in which 'every "Chopinesque" pattern … was worked out by Lyadov with a special kind of heartfelt tenderness and an infatuation with the game of matching sounds to one another'. The music 'convinces' Karatïgin because of the 'aristocratic detachment' and the 'elusive and unsteady' nature of Lyadov's 'soul': the composer retreated behind a 'shell of self-absorption and seclusion in both his life and work', the result of his 'over-acute spiritual sensitivity'. In Lyadov's music Karatïgin hears no 'gloom', no 'profundity', no 'concentratedeness of creative thought', but rather a 'play' or 'kaleidoscope of sounds'. In particular Karatïgin believes Lyadov was 'inscrutably able to endow what seem to be the most "superficial" ideas with inner significance', producing a 'superficial depth' like the the play of light and waves on 'the surface of the sea'; are these, he asks, 'really less of an enigma, less beautiful, less poetic than what takes place in the depths of the ocean?' For Karatïgin, Lyadov's is a 'Wildean' art of beautiful surface: 'Lyadov's exceptional predilection for the miniature helps to resolve the paradoxical question of finding depth in the surface' and explains the music's apparently 'ephemeral', 'fleshless', over-elegant character. Karatïgin understands Lyadov's miniaturism to be a matter not only of form but also of psychological content. Lyadov transposes Chopin's 'natural' or 'human' emotive scale to the artificially enclosed. 'All the reflections of aesthetic emotions, all the movements of the soul, the entire realm of pathos, are presented in Lyadov's art on an exceedingly reduced

---

[19] Taruskin, *Defining Russia Musically*, 85–7.
[20] Vyacheslav Karatïgin, 'In Memory of A. K. Lyadov', *Apollo*, 1914, Nos.6–7, trans. in Campbell (trans. and ed.), *Russians on Russian Music*, 159–67.

scale by comparison with their "natural size". And because all is small and toy-like, everything becomes special, unusual, different from the ordinary.' By contrast with Scriabin's 'magnified', 'cosmic' scale, or Chopin's 'normal "clear sight"', Karatïgin continues, Lyadov demands a musical microscope 'armed with special psychological prisms and lenses' to 'scrutinize attentively the worlds of the inner life of sound opening up before one's eyes'.[21] Thus Lyadov's 'Wildean' art of surface is also 'unnaturally' miniaturized and concentrated.

It is easy to see how Karatïgin comes to this characterization. Lyadov's piano preludes eschew the 'larger' ternary designs of, for example, Chopin's F sharp and D flat major Preludes from Op.28, which introduce contrast and 'otherness' in the middle section. Like Scriabin, Lyadov almost exclusively restricts the prelude form to a single period (as in Chopin's G major and E minor, for example). They are solipsistic aphorisms which do not open up to embrace marked difference. The period is a question which answers itself. Ternary design – the favoured form of miniature musical romanticism, with its suggestions of self–other encounters, or with a sentimental desire to return to 'original', 'natural' material – is rejected. Where Lyadov does expand his enclosed miniature formal model, for example in his Op.10 No.1 in D flat (1885) (Example 5.1), it is by a sort of generic hybridization, extending the sense of ending from the arrival on the final structural dominant by evoking the florid endings characteristic of Chopin's Nocturnes in E flat Op.9 and F minor Op.55, to suggest not 'otherness', but rather a spinning-out of the same (the proportions of the prelude thus become very end-weighted: the final cadence is stretched to occupy thirty bars of a seventy-one-bar piece). This generates a deformation of the miniature model by lingering 'too long' on the ending through elaborate patterning and arabesques. An extravagance of ornament savours and sustains the sense of immanent closure to such a degree that progress is almost suspended, in a manner which we might identify as a characteristically 'decadent' expansion of the Paterian 'moment':

of impressions, unstable, flickering, inconsistent, which burn and are extinguished with our consciousness of them, it contracts still further: the whole scope of observation is dwarfed into the narrow chamber of the individual mind … Every one of those impressions is the impression of the individual in his isolation,

---

[21] In his 'Random Notes on Lyadov' (1945) Gerald Abraham associates Lyadov's miniaturism with exquisite polish, lack of vitality, hollow elegance and stasis; see *Slavonic and Romantic Music* (London: Faber, 1968), 242.

Example 5.1 Anatoliy Lyadov, Prelude Op.10 No.1, bars 41–71

each mind keeping as a solitary prisoner its own dream of a world … each of them is infinitely divisible also; all that is actual in it being a single moment, gone while we try to apprehend it …[22]

Karatïgin notes that Lyadov was 'enraptured by Scriabin' and that 'his love of Chopin was in all probability conditioned by the Chopinism of Skryabin'. In the four 'Scriabinesque' mood pieces of Op.64 (1909–10) – 'Grimace', 'Gloom', 'Temptation' and 'Reminiscences' – none of which lasts more than ninety seconds – Lyadov offered a late homage to his decadent, miniaturist compatriot. Reciprocally, Lyadov clearly influenced Scriabin's early piano miniatures. The extreme 'interiorization' which Karatïgin hears in Lyadov's music compares with Engel's 1909 image of Scriabin's expressive intensity concentrating within four closing-in walls. Engel saw Scriabin's music as

a product of the most recent times, when we have been living a life of heightened intensity, anxiety and nerviness; art has lost touch with the healthy and fixed moods of the multitude, with the broad fragrant expanse of fields, woods and meadows. The city, four walls, the refined and complicated *moods* of the 'upper-most ten thousand' – that is the sphere of this art.

For Engel, in his musical aristocraticism Scriabin is 'closely attached to Chopin' (and also to Wagner).[23] In summary, for Engel, Scriabin's music is elitist, claustrophobic, intense, unhealthily cut off from nature, intimately derived from Chopin. Engel's characterization can be illustrated by Scriabin's Prelude Op.39 No.3 (1903), which can be heard as a 'decadent' reworking of Chopin (Example 5.2). The turning motivic shapes in the 'tenor' register overtly recall Chopin's F sharp major Prelude; the super-imposition of complex, 'irregular' divisions of the beat (common also in Lyadov) is a 'maximilization' of a procedure in several Chopin works; the derivation of melody from accompaniment (or the other way round) recalls, in a much more complex form, involving inversions and mirror-ings, Chopin's procedure in his prelude in the same key, G major. This sounds decadent because the combination and extension of these Chopinesque techniques turns the piece, marked 'Languido' and with its cadences instructed to be played *carezzando*, into an exercise in solipsistic complexity and concentration. It expresses a subject obsessively, repeatedly 'turning in' on itself in self-reflective, self-caressing languor.

---

[22] Pater, 'Conclusion', in *The Renaissance*, 151.

[23] Yuly D. Engel, 'The Music of Skryabin', *Russian Bulletin* 44 and 45 (24 and 25 February 1909), trans. in Campbell (trans. and ed.), *Russians on Russian Music*, 198–205.

Example 5.2 Alexander Scriabin, Prelude Op.39 No.3, bars 1–4

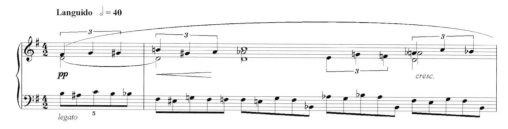

In a 1914 essay, 'The Most Recent Trends in Russian Music', Karatïgin also compares Scriabin with Chopin. He describes Scriabin's 'soul' as 'fragile, tender, less strong but more refined than Chopin's'; it nonetheless 'shows all too clearly through the wrapping of the Chopinized sound-world' – manifest in a style in which 'here a convulsively compressed rhythmic figure, there a nervously, morbidly soft suspension, now an explosion of pathos from heaven knows where, which in a flash attains extraordinary intensity before immediately petering out'. He identifies two types of modern composer – the 'impressionist' and the 'neoclassicist'. The former are 'artists who like to reopen their wounds – even with a certain sensuality, so to speak, the wounds in general of the contemporary soul, over-refined, over-delicate, fragmented and slack in the manifesta-tions of its emotional and volitional life' – in short, decadents – to all of which the 'neoclassicists' seek an 'antidote'. For Karatïgin, who wrote one of the earliest biographies of the composer (Petrograd, 1915), Scriabin is 'antinomian in the extreme' because 'in the midst of the complete disintegration of his mental experiences, in the midst of his fantasies of every possible kind, in the midst of the utmost chaos of ideas rushing about convulsively, it would seem, on all sides – in the midst of all that, there reigns an iron logic'.[24] We can partly attribute this compulsive

---

[24] Karatïgin, 'The Most Recent Trends in Russian Music', *Northern Notes* 6–7 (1914), trans. in Campbell (trans. and ed.), *Russians on Russian Music*, 225–8.

logic to the legacy of the contrapuntal and formal rigour inherited from Rimsky and Lyadov's technical fastiduousness. In this classical–anti-classical paradox we can identify Scriabin as mannerist.

Scriabin's mannerism, in its 'anti-classical' and 'anti-natural' aspects, is intimately tied with his miniaturist aesthetic. Karatïgin's essays on Lyadov and Scriabin compare closely with those passages of Bourget's 1881 essay on Baudelaire, which provided the most famous definition of decadent miniaturist style. Similar terms were often coined in Scriabin's critical reception in Russia. Scriabin's one-time friend the dilettante Yuri Sakhnovsky wrote in 1914:

Standing as a decadent, Mr. Scriabin all the same tries to stand on his own feet. He writes endlessly long orchestral compositions and, in reverse, exceptionally short piano pieces. Formerly we laughed at composers when they could not devise a melodic phrase longer than a sparrow's beak. Now, Mr. Scriabin flaunts them before us. He does not even write phrases, but compositions which are shorter than a bear's tail. His short musical fictions have sounds not at all appropriate to their titles as 'Poem', 'Sonata'. But these poems, preludes, or sonatas are as alike as two drops of water – they have one mood, as if the author has fallen into a quagmire and cannot extricate himself.[25]

Compare those phrases with Grigori Prokofiev's review of the first per-formance of Scriabin's Seventh Sonata, Op.64 (Moscow, February 1912):

Its form is so condensed, its writing so ethereal, and its harmonies so far from the ordinary that we could not grasp it during its rendition. It has something endearing about its soaring flight, but for our planet, it is too flighty, too ephem-eral. The volatility of the sonata is unpleasant. Even the very beginning of the first theme, where the rhythm struggles toward something more concrete or corporeal, is shot through with flight.[26]

The sonata is saturated with octatonic pitch organizations in a 'maximili-zation' of techniques developed by the Belyayev group. This is combined with an intensification of Scriabin's concern for the meticulous control of voice-leading, his manner of proceeding by four-square sequential repetitions, and the preoccupation with symmetry and periodicity that are typically condemned by Germanic criticism as superficial, surface patternings, as mechanistic rather than organic 'developing variation', as

[25] Bowers, *Scriabin*, 234.　[26] Bowers, *Scriabin*, 233.

cut-and-paste mosaics rather than subjective, teleological process.[27] Dahlhaus sees Scriabin finding a miniaturist solution to the 'problem' of the 'exhaustion' of sequential presentation and motivic juxtaposition. Halfway through the Ninth Sonata, Op.68 (1913), at bar 111, Dahlhaus notes that the formal principle changes from that of the sonata to that of the 'virtuoso lyric piano piece' developed by Chopin and Liszt, where lyricism gradually moves into 'drama or brilliance', an intensification which overrides the sonata principle of recapitulation.[28] We can see precedents for this in Chopin's generic interpolations of miniatures in the larger works, but it is also a manifestation of Scriabin's overall miniaturization of the sonata, which began with the eight-minute-long Fourth Sonata, Op.30 (1903). In terms of content this is reflected in the late sonatas' exploration of a highly restricted repertory of symbolic types, perhaps based on Ivanov's gendered symbolism, in a single plot archetype which leads to ecstatic dissolution in the flight of the subject.[29] This is 'late' music in the sense that, with the bourgeois illusion of the possibility of progress towards subject–object synthesis dead and buried, instead of dialectical argument and development to some higher synthesis there is eschatology as we approach the apocalyptic end of history.[30] (Perhaps a comparable sense of lateness explains Lyadov's rejection of sonata form as 'obsolete'[31] in favour of condensed formal expressions of single moods.) Even *The Poem of Ecstasy*, Op.54, with its gargantuan forces and tumultuous climax, is the colossal magnification of a single gesture – a massive projection of the orgasmic 'little death'.[32] Scriabin's later sonatas can be heard as miniature mood music (Karatïgin described Scriabin's music as 'moods in sound – moods which are contradictory and demonic'; Scriabin's subtitle for the Third Sonata, 'États d'Âme' – moods or soul-states – comes to seem prophetic). In this way their relationship with the highly wrought miniatures which he composed around them is

[27] Richard Taruskin, review of James M. Baker, *The Music of Alexander Scriabin* (New Haven: Yale University Press, 1986) and Boris de Schloezer, *Scriabin: Artist and Mystic*, trans. Nicholas Slonimsky (Berkeley: University of California Press, 1987), *Music Theory Spectrum* 10 (1988), 160.

[28] Dahlhaus, 'Structure and Expression in the Music of Scriabin', 201–9. In his review of Baker and Schloezer, Taruskin declares that Dahlhaus's essay on Scriabin 'quite misses the point' of the Seventh Sonata.

[29] Susanna Garcia, 'Scriabin's Symbolic Plot Archetype in the Late Piano Sonatas', *19th-Century Music* 23 (2000), 273–300.

[30] See Rose Rosengard Subotnik, 'Adorno's Diagnosis of Beethoven's Late Style: Early Symptom of a Fatal Condition', *Journal of the American Musicological Society* 29 (1976), 242–75.

[31] Karatïgin, 'In Memory of A. K. Lyadov', 162.

[32] Taruskin describes it as an 'agonizingly prolonged anacrusis' modelled on and outdoing the effect of Wagner's Prelude to *Tristan*: review of Baker and Schloezer, 167.

perhaps clarified.[33] And in this way we can also understand their relationship to Lyadov's mannered miniatures.

Strauss and mannerism: *Der Rosenkavalier*

In a classic study Arnold Hauser traced the emergence of mannerism from the Renaissance and assessed its significance for art of the modern world. He identified a number of characteristics which together define mannerism:

1. It can be properly understood only in terms of tensions between apparently irreconcilable opposites: between 'classicism and anti-classicism, naturalism and formalism, rationalism and irrationalism, sensualism and spiritualism, traditionalism and innovation, conventionalism and revolt against conformism'.

2. Its distinctive 'hallmarks' are 'a certain piquancy, a predilection for the subtle, the strange, the over-strained, the abstruse and yet stimulating, the pungent, the bold, and the challenging'. The 'virtuosity that is always displayed contributes greatly to that piquancy. A mannerist work of art is always a piece of bravura, a triumphant conjuring trick, a firework display with flying sparks and colours.'

3. There is a 'defiance of the instinctual, the naively natural or rational, and the emphasis laid on the obscure, the problematical, and the ambiguous, the incomplete nature of the manifest which points to its opposite, the latent, the missing link in the chain'.

4. There is an emphasis on excess: 'beauty too beautiful becomes unreal, strength too strong becomes acrobatics, too much content loses all meaning, form independent of content becomes an empty shell'.

5. The key social concept is alienation, arising from institutionalization and rationalization, which Hauser associates with Max Weber's notion of 'disenchantment' and Karl Marx's definition of 'commodification'. The atomization and reification of cultural functions produce an 'illness of the social body'. There is a concomitant 'illness of the individual mind', which is manifest in 'narcissism'. This complex of isolation and withdrawal generates mannerism's esotericism, allusiveness and formal complexities.

6. Modern mannerism emerges from the decadence of Baudelaire, aestheticism and Huysmans, out of the rejection of romanticism's appeal to

---

[33] Bowers notes that Scriabin marked 'Masque' as expressing 'douceur cachée' (hidden sweetness) and instructed that 'Etrangeté' be played with 'fausse douceur' ('false sweetness').

nature and a turn to the artificial. The 'flight' from social reality is no longer aimed towards some pastoral idyll.

7. A doom-laden sense of lateness is one of the 'basic features that modern art and the modern outlook share with mannerism'.
8. Mannerism shares with decadence a cult of form and a revulsion at the untamed and crudely natural: pleasure is sought in the overwrought and the exquisitely drawn line for their own sake.[34]

In summary, according to Hauser mannerism is an art of unresolved oppositions, shamelessly overt virtuoso technique, esotericism, excess, artifice and fastidious forms. The modern forms of mannerism are a vital artistic phenomenon because they are reflections of the subjective crisis of the times. Hauser's definition remains one of the most useful in the literature. It is closely comparable with Kienzle's discussion of the depiction of the *Casa di Maschere* in Schreker's *Der ferne Klang*. For Kienzle this scene is an example of modern musical mannerism because of its complex knots, masks, illusions and 'hieroglyphic and labyrinthine construction'. He compares its effect with Gustav René Hocke's identification of the loss of self-direction in a labyrinth as a cipher of mannerism. By contrast with the 'clean' lines of classical order, this leads to an enigmatic and esoteric tendency to dispel the real with the hallucinatory. In Schreker's opera Kienzle notes that this mannerism has significant resonances with the 'neue Psychologie' of Mach, Freud and Bahr, which explored the complex inner labyrinths of the modern mind.[35] This suggests that mannerism can move into realms more usually associated with expressionism. As Maniates noted, this similarity to a widely valued aspect of modernism allowed critical merit to accrue to mannerism's morbid and excessive distortions. But Maniates also noted the close comparison between mannerism and the 'ornamental preciosity' characteristic of the rococo.[36] Indeed, John F. Moffit, in a review of Hocke, suggests that rococo style, with its emphasis on the sensual and epicurean, and *art nouveau*, with its opulent stylizations, offer better examples of modern mannerism than the neurotic art of expressionism and surrealism.[37]

Rococo is a style of refined, delicate decoration, of the curved, capricious lines associated with the arabesque. It was often associated with an affected

[34] Arnold Hauser, *Mannerism: The Crisis of the Renaissance and the Origin of Modern Art* (London: Routledge & Kegan Paul, 1965), 12–13, 364–5.

[35] Kienzle, *Das Trauma hinter dem Traum*, 202; Gustav René Hocke, *Die Welt als Labyrinth: Manierismus in der europäischen Kunst und Literatur* (Hamburg: Rohwolt, 1957).

[36] Maniates, 'Musical Mannerism', 288.

[37] John F. Moffit, review of Hocke, *Die Welt als Labyrinth*, *Art Journal* 28 (1969), 446–8.

aristocratic taste. Its florid, sometimes exaggerated gestures led to a loosening of classical formal strictures and an obfuscation of structural clarity. These stylistic features were resurrected in the 'neo-rococo' of Paul Verlaine's highly influential *Fêtes galantes* (1869), whose inspiration was Watteau's iconic canvas, *L'Embarquement pour Cythère* (1717). The attractions of the decorative rococo style of the *ancien régime* and its cults of love, beauty and eroticism were part of the *fin-de-siècle*'s fascination with 'late' aesthetic cultures. After Verlaine there was in the 1890s an international artistic response to rococo's charms. In Austria this was manifest by Bahr's essay on rococo in his *Zur Kritik der Moderne* (Zurich, 1890), aspects of early poems by Stefan George, the enthusiasms of Hugo von Hofmannsthal and the contents of periodicals such as *Die Insel*, edited by Otto Julius Bierbaum, who was seduced by rococo's 'capricious, superficial and mendacious tendencies'.[38] In 1900 Strauss sketched a scenario for a Watteau ballet, *Kythere*, which Hofmannsthal later considered 'pretty and picturesque'.[39] But neo-rococo's heyday seemed to have passed by the turn of the century, and the Hofmannsthal–Strauss collaboration on *Der Rosenkavalier* began against a darkening, doubting disintegration of rococo's hedonistic harmonies.[40] Where delight in decorative pastiche persisted it coexisted uneasily with aesthetic impulses of anxious instability and disturbing exposure. The overcooked was often served up with the raw.

Thus it is telling that Slavoj Žižek and Mladen Dolar describe the Introduction to *Rosenkavalier* as 'an outburst of raw sexual passion muffled by affected rococo manners, in accordance with the half-imaginary, half-real mode of the opera itself'.[41] There is a mannerist heightening of the contradiction between a surface of decorative excess and the elemental nature of what lies beneath. The intensified opposition characteristic of mannerism also pertains to the harmonic process and phrase construction, which poses neo-rococo extension against the balancing, closural demands of classical form. The opening bars establish a tonal mixture of E and E flat, a musical parallel to the erotic entwinement of Octavian and the Marschallin. The allusion to E flat (a second-inversion A flat triad) is

---

[38] K. R. Ireland, 'Aspects of Cythera: Neo-Rococo at the Turn of the Century', *The Modern Language Review* 70 (1975), 727.

[39] See Strauss's letter to Hofmannsthal, 14 December 1900, and Hofmannsthal's to Strauss, 26 June 1909: *The Correspondence between Richard Strauss and Hugo von Hofmannsthal*, trans. Hanns Hammelmann and Ewald Osers (Cambridge University Press, 1980), 2, 36.

[40] Ireland, 'Aspects of Cythera', 729. See also Lyle F. Perusse, '*Der Rosenkavalier* and Watteau', *The Musical Times* 119 (1978), 1042–4.

[41] Slavoj Žižek and Mladen Dolar, *Opera's Second Death* (London: Routledge, 2002), 206–10.

Example 5.3 Strauss, *Der Rosenkavalier*, Introduction, bars 1–7

set over the dominant of E, so that is heard as a chromatic (enharmonic) reinterpretation and enrichment of the leading note, D♯. The intensifying and dissolution of leading-note tension – familiar musical symbol of erotic desire – becomes the basis of structure and effect. All the main motifs and harmonic shifts of the opening paragraph are based on transformations of the D♯–E relationship (see Example 5.3).[42] This procedure is maintained and heightened through *Steigerung* to the infamous musical orgasm, which Strauss instructs must be approached with parodistic effect. This intensification is built initially on complex chromaticisms prolonging a second-inversion E flat triad. This increases the expectation of a cadence in what will later be understood as the Marschallin's key. But at the highpoint, with whooping horns, the harmony shifts to an E major 6–4 (Octavian's orgasm prevails, or at least it is the noisiest). After such hyperbolically – one might say hyperventilatingly – intense erotic excitement the dissolution to repose is daringly, sumptuously, deliciously and extravagantly extended. For some, the bounds of taste may seem to be sorely tested (recall Rosen's assertion that 'good taste' can limit our understanding and appreciation of nineteenth-century music), but the inordinately sustained dominant is required to balance the transformations and intensities of the preceding music. When the tonic E is finally reached the

[42] Richard A. Kaplan identifies *Rosenkavalier* as the work which confirms Strauss's 'decision to exploit chromatic techniques that are based more or less exclusively on the maintenance of triadic structures'. He states that this 'led to stylistic refinement and mannerism', which was sustained through to the *Four Last Songs*: 'Tonality as Mannerism: Structure and Syntax in Richard Strauss's Orchestral Song "Frühling"', *Theory and Practice* 19 (1994), 19–29.

chromatic motif is marked *seufzend* (sobbing); it is in Octavian's key, but the motif is hers. The tonic is then sustained for even longer than the preceding dominant. One further chromatic shift to the dominant (at a varied return of the opening bars) is all that intrudes through the protracted tonic pedal. This extreme harmonic motionlessness is decorated by sensuous chromatic nuances and florid imitations of morning birdsong. The lovers are in a post-coital semi-embrace: she is reclining, face hidden, her beautiful hand peeping out from her lace nightdress. Seductive beauty deflects attention from the radical nature of the music's patterned stasis.

The formal proportions and phrase structures of this orchestral introduction employ neo-rococo patterning which generates both the overt, bravura virtuosity and the tension between classical and anti-classical identified by Hauser as distinctive of mannerism. It opens with a 'normal'-sized four-bar antecedent of the classical period. Within this there is already modern inflection or colouring as the framing classical tonic–dominant motion incorporates the anti-classical tonal dualism of E and E flat. The consequent is condensed to only three bars. It thus disturbs the classical symmetry, but ends 'classically' with a perfect cadence in the balancing tonal answer to the open-ended antecedent. The source of the condensation is a subtle elision in bar 4. Here what at first seems to be mere patterning of the dominant seventh actually becomes a secretive and decorative variant of the opening motif of the antecedent: the B–G♯–C♯–B is transposed and elaborated as F♯–B–D♯–F♯–G♯–F♯ etc. The ambiguity between ornament and thematic substance is functional obfuscation typical of mannerism. To rectify the imbalance created by the four plus three bars of the period there follows a seven-bar codetta or *Abgesang*. Based principally on expansion of the C♯–B relationship, this does not further the tonal argument: it is static and decorative, energetic yet non-progressive. Again there is functional ambiguity, as this is both a balancing phrase and at the same time a decorative supplement or excessive pendant. Once more there is a secretive elision, as by fig.2 restatement of the antecedent phrase is already under way. The emphasis on C♯ in the opening is now replaced by C♮, within a Neapolitan harmony, to offer necessary tonal contrast with the preceding emphasis on C♯. The elision conceals the start of a three-bar antecedent which balances the length of the consequent of the opening period. There follows an enormous, 'parodic' expansion of the consequent to thirty-five bars, harmonically based on the E flat chord functioning as a chromatic pre-dominant. After this there is another combination of the classical impulse to precise formal balance and the mannerist impulse to licentious excess. The codetta or

Abgesang is a static expansion of the tonic to thirty-eight bars, precisely the total length of the previous period of three plus thirty-five bars. The opening paragraph is therefore a remarkable, virtuosic piece of phrase construction containing two enormous expansions. While they balance each other, these expansions have very different characters and are achieved by contrasting means. The first, the expanded consequent, is highly vigorous and chromatically overburdened. It generates tension through the 'parodic' *Steigerung*, which delays arrival of the structural goal. It is overtly a musical imitation of the (male) pleasures towards orgasm, but presented as a parody of the phrase expansions which heighten teleological drive, typical of romantic style and first notably developed by Beethoven.[43] The second expansion contrasts in every way with the first, and is the musical portrayal – reinforcing the sexual stereotypes of the age – of the feminine gasps of pleasure rather than the drive to masculine orgasm. It is static, decorative. It achieves nothing of the energetic functions of the preceding 'Beethovenian' expansion. Its character reflects what Hauser called the 'over-strained, the abstruse and yet stimulating'. It evokes the patterned stasis of the arabesque, both in its motivic shapes – curled and complex – and in its harmonic variations, which are non-progressive and decorate a beautiful moment. The attraction of the arabesque to the adherents of neo-rococo aestheticism is obvious. It is anti-classical as it subverts or contrasts with the concept of musical form as a dramatic narrative of conflict and resolution achieved through teleological progression. The final bars before Octavian initiates the opening dialogue evoke a further mannerist characteristic. The birds are not heard as the intrusion of the real into a scene of ornamental artifice because the identity of the twittering of birdsong and curvaceous arabesque are blended: natural and anti-natural merge into decorative hybridism.

The problematic shadow of kitsch has always accompanied *Der Rosenkavalier*.[44] Many of its passages chime with Hermann Broch's identification of kitsch with virtuosic imitations of aristocratic decorative and amorous art by the ascetic and neurotic bourgeois craftsman.[45] Indeed, kitsch shadows the whole of Strauss's output. 'Tastelessness',

---

[43] See David Beach, 'Phrase Expansion: Three Analytical Studies', *Music Analysis* 14 (1995), 27–47.

[44] For a comparison of *Rosenkavalier* with Erich Korngold's *Das Wunder der Heliane* (1927) in this regard see Taruskin, 'The Golden Age of Kitsch', in *The Danger of Music and Other Anti-Utopian Essays* (Berkeley: University of California Press, 2009), 254–5.

[45] Hermann Broch, 'Notes on the Problem of Kitsch' (1950), trans. in Gillo Dorfles (ed.), *Kitsch: The World of Bad Taste* (London: Studio Vista, 1969), 49–67.

Holloway notes, 'is all-permeating, inseparably part of the very definition of his genius': if kitsch – 'vulgarity, sentimentality, erotic exhibitionism, stylistic provocation' – were 'purged', 'what would be left of him'?[46] Holloway raises *Salome* as the highpoint of Strauss's unique achievement in mixing 'classic art' and 'masterly kitsch' in a provocative juxtaposition demanding 'new definitions of taste'. For Holloway *Salome* is the 'supreme' exemplar of a 'category where it is not necessary to reproach its composer or ourselves for confusing art and kitsch; where the mingling together produces not only the cheap thrill and the naughty chocolate but an emotion too – fugitive but genuine'. In *Salome* 'kitsch is raised to *Kunst*', and Strauss thereby opens up 'new aesthetic territory'.[47] But in *Rosenkavalier* are we only served the 'cheap thrill' and the 'naughty chocolate', with kitsch and no *Kunst*, left to decay in tired old scenarios rather than cajoled into new challenges? Paul Bechert considered its 'preponderance of form over content, of means over matter, of dexterity and trifling playfulness over seriousness of purpose – indeed over purpose itself' to mark the beginning of a sugary descent into the 1924 ballet *Schlagobers* (*Whipped Cream* in Viennese dialect).[48] Such a view confirms the sagacity of Hofmannsthal's remark that Strauss 'has a dreadful tendency towards triviality and kitsch. Whatever he requests in the way of small revisions, expansions, etc. always leads in this direction.'[49] But Strauss seemed to relish the pursuit of a productive, innovative and dialectical relationship between kitsch and art. This is one way in which *Rosenkavalier* represents a continuation of *Salome*, not a retreat.

With its striking parody of intensification to climactic release and exaggerated elaboration of old forms, Strauss's introduction raises two of the bases for Adorno's condemnation of kitsch. (There is no more coruscating critic of kitsch – and of Strauss – than Adorno.) Adorno asserts that kitsch 'parodies catharsis' through the heightening of aesthetic stimuli, as found in the 'sensations' typical of Wilde, D'Annunzio and Maeterlinck, which are 'manipulable', 'reifications' of the 'most fleeting individual reactions'. Strauss's *Steigerung* overtly parodies the cathartic experience of (male) orgasm, the most deliciously heightened

[46] Robin Holloway, 'Strauss: Two Pieces on the Fiftieth Anniversary of his Death' (1999), in *On Music*, 104–5.

[47] Holloway, '*Salome*: Art or Kitsch? (1989), in *On Music*, 107–21.

[48] Paul Bechert, 'The New Richard Strauss Ballet', *The Musical Times* 65 (1924), 547.

[49] Letter of 12 June 1909 to Harry Graf Kessler, trans. in Wayne Heisler Jr, 'Kitsch and the Ballet *Schlagobers*', *The Opera Quarterly* 22 (2007), 44. Heisler's article offers an extended discussion of kitsch based on the ballet, including comments on Bechert's review.

moment of (male) bodily stimulation. It is exaggeratedly 'sensational'. If, after Wilde, one can say here that it is only the shudder that counts, then Strauss's instruction 'die ganze Steigerung von hier ab durchaus parodistisch' means that the music, if not Octavian, is faking it. Decadence always seeks the artificial alternative to the natural. The natural act is replaced by a synthetic substitute or simulation. The rising sequences are not an organic tumescence. They are a musical prosthesis. It is all perhaps a bit kinky. Adorno considered kitsch to be 'a poison admixed to all art'.[50] It is always there as a threatened infection to the artistic health of the work. 'Catharsis' comes from the Greek *kathairō* – to cleanse, as in a purgative medicine. In Adorno's view, then, kitsch as a parodic catharsis is the medicinal turned to the toxic. Those who fall for kitsch's charms have been duped into taking the wrong draught. They have been drugged by the narcotic sold by the dealer disguised as artist. Adorno also stated that 'kitsch is the precipitate of devalued forms and empty ornaments from a formal world that has become remote from its immediate context … kitsch precisely sustains the memory, distorted and as mere illusion, of a formal objectivity that has passed away'.[51] From the neo-rococo decorations and distortions of old classical periodic forms in Strauss's introduction it seems on this count too that the work is from its opening steeped in the 'guilty', artificial pleasures of kitsch. *Rosenkavalier* stands apparently condemned in Adorno's high court of authentic judgement. But, as counsel for the defence, we need to heed Calinescu's reminder that kitsch can be more than merely spurious, disposable, commercial replication based on the luxurious and conspicuous corruption of good taste, more also than the exaggerated sentimentality of *Schmaltz*, the mewling child of romantic nostalgia.[52] Kitsch can fashion an ornately carved knife that cuts to the bone. It can be obviously clever but also mercilessly sharp. Its soft luxuriant exterior can conceal barbed commentary. Calinescu cites Wedekind's note to his play *Kitsch* (1917): 'Kitsch is the contemporary form of the Gothic, Rococo, Baroque.' This, for Calinescu, encapsulates the 'disturbing equation between modernity and kitsch'. In particular, kitsch's characteristic as an 'aesthetic form of lying', as the site of fabricated beautiful illusions, allows the generation of irony – the cutting comment

---

[50] Adorno, *Aesthetic Theory*, 239.

[51] Theodor Adorno, 'Kitsch' [c.1932], in *Essays on Music*, ed. Richard Leppert, trans. Susan Gillespie (Berkeley: University of California Press, 2002), 501.

[52] On such criteria, Joseph Kerman dismisses the opening tableau of *Rosenkavalier*: it is 'already so enervated in sentiment': *Opera as Drama* (New York: Vintage, 1956), 258–60.

which the tooled-up avant-gardist with wounding intent steals from kitsch's cultural cutlery.[53] In this way kitsch and neo-rococo are again closely connected. Neo-rococo mannerism undermines the myths of progress and reveals the world of modernity as exhausted, left with the decorative remnants of a previous age. (Hofmannsthal noted, in an 1893 essay on D'Annunzio: 'it is as if our fathers and our grandfathers have left us, the late-borns, only two things: pretty furniture and over-sensitive nerves'.[54]) Bechert described the Vienna of *Der Rosenkavalier* and *Schlagobers* as a city of superficiality – in effect, as the capital of kitsch – which had seduced Strauss, a Bavarian who lacked the resistance and distance possessed by a north German (for example, Beethoven or Brahms).[55] More productively, in the opera's stylistic dichotomy of old and new Vienna Lewis Lockwood hears 'the modern sensibility of the characters, musing on the fragility of their experience'. This 'reminds us that their city is in the same condition. In 1910 this Vienna was a hollow shell in relation to its former glories, caught up in the dreams of its past, a bastion of antimodernism frustrated by the modern sensibility by which it felt the manifest contradictions between past and present.'[56] *Rosenkavalier*'s stylistic eclecticisms, anachronisms and juxtapositions point to Hauser's defining mannerist features of irreconcilable opposition and subjective alienation. To use Clement Greenberg's antithesis, in the opera the kitsch 'imitation of artistic effects' coexists with a preoccupation with 'imitating imitation', an obsession with formal and linguistic processes and the 'reduction of experience to expression for the sake of expression', all of which he associates with the cultural work of the avant-garde.[57]

Decadence and avant-garde: extremes touch

Decadence and the avant-garde are commonly considered oppositional ideas. They can be understood, however, as divergences from shared ground or as convergences towards similar stylistic procedures – extremes touching as they break the boundaries of cultural rule and taste. This is

---

[53] Calinescu, *Five Faces of Modernity*, 225–33.
[54] See Krobb, '"Die Kunst der Väter tödtet das Leben der Enkel"', 559.
[55] Bechert, 'The New Richard Strauss Ballet', 547.
[56] Lewis Lockwood, 'The Element of Time in *Der Rosenkavalier*', in Gilliam (ed.), *Richard Strauss: New Perspectives*, 243–58.
[57] Clement Greenberg, 'Avant-Garde and Kitsch' [1939], in *Art and Culture: Critical Essays* (Boston: Beacon Press, 1961), 3–21.

especially discernible in the nineteenth-century *fin de siècle* and the early years of the twentieth century, a period when notions of decadence and avant-garde were concurrently in vogue as millennial anxieties combined with a loss of faith in the redemptive romantic project and scepticism mounted concerning the prospects of continuing cultural progress. Daniel Albright has proposed that a theory of the modernist movement which is able to encompass its manifold manifestations might be one based upon the central notion of a 'testing of the limits of aesthetic construction' in a search for 'ultimate bounds'. The aesthetic extremes so reached are often paired in binary opposition: 'each limit-point pre-supposes an opposite limit-point, a counter-extreme toward which the artist can push. Much of the strangeness, the stridency, the exhila-ration of modernist art can be explained by this strong thrust toward the verges of the aesthetic experience.' This shifts the artistic project away from the safe haven of romanticism's 'interior centre' towards 'the freakish circumferences of art'.[58] Decadence and avant-gardism might be identified as two such dangerous and disturbing polar extremes. As we shall see, however, at such extremities certain central tenets of modern-ism are rejected.

The decadent, like the avant-gardist, rejects bourgeois institutions, their codes of behaviour and morality, their investment in traditional values and hopes of cultural progress. Decadents seek the illicit pleasure and pain generated by the exquisite, with pessimistic disregard for the future. Avant-gardists seek the illicit power and panic generated by the explosive, with provocative disregard for the past. Both are based on a fundamental dissatisfaction with the practices of ruling social structures, which they view as restrictive, moribund or alienating. They character-istically seek vital links between art and lifestyle, sharing a fondness for the bohemian. In his study of the avant-garde Poggioli noted that decadent discontent with the present as the result of the negative consequences of apparent progress in the modern world is closely comparable with the distinctively antihistorical, prospective view of the avant-garde; the end of the series meets the beginning of the new. Indeed, Poggioli argues that 'decadence and avant-gardism are related, if not identical'; the avant-gardist awaits 'tremulously', the decadent awaits 'passively, with anguished fatality and inert anxiety':

[58] Daniel Albright, '"Border Crossings": Series Editor's Foreword', in Charlotte M. Cross and Russell A. Berman (eds.), *Schoenberg and Words: The Modernist Years* (New York: Garland, 2000), ix.

degeneration and immaturity equally aspire to transcend the self in a subsequent flourishing; thus the generations that feel themselves decrepit, like those that feel themselves adolescent, are both lost generations, par excellence. If agonistic tendencies triumph in avant-garde futurism, a passive agonism dominates the decadent mentality, the pure and simple sense of agony. Decadence means no more than a morbid complacency in feeling oneself *passé*: a sentiment that also, unconsciously, inspires the burnt offerings of the avant-garde to the cultural future.[59]

In that last sentence, while one might dispute the restricted definition of decadence, we can see how the apparent difference between the decadent and avant-garde pose is perhaps only a superficial one.

Decadence and avant-garde also share common initial ground in nihilism. As we saw in Chapter 2, nihilism is a pervasive symptom of modernity's malaise. If 'the spiritual conflict that culminates in nihilism' is an 'archetypal experience',[60] then the possible manners in which one emerges from nihilism – hedonism, absurdism, iconoclasm, or Nietzschean Dionysianism, for instance – converge onto two paths: one decadent, one avant-garde. These are divergent routes which start from the same position of crisis. Nihilism rejects as an illusion the striving for 'Truth' or redemption, both of which it holds to be bankrupt propaganda. Nihilism's radical pessimism can be manifest in passive or ecstatic attitudes. Through such modes of being the allure of suicide, which by contrast with heroic martyrdom is the ultimate gesture of nothingness, is held at a tensed distance. In their shared relationship to nihilism, decadence and avant-garde both lead towards the anarchic. For example, writing of the birth of the avant-garde in France, Maurice Boisson stated: 'Anarchists come from the most varied backgrounds. But a specific mentality links them – the spirit of revolt and its derivatives, the spirit of examination and criticism, of opposition and innovation, which leads to scorn and hate of every commitment and hierarchy in society, and ends up in the exaggeration of individualism. Decadent literature furnished the party with a strong contingent.'[61] Though Albright's notion of modernism manifest in binary extremes is useful, it is one which in the apparent polarity of decadence and the avant-garde leads to the rejection of modernism's faith in progress. Both decadence and the avant-garde, as two sides of a cultural discontent with bourgeois

---

[59] Poggioli, *The Theory of the Avant-Garde*, 75–6.
[60] Charles I. Glicksberg, *The Literature of Nihilism* (London: Associated University Press, 1975), 15.
[61] Maurice Boisson, *Les Attendats anarchistes* (1930), trans. in Roger Shattuck, *The Banquet Years: The Origins of the Avant-Garde in France, 1885 to World War I*, rev. edn (New York: Vintage, 1968), 20.

optimism (whether positivistic or idealistic), seek to *épater le bourgeois*. The difference lies in decadence's preoccupation with the transitory moment by contrast with the avant-garde's determined delight in disjunction. That part of the avant-garde which advocates a (utopian or nihilistic) radical rejection of modernism seeks liberation from the burdens of history and iconoclastically dismantles the 'old' doctrine of progress. That part of decadence which proclaims a (dystopian or nihilistic) rejection of modernism seeks similar liberties. In these scenarios, progress – a central tenet of modernism – is the fictive dialectical other to both the avant-garde and decadence. Nonetheless, the past is a shadow cast over both: as Hans Keller stated, 'our culture is compulsively retrospective, hence introspective … The very concept of an avant-garde is past-laden.'[62]

In his discussion of the opposition between the avant-garde and 'commodity art' Adorno defined the former as autonomous, as resisting dominant social functions, with fragmentation and disintegration as the immanent laws of its form, and as art which does not attempt to conceal its constructive techniques. In commodity forms of art, by contrast, the social hegemony is accepted; a false appearance of integration and wholeness is displayed on a surface which effects the concealment of the labour of production.[63] Such distinctions can also be posited for the decadent opposition to conformity. Decadence, like the avant-garde, is characteristically based on extreme autonomy (suggesting the solipsistic), on the rejection of wholeness, the reified and the reactionary, and on the display of technique. Indeed, Adorno declared that 'the possibility of music itself has become uncertain. Not that it is endangered because it is decadent, individualistic, and asocial, as the reactionary reproach claims. It is all too little that.'[64] In Dahlhaus's view the avant-garde and the 'music of the future' shared common ground in their exploration of extreme forms of individualism, the 'dissolution of genre' and a 'tendency to favour the exceptional'.[65] Again, these characteristics can equally be identified in artistic manifestations of decadence. The avant-gardist seeks, among other things, liberation

---

[62] Hans Keller, 'Stravinsky v. Stravinsky' [1971], in *Essays on Music*, ed. Christopher Wintle (Cambridge University Press, 1994), 104.

[63] See Paddison, *Adorno's Aesthetics of Music*, 54–5.

[64] Adorno, 'Avant-Garde and Doctrine', in *Philosophy of New Music*, trans., ed. and with an introduction by Robert Hullot-Kentor (Minneapolis: University of Minnesota Press, 2006), 87.

[65] Dahlhaus, 'New Music and the Problem of Musical Genre', in *Schoenberg and the New Music*, 32–44.

from Platonic or Universal formal norms and offers a devastating critique of organic form,[66] which of course the avant-gardist would seek to avoid or destroy completely. The decadent delights in deformation, in the denigration of Universal formal norms, in celebration of the abnormal. It represents a critique or rejection of natural form in favour of the artificial; in place of organic form it characteristically seeks form based on the sensual moment – the shudder, the paroxysm, the orgasmic, the algolagnic. The emphasis in both is characteristically placed on the material and the sensual, as faith in some unrepresentable 'Idea' is rejected. As John Goode has written, the decadent movement's '"materialist" perspective reveals a "break" with the hegemony ... that modernism only repairs by assimilation'.[67] The wide assumption that decadence is a precursor to modernism is thus problematic, for decadence shares with the avant-garde an anti-modernist persuasion, even if the modernist hegemony seeks to co-opt the resuts of both. For both the decadent and the avant-gardist God is dead: they both dare to speak the heretical, the cry of the Nietzschean madman. Both extremes threaten the centrally established, reactionary authority which seeks to pull everything centripetally into its centre. Both seek to inhale the air of forbidden planets.

In Chapter 3 the romantic notion of doubleness was invoked to analyse the coexistence of polar forces of degeneration and regeneration, decline and intensification. Strauss was shown to pursue the implications of such doubleness in Wagner to new ends. The meeting of extremes of decadence and the avant-garde can be seen as a further dimension of this doubleness. In the next section *Salome* returns to reconsider this dual characteristic. But substantial critical leverage can also be generated by considering decadence and avant-garde as extremes which work in a dialectical relationship. It is a question of applicability to different musical projects. Schoenberg is a much more fundamentally dialectical thinker than Strauss, and his creative relationship to decadence is best understood as an under-explored aspect of his dialectical music.

The most complete discussion of the dialectic of decadence and the avant-garde has come from the art critic Donald Kuspit, whose primary critical tool is Freud's theory of the return of the repressed. At the heart of

---

[66] Gianmario Borio, 'Dire cela, sans savoir quoi: The Question of Meaning in Adorno and in the Musical Avant-Garde', in Berthold Hoeckner (ed.), *Apparitions: New Perspectives on Adorno and Twentieth-Century Music* (London: Routledge, 2006), 41–68.

[67] John Goode, 'The Decadent Writer as Producer', in Ian Fletcher (ed.), *Decadence and the 1890s* (London: Edward Arnold, 1979), 109–10.

Kuspit's argument is the conviction that the continuing existence of the notion of advanced art is based upon the repression of decadence. Furthermore, advanced art's 'curiosity' about decadence 'remains unconsciously intense, even as it is consciously avoided by repression'. Decadence is felt to be a perpetual threat or 'contagion', and so its repression, or removal into 'quarantine', must be continuously sustained and strengthened. Crucially, however, 'advanced art does not, unconsciously, want to destroy or even contain decadent art'. The paranoia is necessary to vitalize and authenticate the new and advanced, to sustain the 'progressive' or radical artist's narcissistic self-belief, to displace fears of impotence, to distance one's own inevitable decadence. Thus advanced and decadent art exist in a 'perverse dialectic'. Novelty, surprise, the shock of the new, soon wears out. Advanced art is 'born with the seed of its death in its soul'; it is 'peculiarly stillborn: after the excitement of its birth its inertia becomes self-evident'. Decadence is always already in the material of advance. 'Decadent art, then, is not eliminated by its repression, but deeply internalized as advanced art's necessary opposite. Repressed decadence is the unconscious springboard of self-conscious advance.'[68]

As Kuspit develops his argument there emerge a number of ways in which this dialectic might be identified in musical styles and forms. First, Kuspit proposes that 'to face the fate of one's own decadence would make it an unnerving expectation, discomforting one's intention to advance'. This is suggestive of aspects of the tone of 'Erwartung' which is so important in Schoenberg's music. When Kuspit continues by identifying in decadence and avant-garde a shared awareness of 'helplessness' and 'trauma' in the face of a 'sense of catastrophe',[69] the correlation with the expressive quality of much of Schoenberg's work from before the First World War becomes even stronger. It raises the issue of how decadence might be sustained, through repression and return, in what is more commonly called his 'expressionistic' music. Secondly, this relationship of decadence and expressionism is also raised by Kuspit's discussion of the avant-garde ambition towards the direct expression of desire – the desire which contradicts the semiotic system and formal law and hence confirms the impossibility of artistic 'wholeness' and the persistent resistance to meaning. The avant-garde search for authentic, immediate articulation of the modern in the pure moment – the improvised, unstable and precarious 'now' – is the

---

[68] Donald Kuspit, *The Dialectic of Decadence: Between Advance and Decline in Art* (New York: Allworth Press, 2000), 24–6.

[69] Kuspit, *Dialectic of Decadence*, 25, 28.

'advanced' correlative to the decadent ruination that Nietzsche deplored in Wagner's miniaturism, manifest in the fragment whose demise is always at hand. In both, classical wholeness is recognized as a previously necessary illusion which is now rejected. Thus, Kuspit concludes, 'disintegration and artifical wholeness – the sum of decadence – is the only way of being modern'.[70] This is redolent of Pater's famous dictum: 'For art comes to you proposing frankly to give nothing but the highest quality to your moments as they pass, and simply for those moments' sake.'[71] It also recalls Baudelaire's famous definition of 'modernity' as 'the transitory, the fugitive, the contingent'. But Baudelaire identifies this as 'one half of art, the other being the eternal and the immovable'.[72] This stable undying half of art is what is blown asunder by decadent immediacy and avant-garde 'nowness'. Kuspit's dialectic is especially appropriate to Schoenberg. But first, and for the last time, the *Doppelgänger* Strauss.

Strauss as decadent and avant-gardist

In the years around the turn of the century Strauss's music provoked critical reaction which aligned him with both avant-garde and decadent tendencies. In 1892 Hanslick concluded that Strauss's orchestral virtuosity in colouristic effect 'has become a vampire sapping the creative power'. He described *Don Juan* as a 'musical-sensual stimulation' equivalent to a 'stupefying pleasure gas', as an unhealthy 'narcotic'.[73] Arthur Symons, in his essay 'The Problem of Richard Strauss' (1905), identified Strauss as 'the only decadent in music', for 'he has tried to debauch music'. For Symons, whose sympathies for literary forms of decadence are well known, Strauss's degradation of music's 'sensuousness' and 'passion' lay in his 'satisfaction of a craving which is … elaborate, intellectual, and frigid'.[74] Hanslick heard decadence in the victory of the colouristic over the formalistic; Symons heard it in the triumph of the excessively complicated and ingenious over the directly seductive and vital. Others heard similar effects but with different aesthetic and expressive results. In 1897 Robert Hirschfeld described *Thus Spake Zarathustra* as the explosion of an 'anarchic music-bomb'. The 'fragments of the score were simply

---

[70] Kuspit, *Dialectic of Decadence*, 53–4.   [71] Pater, *The Renaissance*, 151.

[72] Baudelaire, 'The Painter of Modern Life' [1863], in *Selected Writings on Art and Literature*, 403.

[73] Eduard Hanslick, *Music Criticisms 1846–99*, rev. edn, trans. and ed. Henry Pleasants (Harmondsworth: Penguin, 1963), 291–2.

[74] Quoted in Schmidgall, *Literature as Opera*, 268.

flying', he continued, and 'only the hacked, dislocated, torn, and cut-up pieces of motives remained'. Although Hirschfeld did not employ the term 'avant-garde' his language amounts to a pretty convincing description of the avant-garde's iconoclastic effect and motivation. This musical avant-gardism can be related to Strauss's cultural allegiances in the last years of the nineteenth century. Recent Strauss scholarship has highlighted Strauss's enthusiasm for anarchistic, individual liberalism in the 1890s. Nietzsche's brand of radical, anti-metaphysical revaluation of values was, of course, central to this intellectual climate. Musically, we can hear it manifest in the B major section near the end of Strauss's *Thus Spake Zarathustra* which evokes the 'impossible' redemption or transfiguration of Wagner's *Tristan* but only, through the turn to B minor and its unresolved dissonant relationship with C, to affirm the Nietzschean, all-too-human revolt, the disgust at humanity's metaphysical yearnings, and to proclaim the struggle of a 'post-metaphysical worldview'.[75]

Till Eulenspiegel is a further example of the anti-Wagnerian, anti-metaphysical turn in the mid-1890s which is encapsulated in Strauss's shift of philosophical allegiance from Schopenhauer to Nietzsche and reflected in musical-structural deformations whose effect is turned to 'avant-garde', Nietzschean ends. The targets here are the yearnings and idealism of romantic metaphysics. Through emphasis on surface material sensation and the deformations of processes of *Steigerung* (which in romantic form is the intensification generated through the struggle from polar opposition towards a higher synthesis), the music of *Till* is turned against the Wagnerian metaphysical aspiration, with the orchestra now celebrated as visible musical machine rather than as a hidden, other-worldly ideal source, as the producer of sensual effects and noise, and emphatically not some metaphysically symbolic *Ton*. It poses the continuous excitement (and threat) of immediate material stimulus. Endless colour replaces endless melody, as Julius Korngold said of *Salome*.[76] The work's impudent tone is, as Hepokoski notes, one of laughter's 'socially destructive power': it 'defies the [conventional] criteria for aesthetic legitimacy' which had underpinned the romantic orchestral concert canon. In Strauss's tone poem, Till possesses an iconoclastic, Nietzschean laughter.[77] He is, in effect, portrayed as an

---

[75] Charles Youmens, *Richard Strauss's Orchestral Music and the German Intellectual Tradition: The Philosophical Roots of Musical Modernism* (Bloomington: Indiana University Press, 2005), 194.

[76] *Neues Wiener Tagblatt*, 28 May 1907, trans. Susan Gillespie in Gilliam (ed.), *Richard Strauss and his World*, 349.

[77] Hepokoski, 'Framing *Till Eulenspiegel*', 4–43. On *Till* as a precursor of *Thus Spake Zarathustra* see Youmens, *Richard Strauss's Orchestral* Music, 190.

avant-garde prankster. Hepokoski describes how at the close of the opening paragraph of the piece the process of *Steigerung*, which in Wagnerian style would lead to some clinching, transporting *Höhepunkt*, leads to

sudden sonorous deflation, effected by the instant shift of timbre, the unexpected isolation of a single, squeaky voice, *mezzo forte*, and the chuckling, lustig impudence of the motive itself. Hurled out once the prank is underway or completed the Kobold (sprite) idea typically suggests Till's eagerness to sound forth with a finger-pointing jeer, ridiculing those that he has just taken in: 'Gotcha!'.[78]

Furthermore, the treatment and character of the chromatic chord of the Kobold idea generate a 'derisive distortion' of the musical icon of Tristanesque yearning for redemption or erotic fulfilment. It is a mockery of the most revered harmonic mark of Germanic musical, metaphysical modernity.

On *Salome* Hirschfeld wrote, in a manner closely comparable to his review of *Zarathustra*, that 'music no longer wants anything but explosions', 'monstrous' virtuosity and 'cruel harmonic jokes'.[79] His reaction was not unique. In the same work Max Kalbeck described 'dazzling and deceiving inessentials', 'thousands and thousands of tone particles that are shaken up in kaleidoscopic fashion, colourful images and bright constellations emerge as if of their own volition'; there was 'no order and rule over the whole', only 'artificially created chaos'. Kalbeck concludes with a decadent image of the work as unhealthy artificiality, as a 'poisonous plant that has been cultivated in the greenhouse of modern hyperculture'.[80] Strauss appears to be the composer who dares to throw avant-garde stones in decadent glasshouses. It was these kinds of effect which underpinned Adorno's condemnation of Strauss's music because he heard them as founded upon shocks and sudden surprises (the post-Berlioz *imprévu*) rather than on developmental, musical 'logic', as music which is 'forgetful on principle', as the listener is not required to make connections, expect certain continuations or anticipate coherent endings. The music is therefore a disintegration of form. In terms of content it represented a decline through 'externalization' at the expense of the 'inwardness', which can be developed only through 'sustained reflection'.[81] This is clearly related to Nietzsche's

---

[78] Hepokoski, 'Framing *Till Eulenspiegel*', 22.

[79] *Wiener Abendpost*, 26 May 1907, trans. Gillespie in Gilliam (ed.), *Richard Strauss and his World*, 335–6.

[80] *Neues Wiener Tageblatt*, 28 May 1907, trans. Gillespie in Gilliam (ed.), *Richard Strauss and his World*, 336–42.

[81] Adorno wrote that for Strauss 'presence at every moment becomes the duty of compositions which scorn to place their trust not only in the recollection and anticipation of great form, but

critique of Wagnerian decadent miniaturism, in which the parts are no longer heard to cohere into a whole. As we have seen, for Strauss, Nietzsche's criticisms of metaphysical idealism and resulting emphasis on the physical and the now were important stimuli in his distancing from Wagnerian transcendentalism, in the desacralization which marks Strauss's project. The transcendent and the sacred are, of course, prime targets for the avant-gardist. Decadence and avant-garde are slaying the same sacred cows. Only the weapons are different – as are what a decadent and an avant-gardist might imagine doing with the resulting corpse.

Strauss's musical symbol of the necrophiliac is the notorious chord at the final climax of Salome's monologue (1 bar before fig.361; see Example 3.8). It is both avant-garde and decadent in effect and motivation. Kerman's scathing comments on the opera are well known: 'At one point of his life, and it was certainly his best period, Strauss belonged genuinely to the avant garde, especially in matters of harmony'; but in the operas, where his muse is repeatedly ravished, he turns 'decadent'. Kerman heard avant-garde and decadence combined in *Salome*, especially in the infamous dissonance, 'which carries harmonic audacity farther than ever before', but only to produce banality and sentimentality: 'John the Baptist's head might as well be made of marzipan. And it is for this sugary orgasm that all the fantastically involved aphrodisiac machinery has been required.'[82] The moment has, of course, provoked a plethora of similarly extreme views. Kerman's identification of *Salome* as containing both decadent and avant-garde aspects, however, opens up productive interpretative issues. As a perversion or momentary destruction of organic generation and connection the 'sickening' chord comes as a shock after a passage of mostly rather straightforward, if ecstatic, diatonicism. Indeed, the chord's proximity to the norm heightens its quality of abnormality or deformation. Its layered textural disposition and multiple and conflicting implied resolutions are comparable with Schoenberg's well-known analysis in *Harmonielehre* of an eleven-note chord from his monodrama *Erwartung*. This is one of those characteristic pieces of writing where Schoenberg seems to be pleading that he is not an

---

also, at the best in a fortunate duration': 'Richard Strauss: Born June 11, 1864', trans. Samuel and Shierry Weber, *Perspectives of New Music* 4 (1965), 114. See Richard Wattenbarger, 'A "Very German Process": The Contexts of Adorno's Strauss Critique', *19th-Century Music* 25 (2002), 313–36, who also offers a reading of Anette Unger's attempts, by using Adorno's own aesthetic categories, to rescue Strauss from Adorno's critique in her *Welt, Leben und Kunst als Themen der 'Zarathustra-Kompositionen' von Richard Strauss und Gustav Mahler* (Frankfurt: Peter Lang, 1992).

[82] Kerman, *Opera as Drama*, 258–60.

avant-gardist, but a radical progressive in whose music the 'traditional' background can still (just) be heard. (In the 1923 essay 'New Music' he pointedly wrote: 'I was never *revolutionary. The only revolutionary* in our time was Strauss!'[83]) Schoenberg's analysis of the *Erwartung* chord splits it into elements which contain residual patterns of tonal tension and resolution. The intensity and condensed complexity of the chord, however, undermines the leading-note energies (as famously analysed by Kurth in the music of Wagner) which might drive these resolutions. Excessive 'alteration' has led to obliteration: the chord becomes a kind of harmonic 'black hole', sucking all the energy into its dense centre and resisting the progressive release of these forces. Strauss's chord approaches a similar effect. Both chords displace the effect of musical 'Erwartung' – heady expectation or anxious anticipation – to focus on the immediately explosive moment. With her desire to kiss Jochanaan's mouth now sated, Salome is celebrating in an ecstatic moment of plenitude. Extremes touch in this highpoint, where rapturous, delirious decadence meets radical avant-gardism.

If the 'necrophiliac' chord is decadent through its derivation and association with the chromatic music of Salome's deviant desire, then it is also, through its resonances with the cacophony of the 'Jewish' music (through the elements of the dominant of D minor in its lower parts), symbolic of the musical avant-garde. As Sander Gilman has noted, Strauss's choice of Wilde's text represented the operatic break from Wagnerism and an identification with the cultural avant-garde, understood by Strauss as 'Jewish'. The opera sustains and explores the association between this Jewish avant-garde and Wilde as the embodiment of the homosexual decadent. Gilman compares the reception of Wilde in Germany as persecuted outsider with the perception of Eastern Jewry within German conservatism – the identification of homosexual emancipation with the avant-garde (hence Jewish) left. The term which clarified the link between Wilde, Strauss, the Jews and the avant-garde was *Perversität*. It was introduced by Karl Kraus in articles published in *Die Fackel* from 1903 which included analysis of the critical reception generated by German performances of Wilde's *Salome*. It was employed as a positive term, as a defining mark of the cultural avant-garde with which Kraus himself identified. The position of the homosexual decadent and of the 'unacculturated Eastern Jews' on whom the Viennese projected their anxieties was one of the outsider, the scandalous, the abject, the hysterical,

---

[83] Schoenberg, *Style and Idea*, 137 (emphases Schoenberg's).

the excessive and the execrable. These ideas of 'perversity' became closely associated with Strauss's opera and its characters. Early reactions, for example from Eugen Schmitz, Oscar Bie and Romain Rolland, were either dismissive or diagnostic of the 'sickness' of Jewish modernism. But, as Gilman persuasively argues, by providing signs and symptoms of perversity Strauss played to the Jewish avant-garde gallery and, through his opera's *succès de scandale*, became its operatic figurehead.

Example 5.4 Strauss, *Salome*, Page: 'Sie gleitet langsam dahin'

Example 5.4 (cont.)

Strauss's musical symbol of *Gemauschel* (Jewish discourse) is the noise heard from the banqueting hall in the opening scene (fig.4; Example 5.4). For Gilman, this is a 'cacophony which is musically avant-garde'. It is 'clearly contrasted with the opera's two other principal modes of musical discourse, the shimmering, chromatic world of Salome and the firm diatonicism of Jochanaan'; it evokes the irrational, the incomprehensible, and through the exploitation of the registral extremities evokes both the high, feminized voice of the hysterical male (as influentially and

notoriously described by Weininger) and the low, dark and debased.[84] This
music of 'uproar' and animalistic 'howling' is based on dissonant conflict
between D minor and its 'dark' and deathly Neapolitan, E flat minor.
Its characteristic D–E♭ discord contrasts markedly with the aspirant leading-
note-based idiom of the preceding music of desire. This emerges from the
minor ninth dissonance, B♭–A, over the dominant of D at the cadence
which follows the Page's declaration that Salome is 'like a pale, dead
woman'. Two images of death are thus juxtaposed: the decadently eroticized
Salome as zombie is followed by the avant-gardist demise of old belief
structures. The contrast is manifest in other ways: textural fragmentation
versus the smooth semitonal voice-leading; tonal stasis, largely over a D
pedal, contrasting with the tonal flux of the chromaticism of the opening,
which returns as the D smoothly connects to the dominant of C sharp at
Narraboth's declaration of Salome's beauty. The avant-garde is an ugly
interpolation between discussions of Salome's seductively strange beauty.
Here the decadent and the avant-garde lie cheek by jowl; opposites
approach a forbidden osculation.

Hearing decadence in Schoenberg

Third Reich condemnation aside, decadence is rarely strongly associated
with Schoenberg. His music is more likely to be characterized in terms
which are polar opposites to the common understandings of decadence –
referring to formal rigour, anti-ornamentalism, organic unity and expressive terseness rather than licentious formlessness, decorative excess, artifice
or sentimentality. However, in his ambivalent relationship to Wagner's
music, in particular the chromaticism and eroticism of *Tristan*, which had
by the time of Schoenberg's rise to fame (or notoriety) accrued wide
associations with decadence, there lies a complex and sustained interaction
with decadent themes and styles. (A companion essay could be written on
decadence and Schoenberg's relationship to the 'late' Brahms.) This seems
incontrovertible in some of the early works, which often took inspiration
from poets with overtly decadent sympathies. But decadence remains
important in the apparently 'avant-garde' works composed in the years
from 1908 to the outbreak of the First World War.

   First, an example of decadence in Schoenberg's early idiom. For
Christopher Palmer a defining feature of musical decadence lies in a

---

[84] Sander L. Gilman, 'Strauss, the Pervert, and Avant-Garde Opera of the *Fin de Siècle*', *New
German Critique* 43 (1988), 35–68.

'protracting of the cadence or cadential feeling to vast proportions': decadent music is that which 'luxuriates in this sunset sensation, this "sinking feeling"'.[85] The opening sections of *Gurrelieder* – a musical depiction of twilight – show that Schoenberg could compose decadent effects of protracted cadential fall on a grand scale. The E flat 'nature' music which opens the work inevitably recalls the music at the start of *The Rhinegold*. But by contrast with Wagner's musical evocation of 'natural' organic process of motivic development from a basic cell, Schoenberg produces a 'plane of harmony', which is decorated and 'interwoven with ornamental-like linear elements' comparable with the opulent artifice characteristic of canvases of the *Jugendstil*.[86] The motivic content is telling. The kitsch fall of the added sixth (C) is present from the start. Later, four bars after fig.1, a 3–2 motif (G–F in E flat) is introduced, its repeated statements suggesting the motion to closure (3–2–1), but there is as yet no dominant harmony to drive the melodic urge to cadence. When the dominant is reached (4 bars after fig.2) the 3–2 motif is transformed to become a chromaticized decoration of the leading note of E flat (D–C♯, that is, 3–♯2 or 3–♭3 of the dominant, B flat). Sequential descent then ensues, denying the rising tendency of the leading note D as the music sinks successively through transpositions of the semitonal motivic dyad (D–C♯; C–C♭; B♭–A; A–G♯). Two repeats of this opening paragraph then follow (from fig.4), each successive one transposed down a tone. The tonal structure generated by these three paragraphs is a sinking sequence from E flat via D flat to C flat

---

[85] Christopher Palmer, *Szymanowski* (London: BBC, 1983), 31. Palmer is here seeking to contrast the 'decadent' Zemlinsky, Korngold, Mahler, Rachmaninov, Delius and Elgar with Szymanowski, in whose music he discerns no such 'sinking'. See, however, the analysis of the end of *King Roger* in Chapter 6 below. Palmer cites Zemlinsky's *Lyric Symphony*, Op.18 (1922–3), as an example of this decadent cadential excess. (For Adorno, 'Zemlinsky's outstanding quality is his melodic cadence, cadence in the literal sense – that is to say, an expressive falling of the voice, a melancholic falling away from the outset': Adorno, 'Zemlinsky' [1959], in *Quasi una fantasia*, 121–2.) The 'infinite moment' of the final song of the symphony is undoubtedly one passage Palmer must have had in mind. After extended Molto adagio string and horn polyphony, expressive dissonances resolve to the *Augenblick* at the lines 'Steh still, o wundervolles Ende, für einen Augenblick, und sage deine letzen Worte in Schweigen' ('Stand still, O beautiful End, for a moment, and say your last words in silence'). Stretching or slowing increases as part of the final cadence onto a 'pan-diatonic chord with a Lydian G♯'. In the prominent celesta and an unresolved upper-voice sixth lie the cases for calling this Zemlinsky's response to Mahler's *Song of the Earth*. But there are also striking differences between Mahler's 'Ewig' and Zemlinsky's 'Ende'. Zemlinsky's slow closing of the eyes is an attempt to preserve a moment of inward rapture and the lush, luxuriant orchestral sonority which contrasts with Mahlerian clarity. See Anthony Beaumont, *Zemlinsky* (London: Faber, 2000), 315–19. Zemlinsky's music might be called 'endful', not endless.

[86] Klaus Kropfinger, 'The Shape of Line', *Art Nouveau and Jugendstil*, 141.

(I–♭VII–♭VI). The introduction is a massive decline, a descent ending on the romantic's favourite harmony of melancholy instability, the flat submediant. Of course, the next harmony implied by the structural descent is the dominant. This is provided, repeatedly, during Waldemar's opening sentences ('Now dusk mutes every sound on land and sea / the scudding clouds have gathered close, against the margin of the sky. / Silent peace has closed the forest's airy gates, / the limpid sea-waves all have lulled themselves to rest'; 3 bars after fig.9). He is accompanied by repeated chromatic falls in the upper structural line. Five successive descending phrases all descend to end on the dominant of E flat. Berg's comment that the first 145 bars of *Gurrelieder* are a 'gigantic, far-reaching cadence' is apposite.[87] Probably little is contentious about hearing a variety of decadence in the opulent decoration and protracted decline of this example. But to hear how decadence remains a vital aspect of Schoenberg's later music – where such ornamental excess and long-breathed expansiveness seem to be rejected – requires moving into more controversial argument.

In turn-of-the-century Austria the dread of compositional impotency in the face of Wagner's immense achievements – especially in *Tristan and Isolde*, by then already some forty years old – led many to propose that the only way forward was to make a radical break. Thus the musical avant-garde sought emancipation from the grip of the 'music of the future'. In his *Wagner-Probleme und andere Studien* (Vienna, 1900) Max Graf wrote: 'With deep emotion and awe, we, the avant-garde of a new generation, turned away from Wagner's picture and after moments of fear and trembling stepped out together and with head held high towards our own world, our own sun.'[88] Eight years later, in one of the most famous avant-garde leaps in music history, Schoenberg began to produce a series of works in which the Wagnerian past seemed to be irrevocably jettisoned. Schoenberg's breach into apparent atonality, Deathridge notes, was strongly motivated by the need to 'escape the sensual and intellectual force of *Tristan*', the desire for emancipation from 'the tentacles of Wagner's *Tristan*', as Deathridge vividly puts it.[89] Wagner the giant Kraken will drag the unwary, navel-gazing composer under the voluptuous surface of his oceanic erotics. Schoenberg's gaze was on the horizon as

---

[87] Berg, *Gurrelieder-Guide* (1913), trans. in Brian G. Campbell, '*Gurrelieder* and the Fall of the Gods: Schoenberg's Struggle with the Legacy of Wagner', in Cross and Berman (eds.), *Schoenberg and Words*, 45. 145 bars take us beyond this falling initial sentence through to the prolongation of tonic E flat in the rest of Waldemar's opening speech.
[88] Trans. in Glauert, *Hugo Wolf*, 9.   [89] Deathridge, *Wagner*, 114–15.

he navigated a route to new shores. But throughout the heroic voyage there is seepage of the chromatic style of *Tristan* into his vanguard vessel. It oozes into cracks in the new, supposedly atonal edifices which he built employing the techniques of 'intensification' and 'condensation'. In the years from 1908 Schoenberg seemed to make the apparently decisive breakthrough, tearing apart the superficial wrappings and emotional trappings of post-Wagnerian chromaticism and rejecting its sensuous extravagance and excess. The post-Wagnerian style of Dehmel-inspired works such as *Transfigured Night* (1899) seems to be abandoned in an avant-gardist rupture. It is a famous moment of white-hot compositional innovation. The score of *Tristan* is not just smeared; it is seared in the incineration of the icon of Wagnerian eroticism. Adorno, the philosopher of atonality, identified profound syntactical ramifications. He asserted that though the chromatic extremes of *Tristan* played a vital role in the 'elimination of the tendency of the leading tone', and though the weakened force of resolution 'continued into free atonality as a tonal residue' (an aspect of continuity and transition which coexisted with the radical breakthrough), as 'free atonality spread dissonance universally throughout music' triadic harmony became taboo, and the leading note, deprived of force and function, became a dying remnant.[90] If the cinders of the score of *Tristan* remained aglow in Schoenberg's bonfire of Wagner's vanities, then they were soon to be finally extinguished.

   Such is the tenet of emancipated dissonance. In the brave new atonal world where tonal residues remain they become weak, enfeebled, abject. The leading-note function in particular is increasingly problematized, avoided or rejected as moribund. Crucial syntactical consequences of this ambition emerge in the famous last movement of the Second String Quartet (1908). Already by the third bar of the rather conventionally phrased opening theme of the first movement, E♯, the leading note in F sharp minor, is reinterpreted as a falling F, an adumbration of the radical recapitulation of this theme in F major – where the leading-note function of E♯ has been replaced by that of the flat tonic. The theme returns in a shadow key: in a miniature version of Wagnerian sinking 'expressive tonality', leading-note dynamism has turned to darkening.[91] In a work with a number of musical allusions to *Parsifal* (motivated

---

[90] Adorno, *Philosophy of New Music*, 67.

[91] On Wagner's expressive and structural use of keys a semitone down in *Tristan* (an A–C tonal pair sinking to A♭–C♭/B) see John Daverio, *Nineteenth-Century Music and the German Romantic Ideology* (New York: Schirmer, 1993), 189–94. The other famous example of this technique is the repeat of the music of Siegfried's awakening of Brünnhilde in Act 3 scene iii of *Siegfried*

perhaps by the well-known personal wounds that Schoenberg suffered during his wife's affair with Richard Gerstl and, more concretely, by the allusion to Amfortas's plea 'close the wound' in George's 'Litanei', the poem set in the quartet's third movement), this substitution of F for the tonic F sharp may also be heard as a parallel to Wagner's semitonal substitutions in the harmonic structure of Amfortas's prayer to his dead father, Titurel.[92] (If this is Schoenberg seeking salve in techniques drawn from his 'dead father' Wagner then it is a return marked by a darkening and sense of decline at the very structural juncture – the sonata recapitulation – where effects of clarity, release and affirmation are expected to prevail.) In the opening bars of the finale, the 'ascent' or breakthrough into 'rapture', emancipation from tonal 'gravitational' pull is most powerfully felt in the absence of resolutions of leading note to the tonic. When the singer enunciates the famous words 'I feel the air of another planet' the approach to the F sharp major triad at the end of the line eschews any E♯–F♯ connections (the vocal line, meanwhile, exclusively and exhaustively employs the notes of the F major scale, the substitute, flattened tonic). After this, the final resolution of the movement must avoid the resolution of the leading note to the tonic of the perfect cadence.[93] Bryan Simms identifies the quartet as Schoenberg's 'first major confrontation with a compositional paradox with which he would grapple for his entire atonal period – a dialectic between form and expression, constraint and free emotion, Apollonian and Dionysian utterances'.[94] This paradoxical character can be extended to embrace the dialectic of decadence and the avant-garde. In the finale there is not only a raw emotional expression that demands radical escape from old forms and styles, but also an exploration and aesthetic validation of expressive qualities generated by the denudation and enfeeblement of the driving energetic forces of Wagnerian chromaticism. The latter offers a musical parallel to George's pervading poetic images of the weakening of nature ('tired trees') and the extinguishing voice of the desired other.

and the opening of *Twilight of the Gods*, where the original E–C tonal pair is darkened to E flat minor and C flat. See McCreless, 'An Evolutionary Perspective on Nineteenth-Century Semitonal Relationships'. Recall also the conflict between A and A♭ in the first movement of Bartók's First String Quartet.

[92] See David Lewin, 'Amfortas's Prayer to Titurel and the Role of D in *Parsifal*: The Tonal Spaces of the Drama and the Enharmonic C♭/B', *19th-Century Music* 7 (1984), 336–49.

[93] For further analytical observations of this aspect see Severine Neff, 'Presenting the Quartet's "Idea"', in Neff (ed.), *Arnold Schoenberg: The Second String Quartet in F-sharp minor, Opus 10* (New York: Norton, 2006), 128–40 and 166–85.

[94] Bryan R. Simms, '"My dear Herzerl": Self-Representation in Schoenberg's String Quartet No.2', *19th-Century Music* 26 (2003), 276.

Adorno sought to counter the view of Schoenberg's music as the 'exaggeration' of a 'lapsed principle of expression', to clear him of any condemnation as a post-Wagnerian mannerist. To this end he heard the atonal works as a 'breach' into a form of expression 'qualitively different' from the 'Wagnerian *espressivo*' of the early works. This was a break made 'precisely through the "exaggeration" that thinks this *espressivo* through to its conclusion'.[95] But the straightforward, logical, one-directional narrative trajectory of Schoenberg reaching a creative escape velocity to leave nostalgia for the Wagnerian expressive world of chromatic tonality behind is obfuscatory. Julie Brown pertinently asks why in the January 1910 performance of the radical breakthrough works *The Book of the Hanging Gardens*, Op.15, and Three Piano Pieces, Op.11, Schoenberg also included the overtly post-Wagnerian first part of *Gurrelieder*. For Brown this indicates that he wished publicly to declare that his 'avant-garde' project was indebted to the 'spiritual legacy of Wagner's *Zukunftsmusik*', that 'the step into atonality was a response to the revolutionary artist's Wagnerian call to duty'.[96] In this reading Schoenberg has reached a moment of crisis which has Wagnerian provenance. In several well-known essays Schoenberg appropriated Wagner to establish a lineage for his new music: he raised Wagnerian chromaticism as a vital stimulus of his stylistic 'evolution', as part of his self-legitimization. The programme of the January 1910 concert may have been planned to confirm Schoenberg's claim to be the next, necessary stage in that constructed 'evolutionary' history of Austro-German music, to bolster his self-identification as Wagner's natural heir with responsibility to ensure future progeny. *Gurrelieder* indeed shows Schoenberg's Wagnerian 'inheritance', as Taruskin describes it, 'in a "decadent" erotic manner reminiscent of *Tristan*'.[97] But Taruskin has countered the widely held assumption that Schoenberg's 'crisis of tonality' and move into atonality represent a consequence of the chromaticism of *Tristan*. Taruskin argues that Wagner's chromaticism 'actually gave tonality a new source of strength and expressivity', that the delays and denials of resolution only intensified the harmonic tensions which drive tonal syntax.[98] Taruskin

[95] Adorno, *Philosophy of New Music*, 34–5.

[96] Julie Brown, 'Schoenberg's Early Wagnerisms: Atonality and the Redemption of Ahasuerus', *Cambridge Opera Journal* 6 (1994), 51–80. Brown hears the nostalgic, attenuated tonality and ultimate denial of a final cadence in D minor in the last song of Op.15 as marking Schoenberg's resignation and difficulty in making the final step, as wandering 'Jewish' composer, into the wilderness of atonality.

[97] Taruskin, 'The Poietic Fallacy' [2004], in *The Danger of Music*, 319.

[98] Taruskin, 'Wagner's Antichrist Crashes a Pagan Party' [1999], in *The Danger of Music*, 142.

would probably therefore hear *The Book of the Hanging Gardens* as a radical shift away from this post-Wagnerian language. In fact, Op.15 is one of several works in which Schoenberg stylistically swerves between 'Tristanesque' decadence and an 'anti-*Tristan*' avant-garde. In these shifts the decadent forms, those nostalgic remnants of an old language which cling adhesively to the new figures, need to be seen not as debilitating nor as hindrance to future 'progress' (to which Schoenberg felt such a burden of responsibility), but rather as a stimulating presence which is far from silenced or suppressed by apparently more radical voices.

The penultimate song of the cycle is often considered the most advanced or radical. (Adorno considered it to be devoid of traditional form, to be 'dematerialized', with enormously radical implications.) This song represents the highpoint, famously described by Carl Schorske, where the garden, that 'ordered symbol of outer reality and hierarchical culture', is 'pulverised', as thematic form and tonal structure are splintered.[99] The avant-garde character of this horticultural terrorism is clear. But as the lovers part in the final song the garden dries up and dies in a process of desiccation, disintegration and decay which Schorske hears as a pre-echo of the opening of the monodrama of *Erwartung*, where the flowers of the garden are drooping and faded. After the separation of the lovers in its opening stanza the text of the final song of Op.15, 'Wir bevölkerten die abend-düstern', moves from decadent languor and decay – 'high blooms fade and break / pale and fractured is the millpond's glass / And I stumble lost in the rotten grass' – through masochistic expressionism – 'Palms with sharp fingers stab me / crumbling leaves in hissing throngs' – to a debilitating, gloomy prospect – 'Night is overcast and sultry'. The triads in the song are of shifting character. They can sound regressive, like half-heard, attenuated or debilitated resolutions (Lawrence Kramer hears them as 'marking the failure of desire',[100] Simms as a 'wistful' looking back to older styles[101]), while others are shockingly disruptive in an avant-garde sense, as the cruel negation of progress, expectation, anticipation, or hope in the future. In bars 40–1 the two effects sit provocatively cheek by jowl (see Example 5.5). After the vocalist's final line ('Nacht ist

---

[99] Schorske, *Fin-de-Siecle Vienna*, 351.

[100] Lawrence Kramer, *Music and Poetry: The Nineteenth Century and After* (Berkeley: University of California Press, 1984), 166.

[101] Bryan Simms, *The Atonal Music of Arnold Schoenberg 1908–23* (Oxford University Press, 2000), 52.

Example 5.5 Schoenberg, *The Book of the Hanging Gardens*, Op.15 No.15, 'Wir bevölkerten die abend-düstern', (George), bars 33–51

überwolkt und schwül') the piano coda begins a process of liquidation, the dissolving of motivic content to effect a move towards cadence. The upper motifs sink in register and dwindle in character to a three-note minim descent (E♭–D♭–C♭; bb.38–9). This is an augmented version of the motif which has been the basis of the bass descent, now truncated to a repeated A♭–G♭ dyad. The descending third in the right hand suggests a move between E♭ and C♭ through a 'passing' D♭, with these outer structural pitches then 'resolving' onto D and A (bar 40) to form the upper notes of a D minor triad. But this is a debilitated resolution and the triad sounds enfeebled, primarily because the potential leading-note function of C♯ has been replaced by the falling passing motion of the D♭. This absent leading-note drive is then placed as the upper pitch of the low left-hand A major triad of bar 40. The music through this process has slowed and quietened, but now the instruction is *molto cresc.* as beneath the weakened D minor triad the 'dominant' A triad sinks further: first to A minor, then – brutally – to a *fortissimo* G minor. The extreme registeral depth and closed position of this chord make it sound like intrusive, ugly noise. This triad sounds the obliteration of the enfeebled sense of tonal cadence in the preceding bar. The triad, the foundation of the old system, has been employed as a rock upon which progress to resolution founders. It is a recalcitrant jolt to the system, an alien object thrown in to break up the lingering connective procedures of 'post-Wagnerian' chromatic counterpoint. Thus, as alienated fragments or enfeebled echoes of a dead language some of the triads in the song signal the dissolutions and decays of decadence, yet others signal break-through into radical newness in avant-gardist emancipation from old Wagner's 'music of the future'. The endless melody of musical prose, which derives its expressive intensity from a compulsive postponement of cadence that only perpetuates the impending sense of an approaching yet distant end, is brought to a full stop. It is bludgeoned into destruction. The end of Schoenberg's cycle suggests both avant-garde iconoclasm and decadent, degenerative contrast to the expectant, generative musical prose of the opening, which Brown has interpreted as an allegory of mythical Babylonian creation.[102]

The manifest contrasts between the last two songs of *The Book of the Hanging Gardens* are also apparent in the Three Piano Pieces, Op.11, where again they appear to propose two possible routes out of Wagnerian chromaticism. To Adorno's ears the avant-garde credentials of Op.11 are

---

[102] Julie Brown, 'Schoenberg's Musical Prose as Allegory', *Music Analysis* 14 (1995), 161–92.

indisputable. He identifies them in their 'unadorned, naked expression' and 'hostility to art'.[103] In what Adorno considers to be Schoenberg's 'revolutionary', non-Wagnerian *espressivo* there is no decoration or 'simulation' of passions, but instead only the undisguised registering of 'shock' and 'trauma'. This raw truth is wounding: the pieces exhibit for Adorno the 'scars' and 'disfiguring stains' as 'emissaries of the Id, distressing the decorative surface'.[104] In a tactical hearing designed to highlight the piece's radicalism, the 'Tristanesque' echoes in the chromaticisms of the first piece have been interpreted as parodic.[105] But the sense of cool, distanced objectivity required to support such a hearing seems absent. Michael Cherlin is nearer the mark when, invoking Freud's well-known elaboration of the concept of *das Unheimlich*, he hears how the tonal home is made uncanny. In Op.11 No.1, in a return of the repressed, tonality emerges as 'estranged, evanescent spectres': Schoenberg 'usurps Wagner's language … yet the spectre of *Tristan* remains'.[106] Here one can see how Kuspit's dialectic of decadence and avant-garde, in which the return of the advanced artist's repressed decadence can lead to a tone of traumatic anxious expectation ('Erwartung'), is so suggestive. The opening (Example 5.6) suggests that the 'scars' – to borrow Adorno's image for a characteristically avant-garde surface – of Tristan's wounds remain a source of agony. There is no closure, only a sense of an increasingly limping waltz moving through chromatic-semitonal motions which rise and droop in counterpoint of overtly post-Wagnerian provenance. Simms analyses the piece as a 'developmental ternary form', with a B section beginning at bar 12 and a reprise at bar 53.[107] However, the theme returns in bar 17, the material in bars 19–24 has a strong cadential feel, and the contrapuntal texture of bar 25 onwards marks a move into a more obviously developmental phase. The more fragmentary textures and gestures in the second half of the middle section (which take their cue from the fleeting fragment of

---

[103] Adorno, 'Arnold Schoenberg, 1874–1951', in *Prisms*, 161.

[104] Adorno, *Philosophy of New Music*, 66.

[105] Thomas Christensen, 'Schoenberg's Opus 11, No.1: A Parody of Pitch Cells from *Tristan*', *Journal of the Arnold Schoenberg Institute* 10 (1987), 38–44. John Joseph Reible III, 'Tristan-Romanticism and the Expressionism of the Three Piano Pieces Op.11 of Arnold Schoenberg', unpublished PhD thesis, University of Washington, 1980, argues that the parallels were consciously motivated by parallels between Schoenberg's personal life and Wagner's music drama.

[106] Michael Cherlin, 'Schoenberg and *Das Unheimliche*: Spectres of Tonality', *The Journal of Musicology* 11 (1993), 362–3.

[107] Simms, *The Atonal Music*, 62.

Example 5.6 Schoenberg, Piano Piece Op.11 No.1, bars 1–11

bars 12–14) evoke a contrastingly 'extensive', free-floating or fleet-of-foot eschatology. But this flight, escape or leaving-behind is then denied by the return of the opening material, at the original pitch, in accordance with the obligations of traditional ternary design (b.53). This material, as one would expect from Schoenberg, is a condensed return, but the main effect is one of decay and decline. The *crescendo* and rising bass motif of bars 54–6 cannot counteract the melancholic effect produced by the falling character of the upper parts, which are based on the extension of the F–E motif originally exposed in bar 3 to produce a line which descends chromatically from F to C♯ over five bars. The cadential effect is confirmed by the return to prominence of augmented triad chords, which had dominated the cadential bars of the A section (bb.19–24).[108] The texture returns to the overtly Wagnerian chromatic counterpoint of the opening bars. In tonal music, as Wintle says, ternary form 'distils many kinds of feeling – the return of the known, the joy and relief of a child at a parent's return'.[109] In Schoenberg's piano piece the recourse to formal obligations from tonal music brings no such joyful homecoming, though it does suggest the return of the familiar voice of Wagner the father, if now in more aged and weakened form. It calls forth the return of Tristanesque yearning, but also marks its decline in a musical variety of the law of diminishing returns. The contrasting

---

[108] In an example of post-Brahmsian 'linkage technique' these augmented triads continue to inform the harmony at the start of the developmental B section.

[109] Wintle, *All the Gods*, 82.

character of material in the A and B sections led Brinkmann to propose a fundamental opposition between the 'thematic' and the 'eruptive'.[110] Through this double character the first piece becomes the source of both the second piece's yearning tonal nostalgia (not only engendered by the D–F ostinato but also by the shifting leading-note energies or flat-tonic darkenings of the D♭'s uncertain relationship to D) and the apparent lawlessness, athematicism, textural radicalism and uncompromising intensity of the notorious third. Extreme opposites emanate from implications exposed in the opening piece, in which we hear potential for both the decadent (obsessively nostalgic, allusive, melancholic, pessimistic, agonisingly exposing old wounds) and the avant-garde (explosively anarchic, iconoclastic, recalcitrant, bellicose, the point of no return).

In such perilous circumstances as are found at the end of Schoenberg's setting of *The Book of the Hanging Gardens* the decadent might do better to withdraw from the garden to the even more artificial environment of the greenhouse. Schoenberg does precisely this in his Maeterlinck setting *Herzgewächse* (*Heart's Foliage*), Op.20 (1911). The song was famously published in facsimile in *Der blaue Reiter*. The central aim of the almanac was to propose revitalization of dying art through recourse to the primitive, as exemplified by cubism, and the psychological drive of inner necessity manifest in the spontaneous creativity associated with expressionism.[111] In this context the Schoenberg facsimile gains symbolic status as the trace left by the creative impulse which compelled the movements of the composer's pen (songs by Berg and Webern appeared, by contrast, in their printed form). The presentation in the composer's scrawling hand adds to the song's avant-garde veneer, to its apparent newness, implying that it is 'hot off the press'. But it is not all news. Deathridge comments that *Herzgewächse* is

clearly indebted to the radically modern aspect of *Tristan*: not only does the vegetal imagery of Maeterlinck's poem *Feuillages du coeur* (1889) resemble Mathilde Wesendonck's *Im Treibhaus*, which Wagner described as a 'study' for *Tristan* after he had set it to music; but each strand of musical material also grows forward without insisting on closure and remains, so to speak, ecstatically deaf to the past.[112]

---

[110] Reinhold Brinkmann, *Arnold Schönberg: Drei Klavierstücke, Op.11* (1969), quoted by Simms, *The Atonal Music*, 62.

[111] Thomas Clifton, 'On Listening to *Herzgewächse*', *Perspectives of New Music* 11 (1973), 87–103, relates musical gestures and shapes to features of cubism (Picasso) and expressionism (Kandinsky).

[112] Deathridge, *Wagner*, 224.

Example 5.7 Schoenberg, *Herzgewächse*, Op.20 (Maeterlinck), opening gesture

However, what was 'radically modern', or avant-garde, in Wagner is now heard as decadent expiration of the last breaths of a Tristan on life-support in a modern hothouse. In the German version which Schoenberg set, Maeterlinck's second line, 'De mes lasses mélancholies',[113] is shifted to open the poem and rendered as 'Meiner müden Sehnsucht', a poetic line encapsulating the sense of Wagnerian yearning now exhausted. Schoenberg's introductory gesture suggests a remnant D minor through the initial melodic shape G♯–A–D–E♭–D and the bass motif, D–F–D♭ (Example 5.7). But it also alludes to elements of Wagner's *Tristan* opening: the first two notes of the upper line (G♯–A) echo the same pitches at the start of Wagner's upper rising chromatic motif, they sound over an A–C minor third which (very briefly) suggests the tonic A minor of the Tristan Prelude, and the E♭–D which ends Schoenberg's opening motif echoes the D♯–D♮ motion in the 'alto' of Wagner's chromatic counterpoint.[114] This opening musically encapsulates the initial poetic sense of decadence. The second half of the poem, with its image of the rising orchid, symbolizing a mystical hope unusual

---

[113] See Maurice Maeterlinck, *Hothouses: Poems 1889*, trans. Richard Howard (Princeton University Press, 2003), 20–1.

[114] The opening of *Herzgewächse* also offers a motivic and tonal recollection of the climactic fate motif of Schoenberg's other Maeterlinck piece, the contrastingly gigantic symphonic poem *Pelleas and Melisande* (1902). At the start of this earlier work Schoenberg raises the *Tristan* spectre more overtly. Kropfinger considers Schoenberg's to be a contrapuntal and motivic transformation of Wagnerian 'endless melody' such that by contrast with the 'integrating function' performed by Wagner's Tristan chord there is 'constructive linearity' free from a centralizing harmonic function: Klaus Kropfinger, 'The Shape of Line', 144–5. The Tristan chord is now an ending, not an implicative alteration of a pre-dominant: what in Wagner was integrative and generative is now a terminus.

in Maeterlinck's 1889 collection, chimes with the aims of the *Blaue Reiter* project: utopian, evolutionary, spiritual regeneration. And thus, as Bonny Hough concludes, 'the composition has a bipartite form, the first half being the descent into melancholy and inertia, and the second half the elevation to enlightenment'. The song's overall design is an 'inversion of the structural arch'.[115] It is also an inversion of the paradigmatic wave form. Decadence is the seed bed which fertilizes the rise of the new.

When Schoenberg finally completed *Gurrelieder* in 1913, among the new styles he imported into the work was the *Sprechstimme* that has become most famously associated with *Pierrot lunaire*, Op.21. In this cycle radical newness coexists with a strong element of mannerism, manifest in the passages of virtuosic, obsessively complex contrapuntal technique and in the way in which the high expressionistic style, which reached its peak in *Erwartung*, is now looked back upon and 'resurrected' as an old style, with its violence placed at an extra level of remove.[116] This supports Kuspit's argument that the avant-gardist's immediate expression of desire is shadowed by its own immanent decadence. Many early critics identified a decadent tone in Schoenberg's *Pierrot*. In doing so they were, of course, seldom complimentary. 'Der Wanderer' reported from Berlin to his American readers in *Musical America* (14 November 1912) that he could find no 'decent, healthy consonant chord', except in the last bars, 'where it appears that [Schoenberg's] foot must have slipped'.[117] Several critics accused Schoenberg of perverting the Wagnerian inheritance. Thus James Huneker writing in the *New York Times* (19 January 1913) declared:

It was new music (or new exquisitely horrible sounds) with a vengeance. The very ecstasy of the hideous! I say 'exquisitely horrible' for pain can be at once exquisite and horrible … And the border-land between pain and pleasure is a territory hitherto unexplored by musical composers. Wagner suggests poetic anguish; Schoenberg not only arouses the image of anguish, but he brings it home to his auditory in the most subjective way. You suffer the anguish with the fictitious character in the poem.

[115] Bonny Hough, 'Schoenberg's *Herzgewächse* and the *Blaue Reiter* Almanac', *Journal of the Arnold Schoenberg Insitute* 7 (1983), 197–221.

[116] Peter Platt, '*Pierrot lunaire* – Mannerist or Baroque?', in *Art Nouveau and Jugendstil*, 233–4. Arnold Whittall characterized the cycle as mannerist rather than expressionist: *Schoenberg Chamber Music* (London: BBC, 1972), 29.

[117] François Lesure (ed.), *Dossier de presse de* Pierrot lunaire *d'Arnold Schoenberg* (Geneva: Editions Minkoff, 1985), 14–16.

For Huneker there is in Schoenberg's musical style no relief from this agony, but only fragmentation and exaggeration: 'There is no melodic or harmonic line, only a series of points, dots, dashes, or phrases that sob and scream, despair, explode, exalt, blaspheme.'[118] Paul Rosenfeld in *The Dial* (April 1923) noted the cycle's rapidity and abbreviation, which chimes with the 'condensation' noted by Adorno as part of Schoenberg's escape plan from Wagnerian emotionalism, but also heard these as violations of Wagner's style: 'In narrow spaces of time he achieves searing, fiery summits of tone. The ecstatically heaving violin-music of the few measures of "Heimweh" in *Pierrot* … are like an oceanic *Tristan*-climax concentrated in tabloid form.' For Rosenfeld, Schoenberg evokes Wagner's 'swooning sensuousness' and 'ecstatic voluptuousness' but the desire is 'smothered'. Rosenfeld then becomes gruesomely anatomical, describing the music as the 'human torso' of the disfigured man in the machine age: 'He is the thing without arms, without legs, without organs of communication, with a phallus. He is the helpless, quivering pulp; blindly stirring, groping, stretching.' This mutilated body is fatally sick: 'Wagner's will, undercut as it was, seems free and direct by the side of this mortally wounded will. In these works, the cry of Amfortas and of the sick Tristan is become shrill, piping, broken': even those 'moments of health are only moments of lessened sickness'.[119] Rosenfeld's is a grim and grisly verdict. Clearly, he, like Huneker, felt that Schoenberg's decadent music was beyond any hope of convalescence into a healthy wholeness. Some serious therapy seemed to be required.

Adorno, inevitably, sees the 'hothouse' return in *Pierrot* to a 'denatured' *paradis artificiel*, and the miniaturism of the musical idiom ('isolated flowing and flashy *pointes*') as producing a 'masterwork in paradoxical proximity to *kitsch*', as a 'retreat' from the expressionistic aesthetic of the monodrama *Erwartung*. Adorno asserts that while there is no 'decline' in Schoenberg's 'compositional power', he has however become 'entangled' in empty, mendacious transitions and the figured ornament of the 'arabesque'.[120] However, a cursory glance at the poem

[118] Lesure (ed.), *Dossier de presse*, 20–1.

[119] Lesure (ed.), *Dossier de presse*, 147–9. The theme continues, unsurprisingly, in post-war critical reaction. Olin Downes in the *New York Times* (23 February 1923) wrote: 'It is the work of a highly gifted decadent, who has led himself and his followers into an impasse' (Lesure (ed.), *Dossier de presse*, 155). H. C. Colles in *The Times* (22 November 1923) asked, 'who wants to live, even for a moment, in this decadent world?' (*Dossier*, 163); and Percy Scholes in *The Observer* (25 November 1923) observed: 'I fear that the normal mind … will sniff a little, and murmur "decadence!"' (*Dossier*, 164).

[120] Adorno, *Prisms*, 163–4.

Example **5.8** Schoenberg, *Pierrot lunaire*, Op.21, 'O alter Duft aus Märchenzeit' (Hartleben–Giraud), bars 1–6

'Der Mondfleck' – which Schoenberg set in one of the most extreme displays of mannerist technical virtuosity – shows that the relationship between the decadent and the new is sharply pointed. The snowy fleck of moonlight that lies on Pierrot's black coat is an immovable source of irritation: it is a stain on his proud outer appearance of fashionable stylishness. Moonlight is a favoured image of decadence: its light is reflected, it possesses no primary source of its own, and it is in this sense parasitical, uncanny, cold and lifeless. This mark of decadence cannot be rubbed out. It is, moreover, stubbornly attached to his back: it points backwards, yet drives Pierrot to further attempts to confirm his pose as a figure of newness. The finely dressed dandy becomes the twitching figure of a neurotic fidget. This parallels the paradox in Schoenberg's music, where a complex weave of extreme technical skill produces an effect of restless unease.

There are several places where decadence assumes a prominent position among the cycle's stylistic diversity. The opening and closing 'cadences', which set the final text, 'O alter Duft aus Märchenzeit', reveal decadence to be especially crucial at the cycle's end (see Examples 5.8 and 5.9). Here, instead of breathing the new, enrapturing air of some far-flung planet, Pierrot is enveloped by the old perfumes of a strangely familiar fairy-tale world. But this aged scent of the dream's imagination retains the power to 'intoxicate' ('berauschen'). The voice doubles the upper notes of parallel thirds in the piano right hand (Adorno called such thirds 'Viennese'). In bar 1 these thirds outline the triad of

Example 5.9 Schoenberg, *Pierrot lunaire*, Op.21, 'O alter Duft…', bars 24–30

E major. In bar 2 this 'tonality' is undermined, first by allusion to the 'old' technique of modal mixture by altering the G♯ to the 'minor third', G♮, then by lowering the 'diatonic' second F♯ to the 'Neapolitan' or 'Phrygian', F♮. As the top part continues its descent these 'altered' pitches (G and F♮) are repeated. Under them the E 'tonality' is further, and in this part of the texture most radically, undermined by avoiding motion to the 'leading note', D♯: F♮ leaps directly to the 'lowered seventh', D♮, which then falls to D♭. After this the E major triad on the downbeat of bar 3 is an insufficient restoration of tonal 'normality'. Principally, in the upper parts, this is due to the preceding avoidance of the leading note. The 'alterations' of bar 2 introduce allusion to a symmetrical 'counter-structure' since, if bar 1 leads the ear to hear chords on the first and second beats as accented 'dissonances' which 'resolve', in characteristic late Romantic style, on the weak beats, then the right-hand dyads here elaborate a D♭–F–A augmented triad. The left-hand line is more sinuously serpentine and elusive in its 'tonal' allusions, conflicting with the 'E-ness' of the upper parts. Its opening gesture, a rising chromatic line, balances the 'tonal' descent in the right hand, but quickly undermines any expectation of a tonal bass, as the rise is deflected downwards, 'enharmonically' spelling the 'leading note' as E♭ as it sinks to D♮. This move is coincident with the 'passing' A–F♯ third in the right hand, thus forming a fleeting 'resolution' onto a 'D triad' – a sense of 'D-ness' strengthened by its subsequent 'resolution' of G to F♯. Thus the second half of bar 1 has a strong scent of D – the triad which will end the second balancing phrase (in bar 6). On the downbeat of bar 2 the lower part strikes the elusive leading note in the 'correct' spelling, but again this potential tonal function is denied as it initiates a transformation of the line from semitonal motion to movement in 'minor third' dyads in more extreme non-diatonic relationships, confirming types of thirds as the most characteristic intervals of the material (of course, the vocal phrase outlines such an interval, G♯–B). The overall effect is to generate tonal allusion, ambiguity and subversion – raising the old tones only to deform them – through chromatic alterations which allude to late romantic techniques which are found in Wagner, but which seem to be on the brink of liberation from such modes. Given the tone of many of the preceding songs of *Pierrot lunaire* one might call this parodic. Alternatively, one might suggest that the 'old' 'intensive alteration style' of 'late' Wagner has leached through, to emerge not as a parody, but as a crucial force, feeding on or clinging to the 'new' apparently atonal forms.

The final bars (Example 5.9) return to the opening poetic line and to a reworking of the opening melodic and harmonic materials. The effect is profoundly nostalgic. The 'E major' parallel thirds are now given to the viola and cello: they slow down and halt on the F–A dyad. The voice enters, with its first three pitches outlining a version of a motif which became prominent earlier in the song. In the motivic version presented here the semitonal C♯–D move is coincident with the arrival on the F–A dyad in the strings. The D minor triad so formed recalls the 'D-ness' of the opening paragraphs. The minor form rekindles the fascination with the melancholic symbolism of the key of D minor in many of Schoenberg's earlier pieces, and the opposition of this key's symbolic associations with the ecstatic key of E major (see, for example, *Transfigured Night*). On the downbeat of bar 28 the voice peaks on C♯, to produce an F–A–C♯ augmented triad with the sustained major third dyad in the strings. This further recalls the opening – the upper parts of bar 2 suggested a symmetrical 'counter-structure' to the E major 'tonal structure'. The piano now returns with highly enigmatic triads. They motivically echo the voice's line: E♭–E–B, with registral dispacements, parallels the C♯–D–A♯. They also emphasize an E♭–E–E♭ neighbour-note relationship in a distant echo of the diatonic relationship of the leading note to the tonic. The bass Es in bar 29, the lowest sound of the song, sustain the tonal feel. Inevitably, the voice seems to deny resolution. Its final pitches, C♯ and F, are remnant echoes of the augmented triad and hence, even more distantly, are echoes of the allusions to D minor. Placed over the bass E in the piano, they also generate resemblances to the 'kitsch' added sixth and the dark Neapolitan or Phrygian flattened second.

In such details lie the decadent effects in this harmonic world of half-remembered, receding and shadowy tonal forms, poetically figured as the whiff of a bygone scent. 'Resemblance' is the key word (hence all the inverted commas around the technical language of tonality in the preceding analysis). This is music which refutes Adorno's assertion that Schoenberg broke free from the expressive idiom of earlier music – the 'true *musica ficta*' which 'presented expression as stylized and mediated, as a semblance of the passions' – to compose music in which 'passions are no longer faked'.[121] Like the character of Pierrot, the music is a series of fleeting resemblances of this expressive semblance. In this song of old perfumes, rather than the emancipation of dissonance Schoenberg parades the invocation and evaporation of tonal resolution and its condensation into fragile residues.[122] All this may also resemble an enfeebling nostalgia for old expressive forms in the manner of Nietzsche's 'weak pessimism'. But there are further, more radical

---

[121] Adorno, *Philosophy of New Music*, 35.

[122] There is a parallel in literature, where the decadent seduction of resemblance and disguise is pursued to its breaking point. In *Bruges-la-Morte* Georges Rodenbach's Viane concludes that 'resemblance is the horizon where habit and novelty meet'. Viane, who sees the resemblance of his dead wife in his new object of desire, Jane Scott, 'possesses what one might call a "sense of resemblance", an extra sense, frail and sickly, which linked things to each other by a thousand tenuous threads …'. Continuity and discontinuity may join at some 'undefined point' by being reconciled by resemblance. But in the climactic dressing of Jane in the refined old-fashioned clothes of his dead wife Viane 'had gone too far. By trying to fuse the two women into one he had only succeeded in lessening the resemblance. As long as they were kept at a distance, with the mists of death between them, the illusion remained possible. Brought too close together, the differences emerged.' This was because as he had pushed resemblance 'to smaller and smaller details, he had ended up tormenting himself over nuances': Rodenbach, *'Bruges-la-Morte' and 'The Death Throes of Towns'*, trans. Mike Mitchell and Will Stone (Sawtry: Dedalus, 2005), 60, 86.

implications. Again, they counter Adorno, who argued that Schoenberg's was the only music that could challenge Nietzsche's manner of 'affirming aesthetic conventions' through 'ironic play with forms whose substantiality had vanished'.[123] For Adorno, Schoenberg affirmed a commitment to truth by negating decoration, semblance and play. But in its ludic and nostalgic resemblances *Pierrot lunaire* turns Adorno's argument on its head. Richard Kurth has proposed that the cycle undermines the image of Schoenberg as believer in the 'Idea' and thus as a Platonicist, organicist and Schopenhauerian. It thus also challenges the notion that Schoenberg, because of his allegiances to classical and romantic ideals, was no avant-gardist. The modern figure of Pierrot – 'master of mirage but also its servant' – emasculates mimesis and calls attention to the 'alienated, artificial, conflicting, disruptive, and fragmentary qualities' of the modernist artwork. It is an 'image of the modern crisis of identity', a 'pushing to the limits of neurosis and fantastic parody, in the ephemeral, the dissolute, the fragment, the mask. In this it touches the avant-garde.'[124] This Pierrot cycle confirms that the avant-garde (once again) touches the decadent.[125] The ambiguity of Schoenberg's music parallels the characteristics of the text. Hartleben's German versions of Albert Giraud's poetic cycle sustain the Baudelairean decadence, while introducing new layers of irony 'alongside avant-garde attitudes drawn from the commedia dell'arte'.[126] Schoenberg's music sustains this complexity. In its mannerist mixture of *Nervenkunst* and the cerebral, his setting may, to coin Stravinsky's famous dictum, be the 'solar plexus as well as the mind of

---

[123] Adorno, *Philosophy of New Music*, 36.

[124] Richard Kurth, 'Pierrot's Cave: Representation, Reverberation, Radiance', in Cross and Berman (eds.), *Schoenberg and Words*, 205.

[125] In *Die tote Stadt*, Korngold's 1920 operatic treatment of Rodenbach's *Bruges-la-Morte*, a Pierrot *Tanzlied* is inserted (Act 2 scene iii) to provide a kind of symbolic turning point. Saturated with appoggiaturas on the sixth and ninth in a nostalgically diatonic D flat major, it seeks to express his yearning to return home. Pierrot here offers a fleeting image of security, one that is recognized as irretrievably lost. It exudes a kitsch quality far from that which might touch the radical, avant-gardists' break with the past. When the doomed Marietta recalls this music towards the end of the opera the diatonicisms are clouded by more cloying chromaticisms. Korngold's opera only very partially 'resembles' the grey, decadent pessimism of the literary original: the music often exudes a late romantic energy and melodramatic passion, both of which are entirely absent in Rodenbach's enervated, elegiac style.

[126] Glenn Watkins, *Pyramids at the Louvre: Music, Culture, and Collage from Stravinsky to the Postmodernists* (Cambridge, Mass.: Harvard University Press, 1994), 284. For a perceptive comparison of Hartleben and Giraud see Robert Vilain, '*Pierrot lunaire*: Cyclic Coherence in Giraud and Schoenberg', in Mark Delaere and Jan Herman (eds.), Pierrot lunaire: *Albert Giraud – Otto Erich Hartleben – Arnold Schoenberg* (Louvain: Editions Peeters, 2004), 127–44.

early twentieth-century music',[127] but in his 1935 *Chroniques de ma vie* Stravinsky also famously, and inevitably (given his aesthetic creed at the time) denounced the work as a 'retrogression to the out-of-date Beardsley cult'.[128] It is a condemnation which identifies a key aspect of the cycle, the decadence which must be heard as it coils round the music's explosive gestures and esoteric constructions, in a mix, as Holloway puts it, of 'luxuriant and refined, *fin-de-siècle* and futuristic'.[129] The cycle, furthermore, is not an isolated or unique event in Schoenberg's output, but rather a continuation, indeed the pinnacle of his creative engagement with decadence. Schoenberg's *Pierrot* is a cycle of powerful paradox, if one has the nerves, mind and stomach for it.

[127] Igor Stravinsky and Robert Craft, *Dialogues and a Diary* (London: Faber, 1968), 105.
[128] Stravinsky, *An Autobiography*, 43–4, quoted in Taruskin, *Stravinsky and the Russian Traditions*, 826.
[129] Holloway, 'The Great Mutilator' [1989], in *On Music*, 155.

6 | Convalescence and primitivism

> My greatest experience was a recovery. Wagner is merely one of my
> sicknesses. Not that I want to be ungrateful to this sickness…
>
> Nietzsche, The Case of Wagner (Leipzig, 1888)

> Pain is the mental correlate of destruction. (Sickness and death.)
> Pleasure is the mental correlate of creation.
> Lust is accompanied by intense pain, because in it creation and
> destruction are merged.
>
> Otto Weininger, On Last Things (Vienna, 1903)

Introduction

Max Nordau held absolute faith in the methods and progress of 'modern'
science. A qualified medical practitioner, he was an advocate of Darwinian
evolution. He declared that the survival of the fittest in the natural world
contrasted with the weakness of the 'degenerates' who withdrew from the
struggles of life into an artificially enclosed environment of self-indulgent
despair.[1] He proposed a 'diagnosis':

the physician, especially if he has devoted himself to the special study of nervous
and mental maladies, recognises at a glance, in the *fin-de-siècle* disposition, in the
tendencies of contemporary art and poetry, in the life and conduct of the men who
write mystic, symbolic and 'decadent' works, and the attitude taken by their
admirers in the tastes and aesthetic instincts of fashionable society, the confluence
of two well-defined conditions of disease, with which he is quite familiar, viz.
degeneration (degeneracy) and hysteria, of which the minor stages are designated
as neurasthenia.[2]

---

[1] Nordau's *Degeneration* was dedicated to Lombroso, who in *Genius and Insanity* (1863) proposed
that the criminal mind was a product of developmental retrogression, revealing his debt to
Morel's *Traité des dégénérescences physiques, intellectuelles et morales de l'espèce humaine* (1857);
see George L. Mosse, 'Max Nordau and his *Degeneration*', introduction to Nordau, *Degeneration*,
xiii–xxxiii.
[2] Nordau, *Degeneration*, 15.

Nordau's sick 'mystics' include Leo Tolstoy and Wagner.[3] The latter is especially condemned. He is 'charged with a greater abundance of degeneration than all the degenerates put together with whom we have hitherto become acquainted. The stigmata of this morbid condition are united in him in the most complete and most luxuriant development.'[4] Other 'sick' artists are the 'ego-maniacs' (who include Ibsen and Nietzsche) and 'false' and 'pessimistic' realists (for example Zola and '"Young German" plagiarists'). Nordau then pronounced his 'prognosis'. After a 'long and sorrowful wandering through the hospital' the various observed 'pathologies' are declared as types of 'melancholia, which is the psychiatrical symptom of an exhausted central nervous system'. Standing 'in the midst of a severe mental epidemic; of a sort of black death of degeneration and hysteria', he asks if we shall see a bleak future of massed suicides, drug addiction and sexual perversion. His answer is no, for the strength of the evolutionary process remains in the human species: the degenerates will not adapt, but will succumb. The senile art of fatigue has no future; instead there will arise an art of 'stimulating variety'. The end of the twentieth century, he prophesies, will see a generation with 'nerves of gigantic vigour'. In his last section he recommends various 'therapeutics' to hasten recovery into this future vitality, to counter and offer healthy protection from the forces of 'retrogression' and 'relapse', the advocates of which must be 'unmasked' and 'stigmatized as enemies of society' – in short, named and shamed.[5]

Doctor Nordau's therapeutic plan for the recovery from degeneration, his medical diagnosis of the case of decadence, betrays his origins (born in Hungary in 1849) in a generation which characteristically held faith in

---

[3] This is a curious pairing. In his essay *What is Art?* (1898) Tolstoy berates the elitism and esotericism of modern art produced 'under the guidance of Nietzsche and Wagner'. He identifies Baudelaire and Verlaine as the perverted sources of decadence, as producing work poor in content and increasingly incomprehensible in form. Their work is a 'simulcrum of art'. These decadent characteristics he also attributes to Wagner, whose work is similarly a simulcrum, an inorganic music where individual lines, figures or bars can be freely moved around as there is no organic unity binding the parts together in wholeness. He offers a lengthy description of a performance of *Siegfried* in Moscow. He writes of Wagner's 'mastery and power' in the techniques of 'counterfeiting art': the music is 'diverting', yet lawless; there are new modulations and dissonances which are 'striking' but they 'affect the spectator by hypnotizing him'. In sum, the audience was 'enraptured' in an 'abnormal state', of the kind which 'can be achieved in a still quicker way by drinking wine or smoking opium'. For Tolstoy, Wagner did not create art of value and true content because he failed to meet three fundamental artistic criteria, the conditions of 'particularity', 'clarity' and 'sincerity': Leo Tolstoy, *What is Art?*, trans. Richard Pevear and Larissa Volokhonsky (Harmondsworth: Penguin, 1995). Taruskin describes Tolstoy's treatment of Wagner as 'hilarious abuse': 'Wagner's Antichrist Crashes a Pagan Party' [1999], in *The Danger of Music*, 139.

[4] Nordau, *Degeneration*, 171.   [5] Nordau, *Degeneration*, 536–41.

positivistic method and the progressive achievements of 'rational', scientific thinking. Nietzsche, of course, scandalously rejected these bourgeois models of 'truth'. But he shared Nordau's concern to develop a healthy prognosis for the future of a culture which he saw as steeped in decadence. As Nietzsche declared decadence unavoidable, he developed a crucial distinction between its 'weak' and 'strong' varieties, a 'hierarchy of decadents' analogous to the distinction between weak and strong pessimists. Enfeeblement arises through the decay of the species brought about through preservation of the weak individual. (This, at least, chimes with Nordau.) Nietzsche's strong decadent creates values which are radically and pitilessly different. This is achieved, as Jacqueline Scott summarizes it, by attempting to 'maintain a position between the two types of weak decadent values: fabricated optimism and the pessimism of resignation'. It was a kind of 'metaphorical suicide as a self-overcoming; a destruction of the decadent within by revaluing one's expression of this decadence … one must learn to see decadence as a stimulant to life as opposed to a disease to be eluded. Just as by contracting a disease one can actually, if one survives, emerge stronger and more resistant to it.'[6] We have seen how Nietzsche describes his convalescence from Wagnerian decadence[7] and how this places Nietzsche's work as part of a 'rhétorique obsédante', with its oppositions of sickness and health, decay and degeneration, pathology and normalcy. Many decadents sought the experience of convalescence as a transitional, altered state of heightened creative possibilities lying between these oppositional conditions.[8] For Nietzsche, the intoxication of convalescence is an antidote to degenerative decay, one which allows a passage of recovery into rude and childish health. This transitional state heightens the sense of double character, so that Nietzsche can proclaim his wisdom to be a product of his 'two-fold origin', declaring himself a *Doppelgänger* who is 'at once *décadent* and beginning', one able 'to look from a morbid perspective towards healthier concepts and values, and again conversely to look down from the abundance and certainly of rich life into the secret labour of the instinct of decadence – that is what I have practised most …'.[9]

In June 1887 Nietzsche fled from a concert performance of Schumann's music, exasperated by the experience of a 'softening of sensibility' created

[6] Jacqueline Scott, 'Nietzsche and Decadence: The Revaluation of Morality', *Continental Philosophy Review* 31 (1998), 61, 68.
[7] Nietzsche, *The Case of Wagner*, 155–6; *The Will to Power*, 25.
[8] Spackman, *Decadent Genealogies*, vii–viii, 37, 94.   [9] Nietzsche, *Ecce homo*, 38–41.

by music which he described as 'a sea of fizzy lemonade'.[10] Meanwhile, from his self-imposed seclusion Huysmans's Des Esseintes recounted that 'certain settings for the violoncello by Schumann had left him positively panting with emotion, choking with hysteria'.[11] Both are reactions to Schumann's music that result in gagging, one through weakening and over-sweetness and the other through breathless frenzy. Both listeners are left physically drained, momentarily incapacitated or inebriated. Not only is Schumann's music a health hazard: it is itself sickly. Des Esseintes further reported that 'it was chiefly Schubert's *Lieder* that had excited him, carried him away, then prostrated him as if he had been squandering his nervous energy, indulging in a mystical debauch'. But Alma Mahler, in response to viewing Klimt's *Schubert am Klavier* (1898), redressed Des Esseintes's 'error' of decadent taste when she wrote: 'It's Schumann's music that's more sickly and ultra-romantic, hence also more modern.'[12] In adolescence Nietzsche was infatuated with Schumann's music. His attempt at overcoming this youthful obsession with this 'sickly' music provides the first of four examples of compositional 'convalescence'.

Nietzsche *contra* Schumann? The convalescent philosopher-composer

In the mid- to late 1870s Wagner provocatively (if not spitefully) implied a causal relationship between Nietzsche's failure as a composer and the weak health and sexual problems which beset this problematic philosopher (specifically, the debilitating effects of his onanistic excesses). He suggested that conjugal union would solve Nietzsche's problems on both musical-creative and physical counts.[13] Of course, Wagner's diagnosis of the creatively enfeebled masturbator and belief in the success of marital convalescence is nonsense. But the inadequacies of Nietzsche's music have always been noted. One hundred years later, Frederick Love argued that the musical works were 'charged with significance for Nietzsche that is completely disproportionate

---

[10] Trans. from Christopher Middleton, 'Introduction' to Friedrich Nietzsche, *Selected Letters*, trans. Christopher Middleton (Chicago University Press, 1969), xvi.

[11] Huysmans, *Against Nature*, 205.

[12] Alma Mahler-Werfel, *Diaries 1898–1902*, ed. Anthony Beaumont (London: Faber 1998), 23 May 1899, 143. Quoted in Scott Messing, 'Klimt's *Schubert* and the *Fin-de-Siècle* Imagination', in James Leggio (ed.), *Music and Modern Art* (New York and London: Routledge, 2002), 14.

[13] See Marc A. Weiner, 'Opera and the Discourse of Decadence: From Wagner to AIDS', 128–9.

to their intrinsic importance'.[14] Masterpieces they certainly are not, but the importance and effort that Nietzsche invested in them means that they should not be too quickly dismissed as unworthy of critical attention. For Curt Paul Janz, editor of the Nietzsche *Musikalische Nachlass* (1976), they contain important intellectual and spiritual content because the act of writing music lay close to the working-out of Nietzsche's central ideas in the 1860s and 1870s.[15] Though it would be, as Hollinrake warns, 'fallacious' to 'treat Nietzsche's musical compositions, striking as they may be, on a par with his published books',[16] they do represented a crucial aspect of Nietzsche's self-analysis. They have, nonetheless, largely been viewed as texts of only passing curiosity, and the relationship of their musical contents to the development of philosophical themes has yet to be closely analysed.[17] For example, Gary Lemco's essay on Nietzsche and Schumann, which seeks to understand Nietzsche's relationship to the composer through both philosophical and musical argument, makes no reference to Nietzsche's compositional output, despite its initial claim that 'the art of music functions organically as part of [Nietzsche's] ongoing philosophical methodology'.[18] Lemco's essay is, however, a valuable one. In particular it points to the philosopher's and composer's shared aesthetic devices of mask, illusion and irony. It reveals how Nietzsche's self-identification as *Doppelgänger* might compare with the creative duality of Schumann's Florestan and Eusebius, characters who in many aspects might also be related to the dualism of Dionysus and Apollo. Lemco also shows how Nietzsche and Schumann share a comparably polemical relationship to the past, manifest in specific forms of critical 'antiquarianism'. He surveys a tripartite division of Nietzsche's philosophical development. In the first 'metaphysical period' Schumann is raised as a kindred spirit in the fight against philistinism and as

---

[14] Frederick R. Love, 'Nietzsche, Music and Madness', *Music and Letters* 60 (1979), 191.

[15] Curt Paul Janz, 'Die Kompositionen Friedrich Nietzsches', *Nietzsche Studien* 1 (1972), 173–84. See also Janz's 'Friedrich Nietzsches Verhältnis zur Musik seiner Zeit', *Nietzsche Studien* 7 (1978), 308–26; 'Die Musik im Leben Friedrich Nietzsches', *Nietzsche Studien* 26 (1997), 72–86; and 'Friedrich Nietzsches Frage nach dem Wesen der Musik', *Nietzscheforschung: Jahrbuch der Nietzsche-Gesellschaft* 5/6 (2000), 23–31. Love, however, proposes a weaker link than Janz: 'Beyond the central Wagnerian experience Nietzsche's musical taste has only a very tenuous relationship to the main stream of his thought' (Love, 'Nietzsche, Music and Madness', 193).

[16] Hollinrake, *Nietzsche, Wagner and the Philosophy of Pessimism*, 18.

[17] There have of course been studies from the other direction, looking for the 'musical' in Nietzsche's philosophy; see, for example, Michael Allen Gillespie's discussion of 'musical forms' in Nietzsche's writings: 'Nietzsche's Musical Politics', in Michael Allen Gillespie and Tracy B. Strong (eds.), *Nietzsche's New Seas: Explorations in Philosophy, Aesthetics and Politics* (University of Chicago Press, 1988), 117–49.

[18] Gary Lemco, 'Nietzsche and Schumann', *New Nietzsche Studies* 1 (1996), 42.

an artistic model in the development of an aphoristic style. Nietzsche's second, anti-metaphysical, positivistic period (from 1876 to 1883) demanded a critical reappraisal of Schumann, but this was achieved, Lemco notes, through recourse to masking techniques which involved sublimating the Schumann influence. The third 'physiological period' promises a kind of synthesis, via the transition begun with the de-deification, perspectivism and 'incorporization' of knowledge espoused in *The Joyful Wisdom* (1882), by picking up former passions for myth-making (including the return of a transformed Dionysus). Work in this period also brings together new and old values, with the famous valorization of Mediterranean lightness of tempo bearing perhaps surprising reminiscences of the 'dancing, masking' side of Schumann's double character.

Two key statements on Schumann from Nietzsche raise issues not discussed by Lemco. In 'The Wanderer and his Shadow', published as an appendix to *Human, All Too Human* (1879), Nietzsche wrote:

The 'youth' as the Romantic lyricists of France and Germany dreamed of him ... this youth has been completely translated into sound and song – by Robert Schumann, the eternal youth so long as he felt himself to be in the fullness of his own strength: there are, to be sure, moments when his music recalls the eternal 'old maid'.[19]

This passage raises the child as a central figure in the romantic reverie, but with withdrawal into the lyric dream posing the dangers of succumbing to weakening, aging, an absorption in the memories of lost youthfulness which sinks the subject into a state of decay and enfeeblement. The second statement is from *Beyond Good and Evil* (1886), where Schumann is condemned as a 'small taste', for his propensity for 'quiet lyricism and drunkenness of feeling' and of being merely of parochial German import, in short, for being a 'sort of girl'.[20] Here Nietzsche invokes inebriated listlessness, lack of physical vitality, other-worldliness, pessimism and effeminacy – a fairly substantial list of the symptoms which Nietzsche diagnosed in the modern cultural malaise of decadence. Two main issues

---

[19] Nietzsche, 'The Wanderer and his Shadow', aphorism 161, in *Human, All Too Human*, trans. R. J. Hollingdale (Cambridge University Press, 1996), 347.

[20] Nietzsche, *Beyond Good and Evil*, trans. R. J. Hollingdale (Harmondsworth: Penguin, 1990), 177–8. For a discussion of Schumann's music, German identity and politics which takes off from Nietzsche's dismissal of Schumann in this passage see John Daverio, '*Einheit – Freiheit – Vaterland*: Intimations of Utopia in Robert Schumann's Late Choral Music', in Celia Applegate and Pamela Potter (eds.), *Music and German National Identity* (Chicago University Press, 2002), 59–77. This recalls Marsop's characterization of the contrast between Bruckner's Seventh Symphony – public, 'manly', monumental post-Beethovenian sublime – and the 'aphoristic beauty' and 'sensibility of private sorrows' (i.e. womanly character) of Schumann, which was noted in Chapter 4.

are raised by these statements: the association of Schumann with youthfulness and pessimism. These form the central topics of the next section, where close analytical and hermeneutic interpretation of Nietzsche's own, neglected music reveals the complexity of his 'convalescent' relationship with Schumann and its significance for his later definitions of decadence.

Manfred-Meditation (1872) is one of Nietzsche's most ambitious musical works. It was, he said, a creative act of furious vengeance, composed in reaction against Schumann's *Manfred* melodrama (1848), which he deemed to be a fundamental misunderstanding of Byron.[21] In *Ecce homo* he recalled that 'expressly from wrath against this sugary Saxon [i.e. Schumann], I composed a counter-overture to *Manfred*'.[22] This is a piece based on an attempt at musical contradiction. For Janz, while the work is on the surface targeted against Schumann's musical interpretation of Byron, at a deeper level it becomes 'the mirror image to a shattering inner struggle with the still mighty daemon of romanticism'.[23] An enthusiasm for Schumann was a dominant feature of Nietzsche's student years. In 1866, aged twenty-one, he wrote: 'Three things are my relaxations … my Schopenhauer, Schumann's music, and then solitary walks.'[24] *Manfred-Meditation* was a creative outlet for the struggle for independence from this immature infatuation. With this apparently accomplished, Nietzsche gloried in the sense of 'liberation that this Schumann-romanticism has been overcome', for Schumann's nature lies with the pessimism of Werther, not the heroic struggle of Byron; he is 'not at all like Beethoven', 'his music for *Manfred* is a mistake and misunderstanding to the point of injustice', and he is 'a noble effeminate delighting in nothing but anonymous weal and woe'.[25] The comparison with Beethoven is revealing. Nietzsche identified with Beethoven as a fellow thinker who straddles two periods, Beethoven the classical-romantic, Nietzsche the romantic-anti-romantic. Here Beethoven is raised as a heroically masculine and affirmative figure who contrasts with the decadent pessimism of

---

[21] On Nietzsche's complex relationship to Byron see Ralph S. Fraser, 'Nietzsche, Byron, and the Classical Tradition', in O'Flaherty, Sellner and Helm (eds.), *Studies in Nietzsche and the Classical Tradition*, 190–8.

[22] Nietzsche, *Ecce homo*, 58.

[23] Curt Paul Janz, 'Nietzsches *Manfred-Meditation*: Die Auseinandersetzung mit Hans von Bülow', in Gunther Poltner and Helmuth Vetter (eds.), *Nietzsche und die Musik* (Frankfurt am Main: Peter Lang, 1997), 49.

[24] Letter to Carl von Gersdorff, 7 April 1866, trans. in Nietzsche, *Selected Letters*, 12. On the relationship of his taste for Schumann and the early encounters with Wagner's music see Frederick R. Love, *Young Nietzsche and the Wagnerian Experience* (New York: AMS Press, 1966).

[25] Nietzsche, *Beyond Good and Evil*, 177; see Janz, 'Nietzsches *Manfred-Meditation*', 46.

Schumann. But to take Nietzsche's retrospective statements at face value would be hasty. The process was more like a Hegelian *Aufhebung* which preserves what is overcome through its transformation. *Manfred-Meditation* is part of Nietzsche's battle against the prevailing cultural philistinism of his age, a cause that Schumann, of course, had taken up thirty years earlier, and its musical contents suggest that the legacy of Schumann's example was revitalized rather than vehemently destroyed.

But first, what was it about Schumann's *Manfred* that especially raised Nietzsche's ire in the early 1870s? Georges Liébert notes that *Manfred-Meditation* was written just four months after the appearance of *The Birth of Tragedy*. The Wagnerian Nietzsche, he argues, is composing *contra* the earlier Schumannian Nietzsche, in particular against the romantic withdrawal into nostalgic inwardness.[26] We can go further and hear the piece as a reaction against the self-reflective unity of Schumann's overture and the redemptive end of the melodrama, that is, to interpret the piece as a polemic with the themes of incestuous narcissism, solipsism and the narrative of romantic pessimism moving to other-worldly deliverance. Schumann's overture is densely motivic. Processes of variation and combination mean that, musically, it can convincingly be demonstrated that 'everything is related to nearly everything else'. This 'organicism' can be heard to lead not to higher, stronger forms but rather to reversion, despair and enfeeblement. For John Daverio, the end of the overture 'signals defeat', collapse, exhaustion and return to 'original forms'; Schumann's 'masterfully handled liquidation in the coda emerges as a cipher for the inwardness, the destructive solipsism of the central character in Byron's "mad drama"'. This emphasizes Manfred's desire to reach a 'spiritualised, disembodied state, the original condition of harmony that he yearns to recapture'.[27] Disembodiment is sought in the consolations of the expressions of the 'Requiem Idea' which informs the end of *Manfred* and other late Schumann pieces.[28] In summary a self-obsessed, monophonic musical

---

[26] Georges Liébert, *Nietzsche and Music*, trans. David Pellauer and Graham Parkes (University of Chicago Press, 2004), 50, 53.

[27] John Daverio, *Robert Schumann: Herald of a New Poetic Age* (Oxford University Press, 1997), 357–61; Daverio continues: 'the memory of forbidden love becomes a cipher for the past from which the title character seeks, with increasing urgency, to extricate himself – Schumann projects this in a dialectic between forgetfulness and memory'. Daverio's view is that Schumann's ending, though a misreading of Byron, is 'despite its consoling tone … fundamentally tragic' (364). On Manfred's narcissism see Elizabeth Paley, '"The Voice Which Was My Music": Narrative and Nonnarrative Musical Discourse in Schumann's *Manfred*', *19th-Century Music* 24 (2000), 6.

[28] Daniel Beller-McKenna, 'Distance and Disembodiment: Harps, Horns, and the Requiem Idea in Schumann and Brahms', *Journal of Musicology* 22 (2005), 47–89.

tone or voice leads to collapse in the search for metaphysical redemption from the preoccupation with the sins of the past. The higher forms of life, for which the typically 'Beethovenian' organic process heroically strives, are rejected or out of reach. Teleology has turned to entropy.

Nietzsche based *Manfred-Meditation* on his previous musical work, *Nachklang einer Sylvesternacht*, which was offered as a birthday gift to Cosima Wagner, whom he revered and adored, in 1871. This musical offering was itself a rewriting of an adolescent work for violin and piano, *Eine Sylvesternacht: Musikalische Dichtung* (1863–4). We should note, then, this music's adolescent origins, and also that its inspiration was drawn from the moment of recollection at the year's end – as Nietzsche wrote to his mother in 1864, a moment when 'the soul stands still and can survey a period of its own development'. But there is a more striking reason for Nietzsche turning to his *Sylvesternacht* music as source material for the Manfred piece. On New Year's Eve 1864 he recorded a willed disembodiment of his 'self': as he played the requiem from Schumann's *Manfred* on the piano at midnight, he described a sinking into a trance and a dream parable, roaming the past, into an awakening at the dawn of the New Year. This world of Schumann-inspired (and not unimportantly, requiem-inspired) reverie is transformed in the new 'Wagnerian' context of composing the *Nachklang* revision as an amorous gift for Cosima.[29] In 1871 Nietzsche described *Nachklang* as containing a serious melancholic tone ('Ernste und Wehmütige') and the 'painfully exuberant' ('schmerzlich ausgelassen'), and as exemplifying a 'Dionysian manifestation' ('dionysischen Manifestation').[30] This description seems to promise much for the convergence of philosophical and musical content in the exploration of countering forces to pessimistic lassitude. Liébert considers the music of *Manfred-Meditation* to be only a 'clumsy prelude' to the 'dominant tonalites of [Nietzsche's] future philosophical work', particularly in the coexistence of 'pleasure, contempt, exuberance, and sublimity'.[31] But the new and recomposed elements in Nietzsche's return to his adolescent, Schumann-period piece in his construction of *Manfred-Meditation* transform the music into a surprisingly rich overture to his later philosophical engagement with decadence. This is located in its attempt to reinterpret and to explore further the extreme dualism of

---

[29] See Siegfried Mandel, 'Introduction' to Lou Salomé, *Nietzsche*, trans. and ed. Siegfried Mandel (Urbana: University of Illinois Press, 2001), xiii.

[30] Letter to Gustav Kruh, 13 November 1871, in Nietzsche, *Werke*, vol.IV: *Aus dem Nachlass der Achtzigerjahre: Briefe, 1861–1889*, ed. Karl Schlechta (Frankfurt: Ullstein, 1972), 639.

[31] Liébert, *Nietzsche and Music*, 52.

melancholy and Dionysian painful exuburence as he rewrites the musical
creative product of his 'Schumann' years.

In this respect there are some telling differences between *Manfred-
Meditation* and the earlier pieces upon which it was based. The opening
sections of the three pieces are shown in Example 6.1. The earliest piece,
Eine Sylvesternacht, presents immediate contrast between melancholic E
minor and playful G major figures before moving to turbulent and tragic
minor keys (Example 6.1a). *Nachklang* retains the contrasting affects, intensifying the chromaticism of the melancholic opening and turning to the
playful material at the start of a transformed version of this opening
(Example 6.1b). *Manfred-Meditation* takes this formal procedure further
(Example 6.1c). Its whole first section is formed from a sequence of varied
statements of the opening material. The playful scalic figures which inform
the second statement (from b.14) are already more expansive flourishes,
while retaining the move to G major, but lead to an extension of the move
back towards E minor, which incorporates new chromaticisms of more tragic
import. These tragic tones are amplified in the third transformed return of the
opening material, which emphasizes C minor (b.67). This is the key in which
the fourth statement begins (b.73), and C and F minor arpeggiations signalling (Beethovenian?) heroic struggle pervade the end of the fifth statement
(bb.57ff.). In *Manfred-Meditation*, therefore, by contrast with the earlier
models, there is more wilful polarity of affect as the ludic is displaced by the
tragic in obsessive returns to transformations of the opening material. There
are also some telling omissions in the Manfred piece: Nietzsche removes the
sweet, 'feminine' second subject of *Nachklang* and thus excludes its topics of
inwardness and sentimentality (the turn, the drooping phrase end and the
chromatic descending accompanimental line of this section of *Nachklang*
recall Eusebius in *Carnival* or the E major theme in the slow introduction of
the *Manfred* Overture). Indeed, nearly every aspect of the earlier composition
suggesting tones of the 'sugary Saxon' is excised. Finally, the *Nachklang* is a
closed tonal structure, beginning and ending in E minor. But in the *Manfred-
Meditation* Nietzsche returns to a tonal aspect of the very first version of
Sylvesternacht, which began in E minor but ended with material in C minor. It
is quite common for Nietzsche to end his earliest compositions in a key
different (sometimes remotely so) from the opening one. In juvenilia one
might legitimately put this down to lack of technical coherence rather than
considered artistic decision. But as this is a tonal scheme avoided in
Nachklang and then reinstated in the later *Manfred-Meditation* Nietzsche's
decision to rework the original 'progressive' tonal scheme represents a significant structural and aesthetic decision. In the *Meditation* Nietzsche

Example 6.1 (a) Friedrich Nietzsche, *Eine Sylvesternacht*, bars 1–18; (b) Nietzsche, *Nachklang einer Sylvesternacht*, bars 1–35; (c) Nietzsche, *Manfred-Meditation*, bars 1–34

expands the conflict between the two keys, and experiments with a double
tonality which is strikingly unmediated – an opening melancholic E minor
versus a heroically tragic (Beethovenian?) F minor and C minor, the key in
which the piece ends. Nietzsche may have been spurred to follow this strategy
as a wilful contrast to the mediated, dialectical relationship of heroic E flat

Example 6.1 (cont.)

(b)   **Sehr langsam**

major-minor and *dolce* E (F flat) major in Schumann's slow introduction. This is a duality later associated in Schumann's work with Manfred's wish to hear the voice of Astarte's shadow (which, as incestual love-object, is the Freudian Manfred's narcissistic self-image)[32] and also with illusion or

---

[32] Paley, "'The Voice Which Was My Music'", 3–20.

Example 6.1 (cont.)

mendacity.[33] But it is ultimately resolved by the E flat of the melodrama's final requiem, which repeatedly resolves C♭ to the dominant of E flat, excluding the disruptive enharmonic potential of C♭ to act as the dominant of E. Rather than displaying compositional ineptitude, Nietzsche's tonal scheme can be heard as a gesture of willed doubleness, one which deliberately flaunts with the dangers of musical incoherence in order to contradict Schumann's resolving requiem. In Nietzsche's music there is unresolved conflict between the E minor mourning figures which seek the closure which is denied to the melancholic, the playful G major figures and the tragic F and C minor evoking the Dionysian opening-up of new territories. In the context of Nietzsche's thinking in the early 1870s this striking musical device has wider resonances, which allow this musical portrait of Manfred to emerge as a tragic Dionysian character of multiple perspectives, set up to contrast with the solipsistic, melancholic Manfred portrayed by Schumann.

[33] Laura Tunbridge, 'Schumann's *Manfred* in the Mental Theatre', *Cambridge Opera Journal* 15 (2003), 177–83.

Example 6.1 (cont.)

Example 6.1 (cont.)

The identification of Schumann with Manfred – as a melancholic, sickly figure on the brink of insanity – is well known.[34] Figures of sickness, madness and nervousness conferred a perverse cultural prestige, one which Nietzsche of course was to come to share with Schumann.[35] For example, Wilhelm Dilthey wrote in 1905: 'Feeling and fantasy proceed unregulated on their eccentric path. Who does not immediately think of Robert Schumann and Friedrich Nietzsche?'[36] and the examples of both Nietzsche and Schumann fed into Mann's creation of Leverkühn. The madman is the messenger of new values and the destroyer of old beliefs: it is the 'madman' of *The Joyful Wisdom* (section 125) who screams 'We have murdered God!', after which there is no power in the other-worldly redemptive ending of the requiem, but a need to affirm eternal return. The little-explored identification of Manfred as a Nietzschean mad double allows a riposte to Hans von Bülow's description of *Manfred-Meditation* as a musical post-coital hangover ('as for the Dionysian', he wrote to Nietzsche, 'it made me think of the morning after a bacchanalian orgy rather than of an orgy itself').[37] The composition is more than a foreshadowing of the denunciation of Schumann in *Beyond Good and Evil*; it also marks the transformation of Manfred into an early version of Nietzsche's 'Dionysian pessimism of strength' and 'forgetfulness', which were set up in later writings in opposition to the romantic renunciation of life, yearning for redemption and debilitating nostalgia, of which Schumann, among others, was accused.[38]

This nostalgia can be heard reflected in the archaisms of the final requiem in Schumann's melodrama. Its redemptive tones function as a double monument, to the memory of both Manfred the romantic hero and Schumann's great predecessors in German musical history. (This contrasts with the critical antiquarianism embedded in the ironic quotation of the seventeenth-century 'Großvater-Tanz' tune in *Carnival*, which in carnivalesque masquerade pokes fun at the enemy through its associations with the bourgeois philistinism and is part of a process of

---

[34] For a full discussion see Laura Tunbridge, 'Schumann as Manfred', *The Musical Quarterly* 87 (2005), 546–69.

[35] Liébert, *Nietzsche and Music*, 166.

[36] Wilhelm Dilthey, *Das Erlebnis und die Dichtung*, quoted in Leon Botstein, 'History, Rhetoric and the Self: Robert Schumann and Music Making in German-Speaking Europe 1800–1860', in R. Larry Todd (ed.), *Schumann and his World* (Princeton University Press, 1994), 5.

[37] Letter of 24 July 1872, trans. in Liébert, *Nietzsche and Music*, 51.

[38] On the possible transformation of Manfred into the Dionysian Zarathustra see Robert Gooding-Williams, *Zarathustra's Dionysian Modernism* (Stanford University Press, 2001), 355 n.89.

recall, allusion and synthesis in which closure and apotheosis are problematized.[39]) Schumann's complex engagement with historicism in his
late period can be seen as part of the curious mélange of classicism and
progressivism which Dahlhaus sees as two predominant, if seemingly
mutually exclusive, tendencies of the 1848–70 period. The present was
deemed prosaic, an 'unhappy middle'; there was abhorrence of the
reactionary but not of the past.[40] Thus 'an intensely self-conscious
historical anxiety characterized Schumann and his contemporaries',
who were 'profoundly ambivalent about the moment in time in which
they lived', and whose position between the utopian future and the
historical past led to reverie and fantasy as escape routes into nostalgic
realms (especially those of lost childhood). In the 1870s Nietzsche was
of course acutely aware of the burdens of history. Just two years after
composing *Manfred-Meditation* he wrote his famous essay 'On the Uses
and Disadvantages of History for Life', in which we read: 'a child which,
having as yet nothing of the past to shake off, plays in blissful blindness
between the hedges of past and future. Yet its play must be disturbed; all
too soon it will be called out of its state of forgetfulness.' Nietzsche
continues:

It is true that only by imposing limits on this unhistorical element by thinking,
reflecting, comparing, distinguishing, drawing conclusions … only through the
power of exemplifying the past for the purposes of life and of again introducing
into history that which has been done and is gone – did man become man: but with
an excess of history man again ceases to exist, and without that envelope of the
unhistorical he would never have begun or dared to begin.[41]

Here lies the thinking which would lead to the condemnation of Schumann
as an old maid losing strength as 'she' withdraws into 'her' world of

---

[39] See R. Larry Todd, 'On Quotation in Schumann's Music', in Todd (ed.), *Schumann and his
World*, 84–5; Erika Rieman, *Schumann's Piano Cycles and the Novels of Jean Paul* (University of
Rochester Press, 2004), 119–23; Lawrence Kramer, '*Carnival*, Cross-Dressing, and the Woman
in the Mirror', in Ruth Solie (ed.), *Musicology and Difference: Gender and Sexuality in Music
Scholarship* (Berkeley: University of California Press, 1993), and 'Rethinking Schumann's
Carnival: Identity, Meaning, and the Social Order', in *Musical Meaning: Toward a Critical
History* (Berkeley: University of California Press, 2002), 129.

[40] Dahlhaus, *Nineteenth-Century Music*, 246–9. Schumann famously wrote in 1835: 'to recall the
past and its music with all the energy at our disposal, to draw attention to the ways in which
new artistic beauties can find sustenance at a source so pure, – then to take up arms against the
recent past as an age inimical to art, intent solely on extending the bounds of superficial
virtuosity, – and finally to prepare for and help expedite the advent of a new poetic age' (*Neue
Zeitschrift für Musik*, trans. in Dahlhaus, *Nineteenth-Century Music*), 247.

[41] Nietzsche, 'On the Uses and Disadvantages of History for Life' [1874], in *Untimely Meditations*,
61, 64.

nostalgia for lost girlhood. By contrast, Nietzsche's 'Zarathustran' moment is bound to a past with no resentment, and the Will to life affirms youth and its passing; through constant resurrection the past is not dead but by each moment transformed through self-creation as self-overcoming.[42]

A gulf seems to open up between the two protagonists, one succumbing to, the other resistant to pessimistic nostalgia. The image of the child suggests, however, a previously unexplored rapprochement between the philosopher and the composer. In *Ecce homo*, the discussion of the motives for composing *Manfred* is preceded by the declaration: 'I must be profoundly related to Byron's Manfred: I discovered these abysses in myself – I was ripe for this work at thirteen.'[43] Here Nietzsche suggests that on the adolescent cusp between childhood and adulthood lies the moment of freshest fecundity. When in his preface to the second edition of *The Joyful Wisdom* he writes of the 'intoxication of convalescence', he describes this as being experienced as a rebirth into a 'more childlike' state. He also seeks to perpetuate the passage of convalescence, holding the state of health as a continuous hope rather than reaching complete fulfilment. This transitional state heightens the senses of necessary or desired repetition and of double character. Gilles Deleuze and Félix Guattari famously noted that Schumann's 'work is full of refrains, of childhood blocks, which he treats in a very special way'.[44] The refrain is an attempt at orientation and stabilization, a song which is, however, 'always in danger of breaking apart', of moving out from home, centri-fugally away from the 'fragile centre'. Deleuze describes processes of territorialization, a marking-out of one's own space, deterritorialization (especially strong in music), linked to the temporal flux of becoming, which is 'antimemory', linear, and thus contra-history, which fixes time into points of force, and reterritorialization, which is linked with the functional re-establishment of memory.[45] The becoming in deterritorial-ization is, in Nietzschean fashion, untimely, forgetful, as in Nietzsche's image of the child. The play of Deleuze's 'becoming-child' involves creating and destabilizing a homely refrain, and it also marks a disruption of dominant codes of binary opposition, an undoing of the forces of the

---

[42] Alan White, *Within Nietzsche's Labyrinth* (London: Routledge, 1990), 130–3.

[43] Nietzsche, *Ecce homo*, 58.

[44] Gilles Deleuze and Félix Guattari, *A Thousand Plateaus: Capitalism and Schizophrenia*, trans. Brian Massumi (London: Continuum, 2004), 342.

[45] For commentary see Ronald Bogue, *Deleuze on Music, Painting, and the Arts* (New York: Routledge, 2003), 35–7.

dialectic. Reterritorialization is that necessary return of the memory of home (history) but only so that deterritorialization can begin again.

This Deleuzian notion of 'childishness' can be related to the detail of Nietzsche's music. By contrast with the *Nachklang*, which quickly moves to new lyrical and then dance themes, the opening section of *Manfred-Meditation* is principally formed by developing repetitions of the main recurring phrase. This refrain is increasingly 'deterritorialized' as in each successive version Nietzsche increases the prominence and role of C and F minor elements within the 'controlling' E minor; thus the level of tonal dominance within the phrase exerted by the apparent 'home' tonality is gradually weakened. The home becomes a site of loss, a location that is defamiliarized from within. Tellingly, it is enharmonic reinterpretation of D♯ (the note which leads home to E) as E♭ which plays a crucial deterritorializing role. In this transformed identity it leads to tragic, passionate realms which we might hear as prefiguring the Dionysian aesthetic, that which 'can be likened to an unstable, dangerous terrain which provides intensity of experience'.[46] Here, in what Deleuze called music's 'thirst for destruction', the music is far removed from von Bülow's Bacchic hangover, and has relinquished Manfred's melancholic search for redemptive, merciful consolations. The music evokes the child's Dionysian narcissism of ludic strength, as opposed to the narcissistic atrophy of nostalgic regret. In this light the retention of a playful dimension, the naïve rapid G major scalic gestures in the second statement of the 'refrain' in *Manfred-Meditation* (bb.14–15), is highly significant, for Nietzsche later tells us (after his hero Heraclitus, for whom all is play and illusion) that *Kinderspiel* is the highest form of play: that is, it is the source of Dionysian creativity and destruction; it is a game, but one taken seriously. The child is the third and highest stage in the metamorphosis of the spirit: 'the child is innocence and forgetting, a new beginning, a game, a self-propelled wheel, a first movement, a sacred Yes'.[47] *Kinderspiel* contains nothing of the metaphysical search for redemption, the nostalgic yearning for the 'original condition of harmony' or the stagnating preoccupation with memory and ending, all of which are so prominent in Schumann's *Manfred*. It sings against the melancholic obsession with the 'last movement'.

[46] Adrian Del Caro, *Dionysian Aesthetics: The Role of Destruction and Creation as Reflected in the Life and Works of Friedrich Nietzsche* (Frankfurt am Main: Peter Lang, 1981), 15.
[47] Friedrich Nietzsche, *Thus Spake Zarathustra*, trans. R. J. Hollingdale (Harmondsworth: Penguin, 1969), 55. For commentary on this passage see Alan D. Schrift, *Nietzsche and the Question of Interpretation* (London: Routledge, 1990), 68–9.

'Whenever a musician writes *In Memoriam*', write Deleuze and Guattari, 'it is not so much a question of an inspirational motif or a memory, but on the contrary of a becoming that is only confronting its own danger, even taking a fall in order to rise again.' When the composer writes 'against' the memory of a predecessor, then, the apparent paradox is overturned: it preserves and transforms.[48] Hans von Bülow, to whom Nietzsche sent his *Meditation* in search of assurance, called the piece a 'fantasy still intoxicated with Wagnerian resonances',[49] and Love states that 'one does not need to search hard to find the imprint of Wagner'.[50] Liébert describes the piece as 'filled with chromatic runs, appoggiaturas, and modulations that break up Schumann's music and subvert it with suggestions of *Tristan*'.[51] But it is hard to hear direct allusions to Schumann's *Manfred* music or to *Tristan*. Janz's ear is more acute when he notes that the piece resonates with Nietzsche's early musical enthusiasms – Beethoven, Schumann, Chopin and early Liszt.[52] Despite composing the piece in the 'Wagnerian' year of 1872, Nietzsche did not turn to Wagner as a musical model. In fact, Nietzsche the composer was never 'Wagnerian' in style. *Meditation* reinterprets aspects of a post-Schumannian musical language to speak against itself. It reveals how Nietzsche the Schumannian adolescent remains a necessary source for the Dionysian thoughts of his maturity. It shows how *Kinderspiel* can move into cosmic play. Nietzsche's refrain of the becoming-child of Dionysus celebrates the eternal return of multiplicity, in which difference is joyous, not a negative other in a dialectic, but affirmed (even in death's shadow) in dance, laughter and play.[53] Deleuze concludes: 'This is Schumann's madness … the cosmic force was already present in the material, the great refrain in the little refrains, the great maneuver in the little maneuver. Except that we cannot be sure we will be strong enough, for we have no system, only lines and movements. Schumann.' We can replace 'Schumann' with 'Nietzsche' in that statement and re-read it thus: 'This is Nietzsche's madness … the cosmic force was already present in the material, the great refrain in the little refrains, the

---

[48] Deleuze and Guattari, *A Thousand Plateaus*, 330.

[49] Liébert, *Nietzsche and Music*, 51.

[50] Love, *Young Nietzsche*, 70. Love goes on to offer a quite detailed description of 'Wagnerian' techniques and allusions in the piece, but these are far from convincing.

[51] Liébert, *Nietzsche and Music*, 53.

[52] Janz, 'Nietzsches *Manfred-Meditation*', 53. The piece was composed before Nietzsche had heard *Tristan*.

[53] 'Nietzsche against the dialectic' is a key aspect of Deleuze's *Nietzsche et la philosophie* (1962); see *Nietzsche and Philosophy*, trans Hugh Tomlinson (London: Continuum, 1986), 8–10 and the final section, 'The Overman: Against the Dialectic', 147–94.

great maneuver in the little maneuver. Except that we cannot be sure we will be strong enough, for we have no system, only lines and movements. Nietzsche.' We can hear in Nietzsche's ambivalent counterpoint with Schumann an uncanny, doubled voicing – overwriting, yet preserving as in a palimpsest: Nietzsche as a becoming-child of Schumann. *Manfred-Meditation*, composed at the height of Nietzsche's Wagner period, when Schumann was ripe for drastic reassessment, sows the seeds for the wider turn against romantic pessimism, dialecticism and metaphysical eschatology which is the focus of Nietzsche's work in the late 1870s, and foreshadows the diagnosis of cultural decadence developed in the late writings.

Wagnerian agony and Wolf's leading-note treatment

Leading-note tension is the central source of contrapuntal and harmonic dynamism in the Wagnerian 'intensive alteration style'. This style, as famously analysed by Ernst Kurth, is a point on the 'evolution' of 'energetic' harmony, driven by the composer's artistic focus on 'interior dynamics' and the 'quivering of psychic energies'. The style is also marked by pervasive 'disintegration of all normal chordal forms' and 'progressive dissolution of all chordal and tonal relations'. The surge and appeasement of leading-note energies bind these apparent abnormalities and dissociations together.[54] These tensions are frequently employed as musical metaphors of unfulfilled erotic desire. As they are denied, dissolved, fetishised or deflected they may symbolize the perverted erotic pleasure found in masochistic physical and/or psychological wounding. In *Tristan* the control of leading-note tensions is central to the expressive effect of yearning and is crucial to vast swathes of the musical process, from the chromatic ambiguities of the Prelude to Act 1 right through to the long-desired resolution in Isolde's Transfiguration. Extensive stretches of *Parsifal* are similar in effect, where *Sehnsucht* is often tied to images of wounding and recovery. Several readings of Wagner's last work identify the intensification and dissolution of leading-note dynamics as a central musical-symbolic feature in these effects. Kinderman's reading of the 'redemptive' narrative of *Parsifal* is based upon curing G–A♭ of its 'diseased' tendency to act as 5–♭6 exposed in the opening phrase of the Prelude to Act 1, to allow the eventual restoration of its 7–8 function in the tonic A flat. Deathridge notes that in those passages of *Parsifal* which seek to express processes of

---

[54] Kurth, *Romantische Harmonik*, trans. in *Selected Writings*, 110–16.

enfeeblement 'the music seems purposefully to avoid forward movement, or rather to propose it at moments, only to take it back again; and the notes seem to repose constantly in motionlessness, reluctant to do anything else'. The score is pervaded by a paradoxical 'fluid stasis' reflecting the 'melancholic sense of stasis and decay among the knights of the Grail'. Technically this is manifest in a 'musical dynamic that paradoxically develops organically by collapsing into itself'. Deathridge demonstrates this with examples of the treatment of the semitonal F–E dyad in various dissonant contexts at crucial symbolic moments such as Gurnemanz's Act 1 recounting of Amfortas's seduction, Kundry kissing Parsifal in Act 2, the opening of the Prelude to Act 3 and Kundry's transformation into a state of religious devotion.[55] In these examples the effects are dependent to a large degree on the dyad's invocation and revocation of the leading-note's 'energetic' tendency to resolution. Deathridge's observations recall Patrick McCreless's reading of the tonal process across the whole work as a purging of the E–F semitonal relationship through a recuperative transformation into E♭–F in A flat, which can then promise to lead up to the redemptive completion of the leading-note-to-tonic relationship;[56] 'wrongness' is turned to 'wholeness', or, one might say, to provoke Nietzsche's body to turn in its grave, holiness.

Manipulations of leading-note dynamics can serve a variety of expressive or symbolic purposes – for example, the ecstatic, the masochistic, the redemptive. When the levels of intensity and alteration – Kurth's two key stylistic indicators – reach extreme points beyond the realms of the romantic imagination some of these dynamics and deformations might promise entry into the world of decadence. Such concentration of effect (intensity) combined with pervasiveness of apparently abnormal variation (alteration) chimes with the characteristically decadent pursuits of exquisite paroxysm and wilful distortion. In *Parsifal* many passages evoke these features, in particular where leading-note tensions and their vicissitudes play a symbolic role in the dramatic opposition between sickness and recuperation. In such music the intensification and dissolution of leading-note tensions in altered chromatic harmony parallel the yearning for convalescence. The anguished sustaining of this ambiguously paroxysmal yet potentially paradisal state is a symptomatic mark of decadence.

---

[55] Deathridge, *Wagner*, 159–77.

[56] Patrick McCreless, 'Motive and Magic: A Referential Dyad in *Parsifal*', *Music Analysis* 9 (1990), 227–65. McCreless's analysis is not cited by Deathridge.

The section in which Gurnemanz announces the entrance of the sick and wounded Amfortas in Act 1 is one such passage where the intensification and dissolution of leading-note energies generate a decadent tone in their syntactical 'excess' or 'abnormality' and their symbolic-dramatic function as indicators of sickness and convalescence (Example 6.2). The section's tonal centre is D minor, but this is subject to continuous weakening through pervasive chromaticism at both surface and deep structural levels. The tonal wounds are grave indeed, but a temporary resolution achieved at the end of the section offers a hallucinatory moment of convalescence. The opening D–F♯–B♭ augmented triad already moves the harmony away from the putative tonic. This chromatically altered D triad incorporates the leading-note tendency of F♯ to resolve to G in the local move to the minor subdominant (traditionally a symbol of suffering) and the grief-symbol ♭6–5 move of B♭–A, manifest at 'Oh weh" and Amfortas's groaning. But as the passage proceeds the inner B♭ 'sticks' in the texture as an internal pedal, producing dissonant resistance to closure (the open wound, the endless inner pain). It then combines with G♭ to form the seventh and ninth of the dominant of D flat at the recollection of Amfortas as strong ruler. The new local leading note, C, is then turned to C–B at 'Siechthum's Knecht', which chromatically sinks back to B♭–A groaning. The scene's second part opens with C♯–F–A augmented harmony, another alteration or distortion of the D minor triad. The leading-note tendency of the C♯ is weakened by the 'resolution' to B♮. Four bars later C♯ sinks to C♮ to initiate a move to prolonged elaboration over the dominant of B flat, at the image of 'morning joy'. This emphasizes the potential function of A to act as a leading note and reverses the previously painful relationship of B♭ and A. But the resolution of A to B♭ is long delayed by the six bars of 6–4 harmony. The 'home' augmented triad of the scene now returns as B♭–D–G♭, to usher in resolution to the passage's most hopefully recuperative key, G flat, at Amfortas's hallucinatory image of convalescence. Thus the tonal structure of the scene is based on the succession D minor–B flat major–G flat major, a large-scale progression outlining the augmented triad which is also its characteristic surface chromatic chord. Parallelism between foreground and middleground chromatic structure is familiar in Wagner's late style: here it combines with reinterpretations of leading-note tendencies within the intensively altered foreground chords to express the move from an image of sickness, wounding and pain to one of hoped-for recovery.

The symbolic legacy of this particularly intensive type of leading-note chromaticism is clear in Wolf's setting of Eduard Mörike's 'Seufzer' (composed on

Example 6.2 Wagner, *Parsifal*, Act 1, Gurnemanz: 'Er naht, sie bringen ihn getragen'

Example 6.2 (cont.)

Example 6.2 (cont.)

Example 6.2 (cont.)

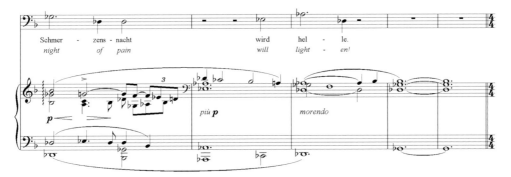

12 April 1888). Kurth devoted close analytical attention to the opening bars of this song.[57] The poem explores the symbolic association of salvation with convalescence, the desire to be redeemed from the pain of damnation:

Dein Liebesfeuer,
Ach Herr, wie teuer
Wollt' ich es hegen,
Wollt' ich es pflegen!
Hab's nicht geneget
Und nicht gepfleget
Bin tot im Herzen –
O Höllenschmerzen!

Thy fire of love,
O Lord, how dearly
I would foster it,
I would tend it!
I have not fostered it,
Have not tended it.
I am dead in my heart –
Oh pains of hell![58]

The expressions of desire in the first half of the poem, with its litany, 'Wollt' ich …', are revoked in the second half by the internal rhyming transformation of the previous 'ich' into 'nicht'. The negation is complete when the final line evokes the pain generated by the burning of the fires

---

[57] Kurth, *Romantische Harmonik*; the passage is translated and discussed in John Williamson, 'Wolf's Dissonant Prolongations', in Kinderman and Krebs (eds.), *The Second Practice of Nineteenth-Century Tonality*, 226–7.

[58] Trans. from Susan Youens, *Hugo Wolf and his Mörike Songs* (Cambridge University Press, 2000), 82.

Example 6.3 Wolf, 'An den Schlaf' (Mörike)

of hell in opposition to the opening line's image of Christ's 'fire of love'. In Wolf's setting the failure of 'heavenly remedies' is expressed in what Susan Youens calls a 'tortured' tonal language created by a delaying of resolution through repeated denial of the leading-note function of D♯. The harmony is

Example 6.3 (cont.)

wie stirbt es sich so leicht!

'twisted' into 'claustrophobic chromaticism', which generates a sense of 'queasiness' as the dynamic energies of altered triads spin out in a 'linear hell'. Particularly striking is the song's climactic intonation of the word 'death', where Wolf most powerfully negates D♯'s function as leading note by turning it to a chromatically falling E♭ (E♭–D–C♯). It is a technique to which he returns in 'Wo find' ich Trost?' (composed 6 October 1888), where Youens hears poetic resonances with *Parsifal* and musical allusions to the spear motif, as the repose promised by resolution of leading-note energy is again repeatedly denied.[59]

For Wolf, Mörike was a poetic exemplification of what he most sought in art, that 'convulsive intimacy', 'voluptuous pleasure in pain'; Mörike embodied the artist as a sufferer drinking 'enraptured torments' from the poisoned chalice which brings knowledge of the terrible truth.[60] In 'An den Schlaf' (composed 4 October 1888) the debt to Wagnerian 'convalescent chromaticism' is once again overt in a musical response to Mörike's poetic expression of the somnalent sublimation of death.[61]

[59] Youens, *Hugo Wolf and his Mörike Songs*, 82–99.

[60] Letter to Emil Kauffmann, 5 June 1890, trans. in Youens, *Hugo Wolf and his Mörike Songs*, 1.

[61] Glauert considers the song to be 'an investigation into the workings of Wagnerian chromatic language', especially that of *Tristan*; see her discussion of the song, *Hugo Wolf*, 65–71.

Schlaf! Süsser Schlaf!
Obwohl dem Tod wie du nichts gleicht,
Auf diesem Lager doch willkommen heiss' ich dich!
Denn ohne Leben so, wie lieblich lebtes sich!
So weit vom Sterben, ach, wie stirbtes sich so leicht!

Sleep! Sweetest sleep!
Although not equal to death,
To my bed I gladly welcome you!
For removed from life, how lovely it is to be alive!
When death seems distant, Oh, how easy it is to die!

The intensive altered chromatic idiom of Wolf's four-bar piano introduction bears notable similarity to the multiple neighbour-note formation of the so-called 'Schlummermotiv' from the 'Abschied' of *Tristan*, Act 2 (Example 6.3).[62] Wolf's is a post-Wagnerian *Satz* notable for the absence of the leading note in the opening two bars. The answering bars 3–4 move to the dominant through intensifying wedge-like formations in which the top line chromaticizes the initial 3–2 motif and sinks to pick up the ♭6–5, the principal chromatic motif of the passage. Wolf's setting is primarily concerned with the enharmonic conversion of these initial 5–♭6 (E♭–F♭) alternations in A flat into the resolution of leading-note to tonic in the final key of E (D♯–E) as the musical expression of the transformation – or transfiguration – of expiring, deathly lassitude. The song's musical materials constitute an obsessive sequence of rewritings of the opening four bars. The 'convalescent' process can be precisely mapped in the tonal transformations. Bars 7–8 rewrite bars 3–4 to undermine the leading-note tension embedded in the dominant by moving G to G♭ (a pitch emphasized by the voice in bar 8). G♭ then becomes (enharmonically) the local dominant of C flat/B minor (the flat mediant of A flat) at the equation of sleep with death. This is an expansion of the fleeting C flat minor harmony which initiated the intensification towards the dominant in bar 3. Bars 9–12 are a transposition of the opening four bars in this minor mediant key; bars 13–17 are a further transposed variant in the subdominant, D flat. Thus the first half of the song avoids modulation to the dominant but does offer a sense of rising hope in the structural ascent of a whole tone from iii to IV. The second, overtly convalescent half of the song begins with the introduction of the dominant of E (enharmonic ♭VI of A flat) at the poetic invocation of life as death's opposite. From the start this reinterprets the opening E♭–F♭ (5–♭6 in A flat) as D♯–E (7–8

---

[62] Geoffrey Chew plots the changes in leading-note tension in the 'Abschied' in his 'Ernst Kurth, Music as Psychic Motion and *Tristan und Isolde*: Towards a Model for Analysing Musical Instability', *Music Analysis* 10 (1991), 171–93.

in E) in the inner part of the accompaniment. The climax of this four-bar phrase lies at the dissonance of bar 21, where the top voice in the accompaniment reinterprets the leading note and tonic pitches of A flat as F𝄪–G♯, which is then transferred into the bass as G–G♯ to drive the move to F sharp minor (the minor supertonic of E). At this point the upper-voice motif is transformed from a falling tone (originally C–B♭) to rising – leading-note-based – semitone motions. These dominate the rest of the song, peaking on the repeated sounding of the D♯–E in celestial registers. These mark the convalescent highpoint. The last line's oscillation between the new tonic (E) and its minor subdominant generates ♭6–5 (C♮–B) motions in the inner voices, as a motivic echo of the chromaticism of the opening. Thus the song moves through various weakenings, reinvigorations and transfigurations of leading-note tensions to reflect the poetic image of sleep as a condition which holds death at bay and sustains a blissful, dream-like state of being.

‘Schon streckt’ ich aus im Bett die müden Glieder’, from the *Italian Songbook* (composed 29 March 1896), is another song in A flat with an initial poetic image of sleep as a state of physical lassitude moving to one of artistic and physical recovery. The lethargic layabout is revitalized by the imaginary portrait of the beloved, which stimulates him into creating charming, teasingly seductive song:

Schon streckt’ ich aus im Bett die müden Glieder,
da tritt dein Bildnis vor mich hin, du Traute.
Gleich spring’ ich auf, fahr’ in die Schuhe wieder
und wandre durch die Stadt mit meiner Laute.
Ich sing’ und spiele, dass die Strasse schallt;
so manche lauscht – vorüber bin ich bald.
So manches Mädchen hat mein Lied gerührt,
indes der Wind schon Sang und Klang entführt.

I was already stretching my tired limbs on the bed
When your portrait, my love, appeared before me.
At once I leap up, put my shoes back on,
And wander through the town with my lute.
I sing and play, so that the streets resound;
Many listen – but I pass quickly by.
Many a girl has been moved by my song,
While its sound was already borne away on the wind.

The piano introduction is closely comparable with that of ‘An den Schlaf’ (and hence once more with the ‘Abschied’ from *Tristan*, Act 2: the four-part writing further recalls Wagner's characteristic use of such textures in *Tristan*

Example 6.4 Wolf, 'Schon streckt' ich aus im Bett die müden Glieder' (*Italian Songbook*)

and in the opening of the Prelude to Act 3 of *Parsifal*). An opening idea based on chromatic neighbour-note motions with an emphasis on the flat sixth is presented twice and then balanced by a phrase which intensifies through to the dominant. These are all based upon the resolution of a chromatically intensified diminished seventh built on the flat sixth (see Example 6.4). Thus, by comparison with 'An den Schlaf', there is more pervasive and greater leading-note tension. At the entry of the voice in both songs, however, there is notable weakening of this 'energy'. In 'Schon streckt'' at bar 4 the leading note, G, sinks unexpectedly to G♭ in the vocal line. This is a precursor to the motion to the Neapolitan B♭♭ harmony (sounded in second

Example 6.4 (cont.)

inversion so that with F♭ in the bass it is heard as a variant on the opening chord of the song) at the poetic evocation of 'dein Bildnis'. The phrase ends with a return to the dominant of A flat as the image of the beloved becomes the inspiration for revitalizing song. The lively music which follows moves from C as tonal centre to E (enharmonic F flat), a symmetrical progression in major thirds which then falls by resolving the enharmonic ♭VI to V. This is a common enough modulation sequence in Wolf's music. Of symbolic significance here are the generation of motivic content and the overall shape of the structural top voice to emphasize this progression's reinvigoration of the G–A♭ relationship, whose leading-note-to-tonic function has previously been so enfeebled (see Example 6.5). When the poet begins singing his new song the tone of folkish simplicity offers a marked contrast to the

Example 6.5 Wolf, 'Schon streckt' ich aus im Bett die müden Glieder', bars 7–12: tonal structure

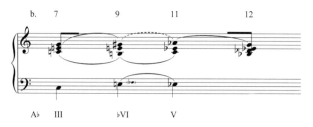

post-Wagnerian languor of the piano introduction. The leading note is initially absent. The rise from the G♭ in the voice at 'manche lauscht' through G♮ to the tonic A♭ in the following bar is a recollection and recovering reversal of the weakening of the leading note caused by the sinking melodic move to G♭ in bar 4. The oscillation between A flat and C triads in the final section is a notable eschewing of a closing perfect cadence which nonetheless maintains the newly vigorous G–A♭ relationship (pointedly emphasized by the voice's repetitions of G and its teasing ending on this pitch). Perhaps most significantly, this ending recalls the beginning of the process of leading-note recuperation, which was initiated by the C major harmony of bar 7. Through this tonal and motivic process the song encapsulates Wolf's investment in developing post-Wagnerian symbols of convalescence. The decadent is refreshed by the adorable image which sparks his imagination, a revival manifest in his new song. The song expresses Wolf's belief that music could be both psychologically and physically restorative.

Szymanowski, pain and recovery: the rehabilitation of Chopin and Dionysian regeneration

An antidote to modern civilization's diseased decline was frequently believed to be available through a rediscovery of the energies and life-affirming qualities perceived to exist in the primitive. Centrally influential were Nietzsche's *The Birth of Tragedy* and Erwin Rohde's *Psyche* (1894), whose chapter on Dionysus informed Mann's description of Dionysian rites in *Death in Venice*. Mann was drawn to myth as site of the primitive and as a vital alternative to naturalism.[63] Dionysian myth played a crucial part in

---

[63] See Herbert Lehnert's study, drawn from Mann's annotated copy of the 1907 edition of *Psyche* and the notes collected before writing *Death in Venice*: 'Thomas Mann's Early Interest in Myth and Erwin Rohde's *Psyche*', *Proceedings of the Modern Language Association* 79 (1964), 297–304.

Mann's search for 'a model of civilization which is strong and flexible enough
to contain (in every sense) its antithesis. Acknowledging the allure of chaos
and the primitive, he asks how order can contain chaos, art incorporate
sensuality, health be not endangered but fortified by contact with sickness.'[64]
In *fin-de-siècle* Poland, as in other 'imperial peripheries', the search for
mythological revitalization was coupled with increased cultural investment
in 'nativist primitivism'. The primitive was highly prized as it provided
examples of archaic cultural survival in the face of apparent modern decline.
With the periphery raised as a site of cultural resistance, regional culture was
appropriated as a symbolic model for the reconstruction and renewal of
national identity. One such site was the Tatra (Podhale) region of southern
Poland. Its main town, Zakopane, became the site of the encounter between
an intelligentsia and ancient tradition (however 'invented'). Here Stanisław
Witkiewicz developed a 'Zakopane style' founded upon a Polish '*ur*-style'
which was believed to have survived because of the region's remoteness and
isolation. This 'direct authenticity' was also claimed by Kazimierz Tetmajer's
collections of stories *Na Skalnym Podhalu* (1903–10) with its evocation of
pastoralism and pantheism. A typical figure is 'Dziki Juhas' (the savage
shepherd), who in his solitary strength existed in a pagan 'deranged wildness'
and exhibited a 'heroic, if self-destructive, pathology' which Tetmajer
infused with notably Nietzschean resonances.[65]

In the imaginary landscapes of romanticism and modernism Poland
seemed an especially appropriate home to the re-energizing forces of the
Dionysian. Nietzsche's constructed 'Polish' identity, his self-appointed
'Polishness', is linked to his proclaimed marginality, his attachment to the
peripheral and the modern, to the disorderly, the particular, the uncontrolled
and the unpredictable, all of which he felt he gained from identifying with the
aristocratic radicalism, cosmopolitanism and struggle through adversity
advocated by the Polish gentry. He considered the wildness and vigour thus
projected onto 'Polishness' to be a Dionysian antidote to the stagnation,
sickness and melancholy of modern Germany.[66] Dionysian pessimism might

[64] Ritchie Robertson, 'Primitivism and Psychology: Nietzsche, Freud, Thomas Mann', in Peter Collier and Judy Davies (eds.), *Modernism and the European Unconscious* (Cambridge: Polity Press, 1990), 86.
[65] Edward Manouelian, 'Invented Traditions: Primitivist Narrative and Design in the Polish *Fin de Siècle*', *Slavic Review* 59 (2000), 391–405. On the constructed cultural functions of Zakopane and the Tatras see Timothy J. Cooley, *Making Music in the Polish Tatras: Tourists, Ethnographers, and Mountain Musicians* (Bloomington: Indiana University Press, 2005).
[66] Peter Bergmann, 'Nietzsche and the Christ among Nations', in Freifeld, Bergmann and Rosenthal (eds.), *East Europe Reads Nietzsche*, 38. In *Ecce homo* Nietzsche wrote: 'I myself am still sufficient of a Pole to exchange the rest of music for Chopin' (62).

therefore be associated or identified with that brand of Polish melancholy – *żal* – prized, for example, by Przybyszewski as a source of expressive power, action and strength. Artists associated with Young Poland modernism were characteristically obsessed with visions of apocalypse or cataclysm, as the modern crisis of religious consciousness was reflected in doubts and disputes over competing claims of resurrection and degeneration, joyful eschatology and oblivion. In such visions Dionysus is often imagined in synthesis with Eros and/or Christ.[67] As Jan Prokop notes, however, the Young Poland hero characteristically 'struggles with elements, and defines his own identity against cosmic chaos, like a fragile boat tossed on turbulent waves. Not only is the cosmos a dramatic event and catastrophe, a tempest and agitation. The inner world too is full of strife and contradiction.'[68] This image of the perils of the maelstrom recalls Schopenhauerian pessimism. The hero who struggles to negotiate a course through these currents may masterfully command his boat over the water's surging tides, only to decline into enfeeblement or hedonism as he lands on the shore of decadent lands. But the 'messianic' tones of much Young Poland work mark a shift from decadent individualism – as explored, for example, in Przybyszewski's comparison of Nietzsche and Chopin in the first volume of *Zur Psychologie des Individuums* (1892) – to a renewal through neo-Romanticism or a turn to the primitive. Nietzschean-Dionysian strength was frequently co-opted in this project.[69] Tadeusz Miciński's drama *Bazylissa Teofanu* (1909), for example, dedicated to Juliusz Słowacki and Nietzsche as heroic people from another shore who become 'mighty' and 'illustrious', has its central character involved in an attempt to confront and assimilate the inner Dionysian.

All these Dionysian, pastoral and primitive enthusiasms exerted considerable influence on Szymanowski's opera *King Roger* (1918–24).[70] The message of the opera is closely comparable with Mann's search for a civilization strong and open enough to acknowledge the allure of the decadent

---

[67] For a detailed discussion of transformations of Dionysus in Young Poland works see also Michał Głowinski, 'Maska Dionizosa', in Maria Podraza-Kwiatkowska (ed.), *Młodopolski świat wyobraźni* (Cracow: Wydawnictwo Literackie, 1977), 353–406.

[68] Jan Prokop, *Żywioł wyzwolony: Studium o poezji Tadeusza Micińskiego* (Cracow: PWM, 1978), quoted and trans. in Edward Boniecki, 'The Lyrical, Young Poland "I" in Songs by Szymanowski to Words by Tadeusz Miciński', in Zofia Helman, Teresa Chylińska and Alistair Wightman (eds.), *The Songs of Karol Szymanowski and his Contemporaries* (Los Angeles: University of Southern California Press, 2002), 14.

[69] See Andrzej Walicki, 'Nietzsche in Poland (before 1918)', in Freifeld, Bergmann and Rosenthal (eds.), *East Europe Reads Nietzsche*, 43–84.

[70] See Alistair Wightman, 'The Book of *King Roger*: Szymanowski's Opera in the Light of his Novel *Efebos*', *Musica Iagellonica* 2 (1997), 202–4.

and the primitive. At the end of the opera Roger emerges to proclaim the dawn of a new age of those heroes who have survived the encounter with decadence to look out to sea at the new dawn. By contrast with Karłowicz's darkly pessimistic tones, Szymanowski's music here is modern Polish music resonating, even glittering, with erotic ecstasy and the promise of regener-ation. Szymanowski's 'convalescence' can be traced from his attempts to emulate and surpass the *Angst* and *Sehnsucht* of Wagner and Strauss through a rescuing of Chopin from the clutches of decadence and a symbolic combi-nation in *King Roger* (the touchstone of his oeuvre) of the experience of Dionysianism and a primitivist Polish pastoralism. Wagnerian yearning and Straussian neuroses are tempered and transformed. Chopin is returned to vital significance, delivered from his disfigurement in decadent imagery, as found for example in Mann's *Tristan* (1902), where the delicate, decaying and beautiful resident at the sanatorium first plays Chopin's Nocturne Op.9 No.2 with 'nervous feeling' as 'the last drop of sweetness clung to her limbs',[71] or in Giraud's *Pierrot lunaire* (1884), where the Chopin waltz marks the depth of decline, the 'swerve' into decadence, an image 'likened to the expectorant of a tubercular patient' expressed in a 'morbid form of art of which we should beware'.[72]

In his early career Szymanowski reflected Young Poland decadent trends by setting many poems by Tetmajer (Op.2, 1900–2) and Miciński (Op.11, 1904–5; Op.20, 1909) in a musical style heavily indebted to the intensive chromatic styles of Wagner and Strauss. He was drawn to the metaphysical anxieties expressed by German poets (Dehmel, Mombert) who were also favoured by Schoenberg and Berg. Like Karłowicz, he left Poland to further his studies in Berlin and mastered the techniques and expressive effects of contemporaneous Austro-German music. He fully felt the perversely seductive allure of the Wagnerian agony: as Adorno noted, 'the suffering that can be sweet, and that the poles of pleasure and pain are not rigidly opposed but are mediated, is something that both composers and audiences learned uniquely from [Wagner] ... And few aspects of Wagner's music have been as seductive as the enjoyment of pain.'[73] This Wagnerism combined with other aspects of decadence and 'Polish' images of yearned-for renewal. The settings of *Three Fragments* from the poetry of Jan

---

[71] Mann, *Tristan*, 110.

[72] Robert Vilain, '*Pierrot lunaire*: Cyclic Coherence in Giraud and Schoenberg', in Delaere and Herman (eds.), Pierrot lunaire, 136. On Chopin's style of 'morbid intensity' see Rosen, *The Romantic Generation*, 398–409.

[73] Adorno, *In Search of Wagner*, 67.

Example 6.6 Karol Szymanowski, 'Święty Boże', Op.5 No.1 (Kasprowicz), bars 106–9

Kasprowicz, Op.5 (1902), are based on repeated pleading to 'Holy God' for merciful deliverance from agony and despair. The first song lays on thickly the blood-soaked imagery: 'blood-stained wings', 'bleeding eyes', 'blood-red rags' and a final entreaty, 'Why must I splutter this bleeding song?' It is a Polish variant of obsessions familiar in 'decadent' Catholicism.[74] The petition is sung to a lugubrious B minor chorale with neighbour-note motions between the tonic and leading note. Its repetitions become cast over chromatic descending motions which weaken the diatonic clarity of the opening. This evokes lament (through the traditional descending chromatic bass line) and the declining power of the 'higher' authority. In the final section of the song (where the poetic fragment tells of a mocking black crow with a beak overflowing with the ashes of the dead) the B–A♯–B motif is reinterpreted as B–B♭–B over G, the tragic flat submediant. Doubly dark harmony (the minor triad on the minor sixth) transforms the symbolic pitch function from A♯, the hopefully redemptive leading note in B, to the melancholic minor third. This motivic transformation is combined with a Tristanesque rising chromatic motion through a minor third which suggests (unsurprisingly) that the origin of the sin is sex (Example 6.6). The close of the song expresses the apparent futility of the sinner's prayer. By contrast, the third fragment opens with a 'blessed moment' when the 'evening hymn', a revitalizing song of the earth, is heard from across the fields. The 'sacred' tune is now no longer the fatally weakened chorale, but a Chopinesque mazurka. The pastoral primitivism is encapsulated in the unaccompanied statement of

---

[74] Ellis Hanson has brought together a voluminous collection of largely British and French varieties in *Decadence and Catholicism* (Cambridge, Mass.: Harvard University Press, 1997).

melodic Lydian fourths and flattened sevenths. In this modal enclave the
♯4–5 semitonal motions take the expressive burden in place of the first
song's motions between the leading note and tonic. The 'primitive' mode
is the alternative to the chromatic tonality which dissolved the first song's
plaintive petition. It evokes a renewing and nostalgic tone. But with the
sinking into darkness of night in the final lines the gory images of sin,
shame and violation return.

   Though they end in gloomy pessimism, the Kasprowicz fragments are in
many ways prophetic of the convalescence which is envisaged more fully at
the end of *King Roger*. Throughout the first decade of the century
Szymanowski sustained and intensified a post-Wagnerian idiom of anguish
and suffering: the image of a recuperative, primitive, Polish pastoral does
not figure again in the musical landscape of these years. 'Die einzige
Arzenei' ('The Only Medicine'), the second of the *Love Songs of Hafiz*,
Op.24 (1911), settings of paraphrases of the Persian poet by Hans Bethge, is
perhaps the most extreme example of poetic imagery dominated by the
association of sickness with unfulfilled erotic desire:

Ja. Ich bin krank ich weiß, ich weiß, doch laßt mich!
Mir kann der beste nicht der Ärtze helfen.
Es gibt kein Mittel gegen diese Wunden,
die so verheerend glühn in meiner Brust.
Nur Eine kann mir helfen, – jene Eine,
die mir das süße Gift gab, dran ich kranke.
Daß sie mich liebte! Ich wäre gleich gesund.

Yes, I am sick – I know, I know, but leave me!
The best doctor cannot help me.
There is no cure for these wounds
That burn devastatingly in my breast.
Only one can help me – the only girl
Who gave me sweet poison, on which I am sick.
If she loved me! I would recover immediately.

Images such as these are pervasive in Young Poland poetry. Przybyszewski
wrote: 'As I took upon my shoulders without complaint the heaviest
burden of pain, as I bore in bloody toil the terrible woes of suffering up
the hill of death and damnation, redeem me Lady!'[75] Felix Dörmann,
librettist for *Hagith*, Szymanowski's ill-fated attempt at a Straussian
Biblical music drama (1912–13), wrote in his tellingly titled *Neurotika*: 'I

---

[75] Trans. in Miłosz, *The History of Polish Literature*, 331.

love all the tormenting thoughts / Which pierce and scar the heart … I love the lamenting and anxious / Songs of the feeling of Death.'[76] Sex, sickness, bleeding wounds and burning kisses – all these are concentrated within Bethge's short text. In response, Szymanowski saturated his setting with chromaticisms whose origins in *Tristan* and *Parsifal* are overt, even celebrated. The intensive altered style expresses the painful predicament of a patient in need of intensive care. The song's opening idea exposes three crucial features – the 5–6 motif, the immediate move away from the putative tonic B to the subdominant minor, and chromatic alteration producing an augmented triad which functions as a local dominant resolving via a passing C major chord (Example 6.7). The legacy of *Parsifal*, and in particular the symbolic association of anguished pain with the augmented chromatic harmony at the opening of Example 6.2, is already clear. Throughout the song the chromatic harmony is based on a limited repertory of three chord types – augmented triads, diminished sevenths and the so-called half-diminished chord, which in this aesthetic and stylistic context resonates with the curse harmony from *The Ring*, the Tristan chord and the magic chord from *Parsifal*. The counterpoint which connects these chords is closely related to procedures found in Wagner.[77] In bars 14–15, the approach to the final climax of the song, the modelling on the Prelude to Act 1 of *Tristan* becomes overt. Example 6.8 shows how upper contrapuntal voices move the harmony from a diminished seventh to an altered dominant, via a Tristan chord. Comparison with the famous *Tristan* opening extends to a top-voice G♯–A–A♯–B and a G♯ inner voice resolving directly to G♮ (omitting the implied A). This is at the poetic introduction of the female figure, the cause of the pain and sickness. Revelation of the source of erotic desire is coincident with revelation of the symbolic musical model. At the climax (on the word 'liebte!') the *Tristan* model emerges once more. But the ecstatic moment is doomed to fail. The song ends by again suggesting descent to the minor subdominant, the tonal symbol of suffering. Yearning continues unabated, and the ceaseless pain, from which healing is denied, is reflected in the alternation of semitone and whole-tone neighbour-note motifs in the final bars. These final alternations are part of a motivic process unfolding through the song, originating with the F♯–G opening motif of suffering, with alterations to the major sixth at passing poetic images of redemption or healing. This climaxes in a

---

[76] Trans. in Schmidgall, *Literature as Opera*, 264.
[77] For more details see my *Szymanowski as Post-Wagnerian*, 102–15, where comparisons are also made with passages in Berg's Op.1 and Schoenberg's *Gurrelieder*.

Example 6.7 Szymanowski, 'Die einzige Arzenei', Op.24 No.2 (Hafiz–Bethge), bars 1–3

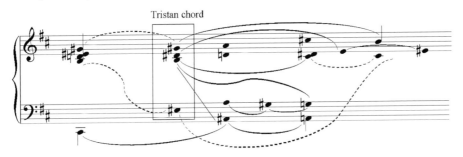

Example 6.8 Szymanowski, 'Die einzige Arzenei', bars 14–15: tonal structure

whole-tone descent under the word 'liebte!', the cry of hope. But life-denying resignation returns in the coda. These motifs combine with a pervasive use of augmented triads to recall again the motif of Amfortas's suffering. Bethge's use of the image of the 'Wunde' (wound) surely suggested *Parsifal* to Szymanowski. The song pursues Wagner's preoccupation with 'redeeming' the sickness of semitonal 5–6 motifs, but with a negative conclusion. It encapsulates in condensed and miniature form Wagner's image of Amfortas as the wounded Tristan 'inconceivably intensified', of the man in 'fearful agony'.

The works up to the Op.24 *Love Songs* mark the highpoint of Szymanowski's post-Wagnerian 'neurotica'. With the second set of Hafiz songs, Op.26 (1914), and the Third Symphony (1913–16) he turned to more explicitly 'Oriental' musical inflexions, in the search for revitalization after years of immersion in what he increasingly considered to be a inward-looking Austro-German style. He expanded the range of his chromatic harmony with new chords from Russia (mid-period Scriabin especially) and France (Debussy, Ravel). His fondness for a Nietzschean image of bodily vitalism in dance was reignited by the new dynamic rhythms he heard in Stravinsky and Bartók. His aim was to generate an eclecticism which maintained his creative distance from what he now saw as an immaturely obsessive infatuation with Strauss and Wagner. Thus, in *Masques* (1916) 'Tantris the fool' mocks Wagner's love-sick hero in a brittle, ironic style especially indebted to Stravinsky and Ravel. The doomed lover is turned into a grimacing clown. Stanisław Witkiewicz (Witkacy) – son of the inventor of the 'Zakopane style' – similarly mocked the world-weary misery and weakened sensibilities of Germanic pessimism and its spread to a symbolic Polish location. His *Insatiability*, written in 1927, describes the mood of the character Zipcio while he is walking in the Tatra mountains:

Suddenly … he was thrust into a very specific springtime despair of the sort that used to be described as '*Weltschmerz*' and which the French, being unfamiliar with the word 'longing', have diluted into some kind of *mal de je ne sais quoi*. This sense of despair was actually a baser, more animal-like and vulgar form of what was essentially a metaphysical bewilderment … the moment of illumination did not recur with its previous intensity: only the memory of it glowed still, slightly altering the contours of the normal process of duration and softening the edges of the contours of known complexes. Its derivatives were that brutelike 'veltshmertz', that subconscious, sexual, ludicrous, and quasi-profound sadness which the Russians express in a manner that's utterly impossible to render: *vsekh ne pro …*[78]

Szymanowski had a turbulent relationship with Witkacy and he is cruelly caricatured in *Insatiablity*. While Szymanowski shared Witkacy's angry impatience with false romantic yearning, for him Miciński's exuberant exoticism and enthusiasm for Zakopane's highland culture held a significant legacy. He pursued a Micińskian brand of 'healthy' eclecticism, seeking fresh development out of new artistic genealogies to revitalize the Polish pastoral inheritance. In this spirit, and at least partially in response to Poland's independence in 1919 (after more than a hundred years of partition and occupation), Szymanowski also reconsidered the legacy of Chopin. Most crucially, Szymanowski moved out of post-*Tristan* Schopenhauerian pessimism and post-*Parsifal* obsessions with sickness, by appropriating revitalizing Dionysian concepts drawn from Nietzsche,

---

[78] Stanisław Witkiewicz, *Insatiability*, trans. Louis Iribarne (London: Quartet, 1985), 139. The complete Russian phrase would be 'vsekh ne proebyosh' – loosely, 'you can't fuck 'em all' (424, translator's footnote).

Pater and Merezhkovsky, and reconceiving decadence as a necessary transition.

Szymanowski's youthful enthusiasm for Wagner and Strauss had been partly motivated by his dismissive disdain for the state of contemporaneous Polish compositions. It was a stylistic allegiance which led to critical attack from conservative critics who despaired at Szymanowski's apparent lack of desire to perpetuate the Polish nationalist line. Szymanowski, however, was derisory of the provincialism he heard in the work of Poland's Chopin epigones. (He held up Scriabin as a contrasting example of a composer who had developed the Chopin style to new and modern effect, rather than languishing in weak imitation.) The influence of Chopin on Szymanowski's early compositions is clear in piano works such as the Nine Preludes, Op.1, the earliest of which date from 1896, when the composer was only fourteen. Ludomir Różycki, fellow composition student of Zygmunt Noskowski, later recalled Szymanowski 'studying in great detail the structure of piano passages by Chopin and Scriabin'.[79] In many of his piano pieces from around the turn of the century the Chopin idiom is frequently overt, channelled into the kind of miniaturism and mannerism also found in Scriabin and Lyadov. But his work soon moved into ambitions strongly imbued by the modern Austro-German manner. Szymanowski was not alone in developing a feeling of discontent with manifestations of the Chopinesque at this time. The dangers of Chopin epigonism had been declared by Władysław Żeleński in his essay 'On the Fiftieth Anniversary of Chopin's Death' (1899). Żeleński asserts that a 'tone' of 'longing' or 'yearning' ('tęskna nuta') is the pervasive expressive characteristic in Polish music. Before Chopin this was 'heard weakly' but was raised to the highest levels in Chopin's compositions, which are of 'purely Polish character'. This was, for example, demonstrated by Chopin's injection of 'profound sorrow' ('żal') and 'quiet complaint' ('skarga') into the genre of the nocturne. For Żeleński, Chopin's compositional process, as revealed by the manuscripts, shows the composer perfecting an idea through 'a true spiritual suffering'. By contrast with this exalted expression of sorrow,

the blind imitators … have fallen prey to a manner of unwelcome sentimentality. They have forgotten that the master, despite his originality, despite the life he led, could not protect himself from a certain morbid melancholy, and that he could not see the truth clearly and express it in a healthy fashion. Whoever wants to understand Chopin and whoever wants to draw from his treasure chest, has to start learning a more healthy classical music. After such a preparation the disciple could

[79] Alistair Wightman, *Karol Szymanowski: His Life and Work* (Aldershot: Ashgate, 1999), 36.

approach with respect, and then begin to research these jewels. This will protect him from falling prey to a *manner*.[80]

Żeleński's is a cautionary message. Chopin's example is a potentially dangerous one. Despite his profound achievements, in Chopin's morbidity lies the potential path to sickly music.

Noskowski's essay 'The Essence of Chopin's Works', also written in the anniversary year of 1899 (it was published in 1902), identifies 'sorrow' ('załosc') as the main tone of Chopin's music, that which is 'neither longing nor pain ('bolesc'), neither pensiveness ('zaduma') nor complaint ('skarga'). It is 'completely different from an elegiac quality. This feeling of sorrow may be discerned in almost all of Chopin's melodies, both in minor and in major; it is the main thread of his thought, and it is what makes him original in his ideas.' Noskowski then introduces the familiar feminizing trope in Chopin reception: 'At times, however, one notices an undue softness or hears a boyish whimpering instead of manly mourning', an 'extreme sensitivity, which was 'amplified' by his 'mental and physical suffering'. He continues by evoking similarly commonplace notions of the relation of art and nature, and the organic or evolutionary development of music. Chopin's 'pure', 'fresh' 'poetry' is a reflection of 'nature' – it is, again in a feminizing image, like a flower (a violet, or a lily-of-the-valley). This character was, however, corrupted by the emergence of 'salon music' in a degraded Chopin style. In the search for fleeting success in the commercial city salon composers pursued artificial 'improvement' or a replacement of 'nature', with works like 'greenhouse flowers', 'artificial roses' or 'exotic fragrances'– a decadent version of Chopin's 'naturally' spirited art.[81]

Żeleński and Noskowski are scornful of the mannered and sentimental music which sought to follow Chopin. Clearly, as figureheads of Polish composition at the turn of the century, they believed that these were artistic weaknesses, and they themselves avoided them. However, in his essay 'On Contemporary Musical Opinion in Poland' (July 1920) Szymanowski declared that neither Żeleński nor Noskowski 'constituted a link in an evolutionary chain', for their work represented an 'artistic level' lower

---

[80] Trans. from Maja Trochimczyk (ed.), *After Chopin: Essays on Polish Music* (Los Angeles: Polish Music Center at USC, 2000), 17–22. On the trope of *żal* (melancholy) in Chopin reception, established by Liszt's biography (1852) and sustained, for example, by Przybyszewski's *Chopin und Nietzsche* (1892), see Maja Trochimczyk, 'Chopin and the "Polish Race": On National Ideologies and the Chopin Reception', in Halina Goldberg (ed.), *The Age of Chopin: Interdisciplinary Inquiries* (Bloomington: Indiana University Press, 2004), 287–9. On racial aspects of Szymanowski's Chopin essays see pp. 300–4.

[81] Trans. from Trochimczyk (ed.), *After Chopin*, 23–45.

even than that of Stanisław Moniuszko (the main Polish composer of the third quarter of the nineteenth century), whom Szymanowski considered to be merely 'talented'. He criticized Żeleński's and Noskowski's music for an 'organic lack of style', especially condemning that of his former teacher, whose works 'came and went, vanishing from our stages and concert platforms, like a sleepy dream, fading gradually in the mists of time'.[82] Thus, in Szymanowski's view Chopin is an isolated figure of greatness in Polish musical history, a paradoxical figure of 'otherness' in relation to the music of his homeland: 'the only musical genius in the history of our art' was a 'mysterious visitant who retained no organic connections with our musical culture. He had no ancestors, just as he had no descendents. Like a lone star shining in the midst of the black night, his absolute "uniqueness" was almost paradoxical. Chopin really was a Pole who composed Polish Music which at the same time is universal art of the highest standard.'[83]

By contrast with Polish musical decline ('Chopin passed fleetingly amongst us like a ghost, in isolation and adversity, arousing no long-lasting echo in the art of the next period'), Szymanowski hailed the Russian moderns as those who understood and sustained the legacy, Scriabin especially maintaining 'genetic links' with Chopin.[84] Provocatively, Szymanowski concluded that for Polish composers 'it is now too late to follow the example of Chopin … He belongs to the past … today he is only a sacred relic, an eternally living and priceless monument to bygone days. We, the living and the free, should be seeking new paths and singing other songs.'[85] Just months before, on his return to the newly independent Poland, when his friend the musicologist Zdzisław Jachimecki urged him to take on the Chopin mantle as leader of his country's national musical culture, Szymanowski's rebuff was curt: 'I'd give you the whole of your Chopin for the fugue from the *Hammerklavier*.'[86] Beethoven is raised as a composer of 'Universal' significance – Chopin's misfortune is that he had spawned merely local art. (Of course, Szymanowski's raising of

[82] Karol Szymanowski, 'On Contemporary Musical Opinion in Poland', in *Pisma*, vol.I: *Pisma muzyczne*, ed. Kornel Michałowski (Cracow: PWM, 1984), 43–4, trans. in *Szymanowski on Music: Selected Writings of Karol Szymanowski*, trans. and ed. Alistair Wightman (London: Toccata, 1999), 91.

[83] Szymanowski, 'On Contemporary Musical Opinion in Poland', 40; trans. in *Szymanowski on Music*, 84.

[84] Szymanowski, 'On Contemporary Musical Opinion in Poland', 41, trans. in *Szymanowski on Music*, 85, in Szymanowski's footnote.

[85] Szymanowski, 'On Contemporary Musical Opinion in Poland', 41, trans. in *Szymanowski on Music*, 85.

[86] Wightman, *Karol Szymanowski*, 239.

Beethoven is deliberately provocative.) To reinvigorate his musical palette Szymanowski sought affiliations with modern styles in non-Polish sources. As Edward Said stated, where filiation apparently fails to sustain or develop a strong legacy, 'compensatory affiliations' beyond the familial boundary are sought and work is produced in a dialectic of 'affiliation' and 'filiation', of loving and belonging.[87] Szymanowski pursued a kind of 'Pan-European', utopian eclecticism.The piano cycle *Métopes* (1915) is illustrative of this ambition. In three pieces evoking mythological images from Homer which he had seen on a trip to Sicily, Szymanowski draws upon the piano styles of Scriabin, Ravel and Debussy, all composers who were heavily indebted to Chopin's music. The Chopin legacy is sustained, but epigonism is avoided by turning to modern models based on its radical transformation.

In the essay 'Fryderyk Chopin', published in 1923, Szymanowski described the failings of Polish music in the second half of the nineteenth century: 'the inexpressibly sad fact that here evolution took place *à rebours*, descending slowly, step by step, from the lofty heights of Chopin's genius, eventually to lose itself in a flat, grey landscape'. In a significant change of heart, Chopin was now a legitimate model, but Chopin's 'rediscovery' 'must not be merely as a 'precious relic' but as a 'living, driving force, the mainspring of new values'.[88] The revaluation of Chopin is motivated by Szymanowski's belief that his music could serve as a medicinal source for the convalescence of Polish music. Through it several potential pitfalls of the romantic legacy could be avoided – sentimentalism, nostalgia, subjective formlessness and exaggerated pathos. He writes: 'The work of a great artist only becomes an eternal source of vital creative power when it takes its proper place in the national cultural consciousness – a position that is precisely defined and devoid of all forms of sentimentalism.' Szymanowski calls for the 'removal of [Chopin's] mummified corpse from the swathing bands of nearly a century's emotional rhetoric'. He compares Chopin with Mozart in the way in which the objective relationship of the artist to his work produces formal beauty and organized perfection. 'His work appears to us to be a play of pure and perfect forms ... that are above all expressive in themselves through the imperturbable harmony of their individual

[87] Edward W. Said, *The World, The Text, and the Critic* (Cambridge, Mass.: Harvard University Press, 1983), 4, 5, 9. For more on this see my 'Szymanowski's Poetics of Paneuropeanism and Edward Said's "Secular Criticism"', in Zbigniew Skowron (ed.), *Karol Szymanowski w perspektywie kultury muzycznej przeszłości i współczesności* (Cracow: Musica Iagellonica, 2007), 93–104.

[88] Szymanowski, 'Fryderyk Chopin' (1923), in *Pisma*, vol.I, 89–102, trans. in *Szymanowski on Music*, 177–95.

elements … I must caution against them being applied in the way that they were until quite recently in those fashionable aesthetic-cum-metaphysical pronouncements concerning music as a means of expression.'[89] Szymanowski is seeking to strip away the layers of romantic expressive critical excess to reveal the music's organic and objective form. Chopin's work will then once more spring to vital significance. He illustrates Chopin's fundamental difference from Wagner by employing oceanic and volcanic wave imagery: 'In the case of Wagner, the uncontrollably rapid, powerful current of his inner experience was not allowed to cool and solidify to form well-defined forms and shapes; it erupted explosively from an inner flame of passion, and the result was an art that was as if a perpetually flowing stream of red-hot lava.'[90] Three years later he made a more general point concerning form and experience:

When one is swept along by deep, but fast-flowing, currents created by the actions of the human spirit, shaping and reshaping itself with a relentless inevitability from day to day and from hour to hour, one's awareness of the eternally enduring forms, raised aloft through the operation of a creative will to the noble station of immortal symbol, is lost in the feeling of immediate reality.[91]

Chopin again is the model for artistic response: 'But surely the great artist yearns instinctively and profoundly to create a work the solid structure of which stands in marked contrast to the unceasing movement and eternally flowing currents of life?'[92] With the 'tragic' nineteenth century over, Szymanowski believed that new perspectives on Chopin could emerge, that the 'black veil of mourning' through which he had been perceived could be torn asunder; Chopin appears from behind a mystifying shroud 'fresher, much more youthful', cured from the ills of 'romantic pathos'.[93] In this context Szymanowski returned to reconsider the traditional identification of a melancholy tone in Chopin's music. In a 1930 lecture delivered at the University of Warsaw he said, 'Is it really a faint, pallid sadness of disillusion, of barren melancholy, a pathetic mask hiding powerlessness and dejection? Is it not instead a creative sadness, but surely that immortal and for us, omnipresent "Melancholy" [*Smętkiem*], that magical,

---

[89] Szymanowski 'Fryderyk Chopin', 95, trans. in *Szymanowski on Music*, 189.
[90] Szymanowski, 'Fryderyk Chopin', 93, trans. in *Szymanowski on Music*, 182.
[91] Szymanowski, 'The Highways and Byways of Contemporary Music' (1926), in *Pisma*, vol.I, 183, trans. in *Szymanowski on Music*, 207.
[92] Szymanowski, 'Fryderyk Chopin', 96, trans. in *Szymanowski on Music*, 191.
[93] Szymanowski, 'Fryderyk Chopin', 94, trans. in *Szymanowski on Music*, 185.

fundamentally Polish Sovereign, who leads us pensive towards our common destiny … the wide expanses of free creative action?'[94]

The reappraisal of Chopin and the composition of the final act of *King Roger* coincided with a crucial fresh encounter with Tatra mountain culture. In Zakopane in 1924 Szymanowski began to write some mazurkas which Jarosław Iwaszkiewicz, the literary collaborator on *King Roger*, sceptically described as 'troubled waters – in which Chopinesque embryos swim like sleepy fish'.[95] Sixteen were written by the end of the year, each a synthesis of highland-style tunes with the rhythms of the lowland mazurka, the Góral culture revitalizing Chopin's legacy. There is a sense of a 'Homeric' return home as well as a Nietzschean convalescence and Paterian pastoralism: the Polish genealogy is reassembled and resituated. By contrast with the 'flat, grey landscape' of late nineteenth-century Polish music, the Tatra peaks were the setting of Szymanowski's idea for the regeneration of Polish music. Chopin was raised once more to the mountain top, from its 'lofty heights' providing the spring for a modern, Universally significant Polish art. *King Roger* evokes the dawn of a new heroic age, a recovery from decadent intoxications to look out to sea at the rising Apollonian sun. The plot is loosely based on Euripides' *The Bacchae*, transplanted to twelfth-century Norman Sicily, a site of geographical transition and of heady cultural mixture comparable to Venice and Byzantium. An ephebic shepherd from the East brings his mysterious religion of love to the Orthodox kingdom of Roger II, breaking taboos and seducing the people with the 'charm' of his smile. The erotic attractions and dangers of his overt narcissism – he gazes into limpid water and declares that his god is 'as fair as I' – open up a theme which recurs in Szymanowski's work.[96] Roger seeks to capture and condemn the disturbing yet seductive visitor, but his queen Roxana and his subjects follow the Shepherd into nocturnal oblivion in the climactic bacchanal. Roger resists, but unlike Euripedes' ill-fated Pentheus he has been regenerated by the encounter, transformed from cold, loveless despot into loving, expressive subject. The work's overt homoerotic dimensions and the contribution of Nietzsche and Merezhkovsky to the opera's symbolic content have all been explored elsewhere.[97] The focus here is on the inspiration drawn from Pater's Dionysian portraits.

---

[94] Szymanowski, 'Chopin' (1930), in *Pisma*, vol.I, 259–60.

[95] Quoted in Wightman, *Karol Szymanowski*, 269.

[96] See my 'Szymanowski and Narcissism', *Journal of the Royal Musical Association* 121 (1996), 58–81.

[97] For these and other related aspects of the opera see Paolo Emilio Carapezza, 'Król Roger między Dionizosem i Apollinem', *Res Facta* 9 (1982), 50–61; Wightman, 'The Book of King Roger'; and my *Szymanowski, Eroticism and the Voices of Mythology*, 54–74.

In 1914 Szymanowski read Pater's *The Renaissance* and *Greek Studies* with great enthusiasm. In Pater's 1876 essay 'A Study of Dionysus: The Spiritual Form of Fire and Dew', which was published in *Greek Studies*, discussion of the Dionysian religion evokes pastoral sensitivity and refinement in a 'world of transformation' achieved through the cycle of life–death–rebirth. The inspirer of 'songs of enchantment', with his vine as symbol of flowing life, Dionysus is the bearer of the gifts of honey, milk and water. In a pantheistic vision he is also the inspirer of the music of the reed 'in which the ideas of water and of vegetable life are brought close together, natural property, therefore, of the spirit of life in the green sap'. As the great inspirer 'he explains the phenomena of enthusiasm … the secrets of possession by a higher and more energetic spirit than one's own, the gift of self-revelation …'. He is the stimulator of intense sensations, the heat of fire and the quench of the cup, the delights of the epicurean. As the source of tragedy he has a double image; he is a *Doppelgänger*, 'bound in winter' but 'unbound in spring'; a 'chthonian god', he contains an 'element of sadness; like Hades himself, he is hollow and devouring, an eater of man's flesh'. Yet he is also regenerative, for out of the Dionysian sorrows of the winter, there is rebirth, purification through suffering.[98] On 'Denys L'Auxerrois', from Pater's *Imaginary Portraits* (1887), Szymanowski confessed: 'this figure is for me some sort of mystical symbol for various personal dreams about life – and it is difficult for me to part myself from him mentally'.[99] Pater's story opens with description of the particularly 'picturesque' qualities of the scenery around Auxerre, and of medieval tapestries depicting listeners to music from the cathedral organ which a stranger had built to recreate the pipe modes of the ancient wine god. In these figures 'a sort of mad vehemence prevails … giddy dances, wild animals leaping, above all the perpetual wreathings of the vine, connecting, like some mazy arabesque, the various presentations of one oft-repeated figure … a flaxen and flowery creature … notwithstanding its grace, and wealth of graceful accessories, a suffering, tortured figure'. This central figure is an ancient pagan returned in the mid-thirteenth century with strange and disturbing powers: 'the sight of him made old people feel young again', and he possessed an irresistible erotic charm. He was also a figure of danger and paradox: 'And yet a darkness had grown upon him', and he was capable of 'strange, motiveless misdeeds … He was making the younger world mad.' Like the wine god he had 'his contrast,

---

[98] Walter Pater, *Greek Studies* (McLean, Virginia: IndyPublish.com, n.d.), 1–22.
[99] Letter to Iwaszkiewicz, 14/27 November 1917, in Szymanowski, *Korespondencja*, vol.I, ed. Teresa Chylińska (Cracow: PWM, 1982), 514, trans in Wightman, *Karol Szymanowski*, 208. See also Teresa Chylińska, *Karol Szymanowski: His Life and Works*, trans. John Glowaski (Los Angeles: University of Southern California Press, 1993), 126–8.

his dark or antipathetic side; was like a double creature of two natures, difficult or impossible to harmonise'. He exuded a 'kind of degeneration, of coarseness – the coarseness of satiety and shapeless, battered-out appetite' leading to wantonness and savagery.[100] Szymanowski was attracted to this figure because of the overt eroticism (with homoerotic elements), his 'charm' and seductiveness, which rejuvenated those who encountered him, but also because of his embodiment of the potentially destructive or degenerative. An encounter with the primitive through this resurrected Dionysus can regenerate ailing modern worlds, but it also contains the perils of formal and personal disintegration.

Pater's descriptions crucially inform the character of the Shepherd in *King Roger*. At the climactic revelation of the Shepherd's Dionysian identity in the final act – the dramatic moment of recognition – there is a stylistic allusion of great symbolic significance. For the first time in the opera Szymanowski introduces a Tatra folk melodic character. This theme of Dionysus is, furthermore, a transformation both of the Shepherd's earlier song of narcissistic love and of an Orthodox chant heard at the ceremonial opening of the opera. Through this thematic relationship the figure of the Shepherd suggests the possibility of regenerating those who have lived by old customs and stultifying dogmas by revealing new versions of eroticism. By offering this transformation in the guise of a Polish folk tune, Polish primitivism is identified with Dionysianism. The Tatra pastoral is raised as site of Paterian regeneration, of Nietzschean convalescence. But the theme is sung within an opera of wild musical eclecticism evoking post-Wagnerian yearning, Scriabinesque ecstasy, Oriental arabesques and French refinement of sound and colour, all of which together informed Szymanowski's musical style from 1914 onwards. In this important regard *King Roger* foreshadows Szymanowski's development of the idea of 'Pan-Europeanism'. In an exasperated tone he asked: 'Is it really necessary for us to rely on the workings of a police state and "customs officer" for the defence of the basic freedom of Polish music from injurious influences? Are we terrified of foreign influences? Are we really that sickly now?'[101] For Szymanowski Pan-Europeanism offered a strong, developmental model; it was

an evolutionary symptom: unheard of refinement of the culture of some individuals, increasing sensitivity on the one hand and intellectual on the other, encompassing more and more wider horizons of a mutual past (historical), and as a result it erases and minimizes the present differences, bringing them down to

[100] Pater, *Imaginary Portraits* (New York: Allworth Press, 1997), 49, 55–6.
[101] Szymanowski, 'The "Ethnic" Question in Relation to Contemporary Music' (1925), in *Pisma*, vol.I, 170, trans. in *Szymanowski on Music*, 129.

'provincialism'. This increased feeling of a common crib – due to the unravelling 'historical thinking' – must in the end lead to a single denominator of all cultured individuals and find a common tongue for communication.[102]

In the final moments of the opera Roger alone decides not to follow the Shepherd into the endless night. He has realized that the Dionysian experience needs to be brought into the world and that blind allegiance to the Shepherd's religion is just another form of dogmatic death. Life is energized by developing the strength to encounter diversity and paradox. By contrast with his condition of declining powers before this realization, Roger now emerges strong and eloquent in the emerging light of a Nietzschean daybreak. He sings to Edrisi, the Arabian sage who stands by him: 'The Sun! The Sun, Edrisi! The sails unfurl on the deep-blue sea like gulls' white wings! They sail away, light and agile as the white sea-spume! Edrisi! The wings are spreading! They embrace all the world! From the abyss of loneliness, of power, I pluck my pure heart, as an offering to the Sun!' The poetic imagery here is the revitalized opposite of the bleeding wings which were the symbols of sinful despair in the apocalyptical Kasprowicz songs. In the Kasprowicz fragments the mazurka tune was heard at twilight before the dark night of torture: in *King Roger* the evocation of the Polish highland tune was the presage for dawn. The wounds seem healed. And yet ambiguities persist in the harmonic and motivic content of Roger's song of recovery. For all the mounting heroic optimism in Roger's voice, for all the poetic images of flight, energetic waves and the rising sun, the harmonic structure is based on descent. The chords are nearly all species of altered dominant – often with strong whole-tone qualities. The symmetries generated by these harmonic alterations weaken the sense of dominant function to virtual non-existence (Szymanowski in part learned this from Scriabin). Leading-note energetics are dissipated. Most significantly, the overall structure is a sinking from D (at the opening of Roger's song) through D flat (at his addressing the rising sun) to C (at his final symbolic sacrifice). The D and D flat tonal areas are prolonged through semitonal descent (through a complete octave in the case of D; through a major sixth to F in the prolongation of D flat). The sinking harmonic successions stop on reaching the final pedal C, but what continues is motivic emphasis on

---

[102] Szymanowski, 'Efebos', in *Pisma*, vol.II: *Pisma literackie*, ed. Teresa Chylińska (Cracow: PWM, 1989), 193, trans. in Chylińska, *Karol Szymanowski*, 135. Szymanowski was a member of the Polish Pan-European Union, founded in 1927. On this, and the relationship with Richard Coudenhove-Calergi's *Pan-Europa* (Vienna, 1923), see Teresa Chylińska, 'Szymanowski and Politics', *Music in Poland* 42 (1990), 5–17.

falling tetrachords.[103] The sinking or harmonic decline is at various points countered by energizing instructions in the score: *avvivando* (three times, alternating with *sostenuto*), *accelerando* and *animato*. The first and third of these occur at moments when the descending harmonic progressions reach chords based on A, the 'key' of the Shepherd's song of love in Act 1. Here also (at fig.71) there are recollections of the dotted rhythms in compound metre that characterized the Shepherd's seductive dancing. These evocations of the vitalizing properties of song and dance are symbols of Nietzschean convalescence. They also reveal the legacy of Roger's encounter with Dionysian eroticism.

Karol Berger considers the close of *King Roger* to be 'a unique comment in the tradition based on the model of the end of *Tristan*'. For Berger, Szymanowski composed a critique of the '*Liebestod* finale' which was the model for Strauss's *Salome* and *Elektra*, and which in Schoenberg's *Erwartung* reached its 'logical conclusion', where it takes over the whole work (the monodrama is all *Liebestod* laid bare). Szymanowski's *Hagith* was a failed attempt to emulate the Straussian version. By contrast, *King Roger* offers a transformative, Nietzschean polemic with the *Tristan* tradition, one which draws heavily on Nietzsche's diagnosis of decadence. Berger persuasively argues that Szymanowski recognized the simultaneous death wish of the post-Wagnerian self and the demise of its language, and in the ending of *King Roger* composed an 'inversion' of *Tristan*, a '*Liebesleben*' as a vital alternative to Wagnerian *Liebestod*.[104] Roger Scruton similarly sees Szymanowski's project as one based on 'redeeming a musical idiom from its inherited decadence' (in particular from Scriabinesque voluptuousness). He identifies this with the symbolic signficance of pedal points as musical 'roots' which counteract the swooning instability and evaporations into nothingness that are the marks of 'true' decadence.[105] The approach to the closing pedal C is made via the last evocation of the rising motif of Tristanesque yearning (Example 6.9), the final swerve away from the Schopenhauerian erotic pessimism which informed Iwaszkiewicz's original ending. (The composer radically rewrote the final scene, to his

[103] These motifs are of two types – diatonic and 'Oriental' – suggesting the interaction of what Pater called European 'centripetal' and Asiatic 'centrifugal' forces: 'The Marbles of Aegina' (1880), in *Essays on Literature and Art*, ed. Jennifer Uglow (London: Dent, 1990), 67.

[104] Karol Berger, 'King Roger's *Liebesleben*', in Michał Bristiger, Roger Scruton and Petra Weber-Bockholdt (eds.), *Szymanowski in seiner Zeit* (Munich: Wilhelm Fink, 1984), 21–8.

[105] Roger Scruton, 'Between Decadence and Barbarism: The Music of Szymanowski', in Bristiger, Scruton and Weber-Bockholdt (eds.), *Szymanowski in seiner Zeit*, 159–78.

Example 6.9 Szymanowski, *King Roger*, Op.46b, from 2 bars before fig.73

collaborator's angry consternation).[106] After this moment the Scriabinesque sequences of 'altered dominant' chords are left behind.

Tristan is not the only Wagnerian model evoked by the final scene. In a manner comparable with Brünnhilde's monologue in *Twilight of the Gods* there are in effect two endings to *King Roger*: the first (for the converts to the Shepherd's religion) a retreat into darkness, the second (for the newly enlightened Roger) an advance into the brightening light of the dawn. But for Szymanowski, as for Nietzsche and so many prominent figures on the modern musical map of Central and Eastern Europe, one had first to become a decadent. In this regard *King Roger* closely maps onto Nietzsche's definition of modern progress as described in *Twilight of the Idols*, where Nietzsche declared that we cannot go back, that 'retrogression' is impossible: 'one has to go forward, which is to say step by step further into *décadence*'. The second ending is a new beginning. Roger emerges as the Nietzschean 'wise man' (his standing shoulder to shoulder with Edrisi at this moment symbolizes his accrual of vital knowledge). The double ending reveals the double origin. 'I am so wise', Nietzsche declares in *Ecce homo*, because I am 'at once *décadent* and beginning'.[107] This experience of decadence is one which eternally returns. Each dawn will always be followed by twilight.

---

[106] For more on this ending see my *Szymanowski, Eroticism and the Voices of Mythology*, 70–4.
[107] Nietzsche, *Ecce homo*, 38–41.

Bibliography

Abbate, Carolyn, 'Elektra's Voice: Music and Language in Strauss's Opera', in Derrick Puffett (ed.), *Richard Strauss:* Elektra, Cambridge University Press, 1989, 107–27.

'Opera as Symphony: A Wagnerian Myth', in Carolyn Abbate and Roger Parker (eds.), *Analyzing Opera: Verdi and Wagner*, Berkeley, University of California Press, 1989, 92–124.

Unsung Voices: Opera and Musical Narrative in the Nineteenth Century, Princeton University Press, 1991.

Abraham, Gerald, *Slavonic and Romantic Music*, London, Faber, 1968.

preface to Tchaikovsky, *Manfred* Symphony Op.58, London, Eulenburg, n.d.

Adams, Byron, 'Elgar's Later Oratorios: Roman Catholicism, Decadence and the Wagnerian Dialectic of Shame and Grace', in Daniel M. Grimley and Julian Rushton (eds.), *The Cambridge Companion to Elgar*, Cambridge University Press, 2004, 81–105.

Adorno, Theodor W., 'Richard Strauss: Born June 11, 1864', trans. Samuel and Shierry Weber, *Perspectives of New Music* 4 (1965), 113–29.

Prisms, trans. Samuel and Shierry Weber, Cambridge, Mass., MIT Press, 1983.

Alban Berg: Master of the Smallest Link, trans. Juliane Brand and Christopher Hailey, Cambridge University Press, 1991.

1992. *Mahler: A Musical Physiognomy*, trans. Edmund Jephcott, Chicago University Press, 1992.

Quasi una fantasia, trans. Rodney Livingstone, London: Verso, 1992.

'On the Score of *Parsifal*', trans. with commentary by Anthony Barone, *Music & Letters* 76 (1995): 384–6.

Aesthetic Theory, trans. and ed. Robert Hullot-Kentor, Minneapolis, University of Minnesota Press, 1997.

Beethoven: The Philosophy of Music, ed. Rolf Tiedermann, trans. Edmund Jephcott, Stanford University Press, 1998.

Essays on Music, ed. Richard Leppert, trans. Susan Gillespie, Berkeley, University of California Press, 2002.

In Search of Wagner, trans. Rodney Livingstone, with a foreword by Slavoj Žižek, London, Verso, 2005.

Philosophy of New Music, trans., ed. and with an introduction by Robert Hullot-Kentor, Minneapolis, University of Minnesota Press, 2006.

332

Agawu, V. Kofi, 'Structural Highpoints in Schumann's *Dichterliebe*', *Music Analysis* 3 (1984), 159–80.

'Concepts of Closure and Chopin's Op.28', *Music Theory* Spectrum 9 (1987), 1–17.

Playing with Signs: A Semiotic Investigation of Classic Music, Princeton University Press, 1991.

Albright, Daniel (ed.), *Modernism and Music: An Anthology of Sources*, Chicago University Press, 2004.

Allen, Warren Dwight, *Philosophies of Music History*, New York, Dover, 1962.

Anders, Henryk, *Mieczysław Karłowicz: Życie i dokonania*, Poznań: Abos, 1998.

Anson-Cartwright, Mark, 'Chord as Motive: The Augmented-Triad Matrix in Wagner's "Siegfried Idyll"', *Music Analysis* 15 (1996), 57–71.

Antokoletz, Elliott, Fischer, Victoria and Suchoff, Benjamin (eds.), *Bartók Perspectives*, Oxford University Press, 2000.

Apter, Emily, 'Acting Out Orientalism: Sapphic Theatricality in Turn-of-the-Century Paris', in Elin Diamond (ed.), *Performance and Cultural Politics*, London, Routledge, 1996, 15–34.

Arscott, Caroline, 'Venus as Dominatrix: Nineteenth-Century Artists and their Creations', in Caroline Arscott and Katie Scott (eds.), *Manifestations of Venus: Art and Sexuality*, Manchester University Press, 2000, 109–25.

Arscott, Caroline and Scott, Katie, 'Introducing Venus', in Caroline Arscott and Katie Scott (eds.), *Manifestations of Venus: Art and Sexuality*, Manchester University Press, 2000, 1–23.

Arscott, Caroline and Scott, Katie (eds.), *Manifestations of Venus: Art and Sexuality*, Manchester University Press, 2000.

Bacht, Nikolas (ed.), *Music, Theatre and Politics in Germany: 1848 to the Third Reich*, Aldershot, Ashgate, 2006.

Baeumer, Max L., 'Nietzsche and the Tradition of the Dionysian', trans. Timothy F. Sellner, in James C. O'Flaherty, Timothy F. Sellner and Robert M. Helm (eds.), *Studies in Nietzsche and the Classical Tradition*, Chapel Hill, University of North Carolina Press, 1976, 165–89.

Bagby, Lewis, *Alexander Bestuzhev-Marlinsky and Russian Byronism*, Philadelphia, Pennsylvania State University Press, 1995.

Bailey, Robert, 'The Structure of the "Ring" and its Evolution', *19th-Century Music* 1 (1977), 48–61.

Bailey, Robert (ed.), *Wagner: Prelude and Transfiguration from 'Tristan and Isolde'*, New York, Norton, 1985.

BaileyShea, Matthew, 'The Wagnerian *Satz*: The Rhetoric of the Sentence in Wagner's Post-*Lohengrin* Operas', unpublished PhD thesis, Yale University, 2003.

'Beyond the Beethoven Model: Sentence Types and Limits', *Current Musicology* 77 (2004), 5–33.

Baker, James M., *The Music of Alexander Scriabin*, New Haven, Yale University Press, 1986.

'Scriabin's Music: Structure as Prism for Mystical Philosophy', in James M. Baker, David W. Beach and Jonathan W. Bernard (eds.), *Music Theory in Concept and Practice*, University of Rochester Press, 1997, 53–97.

Banks, Paul, 'Richard Strauss and the Unveiling of "Salome"', in Nicholas John (ed.), *Strauss:* Salome/Elektra, ENO Opera Guide 37, London, Calder, 1988, 7–21.

'Mahler and Viennese Modernism', in Philip Reed (ed.), *On Mahler and Britten*, Woodbridge, Boydell, 1995, 3–20.

Barham, Jeremy (ed.), *Perspectives on Gustav Mahler*, Aldershot, Ashgate, 2005.

Barker, Andrew, 'Battles of the Mind: Berg and the Cultural Politics of "Vienna 1900"', in Anthony Pople (ed.), *The Cambridge Companion to Berg*, Cambridge University Press, 1997, 24–37.

Barone, Anthony, 'Richard Wagner's *Parsifal* and the Theory of Late Style', *Cambridge Opera Journal* 7 (1995), 37–54.

Barta, Peter (ed.), *Metamorphoses in Russian Modernism*, Budapest, Central European University Press, 2000.

Bartlett, Rosamund, *Wagner in Russia*, Cambridge University Press, 1995.

'Stravinsky's Russian Origins', in Jonathan Cross (ed.), *The Cambridge Companion to Stravinsky*, Cambridge University Press, 2003, 3–18.

Bartók, Béla, *Letters*, ed. János Demény, trans. Péter Balabán and István Farcas, London, Faber, 1971.

Barzun, Jacques, *From Dawn to Decadence: 500 Years of Western Cultural Life, 1500 to the Present*, New York, HarperCollins, 2000.

Baudelaire, Charles, *Selected Writings on Art and Literature*, trans. P. E. Charvet, Harmondsworth, Penguin, 1972.

Les Fleurs du mal, trans. Richard Howard, Brighton, Harvester Press, 1982.

My Heart Laid Bare *and Other Prose Writings*, trans. Norman Cameron, ed. Peter Quennell, London, Soho Books, 1986.

Beach, David, 'Phrase Expansion: Three Analytical Studies', *Music Analysis* 14 (1995), 27–47.

Beaumont, Anthony, *Zemlinsky*, London, Faber, 2000.

Bechert, Paul, 'The New Richard Strauss Ballet', *The Musical Times* 65 (1924), 547.

Beller, Steven (ed.), *Rethinking Vienna 1900*, New York, Berghahn Books, 2001.

Beller-McKenna, Daniel, 'Distance and Disembodiment: Harps, Horns, and the Requiem Idea in Schumann and Brahms', *Journal of Musicology* 22 (2005), 47–89.

Benedyktowicz, Ludomir, *Rodowód Secesyi w malarstwie i rzezbie: Jej kwiaty i owoce na naszej grzędzie*, Cracow, 1905.

Bent, Ian (ed.), *Music Analysis in the Nineteenth Century*, vol.II: *Hermeneutic Approaches*, Cambridge University Press, 1994.

Berg, Alban, *Letters to his Wife*, ed. and trans. Bernard Grun, London, Faber, 1971.

Berger, Karol, 'King Roger's *Liebesleben*', in Michał Bristiger, Roger Scruton and Petra Weber-Bockholdt (eds.), *Szymanowski in seiner Zeit*, Munich, Wilhelm Fink, 1984, 21–8.

'Time's Arrow and the Advent of Musical Modernity', in Karol Berger and Anthony Newcomb (eds.), *Music and the Aesthetics of Modernity*, Cambridge, Mass., Harvard University Press, 2005, 3–22.

Berger, Karol and Newcomb, Anthony (eds.), *Music and the Aesthetics of Modernity*, Cambridge, Mass., Harvard University Press, 2005.

Bergmann, Peter, 'Nietzsche and the Christ among Nations', in Alice Freifeld, Peter Bergmann, and Bernice Glatzer Rosenthal (eds.), *East Europe Reads Nietzsche*, New York, Columbia University Press, 1998, 21–41.

Bernheimer, Charles, 'Unknowing Decadence', in Liz Constable, Dennis Denisoff and Matthew Potolsky (eds.), *Perennial Decay: On the Aesthetics and Politics of Decadence*, Philadelphia, University of Pennsylvania Press, 1999, 50–63.

Decadent Subjects: The Idea of Decadence in Art, Literature, Philosophy, and Culture of the Fin de Siècle in Europe, Baltimore, Johns Hopkins University Press, 2002.

Bernstein, Susan, *Virtuosity of the Nineteenth Century: Performing Music and Language in Heine, Liszt and Baudelaire*, Stanford University Press, 1998.

Blix, Goran, 'Charting the "Transitional Period": The Emergence of Modern Time in the Nineteenth Century', *History and Theory* 45 (2006), 51–71.

Blom, Philipp, *The Vertigo Years: Change and Culture in the West, 1900–1914*, London, Weidenfeld and Nicolson, 2008.

Bogue, Ronald, *Deleuze on Music, Painting, and the Arts*, New York, Routledge, 2003.

Bohrer, Karl Heinz, *Suddenness: On the Moment of Aesthetic Appearance*, trans. Ruth Crowley, New York, Columbia University Press, 1994.

Boniecki, Edward, 'Stanisław Przybyszewski's Berlin Essays on Artists and Art', in Piotr Paszkiewicz (ed.), *Totenmesse: Modernism in the Culture of Northern and Central Europe*, Warsaw, Institute of Art and Polish Academy of Sciences, 1996, 51–64.

'The Lyrical, Young Poland "I" in Songs by Szymanowski to Words by Tadeusz Miciński', in Zofia Helman, Teresa Chylińska and Alistair Wightman (eds.), *The Songs of Karol Szymanowski and his Contemporaries*, Los Angeles, University of Southern California Press, 2002, 11–23.

Bónis, Ferenc, 'Bartók and Wagner', in Todd Crow (ed.), *Bartók Studies*, Detroit, Information Coordinators, 1976, 84–93.

Borchmeyer, Dieter, *Richard Wagner: Theory and Theatre*, Oxford, Clarendon Press, 1991.

Borio, Gianmario, 'Dire cela, sans savoir quoi: The Question of Meaning in Adorno and in the Musical Avant-Garde', in Berthold Hoeckner (ed.), *Apparitions: New Perspectives on Adorno and Twentieth-Century Music*, London, Routledge, 2006, 41–68.

Botstein, Leon, 'The Enigmas of Richard Strauss: A Revisionist View', in Bryan Gilliam (ed.), *Richard Strauss and his World*, Princeton University Press, 1992, 3–32.

'History, Rhetoric and the Self: Robert Schumann and Music Making in German-Speaking Europe 1800–1860', in R. Larry Todd (ed.), *Schumann and his World*, Princeton University Press, 1994, 3–46.

Bowers, Faubion, *Scriabin: A Biography*, New York, Dover, 1996.

Bowlt, John E., 'Through the Glass Darkly: Images of Decadence in Early Twentieth-Century Russian Art', *Journal of Contemporary History* 17 (1982), 93–110.

Brand, Juliane and Hailey, Christopher (eds.), *Constructive Dissonance: Arnold Schoenberg and the Transformations of Twentieth-Century Culture*, Berkeley, University of California Press, 1997.

Bribitzer-Stull, Matthew, 'The A♭–C–E Complex: The Origin and Function of Chromatic Major Third Collections in Nineteenth-Century Music', *Music Theory Spectrum* 28 (2006), 167–90.

Brinkmann, Reinhold, 'On the Problem of Establishing "Jugendstil" as a Category in the History of Music – with a Negative Plea', *Art Nouveau and Jugendstil and the Music of the Early Twentieth Century: Adelaide Studies in Musicology* 13 (1984), 19–47.

Bristiger, Michał, Scruton, Roger and Weber-Bockholdt, Petra (eds.), *Szymanowski in seiner Zeit*, Munich, Wilhelm Fink, 1984.

Brown, Julie, 'Schoenberg's Early Wagnerisms: Atonality and the Redemption of Ahasuerus', *Cambridge Opera Journal* 6 (1994), 51–80.

'Schoenberg's Musical Prose as Allegory', *Music Analysis* 14 (1995), 161–92.

'Bartók, the Gypsies and Hybridity in Music', in Georgina Born and David Hesmondhalgh (eds.), *Western Music and its Others: Difference, Representation, and Appropriation in Music*, Berkeley, University of California Press, 2000, 119–42.

Bartók and the Grotesque, Aldershot, Ashgate, 2007.

'Otto Weininger and Musical Discourse in Turn-of-the-Century Vienna', in Julie Brown (ed.), *Western Music and Race*, Cambridge University Press, 2007, 84–101.

Bucknell, Brad, *Literary Modernism and Musical Aesthetics: Pater, Pound, Joyce, and Stein*, Cambridge University Press, 2001.

Buhler, James, 'Theme and Form in the Andante of the Sixth Symphony', in Jeremy Barham (ed.), *Perspectives on Gustav Mahler*, Aldershot, Ashgate, 2005, 261–94.

Burkholder, J. Peter, 'Berg and the Possibility of Popularity', in David Gable and Robert P. Morgan (eds.), *Alban Berg: Historical and Analytical Perspectives*, Oxford, Clarendon Press, 1991, 25–53.

Burt, E. S., '"An Immoderate Taste for Truth": Censoring History in Baudelaire's "Les Bijoux"', *Diacritics* 27 (1997), 19–43.

Byron, George, Lord, *Complete Poetical Works*, Oxford University Press, 1970.

Calinescu, Matei, *Five Faces of Modernity: Modernism, Avant-Garde, Decadence, Kitsch, Postmodernism*, Durham, Duke University Press, 1987.

Campbell, Brian, G., '*Gurrelieder* and the Fall of the Gods: Schoenberg's Struggle with the Legacy of Wagner', in Charlotte M. Cross and Russell A. Berman (eds.), *Schoenberg and Words: The Modernist Years*, New York and London, Garland, 2000, 31–63.

Campbell, Stuart (trans. and ed.), *Russians on Russian Music, 1880–1917*, Cambridge University Press, 2003.

Caplin, William E., *Classical Form: A Theory of Formal Functions for the Instrumental Music of Haydn, Mozart, and Beethoven*, New York, Oxford University Press, 1998.

Carapezza, Paolo Emilio, 'Król Roger między Dionizosem i Apollinem', *Res Facta* 9 (1982), 50–61.

Carter, A. E., *The Idea of Decadence in French Literature, 1830–1900*, Toronto University Press, 1958.

Cavanaugh, Jan, *Out Looking In: Early Modern Polish Art, 1890–1918*, Berkeley: University of California Press, 2000.

Cavell, Marcia, 'Taste and the Moral Sense', *The Journal of Aesthetics and Art Criticism* 34 (1975), 29–33.

Cherlin, Michael, 'Schoenberg and *Das Unheimliche*: Spectres of Tonality', *Journal of Musicology* 11 (1993), 357–73.

Chew, Geoffrey, 'Ernst Kurth, Music as Psychic Motion and *Tristan und Isolde*: Towards a Model for Analysing Musical Instability', *Music Analysis* 10 (1991), 171–93.

'Introduction: The Geography of Modernism: Reflections on the Theme "New Music for a New Europe"', in Geoffrey Chew (ed.), *New Music in the 'New Europe' 1918–1938: Ideology, Theory, and Practice, Colloquia musicologica Brunensia 38, 2003*, Prague: Koniasch Latin Press and Institute of Musicology, Masaryk University Brno, 2007, 7–14.

Christensen, Thomas, 'Schoenberg's Opus 11, No.1: A Parody of Pitch Cells from *Tristan*', *Journal of the Arnold Schoenberg Institute* 10 (1987), 38–44.

Chua, Daniel K. L., 'Adorno's Metaphysics of Mourning: Beethoven's Farewell to Adorno', *The Musical Quarterly* 87 (2004), 523–45.

Chylińska, Teresa, 'Szymanowski and Politics', *Music in Poland* 42 (1990), 5–17.

Karol Szymanowski: His Life and Works, trans. John Glowaski, Los Angeles, University of Southern California Press, 1993.

Clifton, Thomas, 'On Listening to *Herzgewächse*', *Perspectives of New Music* 11 (1973), 87–103.

Cohn, Richard, 'Maximally Smooth Cycles, Hexatonic Systems, and the Analysis of Late Nineteenth-Century Triadic Progressions', *Music Analysis* 15 (1996), 9–40.

'Introduction to Neo-Riemannian Theory: A Survey and an Historical Perspective', *Journal of Music Theory* 42 (1998), 167–80.

'Uncanny Resemblances: Tonal Significance in the Freudian Age', *Journal of the American Musicological Society* 57 (2004), 285–323.

Collier, Peter and Davies, Judy (eds.), *Modernism and the European Unconscious*, Cambridge, Polity Press, 1990.

Cone, Edward T., 'Sound and Syntax: An Introduction to Schoenberg's Harmony', *Perspectives of New Music* 13 (1974), 21–40.

Constable, Liz, Denisoff, Dennis and Potolsky, Matthew, 'Introduction', in Liz Constable, Dennis Denisoff and Matthew Potolsky (eds.), *Perennial Decay: On the Aesthetics and Politics of Decadence*, Philadelphia, University of Pennsylvania Press, 1999, 1–34.

Constable, Liz, Denisoff, Dennis and Potolsky, Matthew (eds.), *Perennial Decay: On the Aesthetics and Politics of Decadence*, Philadelphia, University of Pennsylvania Press, 1999.

Cooke, Deryck, *I Saw the World End*, London, Faber, 1979.

Cooley, Timothy J., *Making Music in the Polish Tatras: Tourists, Ethnographers, and Mountain Musicians*, Bloomington, Indiana University Press, 2005.

Cooper, David, 'Béla Bartók and the Question of Race Purity in Music', in Harry White and Michael Murphy (eds.), *Musical Constructions of Nationalism: Essays on the History and Ideology of Musical Culture 1800–1945*, Cork University Press, 2001, 16–32.

Corse, Sandra, 'The Voice of Authority in Wagner's *Ring*', in Herbert Richardson (ed.), *New Studies in Richard Wagner's 'The Ring of the Nibelung'*, Lewiston, Edwin Mellen Press, 1991, 23–7.

Cottom, Daniel, 'Taste and the Civilized Imagination', *The Journal of Aesthetics and Art Criticism* 39 (1981), 367–80.

Crawford, Dorothy Lamb, 'Love and Anguish: Bartók's Expressionism', in Elliott Antokoletz, Victoria Fischer and Benjamin Suchoff (eds.), *Bartók Perspectives*, Oxford University Press, 2000, 129–39.

Crawford, John C. and Crawford, Dorothy L., *Expressionism in Twentieth-Century Music*, Bloomington, Indiana University Press, 1993.

Cross, Charlotte M. and Berman, Russell A. (eds.), *Schoenberg and Words: The Modernist Years*, New York, Garland, 2000.

Crow, Todd (ed.), *Bartók Studies*, Detroit, Information Coordinators, 1976.

Czarnocka, Anna, 'Nietzsche, Przybyszewski and the Berlin *Bohême* from the Circle of the *Kneipe "Zum Schwarzen Ferkel"*', in Piotr Paszkiewicz (ed.), *Totenmesse: Modernism in the Culture of Northern and Central Europe*, Warsaw, Institute of Art and Polish Academy of Sciences, 1996, 41–50.

Dahlhaus, Carl, *Richard Wagner's Music Dramas*, trans. Mary Whittall, Cambridge University Press, 1979.

    Between Romanticism and Modernism, trans. Mary Whittall, Berkeley, University of California Press, 1980.

    Schoenberg and the New Music, trans. Derrick Puffett and Alfred Clayton, Cambridge University Press, 1987.

    Nineteenth-Century Music, trans. J. Bradford Robinson, Berkeley, University of California Press, 1989.

Ludwig van Beethoven: Approaches to his Music, trans. Mary Whittall, Oxford, Clarendon Press, 1991.

Dainotto, Roberto M., *Place in Literature: Regions, Cultures, Communities*, Ithaca: Cornell University Press, 2000.

Danuser, Hermann, 'Musical Manifestations of the End in Wagner and in Post-Wagnerian "Weltanschauungsmusik"', *19th-Century Music* 18 (1994), 64–82.

Darcy, Warren, 'The Pessimism of the *Ring*', *Opera Quarterly* 4 (1986), 24–48.

  '*Creatio ex nihilo*: The Genesis, Structure, and Meaning of the *Rheingold* Prelude', *19th-Century Music* 13 (1989), 79–100.

  Wagner's 'Das Rheingold', Oxford, Clarendon Press, 1993.

  'The Metaphysics of Annihilation: Wagner, Schopenhauer and the Ending of "The Ring"', *Music Theory Spectrum*, 16 (1994), 1–40.

  'Bruckner's Sonata Deformations', in Timothy L. Jackson and Paul Hawkshaw (eds.), *Bruckner Studies*, Cambridge University Press, 1997, 256–77.

  'Rotational Form, Teleological Genesis, and Fantasy Projection in the Slow Movement of Mahler's Sixth Symphony', *19th-Century Music* 25 (2001), 49–74.

Daub, Adrian, 'Adorno's Schreker: Charting the Self-Dissolution of the Distant Sound', *Cambridge Opera Journal* 18 (2006), 247–71.

Daverio, John, *Nineteenth-Century Music and the German Romantic Ideology*, New York, Schirmer, 1993.

  Robert Schumann: Herald of a New Poetic Age, Oxford University Press, 1997.

  '*Einheit – Freiheit – Vaterland*: Intimations of Utopia in Robert Schumann's Late Choral Music', in Celia Applegate and Pamela Potter (eds.), *Music and German National Identity*, Chicago University Press, 2002, 59–77.

  '*Tristan und Isolde*: Essence and Appearance', in Thomas S. Grey (ed.), *The Cambridge Companion to Wagner*, Cambridge University Press, 2008.

Daviau, Donald G., 'Hermann Bahr and Decadence', *Modern Austrian Literature* 10 (1977), 53–109.

David-Fox, Katherine, 'Prague–Vienna, Prague–Berlin: The Hidden Geography of Czech Modernism', *Slavic Review* 59 (2000), 735–60.

Deathridge, John, *Wagner: Beyond Good and Evil*, Berkeley, University of California Press, 2007.

Dejans, Peter (ed.), *Order and Disorder: Music-Theoretical Strategies in 20th Century Music*, Leuven, Rodopi, 2004.

Delaere, Mark and Herman, Jan (eds.), Pierrot lunaire: *Albert Giraud – Otto Erich Hartleben – Arnold Schoenberg*, Louvain, Editions Peeters, 2004.

Del Caro, Adrian, *Dionysian Aesthetics: The Role of Destruction and Creation as Reflected in the Life and Works of Friedrich Nietzsche*, Frankfurt am Main, Peter Lang, 1981.

Deleuze, Gilles, *Nietzsche and Philosophy*, trans. Hugh Tomlinson, London, Continuum, 1986.

Deleuze, Gilles and Guattari, Félix, *A Thousand Plateaus: Capitalism and Schizophrenia*, trans. Brian Massumi, London, Continuum, 2004.

Dellamora, Richard, *Apocalyptic Overtures: Sexual Politics and the Sense of an Ending*, New Brunswick, Rutgers University Press, 1994.

Del Mar, Norman, *Richard Strauss: A Critical Commentary on his Life and Works*, vol.I, London, Faber, 1986.

DeVoto, Mark, 'Alban Berg and Creeping Chromaticism', in David Gable and Robert P. Morgan (eds.), *Alban Berg: Historical and Analytical Perspectives*, Oxford, Clarendon Press, 1991, 57–78.

Diakonova, Nina and Vadim, Vacuro, 'Byron and Russia: Byron and Nineteenth-Century Russian Literature', in Paul Graham Trueblood (ed.), *Byron's Political and Cultural Influence in Nineteenth-Century Europe: A Symposium*, Atlantic Highlands, NJ, Humanities Press, 1981, 143–59.

Diamond, Elin (ed.), *Performance and Cultural Politics*, London, Routledge, 1996.

Donington, Robert, *Wagner's 'Ring' and its Symbols*, London, Faber, 1979.

Dorfles, Gillo (ed.), *Kitsch: The World of Bad Taste*, London, Studio Vista, 1969.

Downes, Stephen, *Szymanowski as Post-Wagnerian*, New York, Garland, 1994.

    'Szymanowski and Narcissism', *Journal of the Royal Musical Association* 121 (1996), 58–81.

    'Eros in the Metropolis: Bartók's *The Miraculous Mandarin*', *Journal of the Royal Musical Association* 125 (2000), 41–61.

    Szymanowski, Eroticism and the Voices of Mythology, Royal Musical Association Monograph 11, Aldershot, Ashgate, 2003.

    The Muse as Eros: Music, Erotic Fantasy and Male Creativity in the Romantic and Modern Imagination, Aldershot, Ashgate, 2006.

    'Szymanowski's Poetics of Paneuropeanism and Edward Said's "Secular Criticism"', in Zbigniew Skowron (ed.), *Karol Szymanowski w perspektywie kultury muzycznej przeszłości i współczesności*, Cracow, Musica Iagellonica, 2007, 93–104.

    'Modern Maritime Pastoral: Wave Deformations in the Music of Frank Bridge', in Matthew Riley and Paul Rodmell (eds.), *British Music and Modernism 1895–1960*, Aldershot, Ashgate, 2010.

Drake, Richard, 'Decadence, Decadentism and Decadent Romanticism in Italy: Toward a Theory of Decadence', *Journal of Contemporary History* 17 (1982), 69–92.

Draughon, Francesca, 'Dance of Decadence: Class, Gender, and Modernity in the Scherzo of Mahler's Ninth Symphony', *Journal of Musicology* 20 (2003), 388–413.

Egyed, Béla, 'Nietzsche's Early Reception in Hungary', in Alice Freifeld, Peter Bergmann and Bernice Glatzer Rosenthal (eds.), *East Europe Reads Nietzsche*, New York, Columbia University Press, 1998, 85–106.

Eichhorn, Andreas, 'Melancholie und das Monumentale: Zur Krise des symphonischen Finaldenkens im 19. Jahrhundert', *Musica* 46/1 (1992), 9–12.

Finney, Gail, 'Self-Reflexive Siblings: Incest as Narcissism in Tieck, Wagner, and Thomas Mann', *The German Quarterly* 56 (1983), 243–56.

Fisher, Philip, *Wonder, the Rainbow, and the Aesthetics of Rare Experiences*, Cambridge, Mass., Harvard University Press, 1998.

Fletcher, Ian (ed.), *Decadence and the 1890s*, London, Edward Arnold, 1979.

Foster, John Burt, Jr, *Heirs to Dionysus: A Nietzschean Current in Literary Modernism*, Princeton University Press, 1981.

Franklin, Peter, 'Style, Structure and Taste: Three Aspects of the Problem of Franz Schreker', *Proceedings of the Royal Musical Association* 109 (1982–3), 134–46.
   Mahler: Symphony No.3, Cambridge University Press, 1991.
   '"Wer weiss, Vater, ob das nicht Engel sind?" Reflections on the Pre-Fascist Discourse of Degeneracy in Schreker's *Die Gezeichneten*', in Nikolas Bacht (ed.), *Music, Theatre and Politics in Germany: 1848 to the Third Reich*, Aldershot, Ashgate, 2006, 173–83.

Fraser, Ralph S., 'Nietzsche, Byron, and the Classical Tradition', in James C. O'Flaherty, Timothy Sellner and Robert M. Helm (eds.), *Studies in Nietzsche and the Classical Tradition*, Chapel Hill, University of North Carolina Press, 1976, 190–8.

Frayling, Christopher, *Nightmare: The Birth of Horror*, London, BBC, 1996.

Freeborn, Richard, *Turgenev: The Novelist's Novelist*, Oxford University Press, 1963.

Freifeld, Alice, Bergmann, Peter and Rosenthal, Bernice Glatzer (eds.), *East Europe Reads Nietzsche*, New York, Columbia University Press, 1998.

Freud, Sigmund, 'On Transience' [1916], in *Complete Psychological Works: Standard Edition*, vol.XIV, London, Hogarth Press, 1957, 303–7.
   'Mourning and Melancholia' [1917], in *Complete Psychological Works: Standard Edition*, vol.XIV. London, Hogarth Press, 1957, 237–58.

Frigyesi, Judit, *Béla Bartók and Turn-of-the-Century Budapest*, Berkeley, University of California Press, 1998.

Frisch, Walter, 'Music and *Jugendstil*', *Critical Inquiry* 17 (1990), 138–61.
   German Modernism: Music and the Arts, Berkeley, University of California Press, 2005.

Frost, Edgar L., 'Turgenev's "Mumu" and the Absence of Love', *The Slavic and East European Journal* 31 (1987), 171–86.

Furness, Raymond, *Wagner and Literature*, Manchester University Press, 1982.

Furness, Ray (ed.) and Mitchell, Mike (trans.), *The Dedalus Book of German Decadence: Voices of the Abyss*, Sawtry, Dedalus, 1994.

Gable, David and Morgan, Robert P. (eds.), *Alban Berg: Historical and Analytical Perspectives*, Oxford, Clarendon Press, 1991.

Garcia, Emanuel E., 'Rachmaninoff and Scriabin: Creativity and Suffering in Talent and Genius', *The Psychoanalytical Review* 91 (2004), 423–42.
   'Rachmaninoff's Emotional Collapse and Recovery: The First Symphony and its Aftermath', *The Psychoanalytic Review* 91 (2004), 221–38.

Garcia, Susanna, 'Scriabin's Symbolic Plot Archetype in the Late Piano Sonatas', *19th-Century Music* 23 (2000), 273–300.

Gasparov, Boris, *Five Operas and a Symphony: Word and Music in Russian Culture*, New Haven, Yale University Press, 2005.

Gillespie, Michael Allen, 'Nietzsche's Musical Politics', in Michael Allen Gillespie and Tracy B. Strong (eds.), *Nietzsche's New Seas: Explorations in Philosophy, Aesthetics and Politics*, University of Chicago Press, 1988, 117–49.

Gillespie, Michael Allen and Strong, Tracy B. (eds.), *Nietzsche's New Seas: Explorations in Philosophy, Aesthetics and Politics*, Chicago University Press, 1988.

Gilliam, Bryan, *Richard Strauss's 'Elektra'*, Oxford University Press, 1991.

Gilliam, Bryan (ed.), *Richard Strauss: New Perspectives on the Composer and his Works*, Durham, Duke University Press, 1992.

Richard Strauss and his World, Princeton University Press, 1992.

Gilman, Richard, *Decadence: The Strange Life of an Epithet*, New York, Farrar, Straus and Giroux, 1979.

Gilman, Sander L., *Difference and Pathology*, Ithaca, Cornell University Press, 1985.

Disease and Representation, Ithaca, Cornell University Press, 1988.

'Strauss and the Pervert', in Arthur Groos and Roger Parker (eds.), *Reading Opera*, Princeton University Press, 1988, 306–27.

'Strauss, the Pervert, and Avant-Garde Opera of the *Fin de Siècle*', *New German Critique* 43 (1988), 35–68.

Gilman, Sander L., and Chamberlin, J. Edwards (eds.), *Degeneration: The Dark Side of Progress*, New York, Columbia University Press, 1985.

Glauert, Amanda, 'The Double Perspective in Beethoven's Op.131', *19th-Century Music* 4 (1980), 113–20.

Hugo Wolf and the Wagnerian Inheritance, Cambridge University Press, 1999.

Glicksberg, Charles I., *The Literature of Nihilism*, London, Associated University Press, 1975.

Głowinski, Michał, 'Maska Dionizosa', in Maria Podraza-Kwiatkowska (ed.), *Młodopolski świat wyobraźni*, Cracow, Wydawnictwo Literackie, 1977, 353–406.

Goehr, Lydia, *The Quest for Voice: Music, Politics, and the Limits of Philosophy*, Oxford University Press, 1998.

Gogröf-Voorhees, Andrea, *Defining Modernism: Baudelaire and Nietzsche on Romanticism, Modernity, Decadence, and Wagner*, New York, Peter Lang, 2004.

Goldberg, Halina (ed.), *The Age of Chopin: Interdisciplinary Inquiries*, Bloomington, Indiana University Press, 2004.

Goode, John, 'The Decadent Writer as Producer', in Ian Fletcher (ed.), *Decadence and the 1890s*, London, Edward Arnold, 1979, 109–29.

Gooding-Williams, Robert, *Zarathustra's Dionysian Modernism*, Stanford University Press, 2001.

Greenberg, Clement, *Art and Culture: Critical Essays*, Boston, Beacon Press, 1961.

Grey, Thomas S., *Wagner's Musical Prose*, Cambridge University Press, 1995.

'Wagner the Degenerate: *Fin de Siècle* Cultural "Pathology" and the Anxiety of Modernism', *Nineteenth Century Studies* 16 (2002), 73–92.

Grossman, Joan Delaney, *Valery Bryusov and the Riddle of Russian Decadence*, Berkeley, University of California Press, 1985.

Guess, Raymond, 'Berg and Adorno', in Anthony Pople (ed.), *The Cambridge Companion to Berg*, Cambridge University Press, 1997, 38–50.

Guibernau, Montserrat and Hutchinson, John (eds.), *History and National Destiny: Ethnosymbolism and its Critics*, Oxford, Blackwell, 2004.

Gutowski, Wojciech, *Mit-Eros-Sacrum: Sytuacje Młodopolskie*, Bydgoszcz, Homini, 1999.

Hailey, Christopher, *Franz Schreker 1878–1934: A Cultural Biography*, Cambridge University Press, 1993.

Haimo, Ethan, 'Schoenberg and the Origins of Atonality', in Juliane Brand and Christopher Hailey (eds.), *Constructive Dissonance: Arnold Schoenberg and the Transformations of Twentieth-Century Culture*, Berkeley, University of California Press, 1997, 71–86.

Hammond, Andrew, 'The Escape from Decadence: British Travel Literature on the Balkans 1900–45', in Michael St John (ed.), *Romancing Decay: Ideas of Decadence in European Culture*, Aldershot, Ashgate, 1999, 141–53.

Hanslick, Eduard, *Music Criticisms 1846–99*, rev. edn, trans. and ed. Henry Pleasants, Harmondsworth, Penguin, 1963.

Hanson, Ellis, *Decadence and Catholicism*, Cambridge, Mass., Harvard University Press, 1997.

Harrison, Thomas, *1910: The Emancipation of Dissonance*, Berkeley, University of California Press, 1996.

Hauser, Arnold, *Mannerism: The Crisis of the Renaissance and the Origin of Modern Art*, London, Routledge & Kegan Paul, 1965.

Hauser, Renate, 'Krafft-Ebing's Psychological Understanding of Sexual Behaviour', in Roy Porter and Mikuláš Teich (eds.), *Sexual Knowledge, Sexual Science: The History of Attitudes to Sexuality*, Cambridge University Press, 1994, 210–27.

Heisler, Wayne, Jr, 'Kitsch and the Ballet *Schlagobers*', *The Opera Quarterly* 22 (2007), 38–64.

Helman, Zofia, Chylińska, Teresa and Wightman, Alistair (eds.), *The Songs of Karol Szymanowski and his Contemporaries*, Los Angeles, University of Southern California, 2002.

Helms, Cynthia Newman, Miller, A. D. and Henshaw, Julia (eds.), *Symbolism in Poland: Collected Essays*, Detroit Institute of Arts, 1984.

Henrichs, Albert, 'Loss of Self, Suffering, Violence: The Modern View of Dionysus from Nietzsche to Girard', *Harvard Studies in Classical Philology* 88 (1984), 205–40.

Hepokoski, James, 'Fiery-Pulsed Libertine or Domestic Hero? Strauss's *Don Juan* Reinvestigated', in Bryan Gilliam (ed.), *Richard Strauss: New Perspectives on the Composer and his Works*, Durham, Duke University Press, 1992, 135–75.

Sibelius: Symphony No.5, Cambridge University Press, 1993.

'Masculine–Feminine', *The Musical Times* 135 (1994), 494–9.

review of Walter Werbeck, *Die Tondichtungen von Richard Strauss* (Tutzing: Hans Schneider, 1996), *Journal of the American Musicological Society* 51 (1998), 617–23.

'Framing *Till Eulenspiegel*', *19th-Century Music* 30 (2006), 4–43.

Hepokoski, James and Darcy, Warren, *Elements of Sonata Theory: Norms, Types, and Deformations in the Late-Eighteenth-Century Sonata*, Oxford University Press, 2006.

Hocke, Gustav René, *Die Welt als Labyrinth: Manierismus in der europäischen Kunst und Literatur*, Hamburg, Rohwolt, 1957.

Hoeckner, Berthold (ed.), *Apparitions: New Perspectives on Adorno and Twentieth Century Music*, London, Routledge, 2006.

Hollinrake, Roger, *Nietzsche, Wagner, and the Philosophy of Pessimism*, London, George Allen and Unwin, 1982.

Holloway, Robin, '*Salome*: Art or Kitsch?', in Derrick Puffett (ed.), *Richard Strauss: Salome*, Cambridge University Press, 1989, 145–60.

On Music: Essays and Diversions 1963–2003, Brinkworth, Claridge Press, 2003.

Hough, Bonny, 'Schoenberg's *Herzgewächse* and the *Blaue Reiter* Almanac', *Journal of the Arnold Schoenberg Insitute* 7 (1983), 197–221.

Houlgate, Stephen, *Hegel, Nietzsche and the Criticism of Metaphysics*, Cambridge University Press, 2004.

Huebner, Steven, *French Opera at the Fin de Siècle: Wagnerism, Nationalism and Style*, Oxford University Press, 1999.

Hutcheon, Linda and Hutcheon, Michael, *Opera: Desire, Disease, Death*. Lincoln, University of Nebraska Press, 1996.

Bodily Charm: Living Opera, Lincoln, University of Nebraska Press, 2000.

Opera: The Art of Dying, Cambridge, Mass., Harvard University Press, 2004.

Huysmans, Joris-Karl, *À Rebours*, trans. as *Against Nature* by Robert Baldicj, Harmondsworth, Penguin, 1959.

Ireland, K. R., 'Aspects of Cythera: Neo-Rococo at the Turn of the Century', *The Modern Language Review* 70 (1975), 721–30.

Izenberg, Gerald N., *Modernism and Masculinity: Mann, Wedekind, Kandinsky through World War I*, Chicago University Press, 2000.

Jackson, Timothy, 'The Finale of Bruckner's Seventh Symphony and Tragic Reversed Sonata Form', in Timothy Jackson and Paul Hawkshaw (eds.), *Bruckner Studies*, Cambridge University Press, 1997, 140–208.

Tchaikovsky: Symphony No.6 'Pathétique', Cambridge University Press, 1999.

'Observations on Crystallization and Entropy in the Music of Sibelius and Other Composers', in Timothy Jackson and Viejo Murtomäki (eds.), *Sibelius Studies*, Cambridge University Press, 2001, 176–9.

Janaway, Christopher (ed.), *The Cambridge Companion to Schopenhauer*, Cambridge University Press, 1999.

Janz, Curt Paul, 'Die Kompositionen Friedrich Nietzsches', *Nietzsche Studien* 1 (1972), 173–84.

'Friedrich Nietzsches Verhältnis zur Musik seiner Zeit', *Nietzsche Studien* 7 (1978), 308–26.

'Die Musik im Leben Friedrich Nietzsches', *Nietzsche Studien* 26 (1997), 72–86.

'Nietzsches *Manfred-Meditation*: Die Auseinandersetzung mit Hans von Bülow', in Gunther Poltner and Helmuth Vetter (eds.), *Nietzsche und die Musik*, Frankfurt am Main, Peter Lang, 1997, 45–56.

'Friedrich Nietzsches Frage nach dem Wesen der Musik', *Nietzscheforschung: Jahrbuch der Nietzsche-Gesellschaft* 5/6 (2006), 23–31.

Kallberg, Jeffrey, *Chopin at the Boundaries: Sex, History and Musical Genre*, Cambridge, Mass., Harvard University Press, 1996.

Kaplan, Richard, 'Tonality as Mannerism: Structure and Syntax in Richard Strauss's Orchestral Song "Frühling"', *Theory and Practice* 19 (1994), 19–29.

Karatïgin, Vyacheslav, 'In Memory of A. K. Lyadov', *Apollo*, 1914, Nos.6–7, trans. in Stuart Campbell (trans. and ed.), *Russians on Russian Music, 1880–1917*, Cambridge University Press, 2003, 159–67.

Karayanni, Stavros Stavrou, *Dancing Fear and Desire*, Waterloo, Ont., Wilfrid Laurier University Press, 2004.

Kárpáti, János, *Bartók's Chamber Music*, Stuyvesant, NY, Pendragon Press, 1994.

'A Typical *Jugendstil* Composition: Bartók's String Quartet No.1', *The Hungarian Quarterly* 36 (1995), 130–40.

Keller, Hans, *Essays on Music*, ed. Christopher Wintle, Cambridge University Press, 1994.

Kemal, Salim, Gaskell, Ivan and Conway, Daniel W. (eds.), *Nietzsche, Philosophy and the Arts*, Cambridge University Press, 1998.

Kerman, Joseph, *Opera as Drama*, New York, Vintage, 1956.

'Beethoven's Opus 131 and the Uncanny', *19th-Century Music* 25 (2001–2), 155–64.

Kielian-Gilbert, Marianne, 'Invoking Motives and Immediacy: Foils and Contexts for Pieter C. van den Toorn's *Music, Politics, and the Academy*', *19th-Century Music* 20 (1997), 253–78.

Kienzle, Ulrike, *Das Trauma hinter dem Traum: Franz Schrekers Oper 'Der ferne Klang' und die Wiener Moderne*, Schliengen, Edition Argus, 1998.

Kinderman, William, 'Dramatic Recapitulation in Wagner's *Götterdämmerung*', *19th-Century Music* 4 (1980), 101–12.

'Wagner's *Parsifal*: Musical Form and the Drama of Redemption', *Journal of Musicology* 4 (1985), 431–46.

Kinderman, William and Krebs, Harald (eds.), *The Second Practice of Nineteenth-Century Tonality*, Lincoln, University of Nebraska Press, 1996.

Kitcher, Philip and Schacht, Richard, *Finding an Ending: Reflections on Wagner's Ring*, New York, Oxford University Press, 2004.

Klein, Michael L., *Intertextuality in Western Art Music*, Bloomington, Indiana University Press, 2005.

Knittel, K. M., 'Wagner, Deafness, and the Reception of Beethoven's Late Style', *Journal of the American Musicological Society* 51 (1998), 49–82.

Knowles, A. V., *Ivan Turgenev*, Boston, Twayne, 1988.

Koppen, Erwin, *Dekadenter Wagnerismus: Studien zur europäischen Literatur des Fin de Siecle*, Berlin, de Gruyter, 1973.

   'Wagnerism as a Concept and Phenomenon', in Ulrich Müller and Peter Wapnewski (eds.), *Wagner Handbook*, trans. and ed. John Deathridge, Cambridge, Mass., Harvard University Press, 1992, 348–50.

Koritz, Amy, *Gendering Bodies/Performing Art: Dance and Literature in Early Twentieth-Century British Culture*, Ann Arbor, University of Michigan Press, 1995.

Korsyn, Kevin, 'Towards a New Poetics of Musical Influence', *Music Analysis* 10 (1991), 3–72.

   'The Death of Musical Analysis? The Concept of Unity Revisited', *Music Analysis* 23 (2004), 337–51.

Kramer, Lawrence, *Music and Poetry: The Nineteenth Century and After*, Berkeley, University of California Press, 1984.

   'Decadence and Desire: The *Wilhelm Meister* Songs of Wolf and Schubert', in Joseph Kerman (ed.), *Music at the Turn of Century*, Berkeley, University of California Press, 1990, 115–28.

   Music as Cultural Practice, 1800–1900, Berkeley, University of California Press, 1990.

   '*Carnival*, Cross-Dressing, and the Woman in the Mirror', in Ruth Solie (ed.), *Musicology and Difference: Gender and Sexuality in Music Scholarship*, Berkeley, University of California Press, 1993, 305–25.

   Classical Music and Postmodern Knowledge, Berkeley, University of California Press, 1995.

   'Primitive Encounters: Beethoven's "Tempest" Sonata, Musical Meaning, and Enlightenment Anthropology', *Beethoven Forum* 6 (1998), 31–66.

   Musical Meaning: Toward a Critical History, Berkeley, University of California Press, 2002.

   Opera and Modern Culture: Wagner and Strauss, Berkeley, University of California Press, 2004.

Kravitt, Edward F., *The Lied: Mirror of Late Romanticism*, New Haven, Yale University Press, 1996.

Krell, David Farrell, *The Purest of Bastards: Works of Mourning, Art, and Affirmation in the Thought of Jacques Derrida*, Philadelphia, Pennsylvania State University Press, 2000.

Krobb, Florian, '"Die Kunst der Väter tödtet das Leben der Enkel": Decadence and Crisis in *Fin-de-Siècle* German and Austrian Discourse', *New Literary History* 35 (2005), 547–62.

Kropfinger, Klaus, 'The Shape of Line', in *Art Nouveau and Jugendstil and the Music of the Early Twentieth Century, Adelaide Studies in Musicology* 13 (1984), 144–5.

Kurth, Ernst, *Romantische Harmonik und ihre Krise in Wagners 'Tristan'*, Berne, Haupt, 1920.

Kurth, Richard, 'Pierrot's Cave: Representation, Reverberation, Radiance', in Charlotte M. Cross and Russell A. Berman (eds.), *Schoenberg and Words: The Modernist Years*, New York and London, Garland, 2000, 203–41.

Kuspit, Donald, *The Dialectic of Decadence: Between Advance and Decline in Art*, New York, Allworth Press, 2000.

La Grange, Henry-Louis de, *Gustav Mahler,* vol.III: *Vienna: Triumph and Disillusion (1904–1907)*, Oxford University Press, 1999.

Large, David C. and Weber, William (eds.), *Wagnerism in European Culture and Politics*, Ithaca, Cornell University Press, 1984.

Lee, Sherry D., 'A Minstrel in a World without Minstrels: Adorno and the Case of Schreker', *Journal of the American Musicological Society* 58 (2005), 639–96.

Lehnert, Herbert, 'Thomas Mann's Early Interest in Myth and Erwin Rohde's *Psyche*', *Proceedings of the Modern Language Association* 79 (1964), 297–304.

Leichtentritt, Hugo, *Musical Form*, Cambridge, Mass., Harvard University Press, 1951.

Lemco, Gary, 'Nietzsche and Schumann', *New Nietzsche Studies* 1 (1996), 42–56.

Leoussi, Athena S. 'The Ethno-Cultural Roots of National Art', in Montserrat Guibernau and John Hutchinson (eds.), *History and National Destiny: Ethnosymbolism and its Critics*, Oxford, Blackwell, 2004, 143–59.

Le Rider, Jacques, *Modernity and Crises of Identity: Culture and Society in Fin-de-Siècle Vienna*, trans. Rosemary Morris, Cambridge, Polity Press, 1993.

Lesure, François (ed.), *Dossier de presse de* Pierrot lunaire *d'Arnold Schoenberg*, Geneva, Editions Minkoff, 1985.

Lewin, David, 'Amfortas's Prayer to Titurel and the Role of D in *Parsifal*: The Tonal Spaces of the Drama and the Enharmonic Cb/B', *19th-Century Music* 7 (1984), 336–49.

   'Some Notes on Analyzing Wagner: *The Ring* and *Parsifal*', *19th-Century Music* 16 (1992), 49–58.

Lewis, Christopher, 'Into the Foothills: New Directions in Nineteenth-Century Analysis', *Music Theory Spectrum* 11 (1989), 15–23.

Liébert, Georges, *Nietzsche and Music*, trans. David Pellauer and Graham Parkes, University of Chicago Press, 2004.

Lim, Seong Ae, 'The Influence of Chopin's Piano Music on the Twenty-Four Preludes for Piano, Op.11 of Alexander Scriabin', unpublished PhD thesis, Ohio State University, 2002.

Lissa, Zofia, *Studia nad twórczości Fryderyka Chopina*, Cracow, PWM, 1970.

Locke, Brian, 'Decadence, Heroism and Czechness: The Reception of Ostrčil's *Legenda z Erinu*', in Mikuláš Bek, Geoffrey Chew and Petr Macek (eds.), *Socialist Realism and Music*, Prague, KLP, 2004, 71–82.

Lockwood, Lewis, 'The Element of Time in *Der Rosenkavalier*', in Bryan Gilliam (ed.), *Richard Strauss: New Perspectives on the Composer and his Works*, Durham, Duke University Press, 1992, 243–58.

Lodge, Kirsten, '"The peak of civilization on the brink of collapse": The "Roman paradigm" in Czech and Russian Decadence', unpublished PhD thesis, Columbia University, 2004.

Lorenz, Alfred, *Das Geheimnis der Form bei Richard Wagner* [4 vols.], Berlin, Max Hesse, 1924–33.

Love, Frederick R., *Young Nietzsche and the Wagnerian Experience*, New York, AMS Press, 1966.

  'Nietzsche, Music and Madness', *Music and Letters* 60 (1979), 186–203.

Lukács, György, *Soul and Form*, trans. Anna Bostock, London, Merlin Press, 1974.

  The Theory of the Novel, trans. Anna Bostock, London, Merlin Press, 1978.

Lyotard, Jean-François, *The Postmodern Condition: A Report on Knowledge*, trans. Geoff Bennington and Brian Massumi, Manchester University Press, 1984.

  'Réponse à la question: Qu'est-ce que le postmoderne?', *Critique* 419 (1982), trans. Régis Durand as 'Answering the Question: What is Postmodernism?', in *The Postmodern Condition: A Report on Knowledge*, Manchester University Press, 1984, 71–82.

  The Inhuman: Reflections on Time, trans. Geoffrey Bennington and Rachel Bowlby, Stanford University Press, 1991.

MacDonald, Hugh, 'G♭', *19th-Century Music* 11 (1988), 221–37.

Maes, Francis, *A History of Russian Music*, Berkeley, University of California Press, 2002.

Maeterlinck, Maurice, *Hothouses: Poems 1889*, trans. Richard Howard, Princeton University Press, 2003.

Mahler, Gustav, *Letters to his Wife*, ed. Henry-Louis de La Grange and Günther Weiss in collaboration with Knud Martner, trans. Antony Beaumont, London, Faber, 2004.

Mahler-Werfel, Alma, *Diaries 1898–1902*, ed. Anthony Beaumont, London, Faber, 1998.

Mandel, Siegfried, 'Introduction' to Lou Salomé, *Nietzsche*, trans. and ed. Siegfried Mandel, Urbana, University of Illinois Press, 2001.

Maniates, Maria Rika, 'Musical Mannerism: Effeteness or Virility?', *The Musical Quarterly* 57 (1971), 270–93.

Mann, Thomas, Death in Venice; Tristan; Tonio Kröger, trans. H. T. Lowe-Porter, Harmondsworth, Penguin, 1955.

  Doctor Faustus, trans. H. T. Lowe-Porter, Harmondsworth, Penguin, 1968.

  Reflections of a Nonpolitical Man, trans. Walter D. Morris, New York, Ungar, 1983.

  Pro and Contra Wagner, trans. Allan Blunden, London, Faber, 1985.

  Blood of the Wälsungs, in Ray Furness (ed.) and Mike Mitchell (trans.), *The Dedalus Book of German Decadence: Voices of the Abyss*, Sawtry, Dedalus, 1994, 254–82.

  Buddenbrooks, trans. H. T. Lowe-Porter, London, Vintage Books, 1999.

Manouelian, Edward, 'Invented Traditions: Primitivist Narrative and Design in the Polish *Fin de Siècle*', *Slavic Review* 59 (2000), 391–405.

Marston, Nicholas, '"The sense of an ending": Goal-Directedness in Beethoven's Music', in Glenn Stanley (ed.), *The Cambridge Companion to Beethoven*, Cambridge University Press, 2000, 84–101.

Matich, Olga, *Erotic Utopia: The Decadent Imagination in Russia's Fin de Siècle*, Madison, University of Wisconsin Press, 2005.

McClary, Susan, 'Pitches, Expression, Ideology: An Exercise in Mediation', *Enclitic* 7 (1983), 78.

   Feminine Endings: Music, Gender, and Sexuality, Minneapolis, University of Minnesota Press, 1991.

   'Narrative Agendas in "Absolute Music": Identity and Difference in Brahms's Third Symphony', in Ruth Solie (ed.), *Musicology and Difference*, Berkeley, University of California Press, 1993, 326–44.

McClatchie, Stephen, *Analyzing Wagner's Operas: Alfred Lorenz and German Nationalist Ideology*, University of Rochester Press, 1998.

McCreless, Patrick, 'Motive and Magic: A Referential Dyad in *Parsifal*', *Music Analysis* 9 (1990), 227–65.

   'An Evolutionary Perspective on Nineteenth-Century Semitonal Relationships', in William Kindermann and Harald Krebs (eds.), *The Second Practice of Nineteenth-Century Tonality*, Lincoln, University of Nebraska Press, 1996, 87–113.

McDonald, William, 'What does Wotan Know? Autobiography and Moral Vision in Wagner's *Ring*', *19th-Century Music* 15 (1991), 36–51.

McGlathery, James M., *Wagner's Operas and Desire*, New York, Peter Lang, 1998.

Messing, Scott, 'Klimt's *Schubert* and the *Fin-de-Siècle* Imagination', in James Leggio (ed.), *Music and Modern Art*, London, Routledge, 2002.

Meyer, Leonard B., *Style and Music: Theory, History and Ideology*, Philadelphia, University of Pennsylvania Press, 1989.

Micznik, Vera, '"Ways of Telling" in Mahler's Music: The Third Symphony as Narrative Text', in Jeremy Barham (ed.), *Perspectives on Gustav Mahler*, Aldershot, Ashgate, 2005, 305–16.

Middleton, Christopher, 'Introduction' to Friedrich Nietzsche, *Selected Letters*, trans. Christopher Middleton, Chicago University Press, 1969.

Miłosz, Czesław, *The History of Polish Literature*, Berkeley, University of California Press, 1983.

Miner, Margaret, *Resonant Gaps between Baudelaire and Wagner*, Athens, University of Georgia Press, 1995.

Mitchell, Donald, review of Victor Seroff, *Rachmaninoff* (London: Cassell, 1951), *Tempo* 24 (1952), 35–6.

Moffit, John F., review of Hocke, *Die Welt als Labyrinth*, *Art Journal* 28 (1969), 446–8.

Morgan, Robert P., 'Circular Form in the "Tristan" Prelude', *Journal of the American Musicological Society* 53 (2000), 69–103.

'The Concept of Unity and Musical Analysis', *Music Anaylsis* 22 (2003), 7–50.

Morley, Neville, 'Decadence as a Theory of History', *New Literary History* 35 (2005), 573–85.

Morris, Mitchell, 'Tristan's Wounds: On Homosexual Wagnerians at the *Fin de Siècle*', in Sophie Fuller and Lloyd Whitesell (eds.), *Queer Episodes in Music and Modern Identity*, Urbana, University of Illinois Press, 2002, 271–91.

Morrison, Simon, *Russian Opera and the Symbolist Movement*, Berkeley, University of California Press, 2002.

Mosse, George L., 'Max Nordau and his *Degeneration*', introduction to Max Nordau, *Degeneration*, trans. of 2nd (1895) edn, Lincoln, University of Nebraska Press, 1993.

'Masculinity and the Decadence', in Roy Porter and Mikuláš Teich (eds.), *Sexual Knowledge, Sexual Science: The History of Attitudes to Sexuality*, Cambridge University Press, 1994, 251–66.

Müller, Ulrich and Wapnewski, Peter, (eds.), *Wagner Handbook*, trans. and ed. John Deathridge, Cambridge, Mass., Harvard University Press, 1992.

Murphy, Michael, 'An Aesthetical and Analytical Evaluation of the Music of Mieczysław Karłowicz', unpublished PhD thesis, University College, Cork, 1994.

Musil, Robert, *The Man without Qualities*, trans. Sophie Wilkins and Burton Pike, London, Picador, 1997.

Nattiez, Jean-Jacques, *Wagner Androgyne*, trans. Stewart Spencer, Princeton University Press, 1993.

The Battle of Chronos and Orpheus: Essays in Applied Musical Semiology, trans. Jonathan Dunsby, Oxford University Press, 2004.

Neff, Severine (ed.), *Arnold Schoenberg: The Second String Quartet in F-sharp minor, Opus 10*, New York, Norton, 2006.

Neubauer, John, *The Fin-de-Siècle Culture of Adolescence*, New Haven, Yale University Press, 1992.

'Bartók and the Politics of Folk Music: Musico-Literary Studies in an Age of Cultural Studies', in Walter Bernhart Steven, Paul Scher and Werner Wolf (eds.), *Word and Music Studies: Defining the Field*, Amsterdam, Rodopi, 1999, 59–77.

Newcomb, Anthony, '*Siegfried*: The Music', in Nicholas John (ed), *Wagner: 'Siegfried'*, London, Calder, 1984, 21–41.

Nietzsche, Friedrich, *Nietzsche contra Wagner*, in *The Portable Nietzsche*, trans. Walter Kaufmann, New York, Viking, 1959.

The Joyful Wisdom, trans. Thomas Common, New York, Frederick Ungar, 1960.

The Birth of Tragedy *and* The Case of Wagner, trans. with commentary by Walter Kaufmann, New York, Vintage, 1967.

The Will to Power, trans. Walter Kaufmann and R. J. Hollingdale, ed. Walter Kaufmann, New York, Vintage, 1968.

Selected Letters, ed. and trans. Christopher Middleton, Chicago University Press, 1969.

Thus Spake Zarathustra, trans. R. J. Hollingdale, Harmondsworth, Penguin, 1969.

Werke, vol.IV: *Aus dem Nachlass der Achtzigerjahre: Briefe, 1861–1889*, ed. Karl Schlechta, Frankfurt, Ullstein, 1972.

Ecce homo, trans. R. J. Hollingdale, Harmondsworth, Penguin, 1979.

Untimely Meditations, trans. R. J. Hollingdale, Cambridge University Press, 1983.

Beyond Good and Evil, trans. R. J. Hollingdale, Harmondsworth, Penguin, 1990.

Twilight of the Idols, trans. R. J. Hollingdale, Harmondsworth, Penguin, 1990.

The Birth of Tragedy Out of the Spirit of Music, trans. Shaun Whiteside, ed. Michael Tanner, Harmondsworth, Penguin, 1993.

Human, All Too Human, trans. R. J. Hollingdale, Cambridge University Press, 1996.

Nordau, Max, *Degeneration*, trans. of 2nd (1895) edn with introduction by George L. Mosse, Lincoln, University of Nebraska Press, 1993.

Norris, Geoffrey, *Rakhmaninov*, London, Dent, 1976.

Notley, Margaret, '"Volksconcerte" in Vienna and the Late Nineteenth-Century Ideology of the Symphony', *Journal of the American Musicological Society* 50 (1997), 421–53.

Lateness and Brahms: Music and Culture in the Twilight of Viennese Liberalism, Oxford University Press, 2007.

Novák, Arne, 'Antonín Sova', *The Slavonic and East European Review* 7 (1929), 418–22.

Nussbaum, Martha C., 'The Transfiguration of Intoxication: Nietzsche, Schopenhauer, and Dionysus', in Salim Kemal, Ivan Gaskell and Daniel W. Conway (eds.), *Nietzsche, Philosophy and the Arts*, Cambridge University Press, 1998, 36–69.

'Nietzsche, Schopenhauer and Dionysus', in Christopher Janaway (ed.), *The Cambridge Companion to Schopenhauer*, Cambridge University Press, 1999, 344–74.

O'Flaherty, James C., Sellner, Timothy and Helm, Robert M. (eds.), *Studies in Nietzsche and the Classical Tradition*, Chapel Hill, University of North Carolina Press, 1976.

Paddison, Max, *Adorno's Aesthetics of Music*, Cambridge University Press, 1993.

'Nature and the Sublime: The Politics of Order and Disorder in Twentieth-Century Music', in Peter Dejans (ed.), *Order and Disorder: Music-Theoretical Strategies in 20th-Century Music*, Leuven, Rodopi, 2004, 107–35.

Paglia, Camille, *Sexual Personae: Art and Decadence from Nefertiti to Emily Dickinson*, Harmondsworth, Penguin, 1992.

Painter, Karen, 'The Sensuality of Timbre: Responses to Mahler and Modernity at the *Fin de Siècle*', *19th-Century Music* 18 (1995), 236–56.

Paley, Elizabeth, '"The Voice Which Was My Music": Narrative and Nonnarrative Musical Discourse in Schumann's *Manfred*', *19th-Century Music* 24 (2000), 3–20.

Palmer, Christopher, *Szymanowski*, London, BBC, 1983.

Palmieri, Robert, *Sergei Vasil'evich Rachmaninoff: A Guide to Research*, New York, Garland, 1985.

Parkany, Stephen, 'Kurth's *Bruckner* and the Adagio of the Seventh Symphony', *19th-Century Music* 11 (1988), 262–81.

Paszkiewicz, Piotr (ed.), *Totenmesse: Modernism in the Culture of Northern and Central Europe*, Warsaw, Institute of Art and Polish Academy of Sciences, 1996.

Pater, Walter, *The Renaissance: Studies in Art and Poetry*, ed. Adam Phillips, Oxford University Press, 1986.

  Essays on Literature and Art, ed. Jennifer Uglow, London, Dent, 1990.

  Imaginary Portraits, New York, Allworth Press, 1997.

  Greek Studies, McLean, Virginia: IndyPublish.com, n.d.

Pensky, Max, *Melancholy Dialectics: Walter Benjamin and the Play of Mourning*, Amherst, University of Massachusetts Press, 1993.

Perusse, Lyle F., '*Der Rosenkavalier* and Watteau', *The Musical Times* 119 (1978), 1042–4.

Pick, Daniel, *Faces of Degeneration: A European Disorder c.1848–1918*, Cambridge University Press, 1989.

Pierrot, Jean, *The Decadent Imagination 1880–1900*, trans. Derek Coltman, Chicago University Press, 1981.

Platt, Peter, '*Pierrot lunaire* – Mannerist or Baroque?', in *Art Nouveau and Jugendstil and the Music of the Early Twentieth Century, Adelaide Studies in Musicology* 13 (1984), 233–4.

Podraza-Kwiatowska, Maria, 'Polish Literature in the Epoch of Symbolism: *Młoda Polska*', in Cynthia Newman Helms, A. D. Miller and Julia Henshaw (eds.), *Symbolism in Poland: Collected Essays*, Detroit Institute of Arts, 1984.

Poggioli, Renato, *The Theory of the Avant-Garde*, trans. Gerald Fitzgerald, Cambridge, Mass., Harvard University Press 1968.

Polony, Leszek, 'Program literacki i symbolika muzyczna w twórczości symfonicznej Karłowicza', in Jadwiga Ilnicka (ed.), *Muzyka Polska a modernizm*, Cracow, PWM, 1981, 141–55.

  Poetyka muzyczna Mieczyslawa Karłowicza: Program literacki, ekspresja i symbol w poemacie symfonicznym, Cracow, PWM, 1986.

  'Preface' to Karłowicz, *Rebirth* Symphony, Op.7, *Mieczysław Karłowicz: Complete Edition*, vol.IV, Cracow, PWM, 1993.

  'Preface' to Karłowicz, *Returning Waves*, Op.9, *Mieczysław Karłowicz: Complete Edition*, vol.VI, Cracow, PWM, 1988.

  'Karłowicz – *A Sad Story*: A Musical Study of Young Poland's Melancholy', preface to Mieczysław Karłowicz, *A Sad Story (Preludes to Eternity)*, Op.13, Cracow, PWM, 2000.

Poltner, Gunther and Vetter, Helmuth (eds.), *Nietzsche und die Musik*, Frankfurt am Main, Peter Lang, 1997.

Pople, Anthony (ed.), *The Cambridge Companion to Berg*, Cambridge University Press, 1997.

Poznansky, Alexander, *Tchaikovsky's Last Days: A Documentary Study*, Oxford, Clarendon Press, 1996.

Praz, Mario, *The Romantic Agony*, trans. Angus Davidson, Oxford University Press, 1970.

Prokop, Jan, *Żywioł wyzwolony: Studium o poezji Tadeusza Micińskiego*, Cracow, PWM, 1978.

Puffett, Derrick (ed.), *Richard Strauss:* Elektra, Cambridge University Press, 1989.
   Richard Strauss: Salome, Cambridge University Press, 1999.

Pula, James S. and Biskupski, M. B. (eds.), *Selected Essays from the Fiftieth Anniversary International Congress of the Polish Institute of Arts and Sciences of America*, vol.III: *Heart of the Nation: Polish Literature and Culture*, New York, Columbia University Press, 1993.

Pynsent, Robert B., 'A Czech Dandy: An Introduction to Arthur Breisky', *The Slavonic and East European Review* 51 (1973), 517–23.

Pynsent, Robert B. (ed.), *Decadence and Innovation: Austro-Hungarian Life and Art at the Turn of the Century*, London, Weidenfeld and Nicolson, 1989.

Ramazani, Jahan, *Poetry of Mourning: The Modern Elegy from Hardy to Heaney*, Chicago University Press, 1994.

Rampley, Matthew, *Nietzsche, Aesthetics and Modernity*, Cambridge University Press, 2000.

Rather, L. J., *The Dream of Self-Destruction: Wagner's 'Ring' and the Modern World*, Baton Rouge, Louisiana State University Press, 1979.

Reed, Philip (ed.), *On Mahler and Britten*, Woodbridge, Boydell, 1995.

Reible, John Joseph III, 'Tristan-Romanticism and the Expressionism of the Three Piano Pieces Op.11 of Arnold Schoenberg', unpublished PhD thesis, University of Washington, 1980.

Remenyi, Joseph, 'Endre Ady: Hungary's Apocalyptic Poet (1877–1919)', *The Slavonic and East European Review* 3 (1944), 84–105.

Revers, Peter, 'Liquidation als Formprinzip: Die formprägende Bedeutung des Rhythmus fur das Adagio des 9. Symphonie von Gustav Mahler', *Österreichische Musikzeitschrift* 33/10 (October 1978), 527–33.
   Gustav Mahler: Untersuchungen zu den späten Sinfonien, Hamburg, Wagner, 1985.

Richardson, Herbert (ed.), *New Studies in Richard Wagner's 'The Ring of the Nibelung'*, Lewiston, Edwin Mellen Press, 1991.

Rieman, Erika, *Schumann's Piano Cycles and the Novels of Jean Paul*, University of Rochester Press, 2004.

Riffaterre, Michael, 'Decadent Paradoxes', in Liz Constable, Dennis Denisoff and Matthew Potolsky (eds.), *Perennial Decay: On the Aesthetics and Politics of Decadence*, Philadelphia, University of Pennsylvania Press, 1999, 65–79.

Rimsky-Korsakov, Nikolay Andreyevich, *My Musical Life*, trans. from the 5th rev. Russian edn by Judah A. Joffe, ed. with an introduction by Carl van Vechten, London, Eulenburg, 1974.

Rink, John, 'Chopin in Performance: Perahia's Musical Dialogue', *The Musical Times* 142 (2001), 9–15.

Rink, John and Samson, Jim (eds.), *Chopin Studies 2*, Cambridge University Press, 1994.

Robertson, Ritchie, 'Primitivism and Psychology: Nietzsche, Freud, Thomas Mann', in Peter Collier and Judy Davies (eds.), *Modernism and the European Unconscious*, Cambridge, Polity Press, 1990, 79–93.

Rodenbach, Georges, *'Bruges-la-Morte' and 'The Death Throes of Towns'*, trans. Mike Mitchell and Will Stone, Sawtry, Dedalus, 2005.

Rosen, Charles, *The Classical Style*, London, Faber, 1971.
  'New Sound of Liszt', *New York Review of Books* 29 (12 April 1984).
  The Romantic Generation, London, HarperCollins, 1995.

Rosenthal, Bernice Glatzer, 'Stages of Nietzscheanism: Merezhkovsky's Intellectual Evolution', in Bernice Glatzer Rosenthal (ed.), *Nietzsche in Russia*, Princeton University Press, 1986, 69–93.

Rosenthal, Bernice Glatzer (ed.), *Nietzsche in Russia*, Princeton University Press, 1986.

Rothfarb, Lee A. 'Hermeneutics and Energetics: Analytical Alternatives in the Early 1900s', *Journal of Music Theory* 36 (1992), 43–68.
  'Energetics', in Thomas Christensen (ed.), *The Cambridge History of Western Music Theory*, Cambridge University Press, 2002, 927–55.

Rothfarb, Lee A. (ed. and trans.), *Ernst Kurth: Selected Writings*, Cambridge University Press, 1991.

Rowse, A. L., *The Use of History*, London, Hodder & Stoughton, 1946.

Sabaneyeff, Leonid, *Modern Russian Composers*, trans. Judah A. Joffe, New York, Da Capo, 1975.

Said, Edward W., *The World, the Text, and the Critic*, Cambridge, Mass.: Harvard University Press, 1983.
  On Late Style: Music and Literature Against the Grain, London, Bloomsbury, 2006.

St John, Michael (ed.), *Romancing Decay: Ideas of Decadence in European Culture*, Aldershot, Ashgate, 1999.

Salomé, Lou, *Nietzsche*, trans. and ed. Siegfried Mandel, Urbana, University of Illinois Press, 2001.

Samson, Jim, 'Chopin Reception: Theory, History, Analysis', in John Rink and Jim Samson (eds.), *Chopin Studies 2*, Cambridge University Press, 1994, 1–17.

Sarmany-Parsons, Ilona, 'The Image of Women in Painting: Clichés and Reality in Austria-Hungary, 1895–1905', in Steven Beller (ed.), *Rethinking Vienna 1900*, New York, Berghahn Books, 2001, 220–63.

Schachter, Carl, 'Motive and Text in Four Schubert Songs', in David Beach (ed.), *Aspects of Schenkerian Theory*, New Haven: Yale University Press, 1983, 61–76.

Schloezer, Boris de, *Scriabin: Artist and Mystic*, trans. Nicolas Slonimsky, Oxford University Press, 1987.

Schmalfeldt, Janet, 'Berg's Path to Atonality: The Piano Sonata, Op.1', in David Gable and Robert P. Morgan (eds.), *Alban Berg: Historical and Analytical Perspectives*, Oxford, Clarendon Press, 1991, 79–109.

Schmidgall, Gary, *Literature as Opera*, Oxford University Press, 1977.

Schneider, David E., *Bartók, Hungary, and the Renewal of Tradition: Case Studies in the Intersection of Modernity and Nationality*, Berkeley, University of California Press, 2006.

Schoenberg, Arnold, 'The Orchestral Variations, Op.31: A Radio Talk', *The Score* 27 (1960), 28–30.

   Fundamentals of Musical Composition, London, Faber, 1967.

   Style and Idea: Selected Writings, ed. Leonard, Stein, trans. Leo Black, London, Faber, 1984.

   The Musical Idea and the Logic, Technique, and Art of its Presentation, ed. Patricia Carpenter and Severine Neff, New York, Columbia University Press, 1995.

Schoffman, Nachum, 'D'Annunzio and Mann: Antithetical Wagnerians', *Journal of Musicology* 11 (1993), 499–524.

Schollum, Robert, 'Kodaly, Marx, Szymanowski: Drei Komponisten im Jugendstilbereich', in *Wort und Ton im europäischen Raum: Gedenkschrift für Robert Schollum*, Vienna, Böhlau, 1989, 147–65.

Schoolfield, George C., *A Baedeker of Decadence: Charting a Literary Fashion 1884–1927*, New Haven, Yale University Press, 2003.

Schopenhauer, Arthur, *The World as Will and Representation*, trans. E. F. Payne, New York, Dover, 1968.

Schorske, Carl E., *Fin-de-Siècle Vienna: Politics and Culture*, New York, Knopf, 1979.

Schrift, Alan D., *Nietzsche and the Question of Interpretation*. London, Routledge, 1990.

Scott, Clive, 'The Poetry of Symbolism and Decadence', in Patrick McGuinness (ed.), *Symbolism, Decadence and the Fin de Siècle: French and European Perspectives*, University of Exeter Press, 2000, 57–71.

Scott, Jacqueline, 'Nietzsche and Decadence: The Revaluation of Morality', *Continental Philosophy Review* 31 (1998), 59–78.

Scruton, Roger, 'Between Decadence and Barbarism: The Music of Szymanowski', in Michał Bristiger, Roger Scruton and Petra Weber-Bockholdt (eds.), *Szymanowski in seiner Zeit*, Munich, Wilhelm Fink, 1984, 159–78.

Segievsky, Nicholas, 'The Tragedy of a Great Love: Turgenev and Pauline Viardot', *American Slavic and East European Review* 5 (1946), 55–71.

Shattuck, Roger, *The Banquet Years: The Origins of the Avant-Garde in France, 1885 to World War I*, rev. edn, New York, Vintage, 1968.

Shaw, Jennifer, 'The Figure of Venus: Rhetoric of the Ideal and the Salon of 1863', in Caroline Arscott and Katie Scott (eds.), *Manifestations of Venus: Art and Sexuality*, Manchester University Press, 2000, 90–108.

Shaw, W. David, *Elegy and Paradox: Testing the Conventions*, Baltimore, Johns Hopkins University Press, 1994.

Sheppard, Richard, 'The Problematics of European Modernism', in Steve Giles (ed.), *Theorizing Modernism: Essays in Critical Theory*, London, Routledge, 1993, 1–51.

Showalter, Elaine, *Sexual Anarchy: Gender and Culture at the Fin de Siècle*, London, Bloomsbury, 1991.

Silk, Michael, 'Nietzsche, Decadence, and the Greeks', *New Literary History* 35 (2005), 587–606.

Simms, Bryan, *The Atonal Music of Arnold Schoenberg 1908–23*, Oxford University Press, 2000.

'"My dear Herzerl": Self-Representation in Schoenberg's String Quartet No.2', *19th-Century Music* 26 (2003), 258–77.

Sisman, Elaine R., 'Pathos and the *Pathétique*: Rhetorical Stance in Beethoven's C-minor Sonata, Op.13', *Beethoven Forum* 3 (1994), 81–105.

Smith, Anthony D., *Myths and Memories of the Nation*, Oxford University Press, 1999.

'When is a Nation?', *Geopolitics* 7 (2002), 5–32.

Smith, Charles J., 'The Functional Extravagance of Chromatic Chords', *Music Theory Spectrum* 8 (1986), 94–139.

Soll, Ivan, 'Pessimism and the Tragic View of Life: Reconsiderations of Nietzsche's *Birth of Tragedy*', in Robert C. Solomon and Kathleen M. Higgins (eds.), *Reading Nietzsche*, Oxford University Press, 1988, 104–31.

Solomon, Maynard, 'Beethoven's Ninth Symphony: The Sense of an Ending', *Critical Inquiry* 17 (1991), 289–305.

Solomon, Robert C. and Higgins, Kathleen M. (eds.), *Reading Nietzsche*, Oxford University Press, 1988.

Solvik, Morten, 'Mahler's Untimely Modernism', in Jeremy Barham (ed.), *Perspectives on Gustav Mahler*, Aldershot, Ashgate, 2005, 153–71.

Sontag, Susan, *Illness as Metaphor and Aids and its Metaphors*, Harmondsworth, Penguin, 1991.

Spackman, Barbara, *Decadent Genealogies: The Rhetoric of Sickness from Baudelaire to D'Annunzio*, Ithaca, Cornell University Press, 1989.

Spector, Scott, *Prague Territories: National Conflict and Cultural Innovation in Kafka's Fin-de-Siècle*, Berkeley, University of California Press, 2000.

'Marginalizations: Politics and Culture beyond *Fin-de-Siècle Vienna*', in Steven Beller (ed.), *Rethinking Vienna 1900*, New York, Berghahn Books, 2001, 132–52.

Spengler, Oswald, *The Decline of the West*, trans. Charles Francis Atkinson, London, George Allen and Unwin, 1932.

Spitzer, Michael, *Metaphor and Musical Thought*, Chicago University Press, 2004.

Sponheuer, Bernd, *Logik des Zerfalls: Untersuchungen zum Finalproblem in den Symphonien Gustav Mahlers*, Tutzing, Hans Schneider, 1978.

Steinberg, Michael P., *Listening to Reason: Culture, Subjectivity, and Nineteenth-Century Music*, Princeton University Press, 2004.

Stephan, Philip, *Paul Verlaine and the Decadence, 1882–90*, Manchester University Press, 1974.

Stewart, Suzanne R., *Sublime Surrender: Male Masochism at the Fin-de-Siècle*, Ithaca, Cornell University Press, 1998.

Straus, Joseph, 'Normalizing the Abnorm: Disability in Music and Music Theory', *Journal of the American Musicological Society* 59 (2006), 113–84.

'Disability and "Late Style" in Music', *Journal of Musicology* 25 (2008), 3–45.

Strauss, Richard and Hofmannsthal, Hugo von, *The Correspondence between Richard Strauss and Hugo von Hofmannsthal*, trans. Hanns Hammelmann and Ewald Osers, Cambridge University Press, 1980.

Stravinsky, Igor and Craft, Robert, *Dialogues and a Diary*, London, Faber, 1968.

Subotnik, Rose Rosengard, 'Adorno's Diagnosis of Beethoven's Late Style: Early Symptom of a Fatal Condition', *Journal of the American Musicological Society* 29 (1976), 242–75.

Sutton, Emma, *Aubrey Beardsley and British Wagnerism in the 1890s*, Oxford University Press, 2002.

Swart, Koenraad W., *The Sense of Decadence in Nineteenth Century France*, The Hague, Nijhoff, 1964.

Swartz, Anne, 'Chopin, Politics, and Musical Meaning in Russia during the Reign of Nicholas 1', in James S. Pula and M. B. Biskupski (eds.), *Heart of the Nation: Polish Literature and Culture*, vol.III, New York, Columbia University Press, 1993.

'Chopin as Modernist in Nineteenth-Century Russia', in John Rink and Jim Samson (eds.), *Chopin Studies 2*, Cambridge University Press, 1994, 35–49.

Szczepanowski, Stanisław, 'Dezynfeksja prądów europejskich', *Słowo Polskie* 40 (1898).

Szymanowski, Karol, *Korespondancja*, vol.I, ed. Teresa Chylińska, Crakow, PWM, 1982.

Pisma, vol.I: *Pisma muzyczne*, ed. Kornel Michałowski, Cracow, PWM, 1984.

Pisma, vol.II: *Pisma literackie*, ed. Teresa Chylińska, Cracow, PWM, 1989.

Szymanowski on Music: Selected Writings of Karol Szymanowski, trans. and ed. Alistair Wightman, London, Toccata Press, 1999.

Taruskin, Richard, review of James M. Baker, *The Music of Alexander Scriabin* (New Haven: Yale University Press, 1986) and Boris de Schloezer, *Scriabin: Artist and Mystic*, trans. Nicholas Slonimsky (Berkeley: University of California Press, 1987), *Music Theory Spectrum* 10 (1988), 143–69.

Stravinsky and the Russian Traditions, vol.I, Oxford University Press, 1996.

Defining Russia Musically, Princeton University Press, 1997.

The Oxford History of Western Music, vol.IV: *Early Twentieth Century*, Oxford University Press, 2005.

The Danger of Music and Other Anti-Utopian Essays, Berkeley, University of California Press, 2009.

Todd, R. Larry, 'On Quotation in Schumann's Music', in R. Larry Todd (ed.), *Schumann and his World*, Princeton University Press, 1994, 80–112.

Todd, R. Larry (ed.), *Schumann and his World*, Princeton University Press, 1994.

Tolstoy, Leo, *What is Art?*, trans. Richard Pevear and Larissa Volokhonsky, Harmondsworth, Penguin, 1995.

Treadwell, James, 'The "Ring" and the Conditions of Interpretation: Wagner's Writing, 1848 to 1852', *Cambridge Opera Journal* 7 (1995), 207–31.

Interpreting Wagner, New Haven, Yale University Press, 2003.

Tregear, Peter, '"Stadtluft macht frei": Urban Consciousness in Weimar Opera', in Nikolaus Bacht (ed.), *Music, Theatre and Politics in Germany: 1848 to the Third Reich*, Aldershot, Ashgate, 2006, 237–54.

Trochimczyk, Maja, 'Chopin and the "Polish Race": On National Ideologies and the Chopin Reception', in Halina Goldberg (ed.), *The Age of Chopin: Interdisciplinary Inquiries*, Bloomington, Indiana University Press, 2004, 278–313.

Trochimczyk, Maja (ed.), *After Chopin: Essays on Polish Music*, Los Angeles, Polish Music Center at USC, 2000.

Trueblood, Paul Graham (ed.), *Byron's Political and Cultural Influence in Nineteenth-Century Europe: A Symposium*, Atlantic Highlands, NJ, Humanities Press, 1981.

Tunbridge, Laura, 'Schumann's *Manfred* in the Mental Theatre', *Cambridge Opera Journal* 15 (2003), 177–83.

'Schumann as Manfred', *The Musical Quarterly* 87 (2005), 546–69.

Unger, Anette, *Welt, Leben und Kunst als Themen der 'Zarathustra-Kompositionen' von Richard Strauss und Gustav Mahler*, Frankfurt, Peter Lang, 1992.

Van Den Toorn, Pieter, *Music, Politics, and the Academy*, Berkeley, University of California Press, 1995.

Vilain, Robert, 'Temporary Aesthetes: Decadence and Symbolism in Germany and Austria', in Patrick McGuinness (ed.), *Symbolism, Decadence and the Fin de Siècle: French and European Perspectives*, University of Exeter Press, 2000, 209–24.

'*Pierrot lunaire*: Cyclic Coherence in Giraud and Schoenberg', in Mark Delaere and Jan Herman (eds.), Pierrot lunaire: *Albert Giraud – Otto Erich Hartleben – Arnold Schoenberg*, Louvain, Editions Peeters, 2004, 127–44.

Wagner, Richard, *My Life*, trans. Andrew Gray, ed. Mary Whittall, Cambridge University Press, 1983.

Selected Letters, trans. and ed. Stewart Spencer and Barry Millington, London, Dent, 1987.

Walicki, Andrzej, 'Nietzsche in Poland (before 1918)', in Alice Freifeld, Peter Bergmann and Bernice Glatzer Rosenthal (eds.), *East Europe Reads Nietzsche*, New York, Columbia University Press, 1998, 43–84.

Walsh, Stephen, 'Sergei Rachmaninoff 1873–1943', *Tempo* 105 (June 1973), 17.

Warner, Marina, *Phantasmagoria: Spirit Visions, Metaphors, and Media into the Twenty-First Century*, Oxford University Press, 2006.

Watkins, Glenn, *Pyramids at the Louvre: Music, Culture, and Collage from Stravinsky to the Postmodernists*, Cambridge, Mass., Harvard University Press, 1994.

Wattenbarger, Richard, 'A "Very German Process": The Contexts of Adorno's Strauss Critique', *19th-Century Music* 25 (2002), 313–36.

Weiner, Marc A., *Richard Wagner and the Anti-Semitic Imagination*, Lincoln, University of Nebraska Press, 1995.

'Opera and the Discourse of Decadence: From Wagner to AIDS', in Liz Constable, Dennis Denisoff and Matthew Polotsky (eds.), *Perennial Decay: On the Aesthetics and Politics of Decadence*, Philadelphia, University of Pennsylvania Press, 1999, 119–41.

Weininger, Otto, *Geschlecht und Charakter*, Vienna, 1902.

A Translation of Weininger's 'Über die letzten Dinge' (1904/1907)/'On Last Things', trans. Steven Burns, Lewiston, NY, The Edwin Mellen Press, 2001.

Weir, David, *Decadence and the Making of Modernism*, Amherst, University of Massachusetts Press, 1995.

White, Alan, *Within Nietzsche's Labyrinth*, London, Routledge, 1990.

Whitesell, Lloyd, 'Men with a Past: Music and the "Anxiety of Influence"', *19th-Century Music* 18 (1994), 152–67.

Whittall Arnold, *Schoenberg Chamber Music*, London, BBC, 1972.

'Dramatic Structure and Tonal Organisation', in Derrick Puffett (ed.), *Richard Strauss:* Elektra, Cambridge University Press, 1989, 55–73.

Wightman, Alistair, *Karłowicz, Young Poland and the Musical Fin-de-Siècle*, Aldershot, Scolar Press, 1996.

'The Book of *King Roger*: Szymanowski's Opera in the Light of his Novel *Efebos*', *Musica Iagellonica* 2 (1997), 161–213.

Karol Szymanowski: His Life and Work, Aldershot, Ashgate, 1999.

Wilde, Oscar, *The Picture of Dorian Gray*, Harmondsworth, Penguin, 1994.

Williamson, John, 'Wolf's Dissonant Prolongations', in William Kinderman and Harald Krebs (eds.), *The Second Practice of Nineteenth-Century Tonality*, Lincoln, University of Nebraska Press, 1996, 215–36.

Wilson, Alexandra, *The Puccini Problem: Opera, Nationalism and Modernity*, Cambridge University Press, 2007.

Winthrop, Henry, 'Variety of Meaning in the Concept of Decadence', *Philosophy and Phenomenological Research* 31 (1971), 510–26.

Wintle, Christopher, 'Kontra-Schenker: *Largo e mesto* from Beethoven's Op.10 No.3', *Music Analysis* 4 (1985), 145–82.

'The Questionable Lightness of Being: Brünnhilde's Peroration to *The Ring*', in Nicholas John (ed.), *Wagner:* Götterdämmerung, London, Calder, 1985, 39–48.

'Elektra and the "Elektra Complex"', in Nicholas John (ed.), *Richard Strauss:* Salome/Elektra, ENO Opera Guide 37, London, Calder, 1988, 63–79.

'Wotan's Rhetoric of Anguish', *Journal of the Royal Musical Association* 118 (1993), 121–43.

All the Gods: Benjamin Britten's 'Night-Piece' in Context, London, Plumbago, 2006.

Witkiewicz, Stanisław, *Insatiability*, trans. Louis Iribarne, London, Quartet, 1985.

Wolff, Larry, *Inventing Eastern Europe: The Map of Civilization on the Mind of the Enlightenment*, Stanford University Press, 1994.

Wurz, Stefan, *Kundry, Salome, Lulu: Femmes fatales im Musikdrama*, Frankfurt am Main, Peter Lang, 2000.

Yaraman, Sevin, *Revolving Embrace: The Waltz as Sex, Steps, and Sound*, Hillsdale, Pendragon Press, 2002.

Youens, Susan, *Hugo Wolf and his Mörike Songs*, Cambridge University Press, 2000.

Youmens, Charles, *Richard Strauss's Orchestral Music and the German Intellectual Tradition: The Philosophical Roots of Musical Modernism*, Bloomington, Indiana University Press, 2005.

Zajaczkowski, Henry, *Tchaikovsky's Musical Style*, Ann Arbor, UMI Research Press, 1987.

Zeiger, Melissa F., *Beyond Consolation: Death, Sexuality, and the Changing Shapes of Elegy*, Ithaca, Cornell University Press, 1997.

Žižek, Slavoj and Dolar, Mladen, *Opera's Second Death*, London, Routledge, 2002.

Index